A QUESTION OF JUSTICE

Confluencias

SERIES EDITORS

Susie S. Porter
University of Utah

María L. O. Muñoz
Susquehanna University

Diana Montaño
Washington University in St. Louis

A QUESTION OF JUSTICE

Criminal Trials, Notorious Homicides, and
Public Opinion in Twentieth-Century Mexico

ELISA SPECKMAN GUERRA

Translated by Debra Nagao

University of Nebraska Press | Lincoln

En tela de juicio. Justicia penal, homicidios célebres y opinión pública (México, siglo XX) © 2020 by Elisa Speckman Guerra Translation © 2026 by the Board of Regents of the University of Nebraska

The University of Nebraska Press is part of a land-grant institution with campuses and programs on the past, present, and future homelands of the Pawnee, Ponca, Otoe-Missouria, Omaha, Dakota, Lakota, Kaw, Cheyenne, and Arapaho Peoples, as well as those of the relocated Ho-Chunk, Sac and Fox, and Iowa Peoples.

∞

For customers in the EU with safety/GPSR concerns, contact: gpsr@mare-nostrum.co.uk
Mare Nostrum Group BV
Mauritskade 21D
1091 GC Amsterdam
The Netherlands

Library of Congress Control Number: 2025037051

Set in Quadraat by A. Shahan.

CONTENTS

ILLUSTRATIONS

TABLES

FOREWORD

JOSÉ RAMÓN COSSÍO DÍAZ

Certain authors, given the importance of the subject they deal with and the perseverance of their approach, tend to be identified with these subjects. If anyone raised questions about *amparos* (judicial protection against authorities' violations of constitutional rights) in the 1950s or 1960s, the name of Ignacio Burgoa would surely come to mind. If that same question had been asked in the 1970s and 1980s regarding constitutional procedural law, the name of Héctor Fix-Zamudio would have arisen. The list of examples such as these could go on and on. In any case, they would demonstrate the identification of a specific topic with the name of an author who obviously had written about it.

I begin with this brief observation because, from my viewpoint, it is what has happened among us with the historical development of criminal law and criminology and Elisa Speckman. In other words, if anyone has a question about criminal law—or, better said, the history of Mexican criminal law from the later part of the nineteenth century to this day—the name of Professor Speckman immediately arises, without any point of contrast. This implies and means that, without much debate and further inquiry, she has appropriated this field of study. Furthermore, it would not be a far stretch to say she is that field of study.

Her work began with an article published in 1997 in the journal *Historia Mexicana*, with the interesting and suggestive title "Las flores del mal: Mujeres criminales en el Porfiriato" (The flowers of evil: Women criminals in the age of Porfirio Díaz). From then we move to 2003, when Elisa contributed a work on murders and infanticides during that same period to an anthology about dissidence and dissidents in Mexico, compiled by the Instituto de Investigaciones Históricas of the Universidad Nacional Autónoma de México (IIH UNAM). Based on this work, although at times returning to what I would call her nineteenth-century origins, Professor Speckman expanded the temporal and thematic focuses of her research. She was no longer solely interested in women, maternity, madness, and vice. Gradually, issues that made it possible for a woman to be declared a criminal and sanctioned for it were introduced. That is to say, from female criminal phenomena, there was a step toward institutional conditions that identified certain acts as crimes. With this, Speckman fully entered the criminal field, which by definition deals with the police, Local Prosecutors' Offices, defense attorneys, and judges in the institutional field; codes and legislation in the regulatory branch; and punishment, prisons, and criminals in the social sphere. Elisa Speckman's accumulation of identifications, reflections, and results on all these issues is what I believe has given her work a distinctive stamp. By stamp, I mean not only the fact that she has spent many years focusing on a single phenomenon—criminal matters—but also the way she has approached them. Allow me to elaborate.

The fact that researchers devote themselves to a specific topic—although not always, but largely—is not in itself particularly unusual. In fact, that is what one is supposed to do to know and even master a subject. Just as Elisa has worked in the field of historical criminology, other authors have focused on codification, such as the constituents and origins of the *amparo*. What is new is that she has persisted in this endeavor, incorporating ever more thematic possibilities, from female criminals during the Díaz administration to criminals in general, then to criminal phenomena, and from there to prisons, and finally to judicial processes and codes. In short, she went from the highly specific to the totality to form a comprehensive image of what has happened in criminal matters until recent times.

The second innovation is no less important. One of the reasons those of us who are dedicated to law are not satisfied with works on the history of law from the perspective of general history is that those who write them know very little about law. Consequently, although invaluable, these works end up being confined to those who study general history. In the best of cases, they serve as springboards introducing us to questions of legal interest, often dominated by regulatory and institutional issues. Unlike what is commonly the case, what Elisa Speckman has done with law is to try to understand it not solely from the point of view of history, but rather from the standpoint of law itself. To achieve this skill or use this tool, she has immersed herself fully in the profession.

For years Elisa has participated and directed the Permanent Law and Justice Sociocultural History Seminar held at the IIH UNAM and the Escuela Libre de Derecho, with the participation of the foremost legal historians, such as Andrés Lira, Jaime del Arenal, and Pablo Mijangos, to name only a few. In their monthly sessions, legal history is discussed, but from a legal perspective. I have had the opportunity to attend several of them, so through experience,

I know there are no concessions in terms, so the discussion of the acts that could be characterized as crimes, emphyteusis, and propriety are based on knowledge of the law that was in force in other times.

In addition to her attendance at the seminar and her daily conversations with legal historians, Elisa Speckman has been doing other things in the same field. For years, she has been connected to members of the Academia Mexicana de Ciencias Penales (Mexican Academy of Criminal Sciences). The members of this hallowed, prestigious institution periodically meet to discuss, on a highly technical level, issues related not only to criminal law but also to criminology, criminalistics, forensic sciences, and other disciplines related to the phenomenon of criminality. The fact that Professor Speckman has been accepted, first, to participate in and then to belong to this organization demonstrates her professional qualities. However, beyond that, the fact that she does so regularly and enthusiastically explains why her historical studies are increasingly steeped in solid legal knowledge.

Throughout the works Elisa has written, her growing command of the subject is notable. It is fairly obvious. But not so obvious, her technical expertise mentioned above also shines through. The way she expresses that legal knowledge, however, used to be a bit fragmented; it was evident in works on certain women, crimes, and periods, but not in a sort of unified whole that made it possible to demonstrate not only how much she knows but, above all, the systematic level she has achieved. This book largely aims to accomplish this far-reaching meaning that was lacking in Professor Speckman's prior work.

If we ask ourselves exactly what this book is, it is a bit complicated to classify. On the one hand, it could be considered a sort of encyclopedia on various subjects, in which Elisa has concentrated explorations, sketches, and partial studies that served to shape her other works. For instance, by analyzing the genesis of the codification process, it might be thought that she wished to understand its reasons as a way to understand the way criminal justice itself worked. Likewise, it could be assumed that analyzing the social representation of the murder of this or that individual in their time served to further understanding of the myths or symbols of those crimes at a specific moment. If that had been the way of proceeding, or at least her basic intention, what we have here would be a sort of accumulation of notes or studies instrumental to other, broader purposes. Knowing how Elisa works for the results that she has achieved, I think this idea of a more encyclopedic compilation falls short in explaining this book.

A second way of looking at it would begin by considering that she wished to explain the twentieth-century Mexican criminal phenomena as much as possible, both in extension and in depth. It is the answer to an all-encompassing undertaking of this sort to show what it was from various angles and with various methodological possibilities. This path is, in fact, what it seems to me that Elisa Speckman has sought. Let us see.

In chapter 2, she tells us how the justice system was designed. What did the constituents and legislators want, and what were they able to do by making regulations and, with them, institutions? For instance, she responds to questions such as the following: Why this model of justice and not another? Why these types of judges and not others? Why jury trials and why were they so limited? To resolve these issues, she delved into preparatory works, statements of motives, doctrinal discussions, and other, similar sources. The idea was, in fact, to determine the relationships among many different things. But only in this way, I believe, did she think it would be possible to show the whys and wherefores of the situations expressed in legal regulations.

In chapter 3, the subject is completely different. The idea is to show the image of criminal justice at that time, including its administration. What was intended here supports my idea of Speckman's extra-expository book. It does not cover a sensational case or major or minor cases from yellow journalism. Instead, representative examples have been selected to show how the police, the media, public opinion, academia, and the judiciary created an image of them. With this spelled out, Speckman tries to show us what was considered a crime by contemporaries, how the victim was seen, how the criminal was perceived, how the state reacted, and why punishments were imposed. What had been certain ways of studying some sorts of criminals, whether from the Porfirio Díaz period or otherwise, now became an extension of the behaviors and actions of many, if not all, forms of criminality and thus the form of delinquency. Elisa's intention in this chapter is to show us how criminality was seen at that time. Therefore, as a whole, the book is an attempt to tell us something like "Look at what things were like with the eyes of those times, in the eyes of the victims or injured contemporaries."

Chapter 4 addresses judicial practices. Here we are shown how judges became judges—their origins, backgrounds, actions, and to some degree, personal character—as well as the ways that these individuals central to criminal life acted in famous trials in which they had to intervene.

Dr. Speckman's book is composed of all the above elements. This is what readers hold in their hands. The chapters are impeccable, and analytically, the book is complete. I feel something extra would close what I believe was the proposed cycle: a synthesis of the results. Something like the "Speckman vision" of what all these events, all these developments were for Mexican criminal justice, at least from her perspective. For her to tell us, ultimately, what our justice system was and wasn't, and what it could have been, the alternatives that were available, and what never could have appeared.

Knowing how Elisa Speckman works and the way that her historical journey has reached the present, I think the conclusions will be the subject of a new book—one that is less historical, closer to what is happening to us today and what determines our bad standing in justice. Those are the kinds of reflections that can be decanted with the years and experience that historians make of the present. I hope Elisa does so. Her words about the times we deviated, the reasons with deep roots for not being a complete system, for not having been able to consolidate things despite reflection on them, can be of great use to us. Until that new book arrives, Speckman has given us enough material to understand some of the reasons so much continues to go wrong in criminal matters.

Cossío Díaz is a former Supreme Court justice, member of El Colegio Nacional, and researcher at Member of El Colegio de México.

FOREWORD

SERGIO GARCÍA RAMÍREZ

The author of this work, Elisa Speckman Guerra, gave me the opportunity to accompany her in this new expression of her remarkable academic work. I am honored by the generous invitation to write this foreword and to reflect once again on the merits of the subject analyzed in this book and on those of the author, a scholar of history and law—her double doctorate—with abundant and highly worthy production in this field, which has earned her just recognition.

This work originated as a doctoral dissertation that she developed after years of painstaking and constant research and presented at the Facultad de Derecho of the Universidad Nacional Autónoma de Mexico. It has not arisen solely from the author's commitment to achieve the degree she was awarded with honors (*mención honorífica*); rather, it is a link added to the chain of a long and fertile research career at the Instituto de Investigaciones Históricas UNAM (the national university department where she is currently affiliated), the Academia Mexicana de Ciencias Penales (Mexican Academy of Criminal Sciences), and the Instituto Nacional de Ciencias Penales (National Institute of Criminal Sciences), among others, as well as during her stays in the United States and Spain.

Elisa Speckman has cultivated research on ideas and practices in the field of criminal justice, its institutions and leading figures, and related topics. Alongside experts in criminal dogmatics, procedural doctrine, penitentiary regulations, and criminological and criminalistic disciplines, Speckman is one of the few researchers who have worked in depth examining ideological and political trends and circumstances that affect criminal justice. This effort is fertile and highly valuable for truly comprehending the state of criminal justice in Mexico in its diverse stages and expressions, in connection with reality as well as its historical course.

In Mexico there are not many historical studies on this subject, neither about the regulations developed since the early years after independence—in which colonial law lasted for a long time and amid multiple setbacks—nor about the successive currents of thought and the needs that informed those regulations. However, there are valuable insights and reflections that we should not overlook and that shed light on that succession of regulations, their characteristics, their course, and their consequences.

We have recognized and analyzed the criminal ideas that influenced the development of Mexican law and that continues to do so. French jurists come to mind, in the early years, and then Italian, Spanish, and German jurists. They fuel dogma. But not everything is regulatory, of course: It is necessary to emphasize the practice of justice, the natural history of this function of the state—in which citizens appear in the form of diverse figures and with different accents—to gain awareness of the reality, its high and low points, its tasks and its future. The work of Speckman, collected here and in other publications that we owe to her talent and dedication as a researcher in history and law, contributes to this.

In recent years—let us say the end of the twentieth and early twenty-first centuries—we have proposed and adopted countless reforms to criminal law, with the proclaimed purpose of improving public security and preserving the state of law and the welfare of society. Our legislator is "motorized," to use the expression of Gustavo Zagrebelsky. Political and legal discourse bears witness to these reiterated intentions, which do not always reach their aim. As I write these lines, we are beginning to embark on a new undertaking of reforms that will cover, it is said, both the text of the Constitution, which has already undergone innumerable changes, and secondary law. I resist the temptation to examine these projects, governed by the same old purposes. I can only hope that they result in progress, not in setbacks or regressions, of which we have had many regrettable and flagrant ones. However, in the texts received so far, what stand out are the regressions. The legal state, democracy, and of course, human rights can stumble on them.

I have thought it useful to refer to this background of the author and the subject matter she analyzes to place the work in the framework of her academic exercise and to explain her motives, reasons, and results. She studies the situation of criminal justice—or, better said, the situations of this branch of justice—in Mexico City, formerly the Federal District, starting in 1929, with very pertinent references to earlier periods, and continuing up until 1971. In 1929 the Mexican Revolution more or less started its stage of peace and institution building, and in 1971 powerful winds that promoted greater changes had already appeared.

The points of departure and arrival of Speckman's work are defined by the 1929 legislation, with an enlightened jurist, José Almaraz—although not only him—who imposed a radical change on the federal and local regulations of 1871, and by the local criminal and penitentiary procedural reform of 1971, which incorporated significant novelties that Speckman refers to in detail. Those are the parentheses bracketing the research, which does not overlook earlier and later events. Thus we have in view slightly less than half a century in the evolution of criminal justice in Mexico City, a period in which many innovations of notable magnitude occurred, in the heat of the transformations in the world, in Mexico, and in our capital city, with profound changes in circumstances.

This book describes the political, social, economic, and cultural context that characterized each of the stages that the natural and legal history of justice can be divided into during the forty-plus years covered by this research. The course of the legal history is linked—as it should be in a genuine effort of understanding and evaluating—with the dominant ideas regarding the criminal instrument at the disposal of the state, which it uses because of its liberal or authoritarian, progressive or regressive character. It is essential to ponder this link and to appreciate its implications, as the author does. In general, the prevailing criminal ideology advanced under a liberal model to which social concerns were added. In more recent years, authoritarian influences appeared, which have reached the Constitution and secondary legislation.

Legal works do not usually deal with these questions, more often reserved for political, historical, or sociological works. This work provides indispensable information to delve deeply into the ideas, discourses, norms, and practices that flourished in each specific period of the extensive total time of criminal justice in Mexico City, which simultaneously had an influence or impact on justice throughout the country. As we know, the "province"—a pleasant, also reductionist and reassuring expression—used to welcome the inductions of the powerful and decisive "center," but then things varied to a certain degree, and the innovations that arose affected federal and district legal order.

In the chapters constituting this work, Speckman Guerra refers to the prevailing circumstances during the periods covered or concerning the subject matter examined, including the political conditions—in a remarkable time of changes, which characterized the most violent years of the Mexican Revolution and its immediate aftermath—and the viewpoints, concerns, and projects of the politicians to lead the country forward; the jurists who acted in various capacities, in the forum of proposals and practices; and the diverse social sectors and actors who observed the application of laws or participated in it. This is a great mural, so to speak, of justice and its protagonists, which contributes to our understanding of the ports of transit in the social march and the products of that march, to reach the moment in which we find ourselves.

Elisa Speckman's work contributes, as I have said, to understanding the avatars of criminal justice—and of the society that received or suffered from it—in a long stage of our social life. She recognizes, gathers, and explains the multiple vicissitudes that give "sign and color" to that expression of justice, beyond—or more thoroughly than—a superficial reading of old or new precepts governing it. It is necessary—hence the relevance of Speckman's work—to look back at the past, to extract from it the needs and solutions that have characterized the criminal justice system in Mexico, to compare it with the present to design and evaluate current tasks, and to take advantage of them in outlining the future.

Speckman Guerra reveals the foundations of the criminal system in Carranza's constitutional proposal in 1916 and in the debates of the Constitutional Congress of 1916–17, a foundation full of reproaches of the past and illusions of the future that it wished to build on the ashes of the earlier criminal system, with a strong inquisitive emphasis, albeit dominated first by the legalist orientation of the classical school and later by the naturalist orientation of the criminological-positivist school and its followers in Mexico. The author examines this ebb and flow with relevant and sufficient data, as an entry point to access the stage immediately following it, when the earliest postrevolutionary Criminal and Procedural Codes were ushered in.

The author describes the gestation and stumbling blocks of the short-lived criminal code of 1929 and of the law that followed it in 1931. In both cases, she refers in detail to the conflicting positions: those against the 1929 Codes, including the work of a vigorous generation of criminalists who founded the journal *Criminalia* and the Academia Mexicana de Ciencias Penales, in which Dr. Speckman is a member of number. She then goes on to review preliminary drafts and projects for criminal law reforms. The scholar studying this subject cannot overlook the contradictory opinions that arose with each wave of criminal reforms. They help us understand the times and set out the steps as they occurred in light of the circumstances. In this way, we avoid the lightness with which we tend to qualify codes and welcome their reforms.

The author examines these ordinances and projects that appeared in the 1940s and the following decades, along with their ideological and practical bases, because these elements ultimately influenced the daily functioning of the institutions called upon to apply them and the agents called upon to fulfill tasks in law enforcement, administration of justice, and defense of the accused. In the mid-twentieth century and slightly later, calls arose for criminal unification, whose regulations were disseminated in some thirty ordinances covering each specialty, housed in the states and federal ordinances. The author's reflections on this process are collected in various works.

In this detailed examination, Speckman refers to the authors of projects and codes, a reference that contributes to explaining the solutions they promoted and the reactions they provoked. When a new ordinance appeared on the horizon, accompanied by promises, we tend to ask, Who designed the project? The answer says a lot—although it doesn't tell the whole story—about the motives and quality of the regulations. Here we see a procession of the thoughts and experiences that informed, drove, mobilized, or slowed down the ordinances and reform proposals that determined at different times, in ever shorter stages, judicial organization and whose transfigurations are an important topic in the book.

The "protagonists" of justice are featured in the list of topics in this work. To present issues of justice from this indispensable perspective, it is important to remember with Piero Calamandrei, whom Speckman invokes, that justice is ultimately what its protagonists made of it, not merely what the precepts of the law—or discourses that proclaimed or interpreted them—said about it. Here everything operates as if on the stage of a great theater: first the subject of the drama is outlined by a masterful hand or incompetent happenstance; then the legislators develop it; and finally, there is the staging by the actors, whose evolution in the forum gives meaning, content, and efficacy—or does not, as often happens—to the drama designed by the legislator.

Thus on the stage set up by Speckman, there is a procession of judges of different ranks and jurisdictions, particularly criminal judges of both instances in Mexico City, but also of federal *amparo* courts: Public Prosecutor's Office agents, defense attorneys, and the multitude of observers, more or less "activists," like crime page reporters—who were numerous and very important, and Speckman identifies them—and even the narrators of justice through novels and, especially, movies. The author's journey through the course of Mexican cinematography is quite interesting, filled with trials and prejudices related to criminal acts and actions and reactions of justice.

Naturally, in Speckman's research, judges play a central role: judges and magistrates, in addition to their assistants; those of first instance, initially monocratic, then collegiate, and later unitary again. The author gives a detailed account through her splendid research, on which she spent a long time, and reveals the antecedents of the judges, their lives, and some of their "miracles," under the idea that it is necessary to know their character and person to understand their evolution in tribunals and the product of this: the judicial decisions in which the mandate of the law was applied in one way or another.

At different points of the work, the author refers to the jury trial, a jurisdictional figure that has sparked debates between those who affirm—as occurred in Mexico, following foreign traditions—that it represents a democratic indication in the administration of justice and those who maintain it incorporates elements that distort and distance it from the purposes it is meant to serve. It is justice exercised directly by the people: an expression of democracy, say the supporters of juries. He who judges his fellow citizens is the true ruler of society, to paraphrase Alexis de Tocqueville.

Speckman reviews the debate on juries, which the author has written about in earlier studies, taking into account the genealogy and experiences of that institution in Mexico, excluded by the legislator of 1929—although it was preserved in constitutional regulations for specific causes and was vindicated from time to time, unsuccessfully, under the protection of procedural reform initiatives associated with the accusatory system. The chronicle on the jury trial in Mexico is substantial and makes for enjoyable reading; many observers heaped it with criticism—which it certainly deserved—in contrast to the praise that analysts devoted to the same institution in other national media.

In the roll call of the figures in justice, numerous well-known judges appear along with others whose names are barely known, but not their background and exploits. The author analyzes the prior performance of those judicial office holders and examines the political ties with the highest offices in Mexico, which has continued to this day and will no doubt continue in the future, both under the regime of extreme removability and under that of relative lack of removability during the years covered by this research.

It is always worth reviewing the nominal and real procedures of the appointment and influence of that hand of politics—always and everywhere—as well as other, "invisible" hands. See, then, what Speckman says about the connections between the judges, their generous friends, and their powerful godfathers, situations of clientelism and patrimonialism that slipped into the labyrinths of justice. Reflection on the independence of judges appointed or promoted by politicians in office always leads to this point. And I invoke the confidence of the Potsdam miller in the integrity of the Berlin judges, who would restrain the greed of the king of Prussia, Wilhelm II, as the anecdote goes that refers to the appointment of Robert Badinter as president of the Constitutional Council of France. In 1986 Badinter, a successful combatant against the death penalty, was appointed president of that council. He had been the minister of justice under President François Mitterrand, who advocated for the new appointment. When Badinter was asked if the fact that he had served Mitterrand would hinder his appointment at the head of the court, he replied that the first duty he would fulfill in his new position would be the "duty of ingratitude." Let us understand: ingratitude—if this is how he looked at it—toward the man who appointed him, but gratitude and commitment to the nation awaiting justice.

The judges do not compose the entire roster of characters. I have already referred to other categories, taking into account Speckman's contributions. Among them are the attorneys, both the generous "romantic" defenders, such as the famed (in his time) "Man of the Big Necktie" ("El Hombre del Corbatón") and the others—those whom we don't wish to remember, but who also existed, acted, and influenced—who can be called *abogánsteres*, a term used by Eugenio Aguirre in his superb novel on one of these characters who darkened, but also characterized, some extremes of forensic practice.

A part of the book is devoted to the judgment of justice. It is as if justice appears in a courtroom where it is rigorously put on trial: the court of history. In it, Dr. Speckman is comfortable. Justice has earned this trial and must respond both to the praise that many of its distinguished judges naturally deserve and to the claims that society has addressed and is addressing to it. Public opinion is not usually benign, and was not so in the historical trajectory covered by this research. Luigi Ferrajoli has rightly said that the sum of suffering, devastation, blood, and pain—I translate his words in my own way—that appears in the history of criminal justice is greater than that same sum in the chronicles of crime.

It is interesting to bring up, as the author does, the controversies that occasionally arose between judicial officials—and even collegiate bodies of justice, entire courts—on the one hand, and powerful critics, such as the legislative deputies and senators who questioned them, on the other, in disputes that ended only thanks to the conciliatory intervention of the "invisible hand" of the executive power, the ruler of Mexico City.

Of course, the reiterated opinions—on occasions highly critical—of attorneys, academics, men of science and letters, and large sectors of society, granted voice and vote by the press, are also relevant. Speckman's book addresses this facet of history with an ample contribution of testimonies, which tell us about that severe judgment that never ended and does not seem to have ceased, not to mention the critical opinions of citizens subjected to the "wheels of justice." The work to which my preliminary words are added is a descriptive and reflective record of this.

Another particularly appealing and rich aspect of this book is that it includes accounts of different "notable cases." Perhaps Dr. Speckman Guerra would have liked to augment this examination, bringing to light numerous cases of different entities submitted to the criminal justice system, which fill abundant criminal archives. She made the pragmatic decision, however, to select some outstanding cases that attracted public attention and determined the singular action of the authorities. She looks at the wanderings of justice from this perspective.

These notable cases from between 1931 and 1971, which have very different physiognomies and characteristics from those that we can consider under the same heading, subject to minute-by-minute social scrutiny, highlight the strengths and weakness of justice. Thus they contribute to the author's X-ray of it. Speckman Guerra explains her reasons for selecting these cases and describes the conclusions that can be derived from her examination. All the examples deal with "blood crimes," which inflamed the vision and conscience of both those reporting the facts in the press and those receiving the news. Motives of passion stand out in some crimes and greed in others. The gravity of these crimes pales in comparison to the seriousness of today's crimes, to which we have become accustomed both in quantity and in magnitude; there has since been a multiplication of undefeated and arrogant criminality, a display of uncommon cruelty. I will never forget that José Vasconcelos identified cruelty as a fact rooted in the deepest core of Mexicans.

In these cases, the factors that influenced the performance of the justice machine appeared on the scene: social pressure, political interests, attention-seekers, and various others that the author describes in detail, based on sources that back her reasoning. It is interesting to look at justice from these points that stand out and thus contribute to the judgment of justice.

As I said, the chronological-legal course of the research culminates in 1971, when there were important novelties—all of them promoted by the executive branch, although some were taken up and presented by the legislature. Innovations were deployed, the author explains, on various areas of the criminal justice system: substantive, procedural, executive. The year 1971 brought progressive reforms to criminal and procedural law, such as those related to the summary trial and suppression of criminal courts, and in the implementing law, Minimum Standards on Social Readaptation, based on which penitentiary law of the following decades was built, but not that of recent years, plagued by errors.

The work focuses on procedural matters, particularly on suppression, from the 1971 reforms of the criminal courts that had operated in Mexico City—often with notable members—for several decades. The author reports in detail on the reform process and arguments for and against the courts, and therefore for or against monocratic legal bodies reestablished that year, which have come down to the present in Mexico City (though not necessarily in all the states in the country). Other issues of procedural reform and judicial work, such as summary proceedings, are also examined.

At the start of each chapter the author includes an introduction, a sort of guide to the journey, and at the end she includes some final reflections, recapitulating the main sections of the journey or the protagonists, or both. The book ends with a concluding chapter in which Speckman describes, and provides reasons for (those accumulated in the course of the voyage and those that can be seen, with contemporary eyes, from the vantage point of citizens in 2020), the common landscape of yesterday and today. In the final lines, where she again evokes certain characters from filmography, the author points out that some emblematic figures "died many years ago, and some have disappeared from the collective memory. However, their stories and the history of justice described here have not lost their power. The bases of the justice system and judicial institutions, practices, and negotiation mechanisms from 1929 to 1971, as well as the problems and solutions, ideas and values, persisted in the decades that followed and continue to this day. History has no clear edges or radical cuts; it lives in the present and heralds the future."

I would also like to make reference to the sources considered by the author in the formulation of her work. She consulted numerous books and articles from specialized journals, texts that appeared in multiple newspapers over the course of more than forty years, legislative provisions, regulations, different sorts of official documents, international treatises, sentences (to uphold the motives of judges based on their decisions), and even movies that tell of the wanderings of justice and swayed public opinion no less than the media news. Speckman conducted research in general and judicial archives, and she reviewed a large number of files of this nature, all of which are documented.

From these and other sources, the author put together this remarkable body of information that she provides about different cases illustrating the administration of justice, as well as about the origin, formation, and development of the exercise of judicial officials who, based on Speckman's research, appear in the pages of this book and were arbiters of justice in tens or hundreds of cases.

This information also allows us to know the profiles of other actors I mentioned, such as the social communicators who have always appeared in sensationalistic reporting, either transmitting them with terse severity or adding a little or a lot of rhetoric to each account, which has been another influential factor in legal decisions.

Given that "celebrated" cases often involved the opinions of Public Prosecutor's Office agents, first-instance judges in criminal courts, or magistrates regarding the exclusion of incrimination or other criminal matters set forth in the detention, lawsuits, conclusions, or sentences, an account of the judicial precedents on those matters is also included.

The survey of the subjects I have undertaken—which in no way exhausts those that Elisa Speckman addresses—serves to underscore the importance and relevance of the book as research on justice, a topic of the past and today, which now as yesterday is subject to political, academic, and popular deliberation. Similarly, I want to emphasize that this panorama has strong foundations, consolidated by someone with command of the technique of historical research and who has placed it at the service of researchers on law.

This superb account on these wanderings of justice will serve all readers: those who are venturing into this field or have undertaken its study and will define its calling and performance, and those who are witnesses—beneficiaries or victims—in the vast space, which is all of society, where justice operates and gains or loses credibility and hope.

García Ramírez is a researcher at the Instituto de Investigaciones Jurídicas of the UNAM, professor emeritus of the UNAM, researcher emeritus of the Sistema Nacional de Investigadores, and former president of the Inter-American Court of Human Rights.

PREFACE

In this book, I present a history of the criminal justice system in Mexico City in the twentieth century, between 1929 and 1971, when the criminal courts (Cortes Penales) operated and justice in courts of first instance was collegial.

Intertwining two disciplines, law and history, I describe the state and justice models outlined in legislation, comparing them with the aspirations of jurists and theoreticians of the time, assessing the respect for or violation of their fundamental principles in police and judicial practices, and also examining alternative proposals. I analyze the public image of justice and its possible bearing on the actions of legislators, administrative authorities, judges, attorneys, and citizens. I examine judicial processes considering judges' actions and the subject of judicial discretion (discrecionalidad); the role of attorneys, expert witnesses, investigative actors, and defendants; and the emergence of ideas and values in courts. Finally, I address the impact of journalists on investigations and trials, reconstructing celebrated cases in the press and the array of cultural representations of homicide, murderers, law, justice, punishment, and what was considered prohibited, permitted, legitimate, illegitimate, moral, and amoral.

These pages feature legislators, judges, litigators, jurists, reporters, participants, and well-known murderers, from "self-made widows" (autoviudas) like "Chole la Ranchera" to Olympic medalists like Humberto Mariles. Their stories help us understand the origin and evolution of major problems in Mexico today. During the period under discussion, criminal behavior and the fear of criminality, violent homicides or robberies, and criminal impunity increased. Furthermore, the breach between legal principles and police and judiciary practices widened. The justice system favored the accusatory system, whereas legislation and judicial precedents placed greater emphasis on the rights of the accused and defendants. However, numerous formal complaints targeted the violation of these maxims in police and judicial proceedings. Sanctions for homicide became harsher, and greater attention was placed on punishing crimes than on preventing them. The image of justice deteriorated, as acts of corruption and influence peddling were uncovered. Talk prevailed of a broken promise (the "revolutionary" government's commitment to improving justice) and a failed state (one unable to fulfill its essential mission to protect the people's safety and rights).

This book brings the history of justice to life. It also offers important caveats for the future, because I believe experiences from the past must be considered in designing public policies and legislative reforms in the present.

ABBREVIATIONS

AMCP   Academia Mexicana de Ciencias Penales
(Mexican Academy of Criminal Sciences)

BMA   Barra Mexicana de Abogados (Mexican Bar Association)

CSDPS   Consejo Supremo de Defensa y Prevención Social
(Supreme Council of Defense and Social Prevention)

ELD   Escuela Libre de Derecho

ENJ   Escuela Nacional de Jurisprudencia

MP   Ministerio Público (Prosecutor's Office)

PGJ   Procuraduría General de Justicia del Distrito Federal
(Attorney General's Office of the Federal District)

PGR   Procuraduría General de la República (Attorney General's Office)

SCJ   Suprema Corte de Justicia (Supreme Court)

TSJ   Tribunal Superior de Justicia (Superior Court of Justice)

UNAM   Universidad Nacional Autónoma de México
(National Autonomous University of Mexico)

A QUESTION OF JUSTICE

I. PRELIMINARY QUESTIONS

Criminal courts were created in 1929, when the 1871 Criminal Code and the 1894 Criminal Procedure Code were repealed, and important changes were introduced in the justice system. Instead of trial by jury, collegial courts composed of three judges were created. Much as with earlier reforms, legislators sought to establish an impartial, efficient justice system based on laws and rights to achieve social harmony. Nevertheless, given indications of the failure of all or some of these goals, the collegial model was suppressed in 1971, when criminal courts were replaced by unitary courts (under a single judge). This chapter describes the general characteristics of the criminal courts, the scenarios in which they functioned, and how I address their history in this book.

THE CRIMINAL COURTS

Criminal courts were empowered to judge adults who committed the crimes most heavily sanctioned under the Criminal Code. A criminal court's three judges were each required to hold a law degree. One of them directed the judicial instruction period, in which prosecutor and defendant outlined their positions and presented proofs. This was followed by the plenary phase, in which all three judges participated, along with the other parties involved: the defendants and their counsel and the prosecutor from the Local Prosecutor's Office (Ministerio Público, hereafter MP), responsible for investigating and prosecuting crimes. In a public hearing to air the details of the crime to be tried, both parties, witnesses, and expert witnesses were heard. Later judges had to apply the corresponding legal rules and determine the sentence. Finally, the investigating judge formulated a draft judgment, and the decision was made by majority vote.

Thus criminal court members assessed the evidence determining the existence and circumstances of the manner, time, and place of the crime and later applied the corresponding legal provision. In criminal matters, the court did away with the division of tasks that had been in force since 1869, which had entrusted assessing the facts to citizens as jury members. It thereby moved from a mixed (professional and citizen) justice system to one overseen exclusively by professional judges.

The drafters of the 1929 Code also expanded the judges' margin of discretion. Following Mexican Independence, in response to the broad discretion of judges in New Spain, who at sentencing could base their rulings on different written and unwritten regulations, philosophical or religious doctrines, past sentences, or local customs, Mexican legislators sought to replace that "justice of judges" with a "justice of laws." They opted for the French model, which considered the general will that was expressed exclusively in the law and had to be obeyed by citizens, officials, and judges.[1] Members of the committee that drafted the 1871 Criminal Code took this aspiration to the extreme: The judge could sanction only those acts characterized as crimes, had to apply the punishment stated in the code, and to determine the punishment, had to consider aggravating and attenuating circumstances specifically listed in the code and with a preassigned value. In the 1929 and 1931 codes, judges were granted a wider margin of discretion: In 1929 they could consider aggravating or attenuating circumstances unforeseen by the legislators in determining the punishment, and in 1931 they could start from broad time limits, generally considering the characteristics of the offender and the crime.

In sum, in 1929 the legislators entrusted the administration of justice to professional judges and gave them a vote of confidence, expanding their margin of discretion. Despite this—or perhaps because of it—they did not opt for a unitary justice system, but rather a collegial one. They assumed the three judges would add from their knowledge and experience and would probably monitor each other.

THE SETTING

Criminal courts functioned in three contexts: They were founded when the political and social institutions of postrevolutionary Mexico were being constructed or consolidated; they lived in the context of "presidentialism," the economic "miracle," and the capital city's expansion; and they were abolished in years of disillusionment.

In the late 1920s it was necessary for the Mexican president to reactivate the economy, debilitated by ten years of war; reinstate political control; and restore social order. Shifts in power, political disagreements, and social demands continued to be resolved through violence. In his last State of the Union Address, weeks after Álvaro Obregón (Mexican president 1920–24 and reelected in 1928) was assassinated before taking office, President Plutarco Elías Calles (1924–28) declared it was time to abandon "the historical condition of the country of one sole man" and move on to a "higher and more respected, more productive, more peaceful, and more civilized" stage, in which "men were not mere accidents lacking importance, alongside the perpetual and august serenity of institutions and laws."[2]

Years of political reconstruction, institutionalization, legislation, and professionalization of public servants followed. These reforms included the creation of the National Revolutionary Party (Partido Nacional Revolucionario), expansion of the presidential term, a second wave of legal codification, and reorganization of the army and police.

The Federal District (Distrito Federal, or Mexico City) reflected the thirst for institutionalization and centralization of political power. In 1928 the figure of the governor and city councils (ayuntamientos, organs representing the government through elected members) were abolished, based on the argument that they blocked the centralized control and administration of the city.[3] The Federal District was divided into thirteen administrative divisions, or boroughs (delegaciones), and a Central Department (Departamento Central), which accommodated the former municipalities of Mexico, Tacuba, Tacubaya, and Mixcoac.[4] Mexico City once formed part of the municipality bearing its name, but at that time it was part of the Central Department; therefore, it concentrated much of the population and was the most important of the boroughs.[5] The supreme authority, the jefe (head) of the Central Department, later head of the Department of the Federal District (Departamento del Distrito Federal), was freely appointed and removed by the nation's president. Unsurprisingly, the first head, José Manuel Puig Casauranc, was a follower of Plutarco Elías Calles. The heads of the department appointed the delegates (delegados, or local representatives). Thus the city's inhabitants lost the opportunity to elect their leaders or representatives, for there was no local legislative congress, and laws were issued by the federal legislature. Nevertheless, there was an Advisory Board (Consejo Consultivo) of the Central Department, and until 1941 borough-level boards served a certain representative function because the mayor (regente) and delegates appointed them, but they followed a corporatist logic based on proposals of social organizations.[6]

The city also echoed the desire to professionalize government officials. Justice was professionalized, as evidenced in the suppression of jury trials and the requirement for all criminal judges to hold a law degree.

That said, although criminal courts were born during a historic period of change, they functioned within a stage of consolidation and growth. From the mid-1930s, especially over the next three decades, presidential power grew. This was followed by the electoral victories of the National Revolutionary Party, which, over time, with differences in integration and vision, became the Party of the Mexican Revolutionary (Partido de la Revolución Mexicana) and finally the Institutional Revolutionary Party (Partido Revolucionario Institucional). The country's presidents, also leaders of the party, gained power and asserted their authority over regional forces, while they obtained control of legislative and judicial powers. They not only set the direction of politics but also, as in other countries, defined economic and social spheres.

The state protected national industries, was committed to improving infrastructure, and provided fiscal stimuli. It favored businessmen's interests. The economy grew and the "Mexican miracle" was upheld for two decades. Thanks to the rise of investments, development of industry, and nationalization of petroleum, infrastructure works were carried out, jobs were created, and social expenditure increased in health and education.

The middle class prospered, but privileged sectors benefited the most. Inequality between regions and groups was exacerbated.[7] Social discontent became obvious. The government cracked down on agrarian movements (such as the organization championed by Rubén Jaramillo in Morelos in the 1940s and 1950s), laborers (such as the group of railroad workers led by Valentín Campa and Demetrio Vallejo), and teachers' movements (manifested in strikes expressing urban and rural discontent).[8]

There was also marked ethnic and cultural heterogeneity. According to the 1921 census, 29 percent of the population was Indigenous and 59 percent was "mestizo," but the boundary separating them was tenuous. The Indigenous component of the population was important, as was *indigenismo* (a political, intellectual, and cultural movement that advocated for the defense and recognition of Indigenous peoples and the valorization of their culture) in official discourse. The government continued to glorify the pre-Hispanic past, while it also recovered the culture of Indigenous peoples of the time. Mexico was seen as a mestizo nation, in which the Indigenous people were a part, and racial distances or inherited cultural tendencies were no longer spoken of in favor of thinking of the country in conditions of economic and social disadvantage. However, under a paternalist stance, integration continued assuming the improvement of Indigenous people through eugenics, nutrition, health, education, and incorporation into the market economy.

The nation's population increased: In 1930 Mexico had approximately 16.5 million inhabitants, in 1950 close to 26 million, and in 1970 48 million. Moreover, the number of residents in cities, especially the capital, rose; in fifty years, this population grew tenfold. The center of federal political power and the government's main offices concentrated investments, business, industry, services, education, and cultural activities. The period was marked by growth and dynamism.

Population of the Federal District, 1921–70

1921	906,063
1930	1,229,576
1940	1,757,530
1950	3,050,442
1960	4,870,876
1970	6,874,165

With time, the Central Department took the name of Mexico City. In 1931 two boroughs—Guadalupe Hidalgo and General Anaya—were joined to the Central Department, so only eleven remained. Three years later, Guadalupe Hidalgo separated from the Central Department and became the Gustavo A. Madero borough, which raised the total to twelve.[9] The urban sprawl was expanding. In the 1930s and 1940s Mexico City accounted for approximately 83 percent of the population of the Federal District, but as the number of inhabitants of the boroughs increased, the percentage of Mexico City residents decreased. In the 1950s the city's population fell to 73.26 percent, in the 1960s to 58.14 percent, and at the start of the next decade, to 42.22 percent.[10]

In the political sphere, despite the Department of the Federal District's dependence on the executive branch and the federal public treasury, by mid-century its heads were politically stronger, had their own support within the official party, and enjoyed a degree of autonomy.[11] This was the case with Ernesto Uruchurtu, known as the "iron-fisted mayor," who governed the city between 1952 and 1966. At the local level, Mexico City mayors reproduced corporatist and clientelist politics. They wove alliances with businesspeople, industrialists, shopkeepers, and owners, although they also sought to forge ties with unions and granted favors and bribes to small businesses, employees, workers, and renters. Just as in the rest of the country, starting

Map 1. The boroughs of Mexico City, Mexico. María Cristina Sánchez-Mejorada Fernández-Landero, *Rezagos de la modernidad: Memorias de una ciudad presente*, 43. Ley Organica del Departmento del Distrito Federal de 1941.

in 1940 the real minimum wage in the capital was gradually reduced, but the decrease was compensated by concessions, subsidies, and healthcare and education services.[12]

Taking advantage of the fact that the nation's capital received much of the national budget, its mayors were committed to modernization, although investments and public works were concentrated in targeted urban zones, while most of its roads were in poor condition, it lacked services and safety, and its inhabitants lived in crowded conditions given rising housing costs.[13] At the same time, Mexico City mayors were responsible for the police and the administration of justice. Law enforcement agencies multiplied, and buildings were constructed for the Attorney General's Office of the Federal District (Procuraduría General de Justicia del Distrito Federal, hereafter PGJ), Superior Court of Justice (Tribunal Superior de Justicia, hereafter TSJ), and criminal courts.

The crime statistics of the time had lower numbers than those reported in the final years of the Porfirio Díaz administration: Although 28,182 defendants were recorded in 1910 for their presumed responsibility in committing a crime, in 1922 there were 27,689. The numbers peaked in 1925, with 31,917 accused, then dropped in 1929 to 9,434 or 12,545, depending on the source. They continued falling in the following years, remaining between 3,500 and 10,000.[14] The fact that the criminal indices reported between 1929 and 1971 remained stable, while the population was increasing, shows that the percentage of criminals with respect to the total population in the capital plummeted: In 1930 the number of defendants represented 1.08 or 2.1 percent of the population (varying figures are reported); in 1940 and 1950, 0.35 percent; in 1960, 0.10 percent; and in 1970, only 0.07 percent (see table 1).

Table 1. Presumed criminals by gender, 1929–71

YEAR	MEN		WOMEN		TOTAL	
	ABSOLUTE NUMBERS	% OF THE TOTAL	ABSOLUTE NUMBERS	% OF THE TOTAL	ABSOLUTE NUMBERS	% OF THE POPULATION OF THE D.F.
1929	12,545	81.95	2,762	18.04	15,307	
1930	18,117	81.68	4,063	18.31	22,180	2.15
1931	11,207	84.99	1,979	15.00	13,186	
1932	7,534	87.08	1,117	12.91	8,651	
1933	8,171	85.20	1,419	14.79	9,590	
1934	6,887	85.84	1,136	14.15	8,023	
1935	6,042	87.97	826	12.02	6,868	
1936	5,283	88.27	702	11.72	5,940	
1938	7,129	90.63	737	9.36	7,866	
1939	5,906	90.56	615	9.43	6,521	

YEAR	MEN		WOMEN		TOTAL	
	ABSOLUTE NUMBERS	% OF THE TOTAL	ABSOLUTE NUMBERS	% OF THE TOTAL	ABSOLUTE NUMBERS	% OF THE POPULATION OF THE D.F.
1941	8,225	89.84	930	10.15	9,155	
1942	7,987	90.03	893	9.96	8,880	
1943	7,111	81.89	972	18.10	8,083	
1944	7,484	88.27	995	11.72	8,479	
1945	7,601	88.39	998	11.60	8,599	
1946	9,042	90.12	991	9.87	10,033	
1947	9,604	89.95	1,072	10.04	10,676	
1948	11,364	90.12	1,245	9.87	12,609	
1949	10,835	89.56	1,263	10.43	12,098	
1950	9,851	89.27	1,184	10.72	11,035	0.35
1951	9,853	90.39	1,053	9.60	10,906	
1952	8,723	90.32	934	9.67	9,657	
1953	3,469	89.82	393	10.17	3,862	
1954	5,963	90.10	655	9.89	6,618	
1955	6,073	90.50	637	9.49	6,710	
1956	6,370	90.21	691	9.78	7,007	
1957	6,679	90.87	671	9.12	7,350	
1958	6,388	92.51	517	7.48	6,959	
1959	6,783	92.87	520	7.12	7,303	
1960	5,381	93.19	393	6.80	5,774	0.10
1961	5,387	93.42	379	6.57	5,766	
1962	5,167	93.08	384	6.91	5,551	
1963	5,104	92.74	399	7.25	5,503	
1964	5,324	92.62	424	7.37	5,748	
1965	6,006	92.23	436	6.76	6,442	
1966	6,001	92.69	479	7.39	6,480	
1967	6,002	92.46	489	7.53	6,491	

1968	5,897	93.38	418	6.61	6,315	
1969	5,737	93.48	400	6.51	6,137	
1970	6,050	93.95	389	6.04	6,439	0.07
1971	7,827	93.53	541	6.46	8,368	

Source: Author's compilation based on *Anuario Estadístico*, annual publication of the Dirección General de Estadística del Distrito Federal.

However, criminality statistics contrast with opinions of the time.[15] In 1942 Alfonso Quiroz Cuarón referred to an evolving, more dangerous and barbaric criminality, for he found that primitive, opportunistic delinquents were replaced by astute, organized, and well-armed gangs.[16] In 1967 President Gustavo Díaz Ordaz declared, "The social and economic circumstances of the world today have made formerly rare crimes appear with alarming frequency."[17] Shortly after, Sergio García Ramírez spoke of the phenomena of the time, such as crime occurring in housing projects or linked to drug use.[18] Society's views accompanied expert opinions. Various crimes had an impact on the community and received extensive media coverage, especially serial killings or murders tied to robberies.[19] The growing feeling of insecurity was cultivated by newspapers and magazines that gave ample space to sensationalistic stories and a film industry eager to take advantage of the interest crime aroused in viewers.[20]

The citizenry felt unsafe, the immense metropolis harbored anonymity, and modern life seemed threatened, as new ideas and fashions appeared to weaken traditional values and drive women and young people to break behavioral molds. A discourse of fear was constructed around nightclubs; the press and cinema associated nighttime with evil.[21] "Mexico City is a gigantic den of vice," asserted an *Excélsior* writer in 1943.[22] Cabarets and dance halls were portrayed as sites promoting immorality and crime, so their operations and alcohol consumption were regulated. Alcoholism continued to be seen as a physical and moral disease, and fighting it took on new strength in postrevolutionary Mexico. The nation's presidents—from Emilio Portes Gil to Manuel Ávila Camacho—backed by Federal District mayors, promoted educational campaigns and sports activities, while they limited the sale of alcohol, imposed strict regulations on nightclubs, and shut down those that violated them.[23]

They also controlled prostitution. In the 1920s zones were delimited where it could be practiced; in 1940 the policy went from regulation to abolition, and brothels were banned.[24] Through pimps and police extortion, many women continued practicing the trade, and bordellos survived, some managed by women like Marina Aedo, better known as Graciela Olmos, who went by the alias "La Bandida."[25]

The Miguel Alemán administration eased the crackdown. During World War II, bars and dance halls proliferated, while films mythified scenes of nightlife. In 1940 there were 36 cabarets; in 1945 there were 179.[26] However, Adolfo López Mateos and Mayor Uruchurtu undertook a new moral crusade.[27] Cinema, television, and radio were censored; one couldn't show one's navel, recalled actress and dancer Ninón Sevilla.[28]

There was special concern for women who committed crimes. Female criminality was explained as the result of the growing incorporation of women in the public sphere. Although there was no statistical increase, it was seen as dangerous for the family and youth of the future.[29] In the words of attorney María de la Luz Franco, mothers who committed crimes became the "further cause of their children's wrongs."[30] However, female transgressions generally produced a change in the situation and conception of women after the Mexican Revolution. Women fought to be given greater equality by political parties and unions.[31] Laws that mitigated inequality in the family and society were promulgated, such as the 1917 Law of Family Relations (Ley de Relaciones Familiares), which expanded mothers' rights, contemplated inequality of spouses in the management of community assets, and granted the wife the freedom to manage her own assets without her husband's authorization. Women also won the right to vote and run for office. The state of Yucatán was a pioneer, adopting political equality in 1922, followed by the possibility of voting in municipal elections on the national level in 1947 and then voting in federal elections in 1953.[32]

The number of women in universities and in the workplace increased. In 1930 only 4.6 percent participated, but by 1960 this had grown to 18 percent, and more middle-class women occupied positions formerly reserved for men.[33] When women were granted the municipal vote, the mayor appointed two female borough heads; there were four federal deputies (legislators) between 1955 and 1958, increasing to eight during the next three-year term.[34] The first judge (Guadalupe Zúñiga de Mendoza) of the Juvenile Court (Tribunal de Menores) was appointed in 1926; the first temporary female police force was created in 1930; the first female TSJ magistrate (María Lavalle Urbina) was appointed in 1946, shortly after the first criminal judge (María Teresa Puente);

and in 1962 the first female judge (Cristina Salmorán de Tamayo) sat on the Supreme Court (Suprema Corte de Justicia, hereafter SCJ).

However, restrictions were ultimately as important as advances. Civil legislation continued to reflect gender differences. Fewer women than men had access to basic education (for example, in 1930 women accounted for 55.46 percent of the total illiterate population) and higher education (between 1928 and 1954 only 20 percent of the undergraduate degrees at the Universidad Nacional Autónoma de México [National Autonomous University of Mexico; hereafter UNAM] were awarded to women, and just fifteen women earned postgraduate degrees in the humanities).[35] Women slowly entered the political sphere, and in the professional field, competition was unequal because women received lower salaries and found it difficult to access the highest positions.

At the same time, the traditional notion of gender was reinforced, which regarded the woman's place as the home and her mission as caring for her husband and children. This discourse was defended by Catholic groups and other sectors of society.[36] Periodically, competitions were held to reward women who adhered to the desired model (prizes for mothers with the most children or beauty contests reaffirming aesthetic and moral values, in which the winners had to embody attributes like purity, innocence, sweetness, and modesty).[37] Women who broke away from the "ought to be" model were repudiated, such as the "baldies" (pelonas), young athletic flappers of the 1920s who had short hair and wore loose, short dresses.[38]

The press, radio, and movies attest to the transformations and continuities in ideas and values. In addition to newspapers, translated U.S. comic books such as La Pequeña Lulú (Little Lulu) and Lorenzo y Pepita (Blondie), as well as Mexican comic books like Memín Pingüín and La Familia Burrón, proliferated. In a city where illiteracy prevailed (in 1960 only 37 percent of the capital's residents could read),[39] radio was extremely popular. In 1934 the country had 57 radio stations, and by 1940 this had almost doubled; in 1926 there were about 25,000 radios in the capital, and by 1950 the number had grown to two million.[40]

Meanwhile, Hollywood modified customs and shaped fashions. The same could be said of Mexican movies, which in the mid-1930s saw their "golden age," with films like Vámonos con Pancho Villa and Allá en el rancho grande.[41] Pedro Infante, Jorge Negrete, Pedro Armendáriz, Mario Moreno (Cantinflas), Miroslava, Dolores del Río, and María Félix conquered Mexican and foreign audiences. Movie theaters proliferated, and their tickets became cheaper; to see the movie *En la palma de tu mano* in 1950, the public paid from 1.25 to 5 pesos because some went to "lice" (*piojo*) theaters, the cheaper ones. By that time, workers who earned minimum wage had 4.5 pesos for their daily expenses.[42] Equally important was the impact of the small screen, which became widespread in 1950 with the inauguration of the first commercial channel. Since then, television has occupied a predominant place in the nation's culture.

The panorama changed in the late 1960s, when the suppression of criminal courts heralded an economic, social, and political crisis.

THE BOOK'S COORDINATES

Four research issues in the history of justice converge in the study of this period: the role of justice within the state model and compliance or noncompliance in police and judicial practices of essential premises of the liberal, democratic, or legal state; the public image of justice and its impact on actors who intervened in its administration; judicial experiences and the actions of judges, prosecutors, defendants, victims, and journalists; and the character and context of the 1929 and 1971 judicial reforms.

For the first topic, it is necessary to characterize the liberal, democratic, and legal state. In the late eighteenth and early nineteenth centuries, European nations undergoing liberal revolutions and countries in the Americas that won their independence left behind a jurisdictional state, a state model characterized by the fragmentation of sovereignty (the monarch did not monopolize the exercise of authority), regulatory pluralism (the creation of regulations was not monopolized), and the existence of different norms for different bodies (society was conceived as a sum of groups with different qualities).[43] Instead, they adopted a new model of the state: legal state or constitutional state (*Estado de Derecho*). Based on this model, in each nation there is only one legislation and administration (a federal constitution predominates over the constitutions of states or secondary laws), and pluralism of norms is abandoned. A constitution, understood as the vehicle of expression of the general will, had to be applied to all individuals equally, clearly, and uniformly, adopting the principle of equality under the law. The actions of authorities and officials had to adhere to the law (leading to the mandate of legality); in the case of judges, they had to abide by preexisting laws and respect procedural rights (rule of law).

A legal state can take the form of a liberal state if its constitutions and laws aim to balance powers and set limits on the actions of leaders, effectively protecting rights and freedoms of individuals, and leave room for citizens' participation in public decisions.[44] Effective participation and political repre-sentation would make it possible to speak of democratic states. Some elements are part of both state types: The liberal state also requires the participation of citizens, while, according to various authors, the democratic state could not be defined as exclusively heeding the electoral plane but also considers human rights.[45] With this, two models were fused: the liberal and democratic state.

When Mexico won its independence, it was established as a legal state, and the constitutions since that time have expanded the premises of liberalism. Criminal law and the justice system cannot contravene the essential princi-ples of the state model. Furthermore, some of the essential principles of that state model are based on criminal law, and in the criminal field important elements of the state and the political system are put into play. For this, the study of judicial and police practices allows for reflection on the observance of the principles of the state model rendered in the Constitution.

In the following paragraphs, I refer to the characteristics that law and crim-inal justice must have in a democratic and liberal state. First and foremost is respect for human rights. Members must protect the rights and freedom of the inhabitants of the nation's territory, punishing those who attack them, but they must also protect the offenders' rights. Criminal law intervenes in both tasks: It provides penalties for individuals who violate the rights of others while also protecting defendants' rights. As discussed by Sergio García Ramírez, tension between the two functions is inevitable, and balance is difficult to achieve. On rare occasions, the balance leans toward respect for the dignity and rights of the accused, seen as enemies of society, unfit for respect. A rising criminality and discourse of safety for society tends to tilt the balance toward tightening sanctions and restricting rights. According to García Ramírez, the conflict between the two interests in play may be clearly seen in criminal law ("the sanctioning power of the state and the accused's right to freedom") and two "unequal figures" (political power and the individual), and that is where the state employs its most powerful tools and individuals wait with their most fragile defenses.[46] Therefore, we can speak of a "critical scenario of human rights."[47] Needless to say, without abiding by the law and respect for due process, we cannot speak of a liberal or democratic legal state. As García Ramírez concludes, democracy requires a rights-based criminal system.[48]

Second, to speak of this state model entails compliance with the principle of legality or strict observance of the law and, as part of this, the application of these laws and procedures to all the nation's inhabitants. For example,

Larry Diamond maintains that one can speak of democracy only when laws are clear, publicly known, nonretroactive, and universal, respected and applied equally to all.[49]

Third, legal security and certainty must be considered. Under the liberal model, the state was created to guarantee members' rights, with the effective and accurate application of laws to punish criminals that produces legal certainty. In the opinions of José de Jesús Gudiño Pelayo and Hugo Concha, judges provide that certainty by ensuring the application of the law and by grounding their sentences in laws and facts.[50] The effectiveness of the police and judges would achieve the safety of society, whereas criminality, insecurity, and distrust of institutions would bring into question the efficacy of the state. Nevertheless, a liberal or democratic state must achieve this level of security without abusing repressive measures. García Ramírez maintains that criminal law must be a last resort and preceded by preventive actions.[51]

Fourth, to speak of a liberal democracy, it is necessary to address the division of powers and respect for their autonomy—in this case, the independence of judges, which is connected to the possibility of their resisting the interference of other powers in the resolution of legal proceedings.[52] As Piero Calamandrei clearly states, "In totalitarian regimes judges are not independent, they are political entities." He adds that it is important to assess their independence with respect to higher judges or officials who determine their retention or promotion.[53]

Finally, as Norberto Bobbio postulates, transparency of governmental actions, including criminal processes, is necessary.[54] García Ramírez points out that whereas authoritarianism makes use of secrecy, the openness in a democratic state makes the public the judge of the state.[55]

In sum, the essential premises of a liberal and democratic legal state—citizens' safety and legal certainty, autonomy of judicial power, limits of state power, respect for the rights of the accused and defendants, legality and equality before the law, and transparency of governmental decisions—may or may not be complied with. In this book, I analyze whether these premises were respected in judiciary and police practices based on the opinions of witnesses and trial archives, which will permit an assessment of both the type of justice at the time and the scope of and limits to the process of adopting this type of state.

Up to now, I have spoken of current needs, and it is important to ask whether they were part of the demands at the time. Based on the writing of

Laurence Whitehead, I believe democracy has indispensable components, but it can have various configurations depending on time and place.[56] The same may be said of the components of a liberal state. I do not intend to blame twentieth-century Mexicans for violating premises of our contemporary models. Therefore, in this book, I first identify the premises of justice or the state that were important at that time, and based on this list, I then study the contemporary practices to determine which of these aspects were being consolidated or practiced, ignored, or violated.

The second topic I examine is the public image of justice. I believe there is an interrelationship between society's practices and its cultural expressions. It strikes me as relevant to study the opinions and impressions that different sectors had of the police, judges, and defendants, because I presume it fueled the actions of those who intervened in justice, while at the same time, it affected their actions and decisions. To access these, I analyzed writings by experts and widely disseminated products that had a more direct impact on the community's opinions, such as media coverage of crime stories and films.

Various historians have addressed a matter closely linked to this topic: the dissemination of accounts of crimes in the press and movies and their influence on social ideas and values. Dominique Kalifa proposes that in the early twentieth century, cultural industries were created, and the general public had access to the press. At that time in France, society, restless and in conflict with the effects of the French Revolution and the Industrial Revolution, "fueled an exacerbated sensibility regarding crime, the lower depths, and the 'dangerous classes.'"[57] In the case of Mexico and sensationalistic reporting, Carlos Monsiváis also speaks of the "alarmed and pleasure-seeking" denizens who stopped to observe, as if at a shop window, "the fare of rivers of blood, betrayals, iniquity, perversions, robberies."[58] Additionally, Pablo Piccato claims that both the press and literature occupied a key position in the public sphere and shaped the vision society had of crime and criminal law, justice, and the police.[59] Martha Santillán Esqueda refers to the importance of film and newspaper crime reporting in creating the image of the female criminal and the assessment of her crimes.[60] Finally, Julia Tuñón Pablos maintains that filmmakers obsessively repeated themes that touched society and expressed prevailing concepts; by doing so, they strengthened these concepts while also creating new ones, influencing the ideas and feelings of men and women.[61] Texts by experts and the mass media thus influenced the community's vision of crime and criminals, ethics and amorality, the police, lawyers, judges, and justice in general.

It is important to reflect on the homogeneity and heterogeneity of opinions and representations to determine whether it is possible to speak of an image or images of justice. In addition, it is relevant to assess the possible effects of these conceptions on the vision of the state and on practices connected to the administration of justice. Historians and criminal law experts have also suggested such an impact. Piccato notes that sensationalistic journalism in twentieth-century Mexico "could fuel criticism of the government's efficacy and permitted the formulation of demands and rights that eventually had important political consequences."[62] Additionally, García Ramírez points out that thanks to communication media, "the public enters the courtroom in a virtual tide," and the media "can exert a tyranny on the judge that he will transfer to the accused."[63]

The third general research concern is tied to the criminal process and its actors. As Calamandrei states, knowing the theory and law is not enough to understand them, for "the process, as it is described in the code, is nothing more than an empty mold that assumes different shapes when it is translated onto reality depending on the substances poured into its interior."[64] Hence it is important to study court experiences. By analyzing them, I assess compliance with substantive and procedural laws, as well as the actions and weight of the actors involved in the process.

On the one hand, we have judges and their margin of discretion, which, after codification, means the judges' possibility to select within legally valid options or a legal rule among various options (from legal loopholes or vague laws to the interpretation of facts and legal provisions). Today the positivist, mechanistic conception presupposing that law encompasses all cases that can arise and that legal rules do not lend themselves to interpretation, so judges are limited to applying a major premise (law or general legal rule) to a minor premise (specific case) and thus reach a conclusion (sentence), has been overcome.[65] For instance, Roberto Vernengo subscribes to the idea that "even the strictest applications of law contains a trace of judicial discretion" because it requires a series of decisions, based on assessments or preferences.[66] Alejandro Nieto postulates that within the facts presented in court, judges must choose those that are relevant and sufficiently backed by evidence. Similarly, he understands law as an arrow that points in the direction to take but not to the specific path, for the judge must choose one of various possible laws within the body of law. He concludes, "Like it or not, in each sentence there is a greater or lesser dose of discretion that even the most rigorous legal experts cannot do without."[67] The words of Héctor Fix-Zamudio and José Ramón Cossío Díaz ring clear when they maintain that the intention of the exegetical school and Montesquieu's formula have been discarded, and it is necessary to recognize the creative and integrative activity of judges and, consequently, to speak of "imparters" of justice.[68]

Luis Prieto Sanchís explains how this recognition presents new challenges for researchers, for once the "path of the axiomatic method was closed, many efforts were aimed at the analysis of the conditions and circumstances of the process of interpreting and applying the law."[69] Or as Angélica Cuellar suggests, they were aimed at knowing the "world of life" (space of learned patterns and meaningful structures) common to judges and from which they interpret and issue a sentence. Cuellar affirms that judicial decisions involve subjectivity, and this subjectivity cannot be seen as an isolated or solitary phenomenon; on the contrary, the interpretation of law is carried out based on existing notions, formed by knowledge coming from social and individual experiences.[70] Years earlier, Judge Benjamin Nathan Cardozo maintained that two types of considerations converge in sentencing: conscious and subconscious. According to Cardozo, subconscious considerations often "make judges be consistent with themselves and inconsistent amongst them." Nonetheless, the elements that influence judges' decisions are not entirely beyond the possibility of analysis.[71]

Research on the administration of justice should not overlook earlier considerations or omit reflection on elements that can impact legal decisions. Therefore, in approaching legal processes, I evaluate whether a case can be considered "easy or clear" or "difficult or controversial." In an "easy or clear" case, there are no doubts as to how the event occurred; the case coincides with a general rule, and the applicable law is clear. In a case that is "difficult or controversial," there may be doubts regarding how the event happened, no existing legal rule fits the situation, or the applicable law lends itself to diverse interpretations.[72] As Francisco Javier Ezquiaga Ganuzas states, the latter type of case "can be resolved based on law, but in diverse meanings."[73] And such cases can produce controversies among judges. I used the presence of controversies, which I suppose derive from the different situations I referred to, as the criterion to assign cases as "difficult or controversial." In this book, I discuss both "easy or clear" cases, where there was agreement in the interpretation of facts and the applicable legal provision, at least among the three judges of the criminal court and superior justices, and "difficult or controversial" cases, where there was overt disagreement among the judges on the same criminal court or among judges of a different instance. Later, I explore conflicting positions, and to the extent possible, I try to consider the judges' and even the attorneys' world at the time to seek connections between their sentences and arguments and the ideas and values expressed in other sources of the period.

I am particularly interested in the question of gender. Renouncing the idea that paternalist judges tended to be more benign toward women, recent studies have shown that on the contrary, they were more severe toward woman than men because in general, by committing crimes, women violated not only the law but also the attributes and conduct expected from them.[74] It is important to evaluate whether it happened this way between 1929 and 1971, as well as the general weight of gender considerations in women's sentences.

It is also interesting to reflect on the bearing the accused's socioeconomic condition might have had. In one study on what occurred in Argentina between 1880 and 1920, Ricardo Salvatore claims defendants lacking resources were turned into "special subalterns" because they had fewer tools than others with which to defend themselves, so the principle of equality under the law was more of an aspiration than a reality.[75]

Further, I analyze the actions of attorneys in the process. This factor is particularly important in the case of agents of the MP because it is said they played a key role in the final judgment. That said, the study of the parties' participation makes it possible to evaluate the balance in the trial, for the possibility of contradictions among the actors (analysis, debate, dialogue, confrontation) is a fundamental requirement of the accusatorial system.[76]

Additionally, it is relevant to reflect on the presence of journalists in the courtroom and their potential effects on the actions of legal officials and sentences issued by judges, as well as their immersion in investigations and collaboration with the police. Mexico City saw an increase in journalist participation in crime investigation.[77]

The fourth topic in this book is the 1929 and 1971 reforms to the justice system. I assume laws must be understood based on their political, social, and cultural contexts. In this, I concur with other authors. For example, in studying the thought of penitentiary reformers, García Ramírez began with four "concentric circles": the political organization and society of the time; ideological and cultural trends, as well as desires that would lead to new ideas; specific events that prompted concern and created awareness; and individual circumstances and experiences.[78] Meanwhile, Jaime del Arenal points out that reflection on the law must be anchored in "human and social realities."[79] From there, by analyzing reforms, I consider their historical milieu and link them to the prevailing legal culture.

SOURCES

As sources for this analysis, I first examined legislation and legislative debates. Second, I consulted archival documents: Secret Police reports and prison files (Archivo Histórico del Distrito Federal: Fondo Departamento de Policía, Jefatura de Policía section, Expedientes de Investigación y Servicio Secreto series; and Fondo Cárceles, Penitenciaría), expert opinions (Biblioteca Isidro Fabela: Fondo Alfonso Quiroz Cuarón), trial files (Archivo General de la Nación: Fondo Tribunal de Justicia; Archivo del Tribunal Superior de Justicia), and *amparos* (Archivo Central de la Suprema Corte de Justicia). For information on judges and litigators, I used the archives of the Instituto de Investigaciones sobre la Universidad y la Educación of UNAM.

Third, I turned to defendants' writings. Those of Alberto Gallegos Sánchez stand out, as do those of Soledad Rodríguez "Chole la Ranchera," who published her recollections in the press, and Humberto Mariles, who wrote the introduction to the text of his *amparo* suit request (see chapter 5).

Fourth, to better understand the ideas and visions of justice, I relied on specialized works and journals, theses and dissertations, memoirs from congresses, newspapers, novels, and movies. To access the vision of specialists, I turned to legal journals. Some covered all or much of the period studied; as a whole, the journals of the Universidad Nacional de México (*Revista de Ciencias Sociales*, *Revista de la Escuela Nacional de Jurisprudencia*, *Revista de la Facultad de Derecho de México*) were relevant, as were El Foro, Criminalia, La Justicia, and Anales de Jurisprudencia. I consulted others for specific periods: *Los Tribunales* (1923–53), Jus (1938–58), *Revista Jurídica* (irregularly from 1921), and *Revista Mexicana de Derecho Penal* (1961–82). The journal Anales de Jurisprudencia was published by the TSJ and the *Revista Mexicana de Derecho Penal* by the Procuraduría de Justicia; in both cases, they may represent the vision of their officials. Five other journals were published by lawyers: El Foro, which was published by Orden Mexicana and later by the Barra Mexicana Colegio de Abogados; Criminalia, which first appeared in 1933 and became the organ of the Academia Mexicana de Ciencias Penales; Los Tribunales and La Justicia, which were sponsored by independent parties who funded them from advertising and subscription fees;

and Jus, which was produced by the publishing house backed by conservative Manuel Gómez Morín and was funded by a similar process. The rest of the publications mentioned came from educational institutions. This is the case with the journals of the Facultad de Derecho of the Universidad Nacional, heir to the Escuela Nacional de Jurisprudencia (ENJ), and the *Revista Jurídica* of the Escuela Libre de Derecho (ELD), an institution established in 1912, stemming from a strike organized by ENJ students and sponsored by Porfirio Díaz administration jurists identified with the group known as the *científicos*, Emilio Rabasa and brothers Pablo and Miguel Macedo.

As for the vision of nonexperts, the press was my preeminent source. Given the impossibility of consulting every single newspaper from the time, I selected three paths: searches for specific subjects or dates; digital newspaper archives; and "Economic Archives" of the Ministry of the Treasury (Secretaría de Hacienda), consisting of files with newspaper clippings organized by subject to facilitate quick revision by the minister.[80] This allowed me to access newspapers of different leanings.

On the one hand was El Nacional Revolucionario, later called El Nacional. Founded in 1929, it was the mouthpiece of the National Revolutionary Party, and during the administration of President Ávila Camacho, it was passed on to the federal government. On the other hand were newspapers with widespread circulation. El Universal was founded in 1916 by Félix Palavicini and later came under the control of the Lanz Duret family. Starting in 1922, it had an evening edition, El Universal Gráfico, more open to sensationalistic news.[81] Excélsior was a newspaper in this same line; it was founded in 1917 by Rafael Alducín, and with time, ownership passed to a partnership directed by Regino Díaz Redondo, Julio Scherer, and Manuel Becerra Acosta. In the 1960s it had a conservative to moderate right tendency, but internal questioning led to Scherer becoming the director in 1968 and the paper's receptivity to columnists of a "socialist" bent, which had no place before.[82] Perhaps the newspaper with the highest circulation was La Prensa, founded in 1928, which offered generous space for crime reporting. It started out with a conservative orientation, critical of the regime; the director, Miguel Ordorica, was forced to resign, and it was then run by a cooperative. In the years that followed, it expressed a more favorable opinion of the government.[83]

Newspapers obtained the support of the authorities, who sold them low-cost paper and paid for newspaper advertising, and journalists received monthly retainer fees (*igualas*).[84] However, as Arno Burkholder asserts, they were able to distance themselves from government stances, and published critiques served as escape valves through which writers could express social discontent.[85] Similarly, Carlos Monsiváis suggests that the press spread the economic "miracle ideology" and supported presidentialism; however, significant information was censored, and top politicians were considered untouchables, but minor officials were open to mockery (*choteo*) and became scapegoats.[86] Or at least, this was true of certain officials. In the period studied, the judge of the first criminal court, Rafael Pérez Palma, maintained in *El Universal*, "While the people applaud the work of members of the executive branch of governments of the Revolution, they condemn the Judicial Power."[87] Pablo Piccato concurs that the crime page allowed for criticism of political authorities until the 1960s.[88]

I also consulted supplements and magazines. The most interesting is *Magazine de Policía* (which came out on Mondays) and its supplement (on Thursdays), starting in 1939. *Alarma* was created in 1963 and achieved widespread popularity after the case of the Poquianchis. Targeting sensationalistic news, these publications grabbed readers' attention with splashy headlines and multiple photos.

And finally, starting in the mid-1960s, *Sucesos para todos*, which had a leftist tendency, spread criticism of the opposition. Another major source for gaining insight into the vision of unspecialized sectors was cinema because policemen and judges are featured in numerous films.

It is important to note that works have been published on justice in Mexico and in other countries concerning the years or themes addressed here, and I refer to them throughout the book.

2. THE DESIGN OF JUSTICE

This chapter analyzes the design of criminal courts, laws regulating justice, and requirements for judicial appointments, considering the political, economic, social, and cultural setting. Sources include legislative debates, statements of legislative purpose, code and law reform projects, and opinions, especially from legal experts.

The discussion opens with a panorama of the judicial system during the Porfirio Díaz administration, then shifts focus to the 1917 Constitution, which establishes the direction of twentieth-century criminal and procedural law. I next examine the 1929 Codes creating criminal courts, followed by the 1931 Codes, international treaties and their reflection in Mexican law, legislative projects, and legal changes until 1971

BACKGROUND

Justice before the Mexican Revolution

The 1857 Constitution, 1871 Criminal Code, 1894 Criminal Procedure Code, 1907 Organic Law of Tribunals (Leyes orgánicas de tribunales), and other laws regulating the administration of justice mandated compliance with the law and judge impartiality, balance between procedural parties, observance of the rights and equality of defendants, and public trials.

The foundations were based on the 1857 Constitution, which went back to the principle of separation and autonomy of powers, including judicial powers; carried out the principle of legal equality; and expanded the rights of defendants. Furthermore, its Article 14 reaffirmed the nonretroactivity of laws and added a new component: the precise application of law, under which defendants had to be sentenced with laws adjusted exactly to the case adjudicated (principle of legality).

The legality mandate became viable in 1871 with the first Criminal Code, which enumerated actions that could be considered crimes and assigned a *pena media*, a sentence for each crime that could be reduced or increased by only one-third, considering aggravating and attenuating circumstances established and with numerical values (arts. 35–47, 180–82, 229–36). To ensure judicial compliance, the TSJ reviewed sentences that, for the prosecution or defense, had failed to observe substantive or procedural law. The appeal was filed against final first-instance decisions. Another resource (*casación*) could be presented against final second-instance rulings.[1] In turn, the SCJ judged the demands for the violation of constitutional rights. Individuals could initiate a lawsuit in federal court (*amparo/juicio de amparo*), seeking judicial protection against an action committed by public authorities that violated their constitutional rights through laws or acts.[2] Mexican constitutional guarantees included the precise application of the law, so an *amparo* could be granted for judicial sentences.[3] Moreover, the 1871 Criminal Code established that judges could be sanctioned or removed from their post if, among other reasons, they departed from a strict legal provision or issued a "glaringly unjust" sentence, contrary to trial proceedings or to the jury's verdict (art. 1035). A mixed system of justice was thus configured with important elements of accusatorial proceedings: It prevented procedural secrecy and torture, sought judicial impartiality and compliance with the law, and strove for equality of the parties in the proceedings, ensuring protection of defendants' rights. With this, legislators attempted to meet the demands of a liberal state and a legal state.

That said, the most severely sanctioned crimes were tried by a jury, which the Federal District adopted in 1869. It was composed of judges of law (*jueces de derecho*), with legal training, in the service of the state, responsible for applying the law, and triers of fact, or juries (*jueces de hecho*), who did not necessarily have legal training, assessed the evidence for the crime, the defendant's responsibility, and the circumstances of the case tried.

Some experts, especially sympathizers from the positivist criminal school, expressed their opposition to the jury, claiming it did not correspond to Mexican reality.[4] They believed that the scientific method, besides revealing natural world phenomena, permitted knowledge of and solutions to social problems and that legislators had to observe reality to identify the causes of social problems and thus pass laws remedying them. Their assumption was that a theoretical model could not transform reality; on the contrary, reality should shape the model and ideas, or laws could not be imported. Following this logic, they saw the Constitution and Criminal Code as the result of utopian theories—in Jesús Urueta's words, "courses of rationalist philosophy in legal articles."[5]

The supposed equality of individuals, reflected in equality before the law, seemed particularly utopian to them. The liberal school assumed all people act through free will, are responsible for their actions, and therefore could and should receive the same punishment because everyone was equally capable of decision-making. In contrast, according to positivists, human actions are not dependent on will (while criminal sociologists suppose it depends on environmental factors, criminal anthropologists believe offenders' anatomy is responsible). Thus for that school, it was unimportant whether the offender had committed the crime freely, consciously, and voluntarily; what mattered was whether the criminal was a threat to society, which had to be protected, and that some individuals were more prone to commit crimes than others. For example, if followers of the criminal anthropology school assumed people committed crimes stemming from anomalies in their organisms, they also supposed the degree of inclination to criminality varied, and they concluded that law had to weigh the differences and contemplate different sentences depending on the threat posed by each offender.

Jury trials had defenders but mostly critics. Several jurists considered it unfeasible in Mexico or deemed it unviable in general. Some maintained it did not correspond to Mexican society by referring to the people's ignorance and moral backwardness and the difficulty of forming juries of responsible, enlightened individuals.[6] Others, advocates of the criminal anthropology school, held that jurors had to consider organic differences and the threat posed by the defendant, which only technical judges and those steeped in the subject could do.

Another criticism of jury trials came from jurists who defended a basic tenet of the liberal model: the mandate of legality. Theoretically, as "triers of fact," members of the jury should not intervene in applying the law but should only assess the parties' evidence to determine how the act in question took place. Professional judges applied the law to the verdict. Therefore, in theory, no contradiction arose between jury trials and the principle of legality, and thus juries did not hinder the precise application of the law. However, detractors of jury trials believed there was an insurmountable obstacle. In their opinion, juries tended to issue absurd and irrational verdicts because they let themselves be swayed by attorneys' allegations and tactics, public opinion, defendants' image and chicanery, false impressions, sentiments, values, and prejudices.[7] They asserted that the determination of guilt or intervening circumstances in committing the crime did not always correspond with the evidence presented at trial. Because jury verdicts had to be respected, judges could be forced to apply a law that, in their opinion, might not correspond to the act proven.

This distance between proven acts and the exact correspondence with the law in judgments violated the demand for legality.

In sum, detractors of jury trials defended the need to abolish juries to achieve justice under the law and consider the differences between criminals, arguments stemming from opposing positions and trends.[8]

Professional judges were also criticized for their close ties to Mexican President Porfirio Díaz, who had appointed them, suggesting their lack of independence. However, many jurists thought the solution was not to change the path of selection, but instead to adopt irremovability (lifetime appointments), because if their job was permanent, judges would not let themselves be influenced by the officials who appointed them.[9]

Critics of criminal law and the justice system had little impact on legislation, although changes were made. For instance, in response to criticism of jury trials, legislators reduced their jurisdiction and raised the requirements for their members. When the court was created, it judged all crimes with a *pena media* over two years; however, when the Mexican Revolution broke out, it judged only punishment exceeding six years, but not for "special crimes" (for example, abuse of trust, fraud against property, extortion, and bigamy). Furthermore, although at the start jury members had to know only how to read and write, later a professional degree and minimum income were stipulated.

The 1917 Constitution

The justice system just described was in place at the time of the Revolution, and such were the opinions facing President Venustiano Carranza. Carranza addressed concerns over the lack of autonomy and performance of some judges, whom he accused of violating defendants' rights. When he presented his reform project to the Constitutional Congress, he maintained that although Article 20 of the Constitution stated the rights of the accused, in practice their rights were violated by "truly inquisitorial practices, which generally leave defendants subject to judges' arbitrary and despotic action." He claimed judges carried out unlawful arrests, locked up defendants in filthy jails and isolated them to extract confessions, carried out covert inquiries, altered defendant and witness statements, diminished the right to defense, and extended trials indefinitely.[10] To achieve the principal aim of the Constitution, guaranteeing fundamental rights, he proposed changes to several articles; these changes were submitted to the opinion of a committee and later debated and voted on by all members of the Constitutional Congress.[11]

Among the main reforms were those introduced to Article 14, because it permitted the retroactive application of laws if they favored the defendant, and based on prevailing opinions, the guarantee of precise application of the law was limited to criminal matters.[12] Furthermore, only the administrative authority could issue arrest warrants in emergency situations in the absence of the judiciary (art. 16).[13] Moreover, the Constitution ordered that the alleged crime be specified in the *auto de formal prisión* (document that ordered the formal initiation of the judicial process) and that the proceedings exclusively follow that act; if it was determined the defendant had committed another crime, a new accusation had to be formulated (art. 19).[14] The deadline for suspects to give the preparatory statement (*declaración preparatoria*) was reduced to forty-eight hours after arrest. Compelling defendants to testify against themselves was prohibited; they had to be assigned a public defender if they refused to hire their own attorney. Bail had to be granted to anyone who committed a crime warranting a sentence of less than five years in prison, and depending on the seriousness of the offense tried, a period of four months to a year was set for ruling (art. 20).[15] Finally, the local MP was tasked with the investigation (art. 21).[16]

By expanding rights, Carranza and the members of the Constitutional Congress wanted to avoid violating the rights of the accused and defendants. They modified the way judges were appointed and exempted them from criminal investigations. Carranza proposed that TSJ and first-instance judges be appointed by the Mexican Congress (Congreso de la Unión), in a joint session of both chambers of senators and deputies. To defend the autonomy of powers, deputy José María Truchuelo proposed that they be appointed by the SCJ. However, Congress accepted Carranza's idea. Additionally, based on the principle of the lifetime appointment of judges, they decided that from 1923, judges could be removed only with a trial (*juicio de responsabilidad*).[17]

Constitutional Congress members entrusted criminal investigation to the administrative authority through the MP and judicial police (*policía judicial*). With this, in Carranza's words, judges would recover "the dignity and responsibility of the Judiciary" and would achieve impartiality.[18] Thus they reaffirmed the division of the police into two bodies: the preventive branch, which sought to prevent the commission of crimes, and the investigative (judicial or prosecutorial) branch, which investigated crimes committed.

In sum, they resolved one of the major criticisms of justice: judges' close ties to the executive. However, they did not address a central demand made by

Porfirian jurists: the abolition of jury trials. In fact, they strengthened them. They left it up to states to set up juries, but in doing so, they had to adopt a jury with broad jurisdiction (judged crimes with a *pena media* of a year in prison), and its members had to know only how to read and write. They sympathized with the institution. In addition to juries for common crimes, they created one for crimes committed by the press against public order or national security and another for the crimes of civil servants in performing their duties.[19]

Therefore, in consonance with their suspicion of authorities in the Díaz administration and the broad power assumed by the executive, while championing liberal institutions, sovereignty, and the capacity of the Mexican people, legislators returned the original breadth to juries for common crimes. With this, postrevolutionary Mexico inherited one of the institutions most criticized by legal experts in the late nineteenth and early twentieth centuries.

CRIMINAL COURTS AND THE JUSTICE SYSTEM IN THE 1929 AND 1931 CODES

The Origin of Courts and Rupture with the Classical School: The 1929 Codes

After the 1917 Constitution was promulgated, efforts to issue new codes were considered, and in 1915 the Ministry of Justice called for proposals.[20] However, political instability and the armed struggle delayed the task. Meanwhile, organic laws for tribunals were issued that introduced changes in jury trials. After a suspension between 1914 and 1919, jury trials were reinstated with fewer capacities than initially contemplated by Constitutional Congress members; they covered crimes with *pena media* sentences of more than two years and continued to exclude what were designated as special crimes. Over time, these modifications continued. In 1922 fraud and adultery were added to special crimes, and in 1928 sentences were increased to five years for crimes entrusted to juries. Furthermore, in 1919 it was decided that jury members could only determine the defendant's guilt or innocence, and it was up to the judge to admit attenuating or aggravating circumstances in sentencing verdicts. In 1922 a new requirement mandated that jury members have a primary school education.[21]

In the mid-1920s the call for new codes gained adherents. Among them, Miguel Macedo, chairman of the committee reviewing the Criminal Code early in the century, was inclined to preserve this code, but twenty years later, he asserted it was time to undertake "a true overhaul of our laws, as general and profound as what has been done on political and social orders for more than ten years."[22] Plutarco Elías Calles announced the codes would be replaced, which could be distanced from the liberal school, because the Revolution had promised a sea change and the country was counting on institutionalization. Based on the tradition of the Mexican president possessing the power to issue ordinary laws, in 1926 Elías Calles received congressional authorization to reform the codes.[23]

José Almaraz presided over a committee composed of Antonio Ramos Pedrueza, Enrique Gudiño, Ignacio Ramírez Arriaga, and Manuel Ramos Estrada, in charge of drafting the Criminal Code. After several extensions, in early 1928 the committee presented a draft bill, gave explanatory lectures, and received the opinions of SCJ ministers, TSJ magistrates, officials, jurists, and physicians.[24] The draft was different in character from the 1871 Code. As Almaraz explained, the drafting committee was inclined to positivism, regarding the liberal camp as being in "utter bankruptcy," unable to offer solutions in tune with reality. The committee rejected "the a priori foundations of the classics" and opted to "apply the method of experimentation and observation to investigate the causes or conditions that led to the crime." In sum, it considered that only "criminal reality, compiled and ordered by crime statistics and sentences," could point to "the direction of social defense."[25]

Committee members wavered between organic and social determinism. They believed criminal actions result from physical (temperament) and psychic (character) personality, both determined by psychophysiological inheritance. They rejected the principle of moral responsibility to support punishment. Being "demonstrated that offenders reveal bio-psychic, hereditary, or acquired, permanent or transitory anomalies," Almaraz wrote, the grounds for responsibility were weakened, and "the classical edifice collapses." They constructed the edifice on another foundation: the concept of danger. The legislative purpose reads, "The punishment, instead of being expiation of a sin committed, must offer protection, a defense of society from dangerous individuals."[26] Their position is noted in the definition of crime: "damage to a right protected legally by a criminal sanction" (Criminal Code, art. 11). They did not mention willfulness, as did the 1871 Code.

Regarding criminals as acting based on factors beyond their will and presenting differing degrees of danger would have required, according to Almaraz, classifying offenders into categories and considering different punishments.[27] This solution would have contravened the principle of legal equality under the Constitution. In fact, the president of Mexico asked committee members to limit their proposals for change to "constitutional prescriptions." Therefore, they proposed a "transitional code" and renounced the possibility of drafting a "perfect work based on modern tendencies." They wanted the sentence to consider both the crime and offender. Thus they rejected the crime as the sole criterion in determining the sentence, but they preserved it as a shared criterion, because they deemed the offense to be another symptom that permitted measuring the degree of danger of the criminal.[28]

The compromise was not easy. The committee members determined the code would continue to be based on the crime, and they assigned minimum and maximum sentences for each type of crime, conditioning the severity of the punishment on the presence of aggravating or attenuating circumstances. Nevertheless, they allowed judges to consider the offender's specific characteristics and the possibility of amendment. For this, just as Enrico Ferri did in his project for the Italian code, they listed the defendant's characteristics among aggravating or attenuating circumstances in the code; granted judges the possibility of considering uncontemplated circumstances, raising the sanctions for repeat offenders because they were convinced it indicated antisociality and danger; and introduced the notion of the habitual offender for those who displayed a "persistent tendency to crime."[29]

With this, they expanded the judges' margin of discretion. However, they believed that judges in office did not meet the requirements and that the expansion required "professional training." All too often, they thought, judges were "uncommitted, arbitrary, corrupt," which they attributed to how appointments were made. To avoid the issues of loyalties and cronyism, incompetence, and laziness, it was necessary to appoint judges based on their merit and promote them solely according to the career ladder.[30]

It was not up to the code drafters to change the appointment procedure, but in response to their prioritization of specialized judges, they suppressed jury trials for common crimes. Almaraz argued that anonymous juries, with rudimentary capacities and transitory functions, were no match for professional judges, with a reputation to preserve, permanent functions, and intellectual superiority.[31] He asserted that having conducted "the technical investigation of the offender's personality," it was not possible "to submit the result of that investigation to the sentimental vote of jury members."[32] Thus Criminal Code drafters addressed one of the critiques of jury trials: the inferiority of laymen to professional judges. Their decision contributed to the effort to professionalize public servants.

To replace jury trials, they created criminal courts or collegial courts, composed of three judges each trained in law and possessing an attorney's degree. They also suppressed capital punishment and created the Supreme Council of Defense and Social Prevention (Consejo Supremo de Defensa y Prevención Social, hereafter CSDPS), an agency of the executive branch responsible for individualizing the treatment of convicts by considering their personality.[33]

Positivist opinions of the drafts were published. For instance, members of the Mexican Bar Association (Barra Mexicana de Abogados, hereafter BMA) considered it necessary to have codes "in harmony with modern sociological doctrines that preferentially tend to defend society." They welcomed replacing the principle of criminal liability with that of danger because they considered crime a harmful act requiring defense to preserve society and believed sentences had to be individualized by considering the criminal's conditions. These beliefs coincided with Enrico Ferri's premise that "there are no crimes, only criminals" and Quintiliano Saldaña's modification, "there are no criminals, only men." However, after considering that the age-old dilemma between determinism and free will had not yet been resolved, experts could determine a defendant's degree of abnormality or guilt only on a case-by-case basis; they celebrated the drafting committee's efforts to find a balance and expressed their support for preserving the former system for sentencing by expanding the judge's discretion to consider the offender's particular situation.[34]

The code's orientation was also supported by Luis Chico Goerne, who underscored the importance of considering the defendant as a subject of scientific research.[35] Salvador Mendoza maintained that "there was agreement on the guiding ideas of the reform," and José Almaraz affirmed that they made suggestions only on specific points.[36]

One of these points was the suppression of jury trials. Referring to absurd verdicts, they supported representatives of the Ministry of the Interior (Secretaría de Gobernación) and Attorney General José Aguilar y Maya. Furthermore, editorials in the newspaper Excélsior reported that public opinion hailed the end of juries and questioned the sincerity of those who defended it, including the presidents of debates (presidentes de debates), who participated in juries and promoted their interest in preserving their posts. Clearly, the presidents of debates were opposed to the suppression. They described the court as the "more human and equitable genuine expression of a democratic justice for being dispassionate, impartial, and incorruptible." The use of "dispassionate" is significant because it contrasts with the most common critiques. To confirm that it was not a machine churning out acquittals, they presented figures showing that 75 percent of verdicts had been condemnatory, and only 5 percent of the acquittals made it possible to imagine insufficient attention to the evidence presented, which were attributed to defects in the MP's inquiry or accusation.[37]

Contrary to the *Excélsior* editorialist's opinion, other social sectors were in favor of jury trials. For instance, BMA members claimed judges could never equal the "sentiment of justice among the people who never took their eyes off the reality of life, humanly know the defendant and individualize him in their own imperfections and qualities."[38] El *Universal* also defended juries. Its writers acknowledged the existence of flaws but expressed their belief that a reformed jury had to be preserved to respect defendants' rights and avoid judges' excesses.[39]

Therefore, in 1929 the champions of jury trials revisited two arguments: the possibility that jury trials could prevent abuses by authorities and the capacity of juries to understand criminals, who came from a reality far from that of professional judges.[40] However, their objections failed to convince the drafting committee members.

After three years of work, in 1929 the drafts of two codes were finished. It was the time of the Cristero War and also when the federal government began to regain power after the revolutionary struggle. This paved Álvaro Obregón's way to reelection and his assassination, and against expectations, Calles handed off the presidency to become the power behind the throne. Concern increased over population growth, because the number of Mexicans dropped after the Revolution, and over the population's physical health and racial degeneration, which promoted ideas of eugenics in public campaigns. Moral health was also worrisome, prompting an increase in combating vice, such as through the National Committee for the Fight Against Alcoholism. In this environment around the start of the period known as the Maximato (alluding to Calles's ongoing influence) and during Emilio Portes Gil's provisional government, codes were promulgated by presidential decree: the Criminal Code in September 1929 and the Criminal Procedure Code in October, both entering into force in December.

This gave birth to criminal courts, responsible for processing crimes for which the Criminal Code stipulated a *pena media* sentence of over three years or a fine of more than thirty working days.[41] Three were established in Mexico City, each composed of three courts and therefore three judges. They were part of the Judicial District of Mexico (Partido Judicial de México), which covered the Central Department and Guadalupe Hidalgo, Azcapotzalco, Iztapalapa, and Iztacalco boroughs.[42]

The presidency of the criminal courts was rotational, and the three members of the court occupied the office in turns. The judges had to be Mexican, be lawyers with five years of professional experience, and have CSDPS certification of specialization in criminal matters.[43] After 1928 they were appointed by the whole body of TSJ magistrates, who were appointed by the Mexican president and confirmed by the Chamber of Deputies; they remained irremovable unless found guilty of serious misconduct and sentenced by a specific court.[44]

Criminal procedure was divided into phases. First was the prejudicial stage, which began when the MP knew of the existence of a criminal act because most crimes were followed ex officio, so crimes had to be pursued without a request from the affected party. This stage was conducted not before judges, but rather before the MP, which served as the authority and had the judicial police, responsible for investigating crimes, under its command. It had an Investigations Department, and its agents received criminal complaints or accusations (querellas or denuncias), conducted the inquiries tending to confirm the body of the crime and the guilt of the accused, apprehended suspects, and referred investigation records and evidence to the MP.[45] The preventive police should not have had a police corps dedicated to investigation, but it did: the Investigations and Public Safety Corps (Cuerpo de Investigaciones y Seguridad Pública), which was called the Secret Service beginning in 1939. The secret agents depended on the preventive police chiefs, who were appointed and removed by the head of the Department of the Federal District with the approval of the Mexican president. The agents had more training than the rest of the police force; they had to have completed primary school and be able to speak at least two languages. They were responsible for "confidential surveillance and investigations" that could not be entrusted to uniformed policemen.[46] This was a new sign of the rise of presidential authority.

This first phase ended if there was insufficient evidence to support the existence of the crime and guilt of the accused, upon which the suspect was released. When evidence existed, the accused was sent to court, and a judge took over the process.

With the judge's intervention, the procedure was divided into two periods: judicial instruction, or the second stage of the investigation, and later the plenary or hearing. The heads of the three courts of the criminal courts rotated cases, taking turns overseeing the instruction of a process.[47] Solitary confinement and coercion were prohibited in securing confessions. Within two days (forty-eight hours), the accused had to be informed of the name of the accuser, if one existed, and the nature of the accusation. During the same period, the defendant had to give a preliminary statement before the judge and MP agent, and the defense attorney could attend. Defendants had to know of their right to defense, and if they did not have an attorney, a public defender affiliated with the courts was appointed.[48] All those elements guaranteed a full defense, one of the main requirements of an accusatory system. Later, before another day passed (a total of seventy-two hours after detention), the judge again had to determine whether there was sufficient evidence supporting the existence of the crime and the suspect's guilt. If so, the judge ordered the beginning of the trial (auto de formal prisión); otherwise, an order dismissing charges was issued for lack of merits (auto de libertad). The accused could appeal the court order within two days after notification.[49]

Once the judicial process began, the defendant was identified using the Bertillon system. The judge could grant freedom on bail if the crime did not merit a prison sentence over five years. Those released simply on giving their word (libertad bajo palabra) tended to disappear, and the most common form of security was bail (libertad bajo fianza), overseen by bail bond companies. If bail was not granted, the accused remained in preventive custody.

During the trial, the prosecution and defense provided means of evidence to verify or prove their statements. The MP no longer served as an authority but instead was the prosecutor. Its agents were attached to courts. They were not the only party responsible for the burden of proof, for the defense attorney and defendant also had to prove their claims. The recognized means of evidence was established, and evaluation rules were determined. Confession, public and private documents, reports by experts (who intervened when specialized knowledge was required), judicial inspection, testimonies (witness statements), and presumptions (logical deductions inferred from the facts or evidence) were recognized as means of evidence.[50]

When parties offered evidence, the judge could reject or admit it; in the latter case, the evidence admitted had to be presented (desahogarse). For example, in the case of testimony, the judge had to summon the witnesses to testify in court and respond to judges' and litigators' questions. Furthermore, the judge could order the necessary proceedings to clarify the evidence of the prosecutor or the defense or confirm any important point.

After considering the inquiry exhausted, the judge made the records available to the parties (prosecution and defense), which had to present allegations in writing specifying the facts deemed proven in the process and referring to applicable criminal laws.[51] The process continued if the MP agent formulated an accusation and the judge did not request review of the case. The hearing date was set; it had to take place within ten days and be attended by the three criminal court judges. This fulfilled the requirement for immediacy: the immediate proximity of the judge to the proof and subjects participating in the process.[52] At the hearing, the litigants were heard. Although the MP had to be present, the hearing could be carried out without the presence of the defense.[53] This practice suppressed debate and left the defendant at a disadvantage.

Hearings were public and oral, formerly in the jury trial phase and later under criminal courts. This openness permitted public access to hearings, while orality meant that trial proceedings—although recorded in written records—were primarily conducted verbally.[54] They opened with the presentation of accusations, which established the questions to be debated during the trial. The MP had to limit statements to methodically and succinctly explaining the events; proposing matters of law; citing laws, judicial precedents, and applicable doctrines; and after that, issuing clear, precise, specific propositions.[55] Under *amparo*, this paved the way for final judgments (*ejecutorias*), but opinions of jurists or authors on the matter (*doctrinas*) were also admitted, with which the article was closer to the wording of Mexican legal precepts before the demand for precise application of the law than in subsequent Procedure Codes. Later, the defense presented its conclusions. Then began the debate, in which the parties' evidence was presented. After that, the allegations were presented.

When the hearing was over, the judge in charge of the instruction formulated a draft judgment, which was submitted to the consideration of his court colleagues. For the court to issue a sentence, all members had to be present, and the decision was determined by a majority of votes. If one judge did not agree with the vote of the other two, a private vote could be held. All legal resolutions had to contain an extract of the events leading to the sentence (*resultandos*), the legal bases of the sentence (*considerandos*), and the corresponding acquittal or sentencing (*resolutivos*). The judgment had to be issued within fifteen days after the conclusion of the trial.[56]

According to the Constitution, the first-instance process could not last more than four months (for crimes with a prison sentence less than two years) or one year (for sentences over two years).[57] However, the period could be extended if the defendant needed more time to present evidence. Once the criminal court proceedings ended, on the three days following notification of the final sentence, the MP, defender, or defendant could appeal in writing or orally. If the sentence was expressly approved or the deadline expired, the decision was enforceable and considered irrevocable. After an appeal was filed, the judge, without substantiation or any process, admitted or denied it.[58] Once the judge admitted the appeal, the case was referred to the TSJ chamber, which could confirm, modify, or revoke the criminal court resolution, and the sentence could be increased or reduced no matter which party introduced the appeal. After the sentence was issued, the parties were notified and the judgment was sent to the respective court.[59] The second-instance judgment was definitive because the appeal for annulment (cassation) had already been eliminated.

Faced with a definitive sentence, *amparo* could be invoked, and the SCJ would judge it in a single instance. *Amparo* proceeded if a violation of rights occurred in the sentence or arose during the process, but violations had repercussions on the meaning of the ruling.[60] In criminal matters, the injured party—the prisoners, their legitimate representatives, or defenders—could promote and follow *amparo*. The grievant and responsible authorities (both judges and authorities who enforced or tried to enforce the judicial decision) were considered parties.[61] When the judge was informed that a complaint had been filed, enforcement of the judgment sought was automatically suspended; in the case of a prison term, the plaintiff remained at the disposal of the district judge, who could grant release on bail if appropriate.[62]

The application for *amparo* had to indicate the guarantee violated, referring to the relevant constitutional article, specifying the act in question, and enforcing the concept of violation that demonstrated this transgression. If procedural laws were violated, they needed to be specified, and the processual violation committed had to be described clearly and precisely, justifying why it had left the appellant defenseless and explaining its repercussions on the final sentence. If law enforcement had been improper, the applicable law and omitted law had to be duly specified.[63] Indirect *amparo* could be filed for acts of judicial authorities that had taken place during the process before sentencing or for any acts committed later during its enforcement. The district judge judged them.[64]

A thesis (*tesis*) used the criteria maintained by the SCJ to interpret a legal norm applied to solve a specific case and was expressed in an abstract form and in writing.[65] Five *tesis* upholding the same point in law with unvarying criteria uninterrupted by another contrary decision, and voted on in the full session by more than seven judges (and starting in 1935 also those issued by the chambers and voted on by more than four members), constituted judicial precedent (*jurisprudencia*). After 1951 *jurisprudencia* should have been duly observed by lower federal courts and local courts (those of the states and the Federal District), and thus they served as binding legal decisions.[66] In 1941 jurist Ricardo Abarca maintained that in practice, courts tended to bow to Supreme Court interpretations and also took into account TSJ decisions, although application was not compulsory.[67] Perhaps for this reason, Federal District Attorney General Raúl Carrancá y Trujillo sought to establish the judicial precedents of this court. He argued:

> The security of the law follows the security of judicial precedent as its logical consequence. As an ability of judges, assessing the case as a function of the applicable legal rule can produce a different and even contradictory interpretation of one and the same rule; to avoid the serious consequences derived from it, other organic systems empower Superior Courts to, in plenary, determine which interpretation should be binding for the lower courts.[68]

To establish judicial precedent over essential aspects, he requested the help of magistrates and judges. The measure was disseminated and well received by the press and magistrates, who maintained that the absence of uniformity in the application of the law was recurrent and produced "serious and severe disorders."[69]

This is how the criminal courts functioned starting on December 15, 1929, when the Criminal and Procedure Codes entered into force. However, the rules did not remain in force for long.

The reception of the Almaraz codes was different before and after being promulgated and incurred differing opinions among foreign and Mexican authors. Commentaries were more favorable before they entered into force and outside the country or in articles by foreigners. Officials and theoreticians in the United States, and to a lesser degree in Italy, France, Germany, Spain, Brazil, and Japan, pondered the advanced scientific character of the code, some also applauding the end of juries and the suppression of capital punishment.[70] In an article published in the United States, Salvador Mendoza affirmed that public opinion in several countries "was favorably impressed by the Mexican reform" and followed its implementation with interest because it could serve as an example.[71]

In contrast, in Mexico the codes received little praise after promulgation. Some authors recognized the merit of their having opened the way for reform. For instance, Francisco González de la Vega asserted they managed "to bring together previously dispersed scientific concerns, awakening in Mexican jurists the desire for a holistic reform of criminal legal institutions that resisted being dislodged by law of inertia."[72] Raúl Carrancá y Trujillo considered its main contribution as having repealed "the venerable text of Martínez de Castro."[73] With few exceptions, Mexican authors recognized the boldness of the group headed by Almaraz in transforming a code that had a mythical aura, but they refrained from praising the result.

Criticism abounded. Some reproached the code drafters as coming from an outdated school. These included Alfonso Teja Zabre and Mario de la Cueva, who fought for the incorporation of precepts of historical materialism and preventing justice from being "social class justice." Teja Zabre wrote, "The 1929 Code is alien to the socialization and populism trend. It has the entire configuration of a bourgeois code, complacent for crimes of the privileged classes and worthy, like earlier codes, of being called 'law against the poor.'"[74]

Others thought the code did not put an end to liberal school foundations or adopt positivist premises, but that it presented a weak, rambling character. José Ángel Ceniceros, Luis Garrido, and González de la Vega claimed it was not an offender's code, because it was not based on the criminal's personality, nor did it consider indeterminate sentences, but rather it continued being a crime code, because punishment was based on crimes and sentences had predetermined durations.[75] Manuel Rivera Silva declared, "The 1929 legislation came with a brand-new jersey of positivism, that albeit brand-new did not prevent the contemplation of classical school carrion it carried within. The legislators thought that by hiding the corpse in fashionable attire the coexistence of the new legislation could take place and in their mad enthusiasm, they were unable to see that the jersey of positivism was now the color of a shroud."[76]

More importantly, critics regarded the code as contradictory, digressive, and inapplicable. Several authors, such as Carrancá y Trujillo, Garrido, González de la Vega, and Mariano Ruiz-Funes, reiterated that the code presented shortcomings in wording and structure, duplication of concepts, and flagrant contradictions, all of which hindered its practical implementation.[77]

The suppression of jury trials was also criticized. Jurist Antonio Ramos Pedrueza claimed the measure had been hasty and based on recent criticism. He condemned its replacement by collegial courts, which were no more than "three-judge correctional courts" that presented a "secret, outdated organization explicable three hundred years ago, but that today is incompatible in the atmosphere of freedom, openness, and debate that society aims to practice."[78] Isaac Olivé recognized that juries were problematic (due to influence of public opinion, pressure from defendants' families who visited court members, shortcomings in the integration of and errors in questioning), but he believed the problem was in regulatory laws of the tribunal and not in the juries themselves. He criticized the collegial model and claimed justice would be bogged down in never-ending bureaucracy.[79] Armando Z. Ostos argued that only juries could judge the offender and their decisions were visible because the process was public, while judges sentenced based on written records and their errors remained hidden.[80]

Not only legal theoreticians criticized the 1929 Codes but also editorialists, such as the writer under the pseudonym Marxófilo, who described the Criminal Code as "exotic and inadequate for our social environment," reproaching it for not having adopted revolutionary principles and not being detached from the bourgeois crust.[81] According to Alfonso Romandía Ferreira, Federal District representative to the Chamber of Deputies, "No one praised the new code."[82] Garrido maintained, "The press, experts, and even members of Congress undertook a campaign that ruined the law."[83] Ceniceros affirmed that the environment for the legislation was unfavorable among judicial officials responsible for enforcing it, lawyers, and professional associations, as "the whole world was convinced of the failure of the codes," and the need to reform them prevailed.[84]

In an atmosphere of opposition and criticism, in May 1930, four months after the Criminal Code entered into force, President Pascual Ortiz Rubio formed a committee to draft a new law.

José Almaraz defended his project to the bitter end. In a message to the president and members of the review committee, he said it was absurd to accuse the 1929 Code of being casuist, because the constitutional requirement of exact enforcement of the law made it necessary to include most cases that could arise and to do so with clarity, precision, and abundant details, thus preventing crimes from having no judgment. Only this could permit the law from being changed in courts that were just being established.[85] Almaraz, devoted to legal standardization, seemed to distance himself from the inveterate positivist.

Synthesis and Reconfiguration: The 1931 Codes

In December 1930 Pascual Ortiz Rubio asked the Chamber of Deputies for authorization to issue new codes. He argued that the earlier codes were difficult to enforce and urged the elimination of doctrinal statements and superfluous articles. He received authorization in January 1931.[86]

The code drafting committee was composed of José Ángel Ceniceros (representing the Ministry of the Interior), Luis Garrido (PGJ), Ernesto G. Garza Ochoa (TSJ), José López Lira (attorney general of the nation), and Alfonso Teja Zabre (criminal courts).[87] In general, a new generation of theoreticians and law scholars rekindled investigation and legal debate, which was weak between 1910 and the early 1920s. They stood out as distinguished authors of books and articles on criminal law between 1920 and 1940. In 1933 they founded the journal *Criminalia*, which guided the direction of criminal sciences in the following decades. Shortly after, in 1940, they created the Mexican Academy of Criminal Sciences (Academia Mexicana de Ciencias Penales, hereafter AMCP).[88]

The draft was submitted to the consideration of judicial officials and attorney associations.[89] In April 1931 *El Nacional Revolucionario*, the National Revolutionary Party organ, announced a new penal code was ready, described it as the "shortest in the world," and published matching opinions, including those of Deputy Minister of the Interior Octavio Mendoza González, Raúl Carrancá y Trujillo, and jurist Juan José González Bustamante.[90]

The codes were promulgated in August 1931 and entered into force in September. Although they lacked a statement of the statutory or legislative purpose (*exposición de motivos*), this was covered in a presentation given by Teja Zabre on behalf of the criminal law review committee in the National Juridical Congress held in May.

Members of the drafting committee believed the liberal school had failed, but they did not think positivism provided the "remedy." They did not adhere to a particular school of thought because they held that "no school, no doctrine, no criminal system can serve to integrally establish the construction of a Criminal Code," while eclecticism "permitted escape from unilateral dogmatism and the narrow sectarianism of a school or system." They presented themselves as in favor of a "third school," or a critical school.[91] This belief system originated in Italy, and in Mexico it originally spread through an article by Emmanuel Carnevale, one of the foremost proponents of this stance, published in 1892. The school respected the scientific character of positivism, but it was not openly defined by determinism, nor was it inclined to voluntarism. It rejected both extremes but considered it necessary to know the factors that shaped will.[92] Many Mexicans sympathized with this alternative, or as sociologists, literati, architects, and artists did, they took elements from different belief systems, without undue concern over the mixture.

Thus drafting committee members of the 1931 Criminal Code drew much from the classical school, but following the positivist school, they adopted the principle of "social responsibility and overcoming the afflictive concept of punishment."[93] They believed the natural sciences and biology had a lot to offer. In addition, they considered the contributions of schools of thought such as historical materialism and began with the "review of social and spiritual values formulated based on the First World War." Finally, they sought to include "constitutional forms" and Mexican "juridical traditions," while considering the country's "economic and social conditions" and criminality patterns.[94] In the opinion of drafting committee member Garrido, the code was inscribed in the "new criminal positivism adopted in America," which gave preference to criminal sociology above anthropology.[95]

Congruent with the principles of the "third school," the committee members assumed an intermediary position between determinism and voluntarism. They considered the criminal as "a being absolutely equal to whoever has not committed a crime," but they believed criminal acts were conditioned by biological, psychic, and social factors beyond the individual's will.[96] They responded to new tendencies in criminology that opted for a multicausal vision: the influence of economic and social factors was admitted and, with time, they would delve into psychological and even endocrinological elements. From there, they defined crime as "the act or omission that criminal laws sanctioned" without recovering the condition of willfulness included in the 1871 Code but eliminated in 1929. By enumerating the factors that had to be considered when enforcing the sentence, they spoke of the motives driving or leading the criminal.[97]

Therefore, they rejected the postulate of moral responsibility without taking social defense to its ultimate consequences. They did not opt for a justice differentiated based on the danger posed by the criminal because, although they believed the entire code should combine considerations surrounding the act and subject, they continued to focus on the crime. To achieve the combination, they expanded the margin of judicial discretion. In Ceniceros's words, justice demanded "wider discretion for the judge on the grounds of the objective and subjective particularity of each case at hand, as a means of repression is adapted to the nature of the criminal." He added, "The law can provide bases of individualization to the judge, but it cannot carry out individualization itself, because only the judge can know the criminal."[98]

Moreover, Ceniceros said, discretion could be divided into absolute (when the judge chose the sentence deemed appropriate) and relative (when the law determined the sentence and the judge only its duration). The committee members did not believe in absolute discretion. They offered several reasons: constitutional restrictions; Mexican tradition, accustomed to a detailed system of criminal metrics; and the need to have judges with broad knowledge, which were not abundant because they were appointed based on political criteria or cronyism.[99] The last point is particularly interesting and was also discussed by Celestino Porte Petit, who affirmed that the limits to judicial discretion arose in response to the need to reconcile new orientations of criminal science and Mexican juridical life, "which is characterized by the lack of technical and economic elements, and by distrust of judicial officials, whether because their capacity is in doubt [or out of] fear they will yield to power, acquiesce to friendship, or be bought with money."[100]

Thus the drafters opted for a rational judicial discretion, which remedied "the excessive, blind, brutal, and absurd rigidity of the criminal metrics" and gave the judge scope for decisions to consider the circumstances of the crime and its perpetrator.[101] They expanded the margin of judges' discretion between minimum and maximum sentences for each crime, giving the judge the possibility of choosing between the two extremes without taking into account preestablished aspects or values. The judge should consider "the nature of the action or omission, the means to execute it, and the extension of the damage caused and danger represented," as well as special conditions surrounding the criminal when committing the crime and personal characteristics including age, education, customs, prior conduct, motives, economic conditions, and potential danger. It is worth stressing two of these characteristics: economic conditions (a reflection of the social sensibility of postrevolutionary legislators) and potential danger (a former requirement of the positivist school). The drafters also granted the judge the possibility of commuting a prison sentence of less than six months to a fine.[102] They justified the extension of judicial discretion with four arguments:

A) **Its prior and necessary existence.** Not even with the rigid system adopted by the 1871 Code had discretion been successfully eliminated; it existed simply based on determining innocence or guilt, but as it was theoretically eliminated, it became "clandestine and twisted."[103] Ceniceros wrote, "I wish it was possible . . . the law replaced the then supreme judge from saying: I absolve or condemn; but that is not possible, and we accept the judge can throw the criminal out onto the street or send him to prison for a while, but instead, the power to individualize the sentence based on objective and subjective circumstances that come together in the specific case seems to us exaggerated."[104]

B) **Conviction that the rise in judicial discretion would not increase errors.** The drafters rejected the idea the greater the decision-making capacity, the higher the possibility of error. They endorsed the following: "It is argued judges will often make errors in their assessments; but if an error is made in enforcing a measure on a specific individual, whose individuality and behavior he investigates and based on the perception of a specific act whose circumstances he knows, how much more will the legislator in his study not err in establishing sanctions on cases that have not yet occurred and completely unknown subjects?"[105]

C) **Belief that the solution was in the selection and training of judges.** Ceniceros claimed the solution was not to "tie the judges' hands," but to "make them judges." He affirmed, "Since we mistrust our officials, we think by making more detailed laws, we close the doors to arbitrariness, when the only thing we achieve is to create more passageways to reach that arbitrariness." He concluded, "The problem of the judge's integrity does not depend on the law being or not being casuistic" because "good or wise men have never been created by legislative decree." Furthermore, he insisted on the need to create a judicial career to recruit upright and responsible officials.[106]

D) **Differences between Mexicans.** The drafters maintained that "the division of classes and castes by economic and racial differences led to serious difficulties in applying criminal laws in Mexico, particularly given the existence of unassimilated Indigenous groups." They thought inequalities could not be remedied with special laws, which only multiplied the defects of casuistry; instead, broad and generic rules that permitted individualizing judgments were needed.[107]

They touched on two essential points in defining judicial order. First, they believed that despite legislators' efforts, judges had been unable to dispense with a certain margin of interpretation; even the most exacerbated casuistry was problematic in its enforcement; and it was impossible for a legislator to be able to imagine all the circumstances of a crime or the characteristics of a criminal, whereas the judge was close to the specific case. From there arose the need to expand the margin of discretion. Second, they thought egalitarian legislation could not be equitable if it was applied to groups with different situations and cultures, such as Indigenous peoples.

They respected the collegial system and expanded the jurisdiction of criminal courts, entrusting them to judge crimes that warranted a *pena media* exceeding six months (no longer than three years) or a fine exceeding 50 pesos (no longer than thirty days' wages). The number of criminal courts increased from three to eight.[108] The judges on them continued to be appointed by TSJ magistrates and were irremovable, meeting the same requirements to occupy the post, although now the certification of specialty in criminal matters was issued by the TSJ and backed by university degrees.[109]

In addition, the judges' wider margin of discretion gave them greater freedom to make use of evidence, admitting "everything presented as such."[110] Although judges had the freedom to assess expert and presumptive evidence, they had to abide by the rules by assessing the confession, documents, inspection, and testimonies.[111] In general, over time, and as a result of scientific and technological developments and their applicability in criminology, expert witnesses assumed a larger role, and technical proof gained greater weight.[112]

As for procedure, terms were extended, with five days more to prepare the hearing after receiving the parties' conclusions (now totaling fifteen), one more to appeal an *auto de formal prisión* after notification (now three), two more to appeal a judgment after notification (now five), ten more to summon the parties admitted to the appeal (now fifteen), and ten more for TSJ magistrates to issue a trial judgment (now fifteen).[113]

Moreover, the Procedure Code drafters extended the requirements for the presentation of conclusions. They included requirements for the MP's intervention, revisiting the possibility of referring to previous judgments and applicable doctrines when proposing questions of law.[114] They also had an interest in monitoring the prosecutor's actions and expanding the field of the defense. Unlike in the 1929 Code, the conclusions of the MP agent could not be modified unless for supervening causes and the defendant's benefit. In contrast, the defense was only to present its petitions in writing—not subject to any other rule—and could withdraw or modify them at any time; if they were not presented, this was considered a request of innocence. In addition, although the cause could be seen without the defense present, the Procedure Code contemplated sanctions for attorneys not present without the consent of their client, who was assigned a public defender or was allowed to be defended by any of those attending the hearing. Finally, in the appeals submitted by prisoners or their defense, TSJ magistrates could not increase the sentence imposed by lower-court judges.[115] To conclude, it introduced the possibility of requesting the reinstatement of proceedings before second-instance judges.[116]

According to Ceniceros, as a simple law with limited articles, the Criminal Code was "well received by the tribunals and the public."[117] It was also positively regarded by experts. Carrancá y Trujillo and González de la Vega stressed the intention to combine theoretical principles with reality and offer a code based on general concepts and containing clear definitions.[118]

Nevertheless, Ceniceros recognized that "the authors and supporters" of the 1929 Code had criticisms.[119] Referring to Almaraz, Garrido maintained, "In seventeen years he did not abdicate his Aristarchus position before the 1931 legislators."[120] In fact, the most systematic censure of the new code came from Almaraz, who curiously touched on points like those singled out by detractors of the 1929 Code; for example, as a result of the drafting committee's eclectic stance, he considered the code lacking in "harmony and logical consistency" and called it "hybrid legislation that lacked anything modern."[121] He was not the only one who criticized the 1931 Code. Ostos maintained that it had retrograde points, such as extending the investigative power granted to the judge and giving the ability to withdraw bail, because that afforded him intervention like that held before 1917.[122]

Despite criticism, the code was well received. Its parallels with the laws of other European and Latin American nations, its intermediary position in the interpretation of crime and margin of discretion, recognition of its debt to the 1871 Code, and its continuity with the 1929 Code explain how it remained in force for four decades.

THE 1931 TO 1971 PERIOD: OPINIONS ON LEGISLATION AND JUSTICE REFORMS

In the four decades following the promulgation of the 1931 Criminal Code and Criminal Procedure Code, both were reformed, and new laws were enacted. International treaties that defended respect for fundamental rights were also issued. Moreover, drafts of codes were written, and an initiative to reinstate jury trials was presented. This section describes these laws and expert opinions of them.

Fundamental Rights and the Impact of International Law

Shortly before the atomic bomb was dropped on Hiroshima, Celestino Porte Petit asserted that "democracy and freedom were suffering the most serious crisis in their history," and he regarded it as paradoxical, considering that millions of men had just died defending them.[123] Indeed, death on the battlefield and excesses committed against the civil population, along with extreme violence and the lack of ethical principles during the war, horrified the world. To prevent the situation from being repeated, international bodies were created or consolidated, and treaties promoting peace and human rights were issued. "From the most atrocious war that the centuries have known, a humanity arose eager to avoid the repetition of similar horrors and to create a new world where man's dignity was duly guaranteed," wrote Garrido.[124]

In June 1945 the United Nations requested that countries make a commitment to defending human rights, a matter it considered fundamental on the international agenda. Three years later, two important documents were promulgated. In May 1948 in Bogotá, the American Declaration of the Rights and Duties of Man, which vetoed the application of laws that were not pre-existing and contemplated the principles of legal equality and presumption of innocence (the accused could be found guilty only after being tried in an open, impartial court held in a reasonable term).[125] In December of that year, the United Nations approved the Universal Declaration of Human Rights, the first such declaration that was universal in perspective. The document granted greater scope to procedural rights: It sanctioned arbitrary arrests and imprisonment and demanded that defendants have all the means to defend themselves.[126]

Soon concern arose to ensure the preventions were met. In November 1950 the Council of Europe issued the European Convention. It included other procedural rights: limitation of circumstances under which persons could be imprisoned (by judicial sentence or to ensure their appearance at trial) and the defendant's right to know the cause of the accusation. Most importantly, it contemplated the creation of a European Court of Human Rights to monitor compliance with the principles.[127]

The International Covenant on Civil and Political Rights, signed by the United Nations in 1966, integrated other points: the immediate presentation of defendants before a judge, the separation of accused and convicted, the view of first-instance judgments by a higher court, and the right to compensation for individuals condemned by mistake. It also prohibited the use of force to obtain confessions and judging an individual twice for the same crime.

In 1967 the Organization of American States entrusted the Inter-American Commission on Human Rights to promote its observance.[128] Finally, in 1969, just as European countries had done, the nations of the Americas agreed in the American Convention on Human Rights to respect rights and freedoms.[129]

Except for some aspects (such as compensation for judicial error), at that time Mexico contemplated all the points of the treaties. Therefore, it was at the cutting edge of the defense of human rights and the paths to guarantee them. In the Constitution and in law, its criminal system guaranteed rights under rule of law, appropriate for a liberal, democratic, and legal state.

The Justice System and Its Critics: Drafts, Initiatives, and Debates

Between 1931 and 1971 reforms were proposed to the justice system, some general and others specific. It is worth examining the drafts, which allows one to explore the most polemic aspects, such as the expansion of judicial discretion and the reinstatement of jury trials.

The first Criminal Code draft was presented in 1934, three years after the 1931 code came into force. In the following years, three other Criminal Code drafts were formulated (1942, 1949, and 1958) and one Procedure Code (1949). The drafting committees began with the same starting point: They did not debate the theoretical orientation of the codes; they only corrected flaws and introduced changes that experience required. Moreover, an initiative was presented in 1936 to suppress criminal courts, and another in 1937 to reestablish jury trials. In the proposed reforms, four points stand out and correspond with the most debated aspects of the legislation:

A) **Equality of Mexicans and margin of judicial discretion**. The drafters continued debating both legal equality and equality before justice in a heterogeneous society, as well as the scope of discretion.

In 1941, at the inauguration of the Supreme Court of Justice building, President Manuel Ávila Camacho pledged to promote the independence of the judicial power. He argued that it was up to the judges "to fill the gaps and omissions of our legislation and reconcile its contradictions, and above all, to apply law with a high social and human meaning; avoiding the purely logical interpretation of the abstract norm can entail antisocial aims or solutions that overlook economic and cultural inequalities that make it necessary to attenuate the rigor of the law, because its blind application could become a cover for fraud and injustice."[130]

He considered that legal equality should be nuanced in response to extant inequalities among Mexicans. Members of the 1931 Criminal Code drafting committee raised similar arguments by justifying the expansion of discretion. In the same vein, in 1935 Carrancá y Trujillo contended that as long as profound social inequality was not admitted and laws were in place to translate it, "only very broad judicial discretion can temper the tremendous injustice of treating the unequal as equals." He continued, "In countries of such unequal culture as Mexico; of such a disparate moral and philosophical background based on social and economic classes or even races that the individual belongs to, to establish laws of standard application is only an imposition of the democratic lie that organizes us and on which we are founded as a nation; [a] cruel lie for those of inferior culture while it exorbitantly benefits the most cultured."[131]

Postrevolutionary Mexico saw a change in the explanation of crime, in which misery and a lack of education and opportunities occupied an important place. In this logic, Teja Zabre believed punishment should be the last resort, preceded by education and employment. Among criminogenic factors, he emphasized poverty from the crisis in the capitalist system, population growth, the lack of services, and family disintegration.[132] The same vision is reflected in the film *Los olvidados*, written and directed by Luis Buñuel in 1950, for instance, in the words uttered by the director of the reform school, who, after locking Pedro up for having attacked some hens, lamented: "I wish instead of locking them up, we could lock up misery forever."

Significantly, whereas Ávila Camacho spoke of economic and cultural inequalities (a postrevolutionary official could hardly have referred to ethnic distinctions), both Carrancá y Trujillo and the code drafters referred to social, cultural, and racial disparities. In fact, the later discussion focused on Indigenous peoples. The topic took on relevance from the rise of Indigenism and the importance given to Indigenous peoples in official discourse. In 1931, a year before the code was promulgated, Silvio Zavala referred to the impossibility of legislators to issue regulations appropriate for the "Mexican reality," considering the differences between "white" and Indigenous groups. However, he did not believe legislation should be adapted to social conditions.

Instead of accepting backwardness, one should rely on improvement; instead of starting from diversity, one should trust time to mitigate the differences.[133]

As Eduardo Zaffaroni noted in a work probably written in the late 1960s, the authors who reflected on Indigenous peoples and the law opted for two choices: the preservation of juridical equality combined with improvement of marginal groups or the adoption of a tutelary system.[134] Zavala's proposal falls within the first option, as did those of most nineteenth-century intellectuals. In other words, the author believed raising the standard of living or education would achieve uniformity; meanwhile, the principle of juridical equality should be preserved because eliminating it would mean a decline in the ideal of equality. Indigenists, such as Gonzalo Aguirre Beltrán, coincided in the belief that marking differences among groups hindered the national integration project.[135]

Nevertheless, in the nineteenth century protective legislation won the support of experts in Mexico and Latin America (especially in nations with a high percentage of Indigenous population, like Peru and Bolivia).[136] Other major representatives of Indigenism were among its sympathizers. After noting the extant differences between the customs and ideas of legislators and Indigenous peoples, anthropologist Manuel Gamio concluded they should be judged with a law appropriate for them. Concurring with this idea, Lucio Mendieta y Núñez maintained that culturally different communities could not be equal under the law. Moreover, Darío Cruz Ramírez averred that protective legislation should consider judicial aspects, such as the participation of special defenders and translators in cases involving Indigenous peoples.[137] Speakers at the First Convention of Local Jurisdiction Attorneys General (Primera Convención de Procuradores de Justicia del Fuero Común), Carlos Hugo Zayas Lezama, Carlos Cañedo, and Venancio González Ramiro, championed legislation appropriate for the characteristics of "civilization" of these communities.[138]

In addition to these two paths—equality under the law together with policies of social and economic integration or a tutelary system for Indigenous peoples—a third option arose: trust that differences would be accommodated in court. In 1936 a court was established in Chiapas for "crude Indians," and if condemned, they were subjected to the state's tutelary action.[139] Some wanted to transfer this idea to the Federal District. In 1939, at the First Convention of the Attorneys General, Josafat Hernández Islas (attorney general of the State of Mexico) and Claudio Medina Osalde (of the attorneys' union) blamed "civilized men" for keeping the Indigenous population in material and moral backwardness for the sake of domination. They claimed malnutrition diminished the Indigenous people's intellectual capacities and made them prone to disease, while cultural backwardness and misery made them rudimentary, promiscuous, dirty, fanatical, and superstitious (the description was not far from many of nineteenth-century characterizations, although the origin of evils was explained in a different way). They affirmed the state should look after these people. According to Medina Osalde, "Beautiful equality before the law, so fruitful for cultivated men, is nothing more than a derision, injustice, and formidable burden for Indigenous."[140] Hernández Islas insisted on the defenselessness of Natives in courts because they did not know the law and language, lacked the means to defend themselves, and were generally condemned by judges in a hurry to close their cases.[141] Both Medina Osalde and Islas recommended special tribunals. Their idea was well received and adopted as one of the convention's recommendations.[142]

Some thought the possibility of giving judges a wide margin of discretion that would allow them to contemplate the personality and particular circumstances of criminals (including race, which, as it was said, was translated into cultural traits and customs). In other words, to accommodate social, cultural, and racial differences, trust was vested in the individualization of the sentence. Ávila Camacho, Carrancá y Trujillo, and members of the 1931 Criminal Code drafting committee had already proposed it. Years later Ceniceros reaffirmed his position, again backed by Carrancá y Trujillo and now also by Carlos Franco Sodi and Javier Piña y Palacios. These authors denied the possibility of adopting different laws for ethnic groups living in Mexico and entrusted the judge to consider distances.[143]

This was not the sole argument to demand a wider margin of discretion than that of the 1931 Code. In fact, a second demand took on greater force: the need to consider the danger posed by the defendant. Almaraz focused on this aspect. He claimed that by basing the sentence on the crimes, the 1931 Code drafters continued to deal with "legal and not real entities, concepts and not people." He declared that it was urgent to base the code on the somatic, psychic, moral, and social study of the criminal because it was the only way to identify the most appropriate treatment to correct the subject. He criticized the survival of the qualitative predetermination of the sentence and restrictions imposed on the judge in determining the punishment adjusted to the offender. In his opinion, speaking of discretion did not mean expanding the limited range in which the judge moved between minimums and maximums by the law: "It is useless to set the sentence between a very distant minimum and maximum; the qualitative predetermination of the punishment survives and, with it, the judge is left no discretion, because it makes choice impossible in terms of the class of measure suitable for the offender's personality."[144]

Porte Petit supported the idea. He recognized greater elasticity in the application of the sentence in the 1931 Code but believed it was not enough for the judge to consider the defendant's degree of danger. In his opinion, the "code of the future" should contemplate precrime danger (including dangerous states, such as vagrancy and malfeasance) and postcrime danger (considering indeterminate sentences or security measures for criminals in "dangerous states") in the catalog of crimes.[145] For their part, Alfonso Quiroz Cuarón and Alfredo Savido lamented that judges were constrained by a law that left no margin of discretion to consider the offender's characteristics because it did not specify the difference between the two factors leading to crime: biopsychic makeup and exogenous stimuli.[146]

The Criminal Code drafters were aware of these ideas. The committee met in 1934 and proposed that instead of intentional and culpable acts, it should speak of criminal liability (intentional crimes) and social liability (a category including wrongful actions like those committed by minors or persons with mental illnesses, who only deserved safety measures).[147] Furthermore, committee members adopted judicial pardon, defined as "the referral of some penalties corresponding to a defendant, made by the courts at the time of sentencing." They justified it based on the following arguments: "Sometimes judges find their conscience at irreconcilable odds with the law they are required to apply because they consider in that special case the general rule is ostensibly unfair and even harmful, not only for the defendant but also for society," and they are faced with a dilemma—whether to "apply the law in compliance with their duty, ignoring the dictates of their conscience, or follow the [law's] mandates passing over the express letter of the law." The latter was dangerous lest courts of justice become accustomed to breaking legal orders, hence the importance of seeking a solution that allowed the judge to proceed in good conscience but within the law.

Although they proposed an important modification, they did so tentatively: They contemplated judicial pardon only for defendants who confessed they had acted recklessly or excessively in self-defense, which did not require amendment.[148] An example was described by Alberto Vela as "the mother who, extenuated by long nights of anguished vigil at the bedside of her sick

son, confused a medication with a toxic substance and caused his death."
Exacting a penalty in such cases would not benefit society, and true harm
would come with grief, for their families would be left without childcare and
livelihood, and the convicted individuals could be "infected" in prison and
become hardened criminals.[149] The 1949 committee revisited the notion of
judicial pardon, also to reduce the penalty for situations like abortion committed in some circumstances or homicide from adultery.[150] The importance
given to honor is noted here.

Some jurists sympathized with this solution. For instance, Fernando Arilla
Bas saw it as the only way to give greater emphasis to rates of danger.[151] Others
disagreed with judicial pardon and, generally, the expansion of judicial discretion. Instead, they believed it pertinent to limit the margin of discretion granted
by the 1931 Code. Among them, Paulino Machorro Narváez believed judges
should have two guides: a list, within the code, of factors to consider when
setting the sentence duration, and reports submitted by biological, chemical,
and psychophysiological specialists. He also believed judicial pardon could
function only with well-trained judges, who were of upright conscience and
away from "unhealthy influences."[152]

Perhaps as a debated concept, judicial pardon was not included in the
proposal the committee submitted to the Ministry of the Interior in 1949.
Nevertheless, the committee included it in the 1958 draft and expanded it
to cases in which the convict had acted for exceptional reasons, was not a
danger, and had a prison sentence of less than four years.

B) **Reinstatement of jury trials.** After the suppression of juries, initiatives
were presented to restore it. In 1932 a group of attorneys formulated a request
to the Senate.[153] Five years later, in 1937, attorney groups insisted on the proposal and included an innovative aspect: They deemed that it was to be a trial of
peers, with jury members similar to the defendant in class, guild, profession,
or job. That point produced controversy: El Universal editorialists—staunch
jurists—backed restoration, but not the proposal for jury composition. The initiative was approved without debate by the Chamber of Deputies, but the Senate
postponed it.[154] Editorialists of Criminalia applauded the deferment because,
in their opinion, it was a poorly developed and "very lightweight" project.[155]

In support of reinstatement, previously presented arguments were advanced
as proper and essential for a democratic system. Jurists, journalists, and citizens surveyed concurred with this idea. Just as years earlier El Universal writers
had condemned the suppression, in 1941 they opted for restoration, praising

the possibility that the people could participate in the administration of jus-tice.[156] For his part, Rafael de Pina maintained that while "inveterate admirers of totalitarian regimes" were opposed to the court, those who had not lost faith in democracy defended it because it offered defendants greater guarantees.[157] Along the same lines, businessman Felipe Márquez Pacheco described the jury trial as "the most democratic expression of the administration of justice."[158]

Additionally, jurist Fernando Cuen and El Universal asserted that only juries guaranteed openness and transparency, the controversy between the parties, and respect for defendants' rights.[159] In addition, Federico Sodi, deputy Alfonso Francisco Ramírez, and a group of law students thought jury trials served to preserve immediacy. In the words of the students, "There is, without doubt, more probability in jury trials that the crime is better assessed than what can be done by a judge, who has not personally conducted the investigation, and thus has been entirely alien to it."[160]

Finally, it was said that jury members could act as their conscience dic-tated. This argument was recurrent in surveys in the capital: Mexican Navy captain Ignacio González referred to their lack of "ties"; a laborer, Rafael Muñoz, defended the convenience of replacing sentences "dealing with the dead letter of codes" with "the free and honest judgment of members of the collectivity"; and a housewife claimed that courts declared what they felt and thought.[161] Therefore, deputy Ramírez asserted that verdicts reflected "the sentiments of justice" of the community, and Federico Sodi described them as a "thermometer of social mores."[162]

This vision is reflected in cinema. Juries survived on the silver screen because screenwriters preferred them. Rulings did not fail the expectations of persons attending trials and surely the public in movie theaters. Take the example of the 1954 film La infame (Vile woman), directed by Miguel Zacarías. After being deceived by her fiancé, Cristina (Libertad Lamarque) represses her desires to become a mother and develops a resentment toward children. But later, with a doctor's advice, she recognizes her maternal instinct, and to get pregnant, she tries to seduce attorney Esteban (Luis Aldás) before backing out. In a park, she unwittingly meets her old flame's son, polio-stricken and rejected by his mother. Without knowing his identity, she grows fond of him and abducts him when she finds out his mother plans to leave him in a hospital. The mother captures the media's sympathy, and the abductor is the subject of popular ire. When she is put on trial, Esteban represents her. He tells the true story, and at the climax, the boy enters the courtroom, throws his arms around her, and calls her mommy, rejecting his biological mother. The members of the public listening to the trial on the radio outside the courtroom lower their placards insulting the defendant. The jury declares her guilty but recommends a light sentence.

Another movie by the same director, *Legítima defensa* (Self-defense), also serves as an example. The film culminates with the acquittal of scientist Ricardo Morán (Roberto Cañedo), based on a circumstance precluding self-defense. It is his second trial. In the first, Morán is unjustly declared guilty of murdering Arturo Platas (Luis Aldás), who is alive and has faked his death to run away with Morán's wife, daughter, and fortune. In the second trial, he is accused of killing the true Arturo Platas, who was using an alias. Morán's attorney demonstrates the pen the deceased was carrying was a weapon.

Arguments opposing the adoption of jury trials were not new. First, Emilio Pardo Aspe maintained that juries could undermine the fundamental principles of the liberal model, such as legal certainty (everything was "contingent, adventitious, uncertain") and equality (because criminals who committed acts meriting more severe sentences were tried by jury and, ultimately, by judges prone to sentimentalism and benevolence).[163] Second, jurists Alejandro Quijano, Telesforo Ocampo, and Eduardo Pallares revisited the conviction that the court was inviable in Mexico, given the lack of prevailing culture and morals.[164] *La Prensa* columnist Antonio Ruiz Cabañas shared this idea, claiming jury members came from "mobs" of the illiterate or groups that "seek to make a civic function a modus vivendi," because members of the "cultivated classes" avoided involvement in public matters.[165] This explained juries' tendency to acquit. In this sense, deputy José Aguilar y Maya stated that during his administration as attorney general, the jury had acquitted 85 percent of defendants, since it had acted with "pity, sympathy, compassion, misunderstood honor, or any other passionate inclination."[166]

Detractors of jury trials, like Ruiz Cabañas and Franco Sodi, considered that to qualify the acts, it was necessary to know law and other disciplines.[167] Otherwise, judges would easily fall prey to attorneys' strategies and skills. In the words of Quijano, they remained dazzled "by the lure of the beautifully said word."[168] Hence, according to Ruiz Cabañas, justice was not victorious, only the prosecutor or the defense.[169]

In 1941 supporters of jury trials managed to move the initiative forward. TSJ President Ostos, known as the "apostle of the jury trial," championed the cause.[170] The proposal was debated by a Senate Judicial Committee, which summoned jurists and judicial officials. According to Sodi, it interviewed only those opposed to jury trials.[171] The project was rejected by seventeen to four votes.[172] In the following decades, no other important initiative favored jury trials.

c) **Suppression of first-instance collegial justice.** In 1936 the Ministry of the Interior considered suppressing the criminal courts and adopting unitary courts. In their defense, González de la Vega recalled the abuses of judges in Porfirio Díaz's administration. He considered it dangerous "to entrust the solution of trials to a single, sometimes arbitrary and not very controllable judicial will."[173]

The proposal was unsuccessful, and collegial courts functioned for another three decades. This was despite their critics, such as Manuel Rivera Vázquez, who years later stated that collegial courts prevented judges from knowing defendants and from scrutinizing their souls, studying their somatic and physiological characteristics, and assessing the danger they represented, thwarting the legislators' purpose in expanding judges' margin of decision-making.[174]

D) **Reinforcing the accusatory character of the judicial system.** The 1949 Criminal Procedure Code drafters believed it was necessary to repeat proceedings during the plenary and to require the defense counsel to attend and orally present the allegations. Reinforcing the accusatory character of the judicial system was well received. According to Franco Sodi, the diversification of essential functions of the process in three actors—the judge, the prosecution, and the defense—was necessary for "a country like Mexico that has adopted the democratic form of government."[175] *La Justicia* editors thought a more effective confrontation between the parties would allow the judge to better understand the facts.[176]

However, between 1931 and 1971 projects to reform the codes and initiatives to modify the courts failed. The Cold War did not bring changes in Mexican criminal law, only greater rigor in cracking down on vagrancy and malfeasance, and the crime of social dissolution was created to punish individuals who promoted or supported foreign regimes. The possibility of suppressing criminal courts did not come to pass, nor did the reinstatement of jury trials. The Senate rejected the initiative brought by deputies in 1939, and although it did not end the debate on its possible reestablishment, no important initiative appeared from that time on.[177]

Reforms

Between 1931 and 1971 numerous amendments to the Criminal Codes were introduced, but with only minor changes, as detailed in the next two subsections.[178]

ORGANIZATION AND NUMBER OF COURTS

The number of tribunals increased, but at a slower pace than the population. Although in 1929 the capital had about one million inhabitants, in 1970 it had almost seven million. The population was originally concentrated in the Central Department, then in Mexico City, and in the final period studied, throughout the Federal District. However, the TSJ continued allocating only three chambers (the sixth, seventh, and eighth) to criminal matters.[179] As for first-instance courts, in 1929 three criminal courts were created for Mexico City, each composed of three judges.[180] As their jurisdiction expanded, so did their number. In 1931 eight were contemplated.[181] In 1935 the seventh and eighth courts were eliminated, and six courts remained. Criticism was quick. In 1942, in response to accusations of procedural delays made by Lecumberri prisoners, TSJ President Manuel Moreno Sánchez argued that irregularities were the product of the workload being disproportionate to the size of the judicial apparatus.[182] That year two judges, Manuel Rivera Silva and Carlos Franco Sodi, declared there were not enough courts; in the words of the latter, it was unfortunate that "without taking into account population and the rise of criminality," courts were eliminated.[183]

In 1940 La Prensa editorialists noted that states with the same population as the Federal District or less had more courts.[184] Two years later the capital's leading newspapers joined this complaint. María Elena Sodi de Pallares in El Universal and Concha de Villarreal in Excélsior compared population statistics with the number of judges: When there were twenty-four courts, the city had no more than nine hundred thousand inhabitants; in contrast, by 1942 the city had more than a million and a half people but only eighteen courts.[185] As La Justicia and attorney Trinidad García concluded, the number of courts responded to the size of the capital twenty years earlier.[186]

In 1948 it was determined the minimum number of courts would be six, with the possibility of increasing it.[187] However, the number was not increased, and jurists continued to denounce the court shortfall, including La Justicia editorialists, as well as Niceto Alcalá-Zamora y Castillo, Ignacio Moreno Tagle, and BMA members.[188] In response, in 1956 the Seventh Criminal Court was created, raising the number of criminal courts to twenty-one. In addition, throughout the period there was a mixed court in other jurisdictions, with seats in San Ángel, Coyoacán, and Xochimilco.

To many, it seemed the courts were still insufficient. A year after the creation of the new court, attorneys' associations and law schools sent President Adolfo Ruiz Cortines a list of proposals to improve the administration of justice, including an increase of courts. According to Germán Fernández del Castillo, those in existence were only enough for a city eight times smaller, and as Manuel Escobedo calculated, it was necessary to multiply their number by four.[189] Deputy Ignacio Ramos Praslow and attorneys (Javier Gaxiola, Fernando Flores García, Domínguez del Río, and Luis Garrido) agreed with them.[190]

The 1968 Organic Law of Tribunals (Ley Orgánica de los Tribunales) continued with a minimum of six criminal courts. However, that year the three courts ceased to be mixed, and a criminal court was created; jointly, they formed the Eighth Criminal Court.[191] These measures were important, but they did not resolve the problem because the capital's population continued to grow.

In sum, the population grew at a faster pace than its courts. Although at the beginning of the period studied there was a TSJ chamber for criminal matters covering close to 330,000 people, at the end there was just one for three million. Moreover, although in 1932 there was a criminal court for every 45,540 capital dwellers, in 1935 there was one for every 71,121; in 1956 one for every 165,027; and in 1970 one for every 286,424.[192]

THE JUDGES

During the period studied, the path of judicial appointments remained unchanged. As determined in 1928, the Mexican president named magistrates, who were ratified by the Chamber of Deputies, while the TSJ appointed criminal judges.[193] However, changes were made in the profile of judges and the duration of their position.

Under Article 64 of the Organic Law of Tribunals of December 1932, judges now were required to have an official attorney's degree issued by institutions recognized by law, at least five years of professional experience, and proven criminal law studies and practice, and they had to "be of notable morals, and not have been sentenced to prison for intentional crime." In 1935 the law was reformed, adding that they had to be Mexicans by birth in exercise of their political rights, older than thirty, and younger than sixty-five, and they were required to have at least five years of professional experience and not have been given an enforceable sentence handed down by criminal courts. Article 52 of the 1968 law introduced details to the sentence issued by criminal courts, prohibiting appointment when the prison sentence had been more than one year, or any sentence if it was for robbery, fraud, falsification, abuse of authority, or dereliction of duty, because these actions were deemed as "seriously harming the reputation in the public eye."

Furthermore, according to the Constitution, magistrates and judges were irremovable except for bad conduct proven in a jury trial specifically for government officials and employees (*juicio de responsabilidad*). In 1934 removability was returned. President-elect Lázaro Cárdenas sent an initiative to reform constitutional Article 73 that limited the term of justices of the scj and Federal District magistrates and judges to six years. He argued the need to end routine practices and to restore courts, giving entry to young people who "sincerely" felt the Revolution.[194] Approved by the Senate, the initiative was submitted to the consideration of the Chamber of Deputies, which unanimously accepted it without debate.[195]

Thus, starting in 1934, judges occupied the position for only a six-year presidential term. In addition, the free removal of mp agents was permitted by the attorney general, while before they could be removed only through a *juicio de responsabilidad*.[196] The Mexican president's interference in justice was being reinforced. Clearly, the measure responded to the centralization and rise of the federal executive's power over the other branches, or Mexican presidentialism.

Shortly before the Cárdenas administration ended, various jurists expressed their disagreement with removability, including Germán Fernández del Castillo and attendees of the Second National Juridical Congress.[197] Also, BMA members argued that judges could not have freedom or independence of criteria if they feared not being reelected or being removed, because it was enough for the president to request their dismissal. They maintained that at least the coincidence between presidential and judicial six-year terms should be eliminated for several reasons: Once in office, the president had multiple commitments to members of his party; if he had ties of friendship with the previous leader, he had to ratify the judges who did not find a post in other government spheres; and if the former leader was his enemy, he would remove all judicial officials, even when they had demonstrated honor and competence.[198]

The new president, Manuel Ávila Camacho, reversed removability. In December 1940, almost two weeks after taking office, he presented the initiative to the Senate. Once approved, it was sent to the Chamber of Deputies, which voted unanimously without debate the same day. Later, it was submitted for consideration to the state legislatures.[199] Referring to the initiative, Ávila Camacho declared that to guarantee the independence of judges and ensure they act "without rules other than the law nor more dictates than their own conscience," it was necessary to put an end to six-year elections, because in such a short period, judges could not elude created commitments.[200]

Opinions were expressed for and against, although fewer were opposed. Some said that it did not matter how judges had been elected; irremovability would allow them to gain independence (training may also be assumed). The attorney general of the Federal District, Raúl Carrancá y Trujillo, stated, "Only with judicial irremovability is it possible for the judge to declare the law to the powerful and in favor of the defenseless. Man cannot be required to be a hero or saint. Let us welcome irremovability, which will make possible the promise of justice championed by the Mexican Revolution."[201]

TSJ President Daniel Salazar Hurtado claimed judges would be autonomous and less prone to take bribes if they did not need to please a political figure to preserve their jobs.[202] Carlos Franco Sodi argued that it was "true there are ignorant and negligent judges, but also true that hundreds of cultivated and hardworking judges have been tossed out of their posts, after long years of effective and honorable work, only because they lacked an influential figure who backed them."[203] Newspapers expressed similar reactions. After describing the initiative as one of the most important of the time, La Prensa stated, "The judge not liked by any cacique runs the risk that the smooth-talking politician gets him eliminated."[204] The reform to the constitutional article was well received even by SCJ judges, who would have to leave their posts if the measure was approved.[205]

And so went the first three years of Ávila Camacho's administration. In 1943 twenty-two state legislatures approved the initiative and two (Morelos and Zacatecas) rejected it. The matter was referred to the Chamber of Deputies. Some deputies opposed it. For instance, José María Téllez argued it was still possible to find individuals in government who sabotaged the Revolution's accomplishments, and with indefinite tenure in office, "young and honest revolutionaries" could not replace them. Others, like Víctor Alfonso Maldonado, supported the measure, and Fernando Moctezuma asked, "Isn't it enough to trust that the Mexican president [will] issue these appointments?" By seventy-five votes to three, the declaration was approved, and irremovability returned.[206]

Although a certain inclination to choose men close to Ávila Camacho's government for judicial appointments was noted, jurists backed appointments and the end of removability. Ricardo Abarca held that "the umbilical cord where the administration of justice depended on political power has been cut: so irremovable magistrates can now also be unyielding to influence, flattery, threats, power, gold."[207] Francisco Serralde, who published fragments of the work he had written sixty years earlier in favor of irremovability, similarly argued that it permitted judges to be "cautious in their resolutions" and "judicious, fair, and honest in their sentences." Nevertheless, he maintained that irremovability should be accompanied by greater requirements to occupy the position and an effective law of accountability.[208] Many insisted on the need to create a professional law career. La Justicia editors and Fernando Cuen considered a legal career indispensable to irremovability.[209] Excélsior editorialists declared, "If the dignity and independence of new judges is combined with science, irremovability will be a blessing."[210]

Change came fast. Before the Miguel Alemán administration ended, judicial six-year terms returned for Federal District magistrates and judges (irremovability was preserved for SCJ justices). In October 1950 the president presented an initiative to reform constitutional Article 73.[211] One month later the proposal was debated in the Chamber of Deputies. Rafael Corrales Ayala presented it, insisting it addressed social demand. Alberto Trueba Urbina declared the same: "The government has the indisputable merit of having known how to interpret, synthesize, and translate one of the nation's most daunting and profound demands into practical solutions."[212] After being approved by the deputies, removability of judges was voted for by the majority of states and the Senate issued the declaration.[213] It should be noted that judicial six-year terms ceased to coincide with presidential administrations: Presidents appointed judges one year before leaving office and not when taking office.

Irremovability was seen as a solution for shielding judges from political and partisan pressures because it was assumed that the security of not losing their jobs with each six-year change of administration would allow them to find, in the words of Fernando Flores García, "the courage to resist pressures and threats."[214] Similarly, the law career was presented as a solution to remove the weight of influences in judicial appointments and ensure that judges be selected, citing Flores García, for their knowledge, experience, capacity, and morality.[215] Alcalá-Zamora held that it was urgent to replace the play of influences with the contrast of merits, through a regimen of serious oppositions alien to political factors.[216] Based on this argument, several jurists throughout the period studied proposed a system of tiered promotion based on competition.[217] It was said to incentivize judiciary employees, preventing them from falling into apathy and corruption. Take, for example, the words of Luis Garrido: "It is profoundly demoralizing to see old, competent clerks to have never been appointed judges and instead to see politicians and favorites be given high judicial positions."[218]

Irremovability was not adopted, but advances were made in creating the judicial career. The 1968 Organic Law of Tribunals established that "for appointments, background, and experience in the administration of justice will be considered. In the case of other persons, background, and professional capacity."[219] Leaders of the Court Workers Union celebrated the change: "Until yesterday, securing a judicial post was arbitrary. From now, it will be different. The unhappiest employee in the world can, with time, knowledge, and preparation, come to occupy even the most important positions."[220]

FINAL REFLECTIONS

From its inception, trial by jury was criticized. Some condemned it on the principle of legality, claiming that verdicts, when not based on the evidence presented, forced the judge to apply a law not in consonance with the criminal act. Others, starting with postulates of the positivist or eclectic school, in their desire that sentences consider the personality of defendants, denounced the ineptitude of lay judges and demanded the intervention of judges with knowledge of law, psychology, and medicine. Gradually, legislators reduced the jury's power, limited the role of "triers of fact" in trials, and raised the requirements they had to meet to be part of the court.

Considering this criticism and legislative tendency, it is no surprise the 1929 Code drafters—fascinated by positivism—decided to suppress jury trials and professionalize justice. Nor is it surprising that the 1931 committee members—sympathizers of an eclectic orientation—were kept at bay, and the initiatives to reinstate jury trials were not well received by experts and legislators.

Equally expected, the group presided over by Almaraz, willing to accommodate the consideration of danger, would have expanded judges' capacity in decision-making. It is little wonder that—congruent with this intention and tendency, at that moment widely accepted by Mexican, European, and Latin

American jurists—members of the 1931 Code drafting committee would have expanded the margin of discretion. Finally, it is also understandable that in the interest of individualization as truly possible, draft writers and other experts on the subject thought increasing the flexibility of judges in determining the sentence was not sufficient and believed it was necessary to include notions like judicial pardon.

In the logic of jurists and legislators, the commitment to individualization according to the criminal's characteristics required the intervention of professional judges, the only ones who deserved the confidence called for by broad discretion. Therefore, professionalization and broadening discretion had to come together. And they came together in a context favorable for various factors: a mood open to legal change and committed to the institutionalization of political and social life, a ruling elite weary of the victories of "reactionary" attorneys in forums, and public opinion that had been prepared beforehand with the dissemination of verdicts described as erroneous and intimidated by the jury's supposed tendency to acquit criminals, thereby fueling social insecurity.

However, trust in professional judges was not absolute. Years of debate on the path of appointments, suspicion of judicial officials, and a long legislative tradition committed to restricting judicial discretion made it hard for judges to inspire trust. Hence the solution was seen to be the collegial integration of courts, in which the possibility of controlling judges and their discretion was vested, thus preventing abuses and deviations from the law. Criminal courts were collegial courts, where sentences had to be voted on by the majority. It was also believed that debate would improve the quality of sentences and unify judicial precedents.

Unlike the case of jury trials, which underwent multiple reforms during their fifty years of existence, criminal courts experienced few modifications, although they also lasted for almost half a century. Despite the multiple political, social, economic, and cultural transformations in Mexico between 1931 and 1971, apart from shifts in the duration of judges' positions, legislation regulating courts remained largely unaltered. Not even the number of courts changed, as necessitated by the rapid population growth of the Federal District and the public perception of criminality and the lack of safety.

The edifice of justice underwent few modifications, none of them structural. The possibility of reinstating jury trials was unsuccessful, as were proposals predating 1971 on eliminating the collegial nature of first-instance courts.

Those would have been important reforms. However, the edifice kept its shape. It was constructed based on the division of powers and the principle of legality and was upheld by the three major pillars: autonomy of judges, equality before the law, and defense of due process rights. In keeping with international treaties, Mexican legislation accommodated the rights of the accused and contained the instruments necessary to enforce them. The legal system was mixed in character, with elements of the inquisitorial and accusatory system; the latter contained core elements, such as impartiality of judges; balance of the parties, which required ample space for defense; confrontation; orality; and openness.

In sum, the law governing justice corresponded to the premises and requirements of a liberal and democratic legal state.

3. THE PUBLIC IMAGE OF JUSTICE

As *Excélsior* noted in 1943, "It is common and customary that since time immemorial we have heard people's speech or read in the daily press many things and opinions about justice."[1] By word of mouth or in publications, individuals or groups referred to justice, and by doing so, they formulated ideas and opinions, revealed visions and imaginings, and divulged their fears and expectations. In this chapter, I compile their statements, considering the voices of jurists, judges, and litigants (concerning "internal legal culture"), as well as public officials, editorialists, reporters, filmmakers, and citizens (reflecting "external legal culture").

To access the perspectives of experts, I used books, manuals, leaflets, theses, papers presented in meetings of prosecutors of justice or congresses, and articles, columns, and statements in newspapers. My main source was the press, and I cite numerous articles or notes. For the vision of other sectors of society, I turned to cinema, analyzing close to forty movies filmed between 1936 and 1971. In some years, justice generated greater interest than in others. Magistrate Hilario Hermosillo claimed that more notes were published at the end of a judicial period than the beginning because candidates for office wanted to make themselves known or discredit those in office.[2]

Conceivably, at the ends of these periods, which often were concurrent with six-year presidential terms, critics feared fewer reprisals. Furthermore, certain events triggered an explosion of news. There is no better example than when various occurrences coincided in 1942. Early that year, newspapers published denunciations by two women: Concha de Villarreal from Durango, who was apparently close to the Cárdenas camp and a contributor to *Excélsior*, and María Elena Sodi Pallares, from a family of attorneys (daughter of Demetrio Sodi Guergue and cousin of Carlos Franco Sodi), a champion of women's rights, and El *Universal* contributor. Eduardo Pallares, also from a lawyer family (son of Jacinto Pallares) and one of the founders of ELD, who coordinated a section in El *Universal*, joined them with this consideration: "Never as now have the people been as hungry and thirsty for justice, and clearly there is a true clamor that denounces the slowness, irregularities, triviality and bribery in courts, without any effort equal to the evil that must be stamped out." He maintained that the sparse credit given to many judges, the rumors about the real or supposed immorality of quite a few, and generalizations that unfairly discredit the whole "owed in part to the public's poor knowledge of what really occurred in it." Consequently, he proposed "opening the doors and windows of the cloister in which judicial administration has been accustomed to living" and requested signed denunciations, with proof and lacking "insulting and indecent language."[3]

Later that year, in September, when news spread of the murder of several women, presumably by Goyo Cárdenas, the public demanded efficacy from authorities and harsh punishment for the criminals. In December senator Augusto Hinojosa called legislators to intervene in resolving the problems facing the justice system, including corruption. TSJ magistrates were outraged and called for proof of the accusation, also demanding the senator be prosecuted for defamation. Seven senators backed their colleague and asked the president to dismiss the magistrates. Legislative deputies supported them: Enrique Carrola Antuna attacked the PGJ and its agents. The magistrates met again to respond to the attacks, which had assumed a personal tone. Days later the matter was silenced.[4] It was "as if a superior force of serenity had called for concordance," wrote José Ángel Ceniceros.[5] Perhaps the superior force was Manuel Ávila Camacho, as happened later according to Ricardo Garibay, in 1967, when the legislature attacked the judicial power, and thanks to the intervention of the executive power, "the revolutionary union was reestablished."[6]

Legislators and magistrates remained silent, but citizens did not. Other newspapers followed El Universal's lead. La Prensa called for a "nationwide survey":

> In homes, laments; in the streets, clamor; in the highest forums, scandal. Bribes robbery, and murder committed by those who should never be tempted to take bribes, rob, or kill. Delays, prevarication, and bribery by those who should set the example of rectitude and diligence. Without order there is no justice; without justice there is no order, and without one or the other there is no society. Therefore, to defend our society, we ask citizens for their collaboration.[7]

Novedades conducted interviews, and its daily "investigative reporter" took to the street.[8] These efforts reveal the position of the capital's population.

In some years, opinions on justice proliferated. In 1954 and 1957 *Novedades* published interviews with jurists.[9] *Excélsior* did the same in Araldo Prats's column in 1966.[10] In 1967 a new controversy among members of legislative and judicial branches attracted press interest. However, in other years, there were few references. These gaps could be of concern if differences were noted in opinions and visions over time, but this was not the case; on the contrary, I found homogeneity from 1929 to 1971.

The remainder of this chapter looks at the diverse sources offering multiple voices and testimonies. I begin with viewpoints on the importance of justice for social order and the political system. Next, I present denunciations of the insufficient budget, seen as the reason for court shortages, backlogs, deficient installations, and low salaries. Then I trace the (limited) praise and (numerous) critiques of the police, judges, and litigators, as well as proposed improvements. I end with an assessment of their contemporaries on the impact society had or could have on the administration of justice and its eroded image.

THE ROLE OF THEMIS

"All social order revolves around a fundamental axis: the value of justice. Without it, the needs and functions of any government could not be explained. Justice comes before the Constitution, before laws, before authorities. If someone wants to know when a regime is good, just analyze its function."[11] "Since the earliest antiquity, the judicial function has been considered the state's most important activity."[12] "An honest, orderly, and generous administration of justice . . . touches the very essence of the state's function."[13]

The preceding quotes were published over a fifteen-year period, and their authors shared the belief that justice is an essential task of the state and one of its main obligations. Their premise is not strange for liberal logic: Justice protects fundamental rights under the social contract theory, the state's foundational objective. Other judges, jurists, and journalists concurred. Some regarded an efficient administration of justice as synonymous with—even a condition for—the existence of a democratic society respectful of the law and rights. In 1942 an *Excélsior* editorialist wrote that dictatorial governments lost the "notion of the sacred rights of man" and declared, "This cannot happen, it must not happen, in democratic regimes. The people's voice must prevail through their officials and magistrates . . . and the essence of justice found in the direct and immediate protection of the interests of the underprivileged must not be forgotten."[14] Two decades later, members of the Constitutional Points, Judicial, and Legislative Studies Committees of the Chamber of Deputies stated, "No government is justified if it does not fully guarantee the administration of justice, the state's supreme function, a prerequisite for individual freedoms and rights to be respected, and laws effectively complied with."[15]

Furthermore, in the early 1940s prominent voices held that the proper functioning of the judicial system guaranteed public peace; otherwise, social order would be threatened. The Confederation of Mexican Workers (Confederación de Trabajadores Mexicanos) described the judicial system as "the most exact barometer of a country's situation" and affirmed that the courts' prestige, independence, and impartiality indicated the nation "was living normally"; in contrast, mistrust of judicial authorities converted into "instruments of a social class or other powers," and practitioners of prevarication or bribery indicated "a profound crisis in all state institutions."[16] Daniel Salazar Hurtado, TSJ president, asserted that there was a proportional relationship between "perfect justice" or something close to it and social peace.[17]

On the other side of the coin, Franco Sodi maintained, "When any people lacks justice, it dies, for air does not reach its lungs; it is saturated with two mortal toxins called inequality and corruption."[18] A year later *Excélsior* proposed, "Justice is essential and where its nature is distorted and there are magistrates and judges who lack indispensable honesty and integrity, civilization crumbles and the lowest appetites and most intemperate ambitions take preponderance."[19] For his part, attorney Trinidad García noted that if a state does not resolve judicial conflicts, its inhabitants must resolve them on their own, and the "legal regime" is replaced by violence.[20]

The state's image was tied to the image of justice. Salazar Hurtado asserted, "A single case of injustice harms a regime more than a series of flawed administrative measures."[21] Later, *El Universal* editorialists claimed, "The prestige of a government rests on rigor, justice, probity, and good faith."[22]

The state was spoken of in the abstract and specifically as the state arising from the Revolution. Numerous authors considered that since the desire for justice was one of the leading aspirations of the revolutionary movement, achieving a sound judicial system was one of the Mexican state's fundamental commitments. In a speech given in 1893, the politician and intellectual Justo Sierra declared that people were hungry and thirsty for justice. This became a catchphrase reiterated by authors assessing the success or failure of the revolutionary promise in the field of justice.

Discussion focused on justice in general, social justice, and the administration of justice. President Manuel Ávila Camacho professed, "The Revolution can be synthesized in the Mexican people's profound yearning for justice," and Gustavo Díaz Ordaz asserted, "Mexico has a pact sealed in the blood of many of its best offspring to reconcile freedom with social justice," which would be achieved only with the prompt and expeditious administration of justice.[23] Luis Garrido wrote, "The revolutionary work rests on the pedestal of justice, which ensures human dignity and is the most eminent of social virtues."[24] El Nacional Revolucionario maintained, "The general clamor for justice in Mexico was one of the great causes of the Revolution: then it is up to severe, understanding, and upright judges to crown the work."[25] Some jurists, Francisco González de la Vega and Raúl Carrancá y Trujillo, spoke specifically of criminal justice. According to the former, "Criminal reform in Mexico is a genuine product of the Revolution; it obeys its longings and concerns, it meets its needs."[26]

In the opinions surveyed here, the existence of the democratic state or legal state was linked to respect for fundamental rights and the law, and it was viewed as expeditious, impartial, or rights-based and egalitarian. Nevertheless, many believed that justice was not given its due importance and that the low budget revealed the unjust treatment of the justice system.

"TO DIE OF STARVATION": BUDGETARY SHORTFALL

"Judicial power must cease to be the ugly duckling of the budget," lamented an Excélsior editorialist in 1966.[27] Eleven years earlier, magistrate Alberto Bremauntz had complained of the insensitivity of Department of the Federal District heads: "Few public institutions have suffered the indifference of all governments, with regard to meeting even the most indispensable economic elements to efficiently perform the duties entrusted to it."[28] Around the same time, attorneys' associations and law schools deplored the minimal resources allotted to justice.[29]

Statistics backed these assertions. In 1942 Octavio M. Trigo stated that the judicial power of the Federal District was destitute, receiving less funds than the "humblest agencies of the executive branch."[30] The same year, Concha de Villarreal claimed that it was condemned to "die of starvation" because its budget had remained the same since 1927, at less than half the amount allotted to the legislative power.[31] At that time, Bremauntz offered a historical comparison of declining resources in the Federal District budget (see table

2).[32] According to Octavio Hernández, the percentage of decline was accentuated because in 1965 only 0.18 percent of the budget was assigned to the tribunals of the Federal District.[33]

Table 2. Budget allotted to the TSJ (in pesos)

YEAR	D.F. BUDGET	TSJ BUDGET	%
1942		2,626,916	
1946	175,049,000	3,738,220	2.13
1947	179,908,157	4,203,966	2.33
1948	226,809,966	5,297,074	2.33
1949	257,450,308	5,499,024	2.13
1950	297,715,357	5,964,312	2.00
1951	354,334,113	6,826,504	1.92
1952	385,223,049	6,319,896	1.64
1954	517,667,729	9,163,560	1.77
1955	600,000,000	9,667,240	1.61

Sources: Octavio Trigo, "Por una justicia mejor," El Universal, April 11, 1942, ps, 3, 6; Bremauntz, Por una justicia, 137.

Numerous politicians called for a budgetary increase. In 1954, in a Chamber of Deputies debate on the subject, Felipe Gómez Mont affirmed, "Justice cannot proceed [if] economically strangled."[34] A year later Manuel Escobedo, BMA president, declared it "indispensable that before providing other lines of the budget, the administration of justice be assigned what it requires."[35] Meanwhile, others warned of the consequences of the budgetary shortfall. In 1947 La Justicia maintained that unless the amount designated to the TSJ were raised, it could not "perform its civic ministry in favor of society in suitable premises," and as long as salaries allotted to judicial officials did not allow them "to live in accord with their high position," society could not demand better performance.[36] In 1955 Vicente Lombardo Toledano asserted, "The shortage of a suitable budget for the administration of justice means there are few courts and there are poorly paid officials, which makes justice slow and ineffective." Jurists Rubén Robles Guerrero and Fernando Ortiz Cadena agreed, along with Diego Rivera's daughter, Guadalupe Rivera Marín, who stated, "Anyone who goes to court in search of justice deserved has a terrible impression by the physical condition of the buildings and thinks that poorly housed justice cannot be good justice."[37] They cited three consequences of the shortfall: insufficient courts; poorly equipped courts; and poorly paid judges, judicial employees, public defenders, agents, and police.

Shortage of Tribunals and Local Public Prosecutors' Offices

In addition to complaints about the shortage of courts, the same was said of Local Public Prosecutors' Offices (MPS). In 1942 Roberto Guzmán Araujo, Federal District deputy public prosecutor, declared that they did not correspond to population figures.[38] Concha de Villarreal affirmed that the same number of personnel overseeing sixteen to eighteen cases per month ten years earlier now had to oversee fifty-five to sixty. She stated that the same occurred with bench warrants: Courts issued around 2,250 monthly, which were to be processed by "forty-four heroic detectives, who only had three motorcycles and five dilapidated 'vw bugs' that break down on every corner"; hence there were almost ten thousand warrants pending, and these increased by a thousand per month.[39] In 1959 Raúl Cárdenas complained that the workload did not allow the police to gather evidence, making it necessary to accept evidence presented by victims.[40] In the mid-1960s journalist Wilfrido Cantón attributed the impunity of criminals to personnel shortages.[41] There was also talk of insufficient public defenders; in 1940 the TSJ president maintained that each of them had to prepare five cases daily, an impossible task that left defendants defenseless.[42]

"The Dantesque Inferno of Lecumberri and the No Less Filthy Palace of Cordobanes"

In 1950 Fernando Puig asked why taxpayer money was not allotted to "salvaging our courts from the sordid caves where judges and magistrates vegetate that are called the Dantesque inferno of Lecumberri and the no less filthy Palace of Cordobanes."[43] Denunciation of the condition of MPs and courts was nothing new. In a 1942 article María Elena Sodi Pallares reported that MPs had rickety furniture and broken typewriters.[44] Octavio Trigo presented similar images, affirming the offices were "narrow, poorly ventilated, dark, and unclean" and described their furnishings using virtually the same words as the journalist.[45] That same year, Concha de Villarreal asserted they lacked even the most essential equipment.[46] In 1948 Trinidad García wrote, "We attorneys are painfully surprised, despite being accustomed, when we see the sordid offices of many tribunals, dirty, without furniture, and with files piled up as if wastepaper."[47] According to testimonies, the situation produced delays and errors in the performance of judges, court employees, and MP agents. For instance, in 1959 Leopoldo Aguilar spoke of the time wasted taking statements on typewriters instead of tape recording them and the lack of cars to deliver notifications and carry out formalities.[48] Also that year, Raúl Cárdenas held that many MP errors resulted from the lack of investigation laboratories and police cars, and in 1966 SCJ president Agapito Pozo was still complaining about the lack of recording equipment.[49] BMA members concluded, "A good and clean house is needed for justice to be majestic and respectable."[50]

Indigents among Professionals

In 1934 Carrancá y Trujillo contended that an attorney who was given a judicial post could feel rewarded only if that position was of a judge or higher; "not even Local Public Prosecutor[s' Office] agents, public defenders, [or] clerks should enjoy the peaceful slumber if they are men who think seriously about their future."[51] Almost at the end of the period studied, Alfonso Trueba lamented that so much was spent on the Olympiads and so little on justice. He referred to judges' salary and concluded that an "upright judge" could not earn a suitable living, and this made him into "an indigent among professionals."[52] In the words of TSJ president Manuel Moreno Sánchez, it was illogical that judges who decided on high-value assets and the lives of thousands of citizens had to "live almost in misery and among palpable expressions of the low social esteem granted to them."[53]

Throughout the period studied, deputies (Gómez Mont), political party members (Lombardo Toledano, Alberto Lumbreras), judges or jurists (Salazar Hurtado, Rivera Silva, Trigo), attorneys (BMA members, Ignacio Moreno Tagle, Víctor Manuel Ortega), journalists (Sodi Pallares), and editorialists (of Excélsior and El Universal) denounced the situation.[54] Indeed, from 1926 to 1947, despite inflation, judges' salaries were kept at 800 pesos, but they gradually increased after the latter year (see table 3).[55]

Table 3. Salaries of Federal District magistrates and judges (in pesos), 1926–68

YEARS	MAGISTRATES	CRIMINAL COURT JUDGES
1926		800.00
1934	1,216.68	800.00

1935	1,000.00	800.00
1936–43	1,1150.00	800.00
1944–46	1,300.00	825.00
1947–48	1,430.00	1,023.00
1949–51	1,606.00	1,158.00
1952	1,845.00	1,335.00
1953	2,235.00	1,617.00
1954	2,430.00	1,770.00
1955	3,080.00	1,970.00
1957	3,080.00	1,970.00
1968		5,000.00

Sources: Bremauntz, *Por una justicia*, 135; María Elena Sodi Pallares, "Manifiestas injusticias con la justicia en México," *El Universal*, April 29, 1942, ps, 1, 14; "Memorando," 26; Alfonso Trueba, "La otra imagen. Jueces indigentes," *Excélsior*, October 31, 1968, ps, 6A, 10A.

A criminal court judge received a quarter of the salary of an scj minister, less than half that of a circuit court magistrate, and almost the same as judges in other states in the country. Writing in the mid- to late 1960s, Armando R. Ostos and Alfonso Trueba considered this salary insufficient to suitably support a family, based on Bremauntz's calculations: In 1939 judges received double what a working-class family needed to live, but in 1945 only 23 percent more, and after 1950 only 10 percent more.[56] The situation of tribunal employees was even more serious. Trigo affirmed in 1942 that some did not even receive the minimum wages set for laborers.[57] Concha de Villarreal maintained that from her pay of 180 pesos biweekly, 20 pesos was withheld for taxes, pensions, and contributions to the Party of the Mexican Revolution (Partido de la Revolución Mexicana).[58]

According to different authors, this salary shortfall was an attack on quality, honesty, and efficiency. bma members referred to judges as "persons who cannot live suitably in the litigant's professional endeavor or those who accept the post thinking the salary is only a part of their income, and the rest will be produced by the post."[59] Two more points are also addressed by other authors. First, the low salary did not permit the recruiting and preserving of capable people.[60] According to magistrate Pedro Zorrilla, salaries did not correspond "to the specialized service they render nor the legal requirement preventing them from performing other jobs," and only raising them would make it possible to improve the quality of the personnel and demand their dedication.[61] An *El Universal* article said, "Truly valuable men are difficult to preserve, because their training, intelligence, executive capacity, [and] merits make them persistently in demand. Promising opportunities are open to them in private companies that, unless they have a self-denying streak resolved by the public, can only be eluded with difficulty. This causes bureaucratic followers to be reduced to mediocrity or to promote the appearance of thieves."[62]

Second, low salaries encouraged corruption. Niceto Alcalá-Zamora y Castillo wrote:

> With current salaries, only the celibate, without a second family and with an anchorite temperament can survive; if he has a family and is incorruptible he will have to opt to abandon the judiciary or seek supplementary income, which will take away time from his judicial duties or will drag him into entrusting them to aides and subordinates; and if his ethics are not very solid, he will use the jury like a hunting blind and will wield sentences like a saber.[63]

Years later, journalist Mario Rojas Avendaño wrote, "The palace of justice shields in its marble fold hundreds of starving men and women employees, who only have one thought: how to stretch the salary to survive one more week."[64] Agapito Pozo, SCJ president, maintained that gratuities or "bribes" were difficult for public servants who received the lowest salaries to reject.[65] Octavio Trigo held, "What is surprising is not that justice is bad in Mexico and there are bad judges; what is truly surprising is that justice is not worse and it still has proven and competent men in it."[66] David Pastrana Jaimes considered, "Salaries of two, eight, and twelve pesos daily are not the price for a man's honesty. He can begin to be honored with a twenty-five-peso daily salary."[67] Carlos Franco Sodi was opposed to such precise calculations, but he admitted that society excused "weaknesses and transgressions" for the low salaries.[68]

In sum, numerous authors believed the budgetary insufficiency produced delays in justice and encouraged corruption, which led to the failure to observe constitutional rights, such as the expeditious administration of justice.

THE POLICE

"Far from being police proud of the city, based on everyday tranquility, a cause of respect, representation worthy of citizens' values, and the legitimate authority of the government, they are disgraceful, shameful, and dangerous, [so] that the whole world avoids [them], or they use money as a guarantee of impunity. More than public servants, they have come to be a necessary evil, a feared social ill."[69]

As this quote illustrates, the bodies responsible for investigation—the judicial police and especially the secret police, whose functions were juxtaposed—were strongly criticized. As Lucio Mendieta y Núñez stated in 1943, although the police should have reported to the Department of the Federal District, the inspector general of the police was usually a high-ranking military man appointed by the Mexican president, so he was not subordinate to the mayor (regente).[70] Furthermore, there were two corps in charge of investigation, judicial police and secret police, but their functions were the same. The secret police was under the command of the preventive police, but it had to report to the Attorney General's Office (Procuraduría General de la República, hereafter PGR), as stipulated in Article 21 of the Constitution. Rafael Matos Escobedo argued that it operated outside the law, and Excélsior editorialists claimed it operated "outside the constitutional framework."[71]

The situation was serious because the secret police had more personnel than the judicial police (in 1961 the secret police had 450 posts, while the judicial police had 80).[72] In addition, the police force was considered to be inefficient, corrupt, and habitual violators of the rights of the accused.[73]

Neither Intuition nor Science

"The old police must be followed by laboratory men and penetrating observation of concrete facts; only they can lead to the encounter with the truth."[74] "Yesterday's antechamber of justice were tools of torture and today's antechamber of justice must be criminalistic laboratories."[75]

As these quotes show, the capital police were discredited.[76] Luis Garrido affirmed in 1952 that most crimes went unpunished and the perpetrators remained free.[77] In 1959 Raúl Cárdenas noted that "investigations to be conducted were in the thousands."[78] Two years later Ignacio Moreno Tagle affirmed that countless cases were unresolved.[79] In 1969 Alfonso Trueba maintained, "Mexico occupies one of the first places among countries with high criminality and many of the homicides committed were unpunished. Why? Because investigation services are terrible."[80]

Other authors pointed out problems related to apprehending the accused. In 1966 Wilberto Cantón claimed MP agents were accustomed to shelving complaints and bench warrants.[81] In 1942 Concha de Villarreal condemned the existence of 9,515 pending detention orders; in 1959 Raúl Cárdenas claimed there were thousands; and in 1964 *Novedades* editorialists reported 4,000.[82]

Journalists spoke of unjustified releases. According to a 1936 article in *La Prensa*, two individuals quarreled in a hardware store and wounded the owner; no one admitted to the shooting, and the MP agent did not make the accusation. In another *La Prensa* article that same year, a man who had killed his stepfather was released because the MP agent was not at his post, and his secretary refused to cover his absence.[83] Another example comes from *El Universal*, which reported in 1967 that a woman took a man who was forcing her into prostitution to the MP. The agent released him with a 20 peso fine, although "the subject showed signs of being under the influence of an alcoholic or enervating substance and was in a frenetic rage, which could lead even the dimmest to suppose that if he was released he would surely avenge his accuser." After he was released, he stabbed the woman.[84]

Journalists and jurists concluded that deficient investigative work by the investigating agents led to the release of defendants. In 1942 Concha de Villarreal stated that acts poorly substantiated by the MP were hindrances in proving the liability of the accused to the judge, and the number of releases based on the lack of merit was higher than the number sentenced.[85] Almost twenty-four years later, Federal District Attorney General Gilberto Suárez Torres admitted that judicial errors arose from poor investigation.[86]

Wilberto Cantón concluded, "The police institutions responsible for criminal prevention and investigation in our country, as well as those that administer justice, are ineffective as corrupt, inept and mercenaries." He backed this with data from Alfonso Quiroz Cuarón on the last thirty-six years: 48 percent of male murderers and 66 percent of female murderers had been released.[87] According to *La Prensa*, "The city is at the mercy of thugs, and only chance, not technique nor work, make it possible that once in a while some of these criminals end up with their bones in jail."[88]

Violations of Defendants' Rights

In 1961 Ignacio Moreno Tagle maintained that "despite reiterated promises of strict compliance with the law," some policemen continued "committing serious violations of individual rights, detaining individuals without bench warrants and without committing any obvious crime, extending arrest for more than the strict term of twenty-four hours, isolating detainees and inflicting them with acts prohibited by the Constitution."[89] *Novedades* editorialists and Gilberto Keith claimed that many individuals were locked up for days or weeks without a judicial order.[90] Raúl Carrancá y Trujillo denounced the systematic use of psychological coercion and physical violence.[91] Manuel Rivera lamented in El *Nacional Revolucionario*, "We do not know how to describe the inquisitorial conduct of some police, who, in order to appear as skillful investigators and detectives like Sherlock Holmes, inflict physical and psychological torture on miserable prisoners to extract a confession," referring to this as an "abominable, barbaric, and criminal practice."[92] Guillermo Colín Sánchez also held that policemen and MP agents resorted to inquisitorial procedures and methods that "injured human dignity and judicial order" to extract confessions, which continued being regarded as principal evidence.[93] *Novedades* editorialists wrote that the police continued applying "torture expressly prohibited by law and contrary to the most elemental humanitarianism," which gave rise to "irreparable injustice."[94] Alfonso Trueba, with twenty-five years of experience in courts, declared:

> Torture is the most commonly employed method in investigation. A suspect is detained, he is isolated for weeks, threatened with death, beaten, and finally, a confession is extracted. After confessing, he is consigned to the judge. The second phase starts here. The judge receives the "package," and since police pressure has ceased, the first thing the presumed criminal does is to retract his confession. He clarifies he confessed because he was physically and psychologically coerced. The judge says prove it. What will the wretch prove? He has no means. Then the judge issues an order of confinement.[95]

Accusations were accompanied by case reports. There is no better example than a scandal from 1952. José Trinidad Sánchez, accused of raping and killing a girl, confessed and admitted to having buried her body on the highway to Puebla. The police, accompanied by journalists, did not find the body. Hours later, the supposed victim appeared safe and sound. In the hospital, the accused declared he had confessed after being beaten and submerged in a barrel of water. The medical examination revealed he had broken ribs, and a policeman in the MP said he had heard screams. Sánchez died of pneumonia contracted during detention.[96] Periodically, purges and expulsions were conducted of the corps, and the MP agent in charge of the Fifth Local Public Prosecutor's Office and several policemen were dismissed over the Sánchez case.

"More Dangerous . . . Than 'Chucho el Roto' Copycats"

"It's more dangerous to find the night patrol than 'Chucho el Roto' copycats." "We're in the greatest distress. The gendarmes, if you turn to them, are 'bullies.'" "In the police force there are more people who love others' belongings than among professional thieves; whoever arrives at the MP offices becomes a victim of robbery, of the vulgar, shameless 'bribe,' if not of ill treatment and humiliation that decent honorable people could not tolerate." "Local Public Prosecutors' Offices are dens where the worst violations are committed, honor is trampled, and those who have the misfortune to end up there are robbed more and better." The first three statements were published in 1942, and the last in 1952. The first is from the account of a woman who was assaulted by a policeman; the second is from an interview that Miss Consuelo Valdés gave to a reporter; the third was stated by Augusto Hinojosa in a speech to the Senate; and the last was published after a woman was raped by an MP clerk.[97] These types of notes and accusations were published in other years as well. Complaints were made at different levels about requests for bribes from the accused to release them, extortion of innocent parties to exonerate them from a false accusation, or commission of crimes by policemen.

According to criticism, some agents asked for money to release the detainees regardless of whether they were guilty. In 1930 an *El Nacional Revolucionario* reporter discovered that police stations had two different consignment books, one of which was thinner and, he supposed, did not contain the names of the accused who had paid for their release.[98] In 1952 Garrido asserted that MP personnel moved in a world of corruption.[99] That same year, several policemen denounced their colleagues' practices in *La Prensa*.[100] In a 1966 letter to *El Universal*, citizen Javier López Ruiz affirmed, "I have seen many agents of the Local Public Prosecutor's Office in the criminal courts that have an open understanding with defendants."[101] Late in the period studied, journalist Héctor Solís Quiroga wrote, "Each 'case' of a person who might have money or credit, produces daily earnings of several thousand pesos from granting or depriving rights," in addition to practices like falsification or manipulation of statements.[102] Alfonso Quiroz Cuarón concluded in 1970 that agents in expert services had "forgotten the technical lessons of Benjamín Martínez" and understood only "the eloquent language of cash."[103] It was even said that the police fabricated crimes with fines to extort victims or that they directly committed the crimes.

The Magic of Cinema and Television

The image of policemen in literature and movies was different. I do not examine police or crime fiction, but an example would be the stories by Antonio Helú, also a screenwriter, compiled in *La obligación de asesinar* (The obligation to assassinate). One of the protagonists is the clever detective Carlos Miranda; according to Helú, if detective competitions were an Olympic event, he could have been a worthy rival to Sherlock Holmes, Nick Carter, Hercule Poirot, and Ellery Queen.[104]

Cinema also portrayed both capable and upstanding and corrupt and inept policemen. In several plots, they display no interest in finding criminals, and the task falls to other characters, generally the accused.[105] Some of the films I examine have a happy ending, while others do not. In *Paco el elegante* (Paco the Elegant) journalist Luis Camargo (Fernando Galeana) is killed by Paco "El Elegante"(Antonio Badu), boss of a gang that traffics drugs and women. The police blame the sweetheart of Luis's sister, Miguel Labra (Carlos Cores). Knowing the police will do nothing to find the killer, Luis uses the newspaper's influence to secure Miguel's provisional release, surprises the gang, and kills the boss. The police arrive later, only to senselessly shoot and kill the trafficker's innocent girlfriend.[106] In *La muerte es puntual* (Death is on time), Luis (Alfredo Leal) is accused of trafficking drugs and kidnapping a woman; to prove his innocence, he offers himself as bait to lure the true culprit.[107]

In the renowned film *Nosotros los pobres* (We the poor), the police don't bother to find a killer, so they pin it on "Pepe el Toro" (Pedro Infante). He proves his innocence by chance when he is locked up in the same cell as the true murderer, whom he forces to confess.[108] A similar plot, but with a tragic ending, is presented in *Eterna agonía* (Eternal agony). Trinidad (David Silva), the sweetheart of Margarita (Meche Barba), has an affair with the same woman as a secret police member. When a jewelry store is robbed, the jealous agent accuses Trinidad of the crime; the other policemen think he is guilty and release him so he will lead them to his accomplices, but when the actual thief goes in to confess, they kill the man. Trinidad flees the city with Margarita, and to save her, he lets the police kill him.[109]

A final example is interesting for including a reporter's participation: *En busca de la muerte* (Looking for death). The leading suspect in the murder of a man whose body was found in Chapultepec is his wife, beneficiary of his life insurance policy (Lilia del Valle). In her defense, various individuals who hated the victim are mentioned. The case would have been closed if not for *Excélsior* reporter Fernando (Armando Silvestre), who asks for twelve hours to prove the defendant's words. At night they visit the husband's enemies, who admit their motives to kill him, but they all have an alibi. With time running out, a man appears at the police station and claims to have been paid by the husband to kill him; he shows them a letter signed by the dead man confirming the story. Again, the police are on the verge of closing the case. However, the reporter proves that the widow hired the assassin. The film portrays the involvement of journalists and their collaboration with the police. The reporter was the first not only to reach the crime scene and the victim's house but also to solve the crime and cover the story.[110] This is an interesting point that I refer to again below.[111]

The protagonists' ease in finding criminals and the humorous granting of provisional release are hardly believable. Nevertheless, screenwriters employed various strategies to give them credibility. For instance, they "shrank" the city and portrayed it as less anonymous, although at that time the city already had a large number of inhabitants. They gave primary value to the word of the accused or their guardians, although honor was already waning in those years.

That said, although cinema avoided the image of police ineptitude, it did depict corrupt or violent agents. In *Radio patrulla* (Radio Patrol), Rogelio (Arturo Martínez) joins a ring that robs jewelry stores and serves as the lookout.[112] In *La otra* (The other one), María (Dolores del Río) kills her twin sister, Magdalena (also Dolores del Río), and after faking her sister's suicide, she impersonates her twin. Then she finds out the newly widowed Magdalena killed her husband, Fernando, in complicity with her lover, who blackmails María. When the police suspect Fernando's death was not accidental, they arrest the blackmailer and get the truth by beating him.[113]

Conversely, the silver screen also featured honest, dedicated policemen. In *Comisario en turno* (Commissioner on shift), Don Alfonso (Domingo Soler) oversees the Local Public Prosecutor's Office. He acts prudently, with generosity, honor, and respect for the law. His faces his biggest test when his son, who ran over a woman when drunk, appears in his office. The faithful, kind clerk, Manuelito (Carlos López Moctezuma), asks the official, "What are you going to do?" "What I've always done—fulfill my duty," he responds. Manuelito insists on the possibility of releasing his son because there were no witnesses, proposing to cover up the act with attenuating circumstances. "I've been put here to administer justice and I'm not going to change, not for my children, my family, nor my happiness," the commissioner declares. The problem is resolved when doctors miraculously save the injured woman.[114]

The movie *Radio patrulla* has a similar plot. From the start, the director makes his orientation clear, dedicating the film to "the unknown agents who offer their lives day by day in the fight against the criminal underworld, defending society's sacred interests." He tells the story of an investigator who retires, leaving his two sons working in the department: Rodolfo (David Silva), dedicated to investigation, and Rogelio (Arturo Martínez), head of the criminalistics lab. At that time, the office is searching for a band of jewelry thieves. Rogelio collaborates with the gang, but Rodolfo honors his father's name, proves to be incorruptible, and returns every single diamond that reaches him. However, he falls in love with Diana, a member of the gang, and his colleagues believe he is an accomplice. To clear Rodolfo's name, she betrays the gang leader. The retired policeman gets permission to lead the capture, and when he reaches the scene of the robbery, he is surprised to find his son Rogelio, who was the real accomplice. The screenwriter—as in *Comisario en turno*—puts the official to the test: He must choose between duty and fatherly love. The agent prefers his son's death over dishonor to the family, and he tosses Rogelio a gun, suggesting his son commit suicide. "Now I know duty is stronger than a father's pain," the agent declares when he hears the shot. *Ley fuga* (Escape law) has a similar ending: Gabriel (Ramón Gay) is a corrupt policeman who stops at nothing and is arrested by an honest policeman, Mario (Carlos López Moctezuma).[115] Good triumphs over evil and the police are vindicated.[116]

Exemplary policemen appeared not only on the big screen but also on TV, including in two series filmed in the 1950s. The first, *Con el dedo en el gatillo* (Finger on the trigger), featured three protagonists: police commander Aragón (Luis Aragón), private eye Raúl Marín (Raúl Meraz), and Raúl's grandmother (Sara García). Director Luis Spota appears in one episode as a newscaster, interviewing the investigators. The grandmother proves to be the most intelligent and astute of the three, resolving enigmas and even, pistol in hand, saving her grandson on several occasions. The men are not particularly clever, but they are not corrupt or violent, and together they end up solving all sorts of crimes.[117] In the second, *Servicio Secreto* (Secret Service), the agents (Dagoberto Rodríguez and Daniel "Chino" Herrera) display skill and wisdom (wearing disguises, winning over witnesses), in addition to honor and dedication. In a setting reminiscent of Eliot Ness's *The Untouchables*, they lead suspects to the police station without bench warrants and bully them, but with caricaturized violence, which hardly elicits viewers' condemnation.[118]

In sum, in the late 1940s and throughout the 1950s, the magic of cinema offered another vision of the police. This tendency ended in the 1960s, perhaps because by that time there was no magic capable of transforming an image as tarnished as that of the police.

Proposals for Change

Officials of the PGJ, jurists, criminologists, and crime reporters proposed diverse solutions to the problems facing the police. In 1970, assuming the post of attorney general, Sergio García Ramírez deemed it necessary to increase the number of members of the judicial police so they could devote more time to investigation.[119] Earlier, Deputy Attorney General Roberto Guzmán Araujo and journalist Wilberto Cantón had formulated this idea.[120]

García Ramírez also insisted on the need for training. Revisiting a conviction present since the nineteenth century, Alfonso Quiroz Cuarón maintained in 1967, "Progress bears the unmistakable stamp of applied science."[121] In other words—following long-standing desires, as seen in police magazines published late in the Porfirio Díaz administration and overseen by celebrated criminologist Carlos Roumagnac—the hope was for police to be abreast of the latest advances in criminology and criminalistics. Several jurists lamented that this was not the case. José Ángel Ceniceros asserted that the Mexican police did not practice modern techniques and scientific analysis and continued resorting to the "instinct technique."[122] *Novedades* claimed investigation methods were "pharaonic," while *La Prensa* believed it necessary to replace "cantina investigators" with well-trained young people.[123] Finally, Wilberto Cantón and generally those attending the Third Inter-American Congress of the Public Prosecutor (Tercer Congreso Interamericano del Ministerio Público) expressed the urgency of having educated agents knowledgeable about criminology.[124] Otherwise, as noted in the First Mexican Congress of Attorneys (Primer Congreso Mexicano de Procuradores) by José Pérez Moreno, criminal reporter at *El Universal*, the police would be at a disadvantage: "While daily crime is given a technique, the police generally lack the proper means to fight crime."[125] Along the same lines, Quiroz Cuarón maintained that the police had not entered the scientific phase, and therefore instead of being "one of the instruments in the fight against crime," the police were a "cause of crime."[126]

Yet another solution was proposed by the attorneys general of the Federal District and heads of police forces: to bring morality to the organization.[127] Crusades had been undertaken since the 1920s.[128] Pay raises were also proposed. A citizen (who described himself as uneducated but with principles of the "fear of God") said, aware of the bad pay, that whoever joined the force did so "in bad faith." Celebrated policeman Valente Quintana attributed the agents' lack of honor to starvation wages.[129]

José Ángel Ceniceros and Guillermo Colín Sánchez proposed consolidating the police and integrating secret agents into the judicial police, under the MP, as detailed in the Constitution.[130] In the 1960s politicians (such as Senator Rafael Matos Escobedo), jurists (such as Raúl Cárdenas), and journalists (in *Novedades*) spoke of the suppression of the secret police, which had gotten a bad reputation.[131] The vilification of the secret police reached a peak when Arturo Durazo Moreno, better known as "El Negro" ("The Black") Durazo, who was chief of the preventive police, was removed in 1980.

Consequently, journalists, jurists, and officials denounced failures, corruption, and even illicit acts. They spoke of violations of defendants' rights. They also held that the police had failed in their mission: ensuring social order and fighting crime. They believed police acts stained the organization's reputation and of all governmental institutions. According to Francisco Serralde, the fact there were 339 policemen in custody "did no more than generate the hatred and indignation of victims against the government and its disrepute."[132]

ATTORNEYS AND ABOGÁNSTERES

Numerous opinions were expressed on public defenders and private litigators, citing differences between attorneys with and without degrees and between attorneys and *abogánsteres* ("gangster lawyers," or unscrupulous attorneys).

Public Defenders

Various jurists considered public defenders' performance deficient. First District Judge Juan José González Bustamante claimed, "They barely leafed through the records and never bothered to talk to the defendants."[133] Former Deputy Felipe Gómez Mont declared that in his twenty-five years as a criminal lawyer, on only two occasions had he seen the public defenders act assertively; instead, they commonly did not attend proceedings, offer guidance to defendants, or provide proof to invalidate accusations, and they were used to accepting MP agents' petitions requesting the minimum sentence.[134] El Universal Gráfico interviewed remanded prisoners, reporting, "Some said their public defenders had not taken any action to activate their processes; others had not even seen who had been assigned to them or only saw their defenders the day they gave their statement."[135] Movies transmitted the same image: "The poor" had fewer opportunities to be defended. In Nosotros los pobres (We, the poor), Celia "La Chorreada" (Blanca Estela Pavón), seeking a lawyer to defend "Pepe el Toro," offers the attorney her love; he refuses it but is moved to accept the case. His participation is irrelevant. As Julia Tuñón Pablos maintained, "The outside world was governed by a law that meant nothing real for the barrio's inhabitants," and the attorneys "boded problems, more than solutions, and thus, the impotence of the weak was all the greater."[136]

To improve their performance, Gómez Mont deemed their presence at hearings to be mandatory and proposed that litigators perform at least one free defense per year.[137] In 1944 Federal District Attorney General Raúl Carrancá y Trujillo asked attorneys to voluntarily cooperate free of charge in defending prisoners; renowned professionals responded, including Garrido, Ceniceros, Franco Sodi, and González de la Vega.[138] This is important because only in this way could the balance between the parties be guaranteed, providing equality before justice for both those who lacked resources to pay an attorney and those who could pay a lawyer.

From "El Hombre del Corbatón" to Bernabé Jurado: Private Litigators

Private litigators were famous for both better and worse reasons. Better because of greater trust in their capacity. Worse because it was said that some, the abogánsteres, resorted to all sorts of underhanded tactics to get favorable decisions.

In 1966 José Ángel Ceniceros and Pedro Ocampo Ramírez stated that attorneys knew which judges sold justice to the highest bidder.[139] Earlier, in 1940, BMA members affirmed that certain litigators employed "chicanery and bribery" as work methods.[140] Antonio Bennevendo, a student leader, also attributed judges' corruption to mafias of litigators willing to be bought.[141] Garrido held that attorneys, "with their bribes and recommendations," upheld corruption.[142] In El Nacional, Demetrio López Agatangelo affirmed that attorneys with their "kickbacks, duplicity and bad arts have prompted the bad administration of justice."[143] Agapito Pozo, SCJ president, stated, "If there are unscrupulous officials, there are worse litigators."[144]

Even more worrisome was that some attorneys were practicing without degrees. González Franco said that judges made use of them as go-betweens to communicate the amount of the bribe to the defendant and, from this, the severity of the penalty; Crispín Ortiz Alarcón declared that they prostituted justice; a man interviewed by *Novedades* said that they corrupted employees; and *El Nacional Revolucionario* and Concha de Villarreal claimed that they stole money from the unwary.[145] Their effectiveness was not doubted. *Excélsior* affirmed that "coyotes" (persons who offered legal services without holding a degree) achieved more than "attorneys with a solid reputation," who were retiring, leaving the field open to those who "had no objection, as long as they could earn money, suggesting the most twisted methods to make a mockery of justice."[146] According to Concha de Villarreal, police station and court employees warned "coyotes" when a "fine piece of work" arrived, offering freedom in exchange for money; if their clients did not have money, they made messengers available to bring cash or assets to their homes, after bribing guards to allow them to communicate with the outside to buy witnesses and alibis.[147] Earlier, *Excélsior* had claimed that good police investigation work was ruined by the intervention of defenders who did not stop "at the use of resources of the worst kind to mislead justice."[148]

Generally, litigators lacking a degree did not represent individuals accused of serious crimes. The exception was José Menéndez, "El Hombre del Corbatón" ("The Man of the Big Necktie"), a successful litigator who, according to diverse accounts, was highly regarded in courtrooms. Born in Asturias, he had an adventurous spirit that took him first to Cuba and in 1898 to Mexico. He lived on handouts until El Bosque, a restaurant frequented by bullfighting fans, changed his destiny. He earned money writing love letters and defending those in legal peril. In courts he met "El Manco" Valdez, an expert in criminal law. As Menéndez told it, he picked up shrewdness from him, because Valdez learned the doctrine from jury trial lawyers like Jesús Urueta, José María Lozano, and Querido Moheno.[149]

Late in the Porfirio Díaz administration, dressed in a wide-brimmed sombrero and a cravat tied into an oversize bow, Menéndez used the argument of self-defense to obtain the acquittal of a Spanish bullfighter accused of homicide. This brought him fame, which continued into the criminal courts period. He charged some clients but defended destitute prisoners and prostitutes free of charge. "Because prisoners are poor, you need to help them; doing good is the moral person's principle," he would say.[150] A friend of journalists, Menéndez also won the sympathy of judges. In 1924, when he was going to be expelled under Article 33 for defending French prostitutes, the press published notes in his favor, and various groups, including judges, called for President Álvaro Obregón's intervention. The attorney who orchestrated the expulsion also asked that Menéndez be deported from the country because he often defended loose women, to which the president responded, "But, my dear friend, whom will he defend, the eleven thousand virgins?" Menéndez remained in Mexico. On multiple occasions, he used the argument of self-defense, which had earned him his "first forensic success." "With those two words, I have traveled the path. Those two words characterized me. I was the man of 'self-defense' before being 'El Hombre del Corbatón,'" he reminisced. "I owe everything I was and am to 'self-defense.'"[151]

His image contrasts with that of another legendary figure, Bernabé Jurado. Born in Chihuahua around 1910 to a hacienda owner who lost his property and his life to Pancho Villa supporters, Jurado first worked in a mine, then went to Mexico City at the age of twelve to study law. He married fourteen times. He was an attorney to the most famous figures of the time (including Pedro Infante, handling his divorce) and usually met them in La Ópera cantina. He embodied the figure of the abogánster. As Carlos Monsiváis writes, "In a real or induced oversight of employees, he diverts a compromising document from the file and eats it, pays false witnesses, sponsors torture that leads to the confession of innocents, always has an amparo in his pocket, savagely beats his girlfriends, is the image of the influence peddler, the Mexico City criminal attorney, who was never informed of the existence of scruples."[152]

His clients were much like him. Jurado defended William Burroughs for killing his wife and boasted about springing him from jail in just thirteen days. The American writer said entering Jurado's office was like entering a "universe of smiling corruption."[153] Eugenio Aguirre offers an image not far from this in his novel El abogánster, recounting Jurado's life in the first person. Bernabé Jurado is portrayed as a womanizer and drug addict, a violent, corrupt, and unscrupulous person. He cultivated fame because it went hand in hand with his other skill: winning even the toughest cases. A friend of journalists like "El Güero Téllez" and enemy of others like Carlos Denegri, he ensured newspapers paid attention to him, beyond his not infrequent court victories and personal scandals (twice he had to flee the capital, once for being accused of homicide).

The figure of the *abogánster* reached the silver screen in 1951 in the film *Entre abogados te veas* (May you see yourself among lawyers). Attorney Gerardo Barrios (Armando Calvo) threatens his client's wife (played by Carmen Montejo) by accusing her of having an affair with another lawyer, Ricardo Cosío (Luis Beristaín), to pressure her into giving his client a divorce and custody of their son. "We lawyers are the scissor blades around the client," he warns her. However, movies also made room for noble, honest attorneys. Ricardo Cosío defends the *abogánster*'s victim and lays a trap for his rival, recording the conversation in which Barrios admits he faked the husband's signature and sent a hit man to keep her assets. The explanation changes: "We honorable attorneys are obliged to do away with these scoundrels."[154] Thus, just as in police movies, good attorneys prevailed over corrupt lawyers.

Esteban (Luis Aldás) in *La infame*, mentioned earlier, did the same. Likewise, Mario (Octavio Arias) in *La perversa* (The libertine), also filmed in 1953, defends Alicia (Elsa Aguirre), on trial for the murder of Enrique (César del Campo). Alicia, in love with Enrique and threatened by him, sells the honor of her sister Gloria (Alma Rosa Aguirre), causing the death of her mother, who was shocked by the news. Alicia gets no thanks from Enrique, who deceives and humiliates her. When he plans to leave her, she shoots him and tries to make it look like suicide. Mario represents her at Gloria's request and uses expert evidence to convince the jury it was a suicide.[155] Movies also offer appropriate actions by prosecutors. For example *El pecador* (The sinner), which premiered in 1964, involves a student who proves the innocence of his professor, Mario (Arturo de Córdoba).[156]

Although there were diverse perspectives regarding attorneys, the condemnation of the *abogánster* was unanimous. It was deemed necessary to instill moral principles in attorneys and to draft ethical codes, as tasks demanded by jurists (such as Luis Garrido and Jaime Delgado Reyes) that involved a government agency (the TSJ Judicial Cooperation Committee) or group (the BMA, which in 1949 published a professional ethics code).[157] In addition, jurists and journalists proposed compulsory membership in a professional association in the belief that it would oversee the conduct of litigators and the reform of the law of professions by prohibiting litigation by attorneys lacking a degree.[158]

Pedro Ocampo Ramírez wrote in *Excélsior* in 1966, "Mexican justice has been accused of being double-dealing, money-driven, lazy, and tending to cave to anyone who knows how to bombard it with gifts. It might be a falsehood, it might be the product of resentment of those who have not won its favors, but the case is that our justice has a very bad reputation, even among those responsible for administering it."[159]

In this section, I address opinions concerning judges and justice. I begin with those of judges and their appointments. Next, I look at guidelines on judges' inefficacy and lack of interest leading to absenteeism, backlogs, delegation of functions, absence of deliberation in sentencing, and legal errors. This is followed by critiques of influence peddling, corruption, and their result: inequality in judicial processes and sentences. Finally, I discuss proposals made to remedy these problems.

"A True Hospital of Political Invalids": Judicial Appointments

"The judiciary is a true hospital of political invalids. When a political professional falls outside the budget, if he still has influence or favors owed by those in power, he is given a judicial post."[160]

In some years public or judicial officials uttered praise regarding the independence and appointment of judges. Emilio Portes Gil, referring to his own performance, assured, "There was never a case in which my collaborators or I intervened in any judicial matter, even less did we make any profit-motivated recommendation." He added that during his term, judges could be certain they would not be removed and acted freely. He maintained that the same was the case during the administration of Abelardo Rodríguez because the former president too had prevented presidential involvement.[161] In 1945, in the report Raúl Carrancá y Trujillo presented as TSJ president, he supported the appointment of judges made by the magistrates.[162] Judge Ricardo Abarca had applauded the appointment of TSJ judges in 1944.[163] In 1955 another TSJ judge, Alberto Bremauntz, similarly stood up for his colleagues, praising the appointment of judges.[164] Sources reveal the same sentiment expressed by a jurist: In 1948 Germán Fernández del Castillo, a professor at the ELD and a litigator, characterized the selection of judges as proper and hailed the impartiality of appointments.[165]

Nevertheless, criticism outweighed praise. During the period studied, politicians, jurists, litigators, and journalists held that judges appointed did not meet the legal requirements—basically, experience—and they owed their appointment to favors owed, recommendations, and cronyism.

In the 1940s various opinions were expressed on the matter. For instance, Claudio Medina Osalde stated in El Universal, "The policy of 'move over, it's my turn now,'" inspired by cronyism, had brought justice down to [the point it was] misery.[166] La Justicia maintained that at every change in administration, "honest, upright, and wise" judicial officials were replaced by individuals "taken from militant politics, intended to exclusively service the judiciary, as long as the political influence of whoever appointed them lasted."[167]

It was said that some judges had fake degrees issued by governors and even by a military man. La Prensa claimed some of them were simple tricksters with degrees issued in the "pre-constitutional era and in use of extraordinary powers."[168] In response, the TSJ president asked his judges to present their documents, and journalists predicted removals.[169]

Similar opinions continued over the next two decades. Opposition politicians—Juan Gutiérrez Lascuráin, president of the Partido Acción Nacional, and Alberto Lumbares, general secretary of the Partido Obrero Campesino de México—stated that merits and careers held no weight in judge selection, but rather it was based on influences and recommendations.[170] Jurists Ocampo, Bremauntz, Alfredo Domínguez del Río, and Garrido also held this idea.[171] Moreover, reviving a serious accusation, criminologist Héctor Solís Quiroga asserted that not all judicial officials were attorneys with degrees.[172] It was alleged that judges named close friends or relatives for court positions. For instance, when he left the TSJ presidency in 1930, José Ortiz Rodríguez claimed that one of the TSJ judges had appointed his nephew as clerk and another made his father head of the archives.[173]

Judges Wake Up Late: Backlogs, Inefficiency, and Judicial Errors
JUSTICE DELAYED IS JUSTICE DENIED

"The Revolution has successfully attacked a good number of our major social problems; but in that of the speedy administration of justice a satisfactory solution has yet to be achieved."[174] "It has been said the delay of justice is practically tantamount to its denial. A favorable ruling that arrives after the interests have vanished, after families have been torn apart, that the claim itself has perished, what justice can shine?"[175] These quotes exemplify the topic of this section: backlogs and their effects. These were a violation of the constitutional guarantee of prompt and speedy justice and often led to damages for defendants whose cases were not quickly resolved.

Judicial backlog was one of the most severely criticized problems at the time. Much was said of federal tribunals, but *La Prensa*, TSJ President Armando Z. Ostos, *La Justicia*, and attorney Jaime Delgado Reyes also denounced delays in local courts.[176] In 1942 Concha de Villarreal affirmed that when she assumed her post, the first criminal judge had inherited 371 case files, the second 118, and the third 176; because they received twenty-five to thirty new acts daily with requests for court orders to jail suspects, they could not eliminate the backlog.[177] In 1964 the TSJ president indicated that some judges had more than one hundred case files to close.[178] In 1941 Ostos lamented, "No one is unaware that, on the one hand, there are many incomplete processes begun long ago, despite what is foreseen in the Constitution itself, and on the other, there is a vast number of defendants withstanding the rigors of prison although the maximum sentence applicable if they were found guilty has been exceeded."[179] He mentioned two consequences of the backlog: extending procedural time limits and violating constitutional Article 20.[180] Irregularities were detailed as well. Concha de Villarreal maintained that hearings, instead of being held fifteen days from the closing investigation of facts, were carried out three or four months later, while Manuel Escobedo affirmed that agreements that had to be issued within hours took weeks and sentences took months.[181]

Periodically, reporters published prisoner complaints about time limits for determining guilt and that the time for sentencing had ended. In 1954 *La Prensa* published specific cases and names of inmates.[182]

CAUSES OF BACKLOGS

Luis Garrido attributed the backlogs to three factors: "not enough trial and appeal courts, little diligence among much of the staff, and antiquated work procedures."[183] Insufficient courts and personnel have already been discussed; this section focuses on the other factors.

Several jurists complained of delays in work methods, including the lack of tape recorders and vehicles. They also denounced the poor handling of case files. According to witnesses, files were randomly piled up on the floor, making it difficult to find the files for specific cases.[184] In different years BMA members, *El Universal* editorialists, Trinidad García, and other attorneys claimed that the disorder was exploited by litigators, who bribed employees to destroy or remove files.[185] Furthermore, General Martín del Campo attributed irregularities in the trials of two Lecumberri prisoners to the disappearance of the case files or the "lending" of some pages from the files to the attorney wishing to malign a clerk's act.[186]

Other jurists asserted that the legislation retained remnants of the past (Juan José González Bustamante), was rife with confusing and obscure parts (litigators), contained arbitrary or anodyne (literal)/uninspiring procedures (BMA), and just as in other Latin American countries, was overly formalist (Trinidad García).[187] In the words of Luis Garrido, "We are still faithful to colonial paperwork. Proceedings and sentences have useless forms and requirements. Many of our judicial procedures exude the form and spirit of an archaeological obsolescence."[188] Several attorneys claimed that these factors complicated the judge's work and lengthened trials.[189] According to Senator Carlos Soto Guevara, attorneys Trinidad García and Leopoldo Aguilar, and La Prensa, unscrupulous litigators took advantage of legal complications.[190] Therefore, attorneys Gustavo R. Velasco, Javier Gaxiola, Luis Domínguez Carrascosa, and Adolfo Aguilar y Quevedo demanded that laws and paperwork be simplified.[191]

The last argument used to explain delays was absenteeism. In the early 1940s La Prensa claimed, "Neither judges, secretaries, [nor] the rest of the personnel do what is expected of them."[192] José Ángel Ceniceros attributed it to the "organized laziness of some officials, their reiterated negligence that can become the knowing absence of duty."[193] El Nacional Revolucionario writers stated that magistrates and judges arrived in court late.[194] In the following years, private attorneys and public defenders were said to be guilty of the same: Instead of arriving at nine, they reportedly came in at eleven and ended their workday at lunchtime.[195] According to Ernesto Basulto, hearings were never held after one in the afternoon.[196] BMA members noted that activities were suspended on unauthorized days, and limited work hours were spent on matters alien to the court.[197] Moreover, there were even more serious accusations: Jurist and judge Claudio Medina Osalde maintained that two judges did not even show up for five and six years.[198]

DELEGATION OF DUTIES AND JUDICIAL ERRORS

According to sources, the breaches, absences, and delays of judicial officials not only caused the backlog but also created other problems. Litigators claimed that proceedings were not conducted in a timely manner.[199] According to *La Prensa*, sometimes they were never carried out. A reporter described the case of an elderly night watchman sentenced for homicide. When a private attorney decided to help him in the appeal, the lawyer had to request proceedings the judge had never bothered to take care of.[200]

Attorneys and judges asserted that a common practice was the delegation of duties, and they denounced their consequences. In 1931 newly appointed Judge Alfredo Pino Cámara (son of no less than José María Pino Suárez) complained about a custom difficult to eradicate: Some judges did not participate actively in the proceedings; instead, the judge entrusted employees "who were sent as he pleased in the inquiry to receive and record statements, conduct cross-examinations, collect or reject testimonies, all to the best (or worst) of their knowledge."[201] Almost at the end of the period studied, in 1969, Alfonso Trueba wrote, "The judge is very busy in his office, while an old, poorly paid clerk, or secretary who knows them all questions the alleged offender, interrogates witnesses, practices cross-examination, and makes records as he sees fit."[202]

Fernández del Castillo identified the immediate consequence of delegating functions: The judges were signing "false records" that confirmed their participation when they had not actually attended the proceeding; consequently, when determining guilt, they were unfamiliar with the defendant and the case.[203] Rafael de Pina maintained that in certain cases, the pretrial statement was the judge's only contact with the accused.[204] Fernando Arrilla Bas noted that the mixed system contemplated by the law was often reduced to the written document because the trial took place without the judge's presence.[205] Furthermore, Domínguez del Río held that certain judges had no contact with the parties.[206]

This practice defeated the purpose of the 1929 and 1931 Codes, in which the drafters had sought to expand judicial discretion by individualizing the sentences based on the defendants' distinctive characteristics. In 1965 Luis Garrido lamented that this intention bore little fruit because "many judges judge criminals without seeing them, only forming an opinion from reading their files but without the necessary contemplation of the living and effective man."[207] *Sucesos para todos* rued that "those who are judged are not human beings, only lifeless files."[208]

How did these judges issue rulings? In 1930 *El Nacional Revolucionario* argued that sentences reflected a "lack of study."[209] In 1942 María Elena Sodi Pallares wrote of judges, "Given the haste and numerous accusations, they investigate them superficially and do not penetrate the psychology of the accused and accusers, they do not study their living conditions, their background, and the probable motives of their current conduct, nor the credibility of the accusations, the cross-examination is not sound, and a priori an erroneous criterion is almost always formed in cases under their authority."[210] Years later, in 1957, Manuel Escobedo contended that sentences were issued with little thought.[211] A *Novedades* editorialist backed this claim by saying agents determined punishment "by guesswork."[212]

It was said that in this last phase of the judicial process, some judges delegated the task. For instance, Fernández del Castillo asserted that clerks were responsible for drafting the rulings.[213] Trueba claimed that some judgments were based on MP requests, which were generally turned into sentences.[214] Diverse jurists complained of the leading role of the MP agent, who started with the law (with a lack of control over his actions during the preliminary investigation and his later monopoly over criminal action) and took an increasing role in practice.[215] Rafael Zubarán Capmany affirmed that the "deformed, omnipotent, monstrous" MP agent was beyond and above the law.[216] Niceto Alcalá-Zamora y Castillo defined the MP agent as a "key piece of Mexican criminal justice" who "clearly suffers from hypertrophy."[217]

Some jurists lamented that the foundations of collegial justice were also violated. This was affirmed in 1949 by Carlos Franco Sodi: "Day by day, in the overwhelming majority of criminal business, judges make a judgment that his two court colleagues simply sign, the sentence then appearing to come from a collegial court, when in reality it is a resolution dictated by a single judicial official."[218] According to Mario Rojas Avendaño, the carelessness of judicial officials and the delegation of tasks produced judicial errors: "How many times was the attack on an innocent person not only the fruit of the fallibility of the judges as men, but also of the irresponsibility with which they attend to their duties?"[219]

In 1942 *El Universal* published a report on the visit of TSJ president Manuel Moreno Sánchez to Lecumberri Prison: More than 10 percent of the prisoners believed that irregularities had been committed in their trials and that legal standards had not been respected.[220] Twenty-four years later, *Excélsior* reported that a man was in prison for ten months after being unfairly sentenced for homicide and was freed when the guilty party was found.[221] Around the same time, General Martín del Campo considered the list of injustices committed daily to be "as interminable as the suffering of the victims of a crippled justice system."[222] Apparently, judicial errors were not sanctioned. That same year, TSJ President Ignacio Sánchez Vargas recounted the case of a judge who had condemned a man for the death of his stepdaughter, based solely on his confession, but later the victim appeared alive. The reporter asked about the sanction on the judge. The response: "He came to occupy a seat on the Supreme Court."[223]

If the criticism was founded, it shows that essential principles of the justice system were violated. Prisoners without resources did not have the defense described in the Constitution. With the delegation of functions, the requirement of immediacy was not met. Failure to take steps, carelessness, and delegating functions fostered judicial errors and violated the exact application of the law. Furthermore, collegial justice became the justice of a single judge.

Money and Influence Peddling

"Today justice is done based on money and influence."[224] "Systematically, the attorney, instead of invoking the law, invokes with money or power."[225] "Nothing is more disconcerting to the people than a poor administration of justice; especially when social operations are characterized by interest-based predilections, whether by the political position or economic solvency of the probable criminals."[226] "There are killers who do not hesitate to say they will be set free in a few weeks because they have money or 'political influences.'"[227] "Secretaries and judges issue agreements for influences or money."[228] These quotes, published between 1929 and 1965, reiterated the notion that the scales of justice were weighed down by influences or money. This section covers allegations of cronyism, complaints of bribery, and unequal treatment based on economic status.

THE DANGEROUS LINK WITH POLITICS

Some officials believed judges were indeed autonomous. Senator Carlos Soto Guevara maintained that "the machinations of the powerful had crashed multiple times" in the face of justice.[229] Amid the scandal over the declarations of Senator Augusto Hinojosa, TSJ President Daniel Salazar Hurtado, and District Judge Luis G. Corona, they affirmed that judicial power was independent. It was more respected day by day, which, according to Hinojosa, was owed to President Manuel Ávila Camacho, who had never "made a recommendation."[230] Years later, Emilio Portes Gil assured that during his administration, tribunals had been autonomous and respectable jurists filled vacant positions.[231]

However, the contrary opinion predominated. According to politicians, jurists, and journalists, parties, recommendations, and cronyism influenced the appointment of magistrates and judges. Manuel Moreno Sánchez contended, "People lacking vocation and merit were there waiting to improve their luck."[232] Concha de Villarreal asserted, "Political recommendations and kinship with judicial figures are what have made the unfortunate Mexican justice [system] inept."[233] Consequently, as Moreno Sánchez explained, certain judges acted out of gratitude to those who had intervened in their appointment or to ingratiate themselves with those who would determine their ratification. Although friendship or cronyism had a bearing on the election of certain judges, friendship and cronyism had an impact on their resolutions. According to José Castillo Larrañaga, if one appointed friends, one could turn to them in case of need.[234] "What freedom can a judge have to give a fair ruling if gratitude or obligation ties him to his protector?" asked Nicanor Gurría Urgell, founder of the ELD. "Judicial officials, with few exceptions, are more concerned about keeping their jobs by pleasing those who can move them or harm them in any way from blindly applying the law."[235] El Universal stated, "If judges and offenders are brethren, the criminal act is considered to be significantly different."[236] Carlos Franco Sodi imagined the dismissal of a "good judge":

> Sir, I come to dismiss you. We do not want you administering justice even though when appointing you as judge, we told you what we expected you to do. You're just and kind, but we need something different, a man willing to bow to the powerful. You didn't understand what we wanted; we can't keep you. We're sorry because we're glad to see you, over the years, as poor as you were before, a little older, and administering justice up to the end.[237]

Excélsior editorialists contended that having assets or political influences and "kinship with the revolutionary movement" allowed criminals to "escape unharmed by a visible crime."[238] In the same tenor, they assured, "Even judges with their own moral criteria hesitate and yield when the influence of the powerful is involved. There have repeatedly been cases in which an incorruptible judge is disqualified or put on government "blacklists" because they have dared to issue a just verdict against higher interests."[239]

Other examples exist. Magistrate Alberto Bremauntz mentioned that litigators pressured judges by using those who had influenced their appointment, and more judges had ceded to "the official or political slogan or the recommendation of friends or relatives" than to money. BMA members, José Ángel Ceniceros, Luis Garrido, Trinidad García, and Concha de Villarreal spoke of the impunity of influential politicians or their friends, as well as their weight in courts. Froylán López Narváez maintained that "kinship" was decisive in courts, and the Central de Trabajadores Mexicanos recognized that tribunals were benign toward union leaders.[240]

In sum, according to diverse authors, magistrates and judges lacked independence. Raúl Cervantes Ahumada asserted, "When there is a political interest, judges and magistrates forget their dignity."[241] Héctor Solís Quiroga compared this situation to what had prevailed in the Porfirio Díaz regime and claimed that control of justice responded to strengthening executive power: "In a patriarchism of the presidential regime such as ours, the personal interest of the Mexican president acts as a lighthouse for all action anywhere in the country."[242]

"NEITHER THOSE WHO PAY ARE SURPRISED, NOR THOSE WHO CHARGE EMBARRASSED"

According to Gonzalo de la Parra in 1940, "Charging and selling sentences in all sorts of lawsuits is a firmly established business; neither those who pay are surprised, nor those who charge embarrassed."[243] Lucio Mendieta y Núñez pointed to the urgency of limiting abuses and "the unwarranted enrichment of employees and officials."[244] After half a century of experience, Emilio Portes Gil considered corruption to be one of the country's serious ills; he pinpointed its start as 1915, when "the Constitutionalist movement became government" and many officials of the regime amassed "fortunes in the shadow of the Revolution," and he situated its peak between 1936 and 1958, the middle of the period covered in this book.[245] Justice did not elude selling and acceptance of money in exchange for services or favors. Portes Gil contended that tribunals were a place of corruption. For jurist Germán Fernández del Castillo, they were among the places where corruption was flaunted most openly and importantly.[246] It comes as no surprise that most of the criticism of justice was related to bribery and abuse.

Like Portes Gil, I believe that in the field of justice, corruption is characteristic of postrevolutionary Mexico. Before the Revolution, the primary criticism was the influence of the executive in causes that involved political interests or prominent figures of the regime. Francisco Serralde affirmed, "In addition to the vices of the time past to the present should also be added the rotting of the judicial body with the cheap buying and selling of justice, which begins with the bribe and continues to the highest levels of the administration of justice."[247]

Denunciations of judges and judicial employees who committed prevarication and bribery were constant between 1929 and 1971. Before his Senate colleagues, Augusto Hinojosa argued that criminal courts, "with their honorable exceptions, are true dens of larceny. What is worse, even the Tribunal Superior de Justicia, through the goddess Themis's irony, sells judgments, and honest judges are prevented from strictly exercising their functions. It would be necessary, as in the biblical legend, for a new Messiah to cast the merchants out of the temple of justice."[248]

In 1954 Emilio Portes Gil averred that never before had there been so much corruption in the administration of justice and affirmed, "It is public and notorious that many rulings, both criminal and civil, are obtained through money."[249] He was not the only official who denounced the corruption. In 1966 legislative deputy Ignacio Ramos Praslow declared, "Full knowledge that corruption has taken control of the judicial power is not only in the awareness of litigators but also of all citizens. In state courts to promote any matter, you must have money in hand and not in low denominations, instead several blue [bills]."[250] Numerous jurists attested to these accusations, including Fernando de la Fuente, Carlos Franco Sodi, José Ángel Ceniceros, Luis Garrido, Trinidad García, Héctor Solís Quiroga, and Alfonso Trueba.[251] Officials (such as Senator Carlos Soto Guevara) and journalists (Excélsior editorialists and Miguel Bueno) did as well.[252]

However, others expressed the opposite opinion. In the early 1930s Manuel Andrade, José María Lozano, and Víctor Velázquez spoke out in support of judges' integrity.[253] In 1940 the head of the PGR affirmed that during the Cárdenas administration, judges had displayed exemplary honesty.[254] In 1941 Germán Fernández del Castillo praised Octavio Véjar Vázquez's performance at the helm of the PGR, maintaining that he had eradicated corruption and moved aggressively even in cases involving public or political officials.[255] In 1966 litigator Raúl Cervantes Ahumada claimed that in his thirty years of work, he had never given a judge a bribe and had never been asked for one, concluding, "If you delve into the research, it would be discovered, not to the surprise of many, that malfeasance is the exception and not the rule."[256]

It is not possible to generalize about all judges or about all years in the period studied; nevertheless, corruption seemed to be a recognized and accepted problem. Every so often, directors of judicial bodies, such as TSJ Presidents José Ortiz Rodríguez (in the late 1920s), Armando Z. Ostos (in 1942), Carlos Franco Sodi (in 1951), and Julio Sánchez Vargas (in 1964), expressed their intention to expel corrupt officials, as did TSJ magistrates in 1941.[257]

According to witnesses, corruption permeated all levels. Actuaries were repeatedly accused of requesting and accepting bribes.[258] For example, Lucio Mendieta y Núñez held that the problem began with the lack of vehicles in the court's service. It was impossible to ask actuaries with low salaries to pay for car rentals out of their own pocket to deliver notifications, and it was too slow to do so by streetcar, so litigators gave them money to pay their transport, and with this clever actuaries earned more than the salaries of judges and magistrates.[259]

Moreover, according to attorney association and law school representatives, secretaries, clerks, typists, and archivists also expected compensation for their work, as if it were a consecrated "right."[260] Not paying for copies, or even reports of promotions, led to delays and to the loss of files in cases.[261]

Other corrupt practices were also denounced. El Universal Gráfico claimed, "When the remanded did not merit the attention of the defendants, employees of the very tribunal charged them for taking their case, and if they were refused, the process suffered many delays."[262] TSJ President Ignacio Sánchez Vargas expressed the same opinion. He described it as a barbarity in that nowhere else in the world did secretaries and other employees function as defenders of the trials they handled.[263]

Prevarication and bribery were explained away with different arguments, primarily the lack of ethics of some judges and tribunal employees, as well as low salaries. Critics deemed litigants and defendants responsible. According to Ceniceros, "The crime of bribery has a bilateral character and presupposes the participation of two wills, that of the corruptor and that of the bribed official."[264] Attorney General José Aguilar y Maya stated that venality was the fault of bribery and the briber.[265] Raúl Cervantes Ahumada declared, "Both the one who kills the cow sins equally as the one who holds the leg still, and equally immoral is the judge who is sold and the litigator who buys him."[266] Bremauntz maintained that it thus was necessary for the Criminal Code to cover punishment for the briber as well.[267]

Defendants and their families were blamed for offering money to judicial employees through their attorneys. As Concha de Villarreal (in 1942) and Armando R. Ostos (in 1966) averred, they had "more trust in the efficacy of bribes than in laws."[268] Therefore, *Excélsior* claimed they resorted to bribery.[269] Lorenzo Herrera affirmed, "For there to be a venal judge, there has to be an unscrupulous attorney who prefers the path of bribery to obtain the favorable verdict, as it also requires someone who has hired him to provide the money for the judge to depart from the law."[270]

Sergio García Ramírez spoke of the shared responsibility of the citizenry in corruption.[271] And journalist César Lizardi Ramos predicted, "If each of us resisted the bribe, it will prevent the temple of justice from becoming a sordid market."[272] Partido Acción Nacional President Adolfo Christlieb Ibarrola concluded, "There are venal judges because there are corrupt attorneys, and there are attorneys who bribe because there are judges who commit extortion."[273] It was a vicious circle that was difficult to break.

These practices violated procedural rights. As BMA members, *La Prensa* editorialists, and Fernández del Castillo noted, justice continued to have an extraofficial cost.[274] According to Domínguez del Río, in courts everything had "a price and cost."[275] Alfonso Trueba avowed, "The judiciary mechanism doesn't work except through money."[276] Luis Garrido argued, "[The] gratuity of justice is another declaration of the law far from reality."[277] The "buying and selling" of justice also violated the principle of equality before the law.

"THE CIVIL CODE FOR THE RICH, THE CRIMINAL CODE FOR THE POOR"

An editorialist wrote in *Sucesos para todos* in 1969, "Criminal justice is essentially exercised on the poor, who lack the economic means to afford attorneys—public defenders are of no use—greasing the palms of cops, encouraging secretaries and other employees, and softening up judges."[278] Considering the importance of influence and money in courts, the necessary conclusion is that inequality prevailed in the administration of justice, and legal rules did not apply to the influential and rich in the same way as to those who lacked money and influence. *El Universal* editorialists claimed that "despite the theory of equality of all citizens before the law, fundamental in the democratic system, unfortunately the status of criminals affects justice."[279]

Numerous authors denounced inequality or gave examples of it. The divergence began after arrest because some detained individuals were freed after paying a bribe to police officers or MP agents. Given the economic level of those who were arrested, El Universal Gráfico asked, "Is it perhaps only the moneyless lower class [that] commits crimes?"[280] Differences continued in the trial because penniless defendants had to settle for public defenders. Alfredo Domínguez del Río contended, "The poor generally lack good defenders and material resources to dispel the ugliness of their crimes and to be favored with an acquittal or a lenient sentence."[281]

Later, it also affected access to release on bail. Marxófilo, in El Nacional Revolucionario, held that workers could not cover the requirements of bail bondsmen. Therefore, as El Universal contributor Salvador Ponce de León also noted, only the affluent benefited from a prerogative guaranteed to everyone under the Constitution.[282] According to Enrique Basulto, inequality also affected the duration of trials, which were quicker with a competent attorney.[283] Concha de Villarreal said they also affected sentences, and people with a profession and money never wound up there.[284] In Lecumberri, there were many "prisoners forgotten by judges and defense attorneys," La Prensa reported, "poor people who have no money to move the thousand strings that could be pulled by the lucky for justice to release them to the street."[285] A few months before the suppression of criminal courts, Judge Alfonso Trueba noted, "In most cases the poor are not released as soon as those with resources."[286] Similarly, Sucesos para todos explained, "If defendants have money the procedural panorama differed. All facilities are available to them, the acceptance of false witnesses, the favorable interpretation of codes, and release on bail was freely granted."[287] Guillermo Colín Sánchez contended that justice in the country was merchandise and prisons contained only the poor or the foolish.[288]

Newspapers published examples of this inequality. Two legislators from the Partido Revolucionario Institucional, Fluvio Vista Altamirano and Miguel Covián Pérez, and one from the Partido Acción Nacional, Felipe Gómez Mont, denounced the favoritism displayed toward a millionaire's son (possibly referring to Higinio Sobera), who remained unpunished, and a celebrated athlete (Humberto Mariles) who eluded arrest for months.[289] In contrast was the case of a mother who spent months imprisoned for stealing corn to feed her children.[290]

The lack of equality in courts was thus criticized by representatives of the opposition parties. Early in this chapter, I cited the declaration of Vicente

Lombardo Toledano, leader of the Partido Popular. Manuel Terrazas, secretary general of the Partido Comunista Mexicano, similarly decried the notorious impunity of the wealthy classes.[291] Journalists also criticized this inequity, such as in three articles published in 1942: *La Prensa* maintained that some judges showed no mercy to the poor and bowed before the rich, tolerating the staff of justice becoming a bottleneck, "on whose narrow side the reason of the modest could not pass, and on the wide side the power of reason bursts in."[292] *El Universal* denounced the violation of equality of everyone under the law and the existence of "different weights and measures for the powerful and the humble."[293] *Excélsior* declared that justice had two sleeves: "a very wide one for the favored to go in and out, those with political influence; and another narrow one in which the dimwitted, mentally disabled, reactionaries, and those who lacked resources and consideration."[294] Continuing with a metaphor of weights and measures, in the same newspaper, Antonio Armendáriz argued that there were "two scales, one for those who pay and another for those who don't."[295]

Professionals and academics shared the same opinion. Lucio Mendieta y Núñez, director of the Instituto de Investigaciones Sociales of UNAM, said, "No one is unaware how the poor frown over the ease with which the rich mock bench warrants and are released, having committed crimes," concluding, "justice is unilateral, only for the poor."[296] Young attorney Alfredo Bennevendo assured that "class justice has been created in Mexico."[297] *La Prensa* conducted a poll asking, "How to you want justice to be?" One student responded, "But sir, does justice even exist? The poor always bear the entire brunt of the law."[298]

Other sectors of society were of the same mind. According to the results of research conducted by the Facultad de Ciencias Políticas y Sociales of UNAM in 1969, the main complaint of those surveyed was the lack of honesty of judges and equality in courts.[299] Other responses to reporters from various dailies were similar: "If the defendant in the courts is rich, he can prove he is innocent through a thousand means at his fingertips," and "That's justice in Mexico: implacable with those below, who often commit crimes to eat, and exquisitely complacent with those above, who have money to cast at the scales of Themis."[300]

Proposed Solutions

Some solutions that were proposed to correct justice problems required fundamental changes, while others called for minor adjustments.

The most radical proposals came from Communist or Socialist Party members, who thought true change would be achieved only when the state did not obey class interests (for instance, Alberto Lumbreras, general secretary of the Partido Obrero Campesino de México), the economic and social conditions of Mexico changed (Lombardo Toledano, president of the Partido Popular), a true democracy permitted the representation of all social groups and stopped taking into account the interests of just one sector (Manuel Terrazas, general secretary of the Partido Comunista Mexicano), or at least when judges were recruited from the ranks of true revolutionaries.[301]

Some jurists proposed making criminal law reforms and simplifying procedural steps. But others thought that more than reforming laws, it was necessary to guarantee their respect. For example, Carlos Franco Sodi claimed the problem resided in who was applying the law, and Nicanor Gurría Urgell asserted there was no lack of laws, but rather there were not enough men capable of applying and enforcing them.

There were calls for increasing the local justice budget, which would allow for higher salaries and mitigate corruption. In addition, this would permit having more personnel and decreasing delays. Proposals called for the reinstallation of the former Ministry of Justice to intervene in appointments, licenses, and resignations of Supreme Court justices, TSJ magistrates, and local judges, and federal and capital attorneys general.[302]

Furthermore, there was a push for changes in the appointment of judges, with proposals of greater or lesser scope. For years Luis Garrido insisted the plenary of TSJ magistrates had to elect candidates, addressing proposals made by attorney associations and law schools.[303] There was also insistence on the technical and moral training of judges. This demand contained an old request of sympathizers of the positivist school of criminal law, who believed that only judges knowledgeable in medicine, biology, psychology, and sociology could take into consideration the dangers posed by the defendants. It was not an exclusive aspiration of Mexicans, as seen in international meetings and articles published in journals like *Criminalia*.[304] But Mexican jurists were not far behind. They were convinced of progress in science, but specifically thought the expansion of judicial discretion required a new type of judge. For example, in the early 1930s physician-jurist Ramón Pardo held that doctors should be invited to committees responsible for proposing criminal reforms and that judges had to know anatomy, physiology, anthropology, psychiatry, and criminology.[305] José Almaraz wrote that judges who were "not specialists, accustomed to considering all criminals psychologically similar," were superfluous.[306] Luis Garrido and Raúl Carrancá y Trujillo insisted that for criminal judges, purely judicial notions were insufficient.[307] Although law schools taught specialized subjects, emphasis was placed on creating specialties and putting an end to the gap between teaching and practice.[308] As Germán Fernández del Castillo and José María Ortiz Tirado noted, training had little point without specialization (the sum of training and experience).[309]

Finally, some stressed the importance of applying the law to judges who committed errors. Numerous jurists backed this idea.[310] Telesforo Ocampo lamented that although he had accused a magistrate and the breach of the regulation had been established, the file was closed and the official remained in his post.[311] According to Luis Garrido, "The criminal proceeding against only two judges has been recorded for having used economic resources of their office."[312] Antonio Armendáriz believed the application of the law would serve as an example so "bad administrators of justice no longer felt the omnipotence of impunity."[313]

Despite the sweeping range of proposals, the majority focused on the need to end influence peddling and corruption.

THEMIS ON THE SCALES OF JUSTICE

A La Prensa editorialist wrote in 1942, "Here we do not have justice. And so, we avoid the Lady, scales, and blindfold. Instead, we have customary, eternal, unwavering arbitrariness."[314] In this section, Themis weighs herself on her scales.

Between 1929 and 1971 some officials, politicians, and jurists spoke positively of judges and described accusations against them as exaggerated and even slanderous. Bremauntz stated, "The Tribunal Superior has been attacked and is constantly and periodically attacked in an exaggerated and slanderous way: Losing parties malign judges, those who win express their inconformity, often, for not having obtained more. But the most violent attacks are made whenever its members are renewed by the attorneys interested in displacing the elements who occupy the posts to have an opportunity to squeeze in."[315] Domínguez del Río maintained that several judges had been unjustly attacked because of journalism's interest in shocking the public.[316] In 1967 Crispín Ortiz Alarcón affirmed that most judges fulfilled their function.[317]

Nevertheless, complaints about justice were more numerous. In 1930 José Ortiz Rodríguez averred there is no Mexican who had not complained, since Madero's death, about the terrible judicial administration and its venal judges.[318] Ten years later the BMA declared, "The public clamor clearly and resoundingly calls attention to the lack of efficiency of judicial personnel and the lack of integrity of officials and employees in the field."[319] That same year, El Universal asserted that "the good judge" was an exception, and Themis did not preside over the precinct of justice.[320] In 1942 Joaquín Baca Aguirre averred that favoritism, impunity, and corruption persisted.[321] Fifteen years later, noted jurist groups (BMA, Ilustre y Nacional Colegio de Abogados, Academia de Legislación y Jurisprudencia, Facultad de Derecho of UNAM, and ELD) concluded, "It is possible to affirm that the administration of local justice is characterized by its slowness, incompetence, and immorality."[322] In the mid-1960s former president Emilio Portes Gil summarized the opinions on justice in the past twenty-five years, noting mass condemnation of judges; recognition of incorruptible and efficacious magistrates and judges but pointing to many of them as "true traffickers of justice."[323] In the same period, journalist Froylán López Narváez reported that in forums held to collect opinions on justice, no former judicial official or litigator had uttered praise.[324] Carlos Franco Sodi lamented, "Our people do not believe in justice and they are right: It does not exist in Mexico."[325]

Luis Garrido argued that the problem of justice survived the replacement of political authorities.[326] Edmundo Elorduy claimed that no government had "collectively and bravely attacked" the problem of justice.[327] Distinguished journalist Ricardo Garibay said, "The two craftiest bulls that the regentes [mayors] of the city have faced are probably the administration of justice and the police. It might be a euphemism to say they have faced off, and it is more of a reality to say the two bulls who have never faced the city's mayors are the administration of justice and the police."[328] It is important to analyze the repercussions that these problems and the criticism of justice could have in practice or to reflect on the following three areas: the reactions of judges, presidents of jurisdictional organs, or heads of law enforcement institutions to criticism; the consequences of the deficient administration of justice; and the repercussions of the negative image of justice.

The sources do not reveal the reactions of judges and court employees, but they do show the responses of the TSJ. In 1940 TSJ members, outraged by the criticism, demanded proof and threatened to open legal processes against "slanderous" journalists.[329] Two years later, some magistrates began investigations into the irregularities denounced by María Elena Sodi Pallares in the situation of defendants.[330] TSJ presidents José Ortiz Rodríguez, Armando Z. Ostos, Carlos Franco Sodi, and Julio Sánchez Vargas and magistrates expressed their intention to expel or announced the expulsion of corrupt officials.[331] In the early 1940s Federal District attorneys general Antonio Ornelas Villarreal and Octavio Véjar Vázquez encouraged citizens to denounce problems because then they could resolve them.[332]

More opinions addressed the effects of deficiencies in the administration of justice. It was believed that these deficiencies led to impunity. In 1940 María Elena Sodi de Pallares noted, "Criminals in Mexico enjoy their misdeed with impunity and hardworking, honorable people often can find no one to protect and help them."[333] Alfonso Quiroz Cuarón maintained that only 16 percent of those detained in MP borough offices were detained for criminal proceedings before a judge, 33 percent were judged, and 5 percent were found guilty.[334] Felipe Gómez Mont presented a similar scenario to the Chamber of Deputies, stating that more than half of the investigation reports filed were left "sleeping in the files" because there weren't enough agents and that although 75 percent of the cases resulted in guilty verdicts, most of those sentenced were at large.[335] Finally, there was no meaningful relationship between the investigative reports and individuals who were serving a sentence. According to José Ángel Ceniceros, "weak or improper action" by the police, together with the difficulty courts had in gathering evidence and the issuance of erroneous rulings, resulted in impunity, one of the main causes of crime.[336]

According to testimonies, these problems and the negative image of justice produced insecurity among the population, created distrust of institutions in charge of preserving order, and undermined the state's prestige. This produced vigilantism and placed the state's monopoly on the use of legitimate violence at risk.

Concha de Villarreal declared that the population "was not only horrified, but also demoralized because their defense against crime was not guaranteed."[337] There was no confidence in police and judicial institutions, as was indicated by Carlos Franco Sodi, Luis Garrido, and Froylán López Narváez. According to Franco Sodi, it was essential to correct the deficiencies, "since collective life has a mandatory assumption that men secure their rights through the performance of the state."[338] Mistrust was also attributed to contact with MP agents and court employees. According to Pedro Ocampo Ramírez, when interacting with officials, "the common man" felt "run over, robbed, humiliated."[339]

The most immediate consequence of this, according to testimonies, was citizens' lack of collaboration with the police and the justice system. As Humberto Esquivel Medina asserted, no group was as indifferent as Mexicans to authorities in charge of justice.[340] Journalist Jacobo Zabludovsky noted that numerous citizens abstained from denouncing crimes.[341] Luis Garrido shared this idea: "The case of persons who suffer harm to their person or their interests and prefer to renounce any legal complaint is frequent, because they know the failures of our justice and they do not want to risk losing time or suffering unjust counterattacks."[342] He spoke not only of distrust but also of fear. In consonance, Guillermo Colín Sánchez contended that society, "fearful of falling victim to mistreatment and exploitation, covers up for criminals."[343]

Hence Franco Sodi was amazed that men in public office did not realize "the prestige of tribunals is important for the prestige of the entire regime, [and] unjust justice is a stain and unpardonable sin for the government permitting it and a blemish for the people who bear it."[344]

Jurists and journalists foretold the consequences a negative opinion could have on authorities responsible for preserving order. Among them was vigilante justice. In 1942 Antonio Armendáriz warned that "law would be erased from consciences to give rise to violence and the principle that given injustice, robbery, assault, and arbitrariness should not oppose any other logic than guns."[345] In 1968 Raúl Carrancá y Trujillo claimed that Mexico lacked justice and "its law was the law of the jungle," while a newspaper contributor under the pseudonym Gilberto Keith wrote that the population's mistrust, stemming from the absence of state protection, led it to resolve its problems by routes other than judicial ones.[346] Animosity toward the government was also feared. *Novedades* proclaimed, "Keeping those who are absolutely unworthy of command in positions of authority will ultimately again forge violent hostility between the people and governments."[347] Academic Lucio Mendieta y Núñez said, "Mexico City's inhabitants live unprotected, lacking faith in justice, and feeding grudges that greatly damage social stability."[348] The conditions created the risk of a social outbreak. According to *La Prensa*, a people "distrustful, skeptical" or steeped in apathy could experience a "tremendous shock of anger, capable of producing a catastrophe."[349]

In short, authors of the time considered the deficient performance of the police and justice system to have caused the rise in criminality and citizen distrust, which also entailed the lack of collaboration (increasing criminality even more), vigilantism, and potential social upheavals. This led to talk of a crisis in public administration, the state apparatus, or the very state, at least a state with labels: the legal state or the revolutionary state.

Franco Sodi claimed that impunity pushed victims to take justice into their own hands, which was tantamount to "denying state authority, pushing society to anarchy and increasing the immediate exercise of crime."[350] Excélsior affirmed that impunity corroded the foundations of society and destabilized state structure.[351] Furthermore, Alfonso Trueba stated that the lack of punishment had led to people to regress "to the stage of private revenge," demonstrating "an absolute bankruptcy of public administration."[352]

There were allusions to the failure of the legal state. Rubén Salazar Mallén maintained that "the lack of observance of the Constitution is notorious and that lack of observance clearly [means] that Mexico lacks the rule of law, because it is not the abundance of laws that makes the legal state, [but] rather the observance of laws."[353] Allusions were also made to the failure of the revolutionary state—or at least, of one of the leading promises of the Revolution, which had offered not only social justice but also swift justice administered with equality and adherence to the law. Gustavo R. Velasco asserted, "The vices and corruption of the administration of justice were a powerful cause of discontent with the General Díaz regime, as confirmed by Justo Sierra's statement 'The Mexican people are hungry and thirsty for justice.' Today this fulfillment is urgent."[354] Bremauntz argued that the Revolution had not reached courts.[355]

For countless authors, the vices of the Díaz administration continued. Luis Garrido wrote that although Mexicans boasted of having had a social revolution, the problems of the administration of justice remained.[356] The idea was reiterated throughout the time criminal courts existed. For example, Carlos Franco Sodi lamented that the Revolution had not "calmed the hunger and thirst for justice," and the people saw that promise unfulfilled after having taken up arms.[357] Judge Luis Domínguez Carrascosa proclaimed, "After half a century since the start of the Revolution, governments emanating from it are in debt to the Mexican people, because it lacks an administration of justice appropriate for its needs."[358] Raúl Carrancá y Trujillo stated, "If any flag ignited the Revolution [it] was the banner of justice," and the state that arose from this movement had not brought it honor.[359] Jurist Gustavo R. Velasco aptly summarized the situation in 1966: "The improvement of the administration of justice was one of the great promises the Revolution made to the Mexican people. Our people rose to its spell and made it triumph. Fifty-six years have passed since the Revolution began and forty-nine since the Constitution, but the promise has not been fulfilled."[360] *La Prensa* concluded in 1940, "When a revolution does not achieve the value of justice, it is a failed revolution, because always and uniformly, revolutions profoundly fuel a clamor for justice."[361]

Thus there was a broken promise and a failed state.

FINAL REFLECTIONS

Throughout the period studied, sources revealed diverse opinions and representations of justice. Despite the variety of depictions offered, it is possible to speak of an image of justice because, overall, the opinions and representations display few differences and have multiple coincidences.

Some differences relate to sources: The PGJ journal is less critical than other publications (it only denounced the deficient training of agents), and cinema presents a more heterogeneous vision than those of written texts (some films are critical, while other exalt the police or attorneys). Other divergences concern writers: Reporters predominate among critics of justice, while public officials and judges stand out among its defenders; and while jurists ventured to comment on legal reforms and technical questions, journalists wrote about police practices and problems of tribunals.

Nevertheless, similarities prevail, and it is possible to speak of a shared negative image of justice. In the opinions of legislators, politicians, editorialists, reporters, and citizens, published in different years and sources, attacks outweighed praise. Even the press, despite subventions and governmental control, reserved space for denunciation. Uniformed and secret agents, MP representatives, and judges were not untouchable, and we are led to believe the complaints targeting them allowed those who voiced their opinions to vent discontent while leaving members of the executive and legislative branch out.

In other words, according to multiple witnesses, the administration of justice presented serious problems. They considered the meager budget the cause of insufficient tribunals, inadequately equipped MP offices, and poorly paid judges and judicial officials. They also regarded the low salaries as a hindrance to recruiting and keeping capable and dedicated judges, a situation exacerbated by the weight of cronyism and partisanship in some appointments. They thought this explained inefficiency and backlogs, the weight of influences in judicial decisions (because of feeling beholden over appointments or interested in keeping the position), and corruption. Finally, they suggested that influence peddling and corruption led to unequal justice, different for the influential and the wealthy than for the rest.

That said, the criticism expressed in various sources had an impact on the actions and resolutions of citizens, litigators, and judicial officials. According to testimonies, the problems with the justice system produced insecurity and hopelessness, which made citizens rarely report crimes and cooperate with police and judges.

If one gives credence to these statements, one can conclude that in police and judicial practices, some elements of the justice system and the liberal democratic legal state were respected, but others were not. Specifically, regarding the latter, criticisms were made of the following areas:

1. Specialization and experience of judges: According to opinions, appointments were not always made based on the professional capacity of judicial candidates, given the weight of friendship, family ties, cronyism, and recommendations.
2. Judicial rights: According to testimonies, arbitrary and unjustified arrests were made; judicial deadlines were drawn out, and there was a backlog in resolutions; investigative agents used force to extract confessions; and defendants did not always have adequate defense. These are violations of the rights of the accused and defendants under the Constitution.
3. Essential elements of the justice system: The absence or deficient actions of public defenders led to an imbalance between the parties; the delegation of functions by judges and their lack of contact with the defendant and evidence disregarded the requirement for immediacy; and the absenteeism of the three members of the criminal courts at hearings rendered the existence of collegial courts baseless.
4. Essential premises of the liberal or democratic legal state: The weight of influences in courts denoted the lack of autonomy of certain judges with respect to political authorities and, ultimately, failure to respect the independence of powers (judicial with respect to executive); the weight of influences and money suggested unequal administration of justice, which would violate the mandate of equality; inobservance of the law (in the case of the rich or powerful) implied disobedience to the mandate of legality; corruption fueled impunity and insecurity;

and there was a failure of an essential function of the state—namely, ensuring social tranquility and protecting the legal assets of the members.

It is worth highlighting that this assessment is based not on current values and requirements, but rather on criticisms, aspirations, and requirements of the time. In other words, according to witnesses, police and judicial practices made it possible to qualify—or disqualify—the state because essential premises of a model of liberal or democratic law were unmet. As a result, a more general issue emerged—namely, the failed state. It was not said in this way, but indeed, reference was made to breaking the promises of the Revolution, which ultimately would lead to the failure of the revolutionary state.

4. EXPERIENCES IN JUSTICE

JUDGES' APPOINTMENTS AND PROFILES

Analyzing the implementation of the judicial system and its foundations requires two approaches. One is to reflect on the judges and their profiles to determine whether their appointments met the requirements marked by law, thus guaranteeing their experience and independence. The other is to appraise specific cases. Each approach requires different methodologies and sources. Together, they can enrich understanding of the operation of justice and contrast practices not only with respect to laws but also with respect to outlooks and opinions.

Laws concerning the organization of courts had requirements for judges: a lawyer's degree and prior professional experience. During the period studied in this analysis, the duration of the post changed. Between 1928 and 1934 and between 1943 and 1950, if there were no grounds for removal, magistrates and judges were irremovable; between 1934 and 1943 and again starting in 1950, they remained in office for the six-year presidential term (see table 4). Magistrates appointed criminal court judges on the same dates.[1]

Table 4. Magistrate appointments and duration in office

PERIOD	DURATION IN OFFICE	APPOINTMENTS
1928–34	Irremovable	1928 by Plutarco Elías Calles
1934–43	Six years	1934 by Lázaro Cárdenas and 1940 by Manuel Ávila Camacho
1943–50	Irremovable	1944 by Manuel Ávila Camacho
1950 onward	Six years	1951 by Miguel Alemán, 1957 by Adolfo Ruiz Cortines, 1963 by Adolfo López Mateos, and 1968 and 1969 by Gustavo Díaz Ordaz

Source: Created by author.

The *Diario de Debates de la Cámara de Diputados* has the names of the magistrates appointed, because the Chamber of Deputies ratified them. For the list of judges, I consulted magazines, newspapers, and judicial files, but data was incomplete and less precise. After assembling the list, I researched many of the judges to provide a collection of profiles and analyze trends in appointments. For this, I scoured archives (student and professor files in the Instituto de Investigaciones sobre la Universidad y la Educación of UNAM), databases and publications (profiles published by the SCJ, works on members of the AMCP, biographical dictionaries, and legislators' lists).[2]

JUDGES WITH LIFETIME APPOINTMENTS, 1928–34

As Emilio Portes Gil asserted, when he appointed judges in 1928, he selected legal experts who were honest and distanced from any suspicion of immorality, able to guarantee the autonomy of the judicial power, with enough aptitude and experience to "comprehend the progressive tendency of codes," steeped in the spirit of the Revolution, and capable of "satisfying the hunger for justice of all social classes." He wrote, "I knew influences would be moved strongly for the judicial power to be composed of militant political elements; but I firmly resolved not to accommodate any recommendation not fully guaranteed by the three qualities a good magistrate or judge must fulfill: integrity, capacity, and dedication."[3] He gave the Chamber of Deputies a candidate list that, as would become a custom, was accepted unanimously and without debate. Twenty-two magistrates were appointed. Twelve had already occupied the position. The other ten were new, including four who had prior experience. The others didn't and were possibly close associates of the president, such as José Ortiz Rodríguez, a deputy, and Rafael Santos Alonso, a revolutionary general and state deputy.

Thus analysis of their careers suggests they met the degree requirement, but it is unclear whether all of them had five years of experience, and the fourteen that did (some had even worked in courts before the Revolution) were apparently accompanied by improvised judges. Therefore, Portes Gil's claim must be nuanced.

That same year appointed magistrates chose the judges who participated in jury trials and, months later, criminal court members. Portes Gil optimistically asserted that the selection "was the most appropriate, having chosen, with few exceptions, the most prestigious attorneys."[4] Some of the earliest judges in criminal courts were new, but others were not. Most had already been judges or had worked in tribunals, but others, with the exception of Mariano Fernández de Córdova, began their careers after the Mexican Revolution.

Indeed in 1928, by voting for irremovability, legislators expressed their interest in filling court vacancies with young "revolutionaries." Although many of the long judicial careers of the Díaz administration ended with the outbreak of the Revolution, by the end of the 1920s the last step in generational renewal was taken.

In 1931 the number of criminal courts rose to eight, because their jurisdiction had expanded, and they oversaw crimes formerly handled by correctional courts (juzgados correccionales). The magistrates appointed sixteen judges and ratified eight of the judges already serving and ten who had been correctional court judges.

Excélsior stated that courts were the same but "with a new designation" and that the change did not bring "any movement in employees and officials."[5] Besides, two of the new judges (Castaños and Garrido) had already been judges or magistrates in other states. Therefore, only four of the new judges ratified or appointed in 1931 had not previously been judges, but three (Humberto Esquivel Medina, Carlos López Moctezuma, and Raúl Carrancá y Trujillo) were or had been MP agents. Thus, in appointing criminal court judges in 1931, the magistrates respected the requisite prior experience and supported judicial promotion. They were judges who knew the field.

SIX-YEAR ADMINISTRATION JUDGES, 1934–43

During this period, magistrates appointed as irremovable occupied their position for only six years, and judges did so for six or three, because in 1934, at the proposal of President-Elect Lázaro Cárdenas, judicial six-year terms were adopted. The 1932 Ley Orgánica de los Tribunales del Fuero Común had increased the number of magistrates to twenty-five active judges. Once the constitutional reform returning to six-year periods was approved, the president proposed a list of twenty-five magistrates, and his candidate list was unanimously approved by federal deputies with no debate.[6] Seven had already occupied the position, and eighteen were new. Most of the new magistrates were between ages thirty-four and forty-six. At least nine had judicial experience, and three had a political background. Others had only stood out on the political stage and were perhaps appointed because of being Cárdenas supporters; clear examples include Miguel Alemán Valdés, an outstanding member of the Partido Nacional Revolucionario (later Partido Revolucionario Institucional) close to Cárdenas, former deputy, and senator (two years after being appointed magistrate, he became governor of Veracruz), and Enrique

Pérez Arce, who fought in the Revolution, was a deputy, and served as provisional governor of Sinaloa.

By 1934 the number of courts had been reduced to six, so eighteen judges were appointed. Unlike three years earlier, only two (Alberto R. Vela and Rafael Matos Escobedo) were ratified. Of the sixteen newly named judges, around half had prior judicial experience (as with some judges appointed years earlier, Gregorio Ayala Calderón and Hilario Hermosillo occupied more important judicial positions in their home states). Another four apparently did not.

In 1940 Manuel Ávila Camacho presented an initiative to amend the Constitution and return to irremovability. That year, the judicial six-year term ended, and new magistrates had to be appointed for the next period. Awaiting the result of the initiative, he ratified the magistrates in office and only filled vacancies, apparently with temporary appointments. When he proposed five magistrates in 1943 and the candidate list was immediately ratified by the Chamber of Deputies, deputy Víctor Alfonso Maldonado asserted that neither he nor his colleagues had acted under the premise of complying with all proposals of the president, who in fact had urged them not to. Maldonado maintained that the ratification had responded to the quality of the candidates, whom he described as "professionals of solid culture and broad revolutionary dedication." Later, addressing future judges, he transmitted his idea of justice to them, which departed from the strict interpretation of law. He advised them not to limit themselves to faithfully interpreting the law, but instead to resolve legal problems with "revolutionary spirit," because "the peasant and worker masses" hoped judges put "their heart and talent at the service of the Revolution and proletariat."[7]

Of the thirteen magistrates appointed between 1940 and 1943, four had prior experience in courts, but an equal number clearly had a political career, suggesting the influence of cronyism and political comradeship. Perhaps they had the same lack of autonomy attributed to deputies and senators. This was particularly concerning at the time, when adopting irremovability was being debated.

A similar phenomenon can be observed in the appointment of criminal court judges during those same years. The magistrates ratified six and appointed fifteen. Among them, six had judicial experience (Clemente Castellanos and José Trinidad Sánchez Benítez were magistrates, and their appointments could be seen as demotions). Finally, improvisation and possible recommendations may have been involved.

Antonio Armendáriz criticized the appointments in El Universal. He recalled Cárdenas had promised to renew justice with young judges, but that had not happened. He affirmed that the scj appointments responded to "party interests or political or social convenience," turning it into an "executive agency." He warned that this was no different from appointing judges to the criminal courts because "the only young people were already there," and their training was deficient, some having confessed ignorance of criminal matters.[8]

IRREMOVABLE FOR SEVEN YEARS, 1943–50

In September 1944 Ávila Camacho proposed irremovable magistrates. As earlier, the list was unanimously approved by the deputies without debate.[9] Twenty-five magistrates were proposed and approved. Twelve, almost half, were already magistrates and were ratified. Thirteen were new; seven of them had extensive judicial experience, but the others lacked it, such as Alberto Bremauntz, former deputy and senator, and deputies Eduardo Arrioja Insunza and Jesús Nucamendi. Therefore, in 1944 the percentage of ratified magistrates was higher than ever, and almost all new appointments had court experience.

When Miguel Alemán Valdés assumed the presidency in 1946, he faced irremovable magistrates. However, he made new appointments because the number of magistrates had been expanded, and he also had to replace two who had resigned. Of the appointees, two were criminal judges: José Luis Gutiérrez y Gutiérrez and Alberto R. Vela. The president also named former deputy Guillermo Aguilar y Maya, and most importantly, years before Mexican women had the right to vote and be voted for in federal elections, he appointed the first female magistrate, María Lavalle Urbina. She was thirty-nine years old, had received her degree three years earlier, and was the first woman attorney in Campeche.[10]

To examine the appointment of irremovable judges during this period, we must return to 1944. I do not have the list of judges appointed, but seven individuals appointed in earlier periods continued serving in criminal courts. According to Ricardo Abarca and Raúl Carrancá y Trujillo, who presided over the TSJ, the appointed judges were previously court officials, fostering judicial careers.[11] Most had prior judicial experience and occupied or had occupied different positions. María Teresa Puente was named the first female criminal court judge. Therefore, in addition to the seven ratified judges, others had prior experience as judges, and as Abarca and Carrancá y Trujillo attested, the rise through the judicial system was clear.

Irremovability lasted only seven years for officials appointed in 1944. Judicial six-year terms were again adopted in 1950 during the Alemán Valdés administration and, as before, at the president's initiative. With the reform accepted one year before he left office, Alemán Valdés appointed magistrates to serve for the next six years.[12] Again, the list was approved without debate by the Chamber of Deputies. As Edmundo Elorduy maintained, Congress had never rejected any appointment proposed by the president.[13]

Fourteen magistrates were ratified in 1951, so half of the judges in office remained in their posts. Fifteen new magistrates accompanied them; information is available on only nine of them, who all had served as judges.

According to Alberto Bremauntz, the Mexican president left the TSJ free to appoint judges, indicating his respect for the judicial branch's autonomy.[14] By that year there were only six criminal courts, so it was necessary to appoint eighteen judges. Ten of them, more than half, were ratified judges; others ascended from positions such as MP agents. Therefore, ratifications and appointments of officials familiar with courts predominated.

From this time on, judicial six-year terms ceased to coincide with presidential terms. In fact, they were now closer to the end of the presidential term, which is perhaps why ratifications were increasingly common.

In 1957 President Adolfo Ruiz Cortines appointed magistrates.[15] He ratified seventeen (more than Miguel Alemán had) and newly appointed eight. Two were criminal judges with experience (Alberto González Blanco and Aulo Gelio Lara Erosa), two had mixed careers (Pedro Guerrero Martínez and Donato Miranda Fonseca), and one only had occupied political positions (Tito Ortega Sánchez).

I was able to find information about thirteen of the eighteen judges appointed to criminal courts that year. Five were ratified and seven were new. Of the total, with the exception of Salvador Martínez Rojas, former MP agent and judge in Baja California, and Héctor Terán Torres, court clerk and MP agent for years, the rest were apparently new judges.

In 1963, a year before leaving office, Adolfo López Mateos made appointments.[16] He recognized the service of four magistrates who could not be ratified because the law prevented them from occupying the position after turning sixty-five: Alberto Bremauntz, Platón Herrera Ostos, Francisco de Sales Valero, and Ignacio Villalobos Jiménez. Eighteen magistrates were ratified.

Therefore, he appointed only eight new magistrates: three supernumerary magistrates, two criminal court judges with many years of service, and two with long judicial experience. Thus ratifications or judge promotions predominated, but a party quota was covered.

As for judges, Ramón Franco Romero and Salvador Castañeda del Villar (judges since 1944) and Eduardo Urzaiz Jiménez (since 1951) were ratified. Another judge, Rafael Pérez Palma from Hidalgo, was appointed, as was an MP agent, Antonio del Rosal Valenzuela. No information is available on the rest. According to Alfredo Domínguez del Río, they had been appointed without a broad analysis, and they lacked the experience and specialization required by law.[17]

Gustavo Díaz Ordaz made the final appointments. In October 1968 he appointed three magistrates: René González de la Vega, a supernumerary, and José Alfonso Everardo Álvarez and Héctor Terán Torres, both criminal court judges.[18] One year later, in 1969, he appointed those who would occupy the post in the next judicial term, ratifying three he had appointed one year earlier and seventeen other magistrates and making four new appointments.[19] Continuity prevailed.

At the same time, eleven (of a total of twenty-one) criminal court judges were ratified, so slightly more than half remained in their positions.[20] Ten new judges were appointed, seven of them men.[21] Shortly before the appointment, the National Women's Organization of Young Professionals (Organización Femenil Nacional de Jóvenes Profesionales) had demanded the inclusion of more female judges, citing the gender imbalance. Only one female justice was on the SCJ, and two female magistrates were on the TSJ. Criminal and civil tribunals had no female judges, and according to the organization, women officials spent years working as court clerks or judgment drafters without being promoted.[22] Three women were appointed: Victoria Adato Green, former MP agent and TSJ draft writer; Gladys María Cristina García Guerrero, former MP agent; and Martha Herrerías Gutiérrez. Therefore, almost half of the judges were confirmed in their posts; among the new appointees, six MP agents were chosen, including two women, thereby meeting the requirement of prior experience.

FINAL REFLECTIONS

There was no line of continuity between the magistrates and judges of the Díaz administration and those occupying these positions after 1917. Few judges in postrevolutionary Mexico had begun their court careers before the outbreak of the Revolution; there were some exceptions, such as Mariano Fernández de Córdoba, Everardo Gallardo, and Adolfo Valles, but none of them stood out before 1917.

Furthermore, the study of judges appointed between 1929 and 1971 allows us to assume appointments generally met nationality and age requirements. Denunciations that some lacked degrees could not be corroborated. It was not possible to calculate with reasonable precision how many judges did or did not meet the prior experience requirement. This was apart from cases that notoriously demonstrated the persistence of partisanship and cronyism in appointments. Throughout the period, some judges had long judicial careers but worked alongside judges on a lower trajectory. Significantly, in the second half of the period studied, experience played a greater role, and judicial careers of longer duration were observed.

The 1930s and part of the 1940s saw a continuous change of judges. Periods of irremovability did not last more than seven years, and ratifications were infrequent. My research shows that in 1934 only seven (of twenty-two) magistrates and two (of eighteen) judges were ratified, and they had no experience in courts. Regarding the prior careers of appointees, there was a lack of attention to their practical training, as well as evidence of cronyism and partisanship. These factors did not disappear, but the second half of the period studied had more ratifications, such as twenty (of twenty-five) magistrates in 1969.

The appointments extended the careers of many magistrates or judges. Eighteen were judges for fifteen to nineteen years: two appointed in 1928 or earlier, three in 1934, two in 1940, four in 1944, one in 1947, one in 1951, and five in 1957.[23] Eleven served for twenty to twenty-four years: two appointed in 1928, one in 1931, one in 1940, one in 1944, one in 1946, four in 1951, and one in 1957.[24] Three served for twenty-five to twenty-nine years: one appointed in 1931 and two in 1944.[25] Six served for more than thirty years: one appointed in 1928, one in 1931, one in 1934, one in 1940, and two in 1944.[26]

To summarize, of the thirty-eight judges who remained in office the longest, five were appointed in 1928 or earlier, three in 1931, four in 1934, four in 1940, nine in 1944, two in 1946–47, five in 1951, and six in 1957. Therefore, after 1944 judicial careers grew longer, and the number of ratifications increased in the late 1950s, when judges were appointed shortly before the president left office instead of at the beginning of the administration.

The second part of the period studied also reflected an interest in incorporating women, first on the TSJ and then in first-instance tribunals. Although women magistrates remained in office for many years, female judges appointed in the early years did not remain for more than one six-year term in the position.

In sum, appointments in the last twenty-five years of the study period reveal a greater concern that judges have prior judicial experience. Independently of the factors that weighed in their initial appointments, they remained in office longer, which suggests greater respect on the part of Mexican presidents and TSJ magistrates for the experience that magistrates and judges had to have.

However, this latter part of the period did not suggest the presence of influences, cronyism, or partisanship in appointments, and in the entire period studied, there was improvisation that went beyond the demands for training and experience. This impression is reinforced by denunciations made by opposition politicians, jurists, and journalists throughout the period, who claimed that recommendations and influences determined some judicial vacancies. This would clearly affect the autonomy of judges and undermine the principle of the separation of powers and the foundations of the liberal or democratic state.

5. EXPERIENCES IN JUSTICE

JUDICIAL PRACTICES AND NOTORIOUS HOMICIDES

"On occasions, there is a void that cannot be filled between the letter of the law and judges' criteria," wrote journalist Mario Rojas Avendaño in 1966.[1] In referring to the space "between the letter of the law and judges' criteria," Rojas Avendaño chose the word *laguna* (lacuna), an inaccessible, empty space.

Judges were expected to assess evidence offered by the prosecution and defense and later, based on the presentation of evidence and its evaluation, to determine the existence of the crime and guilt of the accused, an analysis that entailed the choice and interpretation of the applicable laws. Indeed, it is difficult for any scholar of judicial practices, and even more so for historians, to know the factors that influenced each of these choices, assessments, and interpretations, given the time that has passed and the dearth of available information. To understand this difficulty, it is essential to consider that judges shape their criteria and make decisions at different moments of the procedure, guided by the prior actions and determinations of various actors: the MP agent, defense attorney, accused, and victim. In grounding in facts or giving reasons for the judgment (*motivar*), they refer to elements that oriented their decision. However, meta-judicial factors remain beyond the judicial file, such as aspects of the unconscious or, as testimonies suggest, influences, bribery, or even the weight of public opinion. Nevertheless, and without any attempt to establish the factors that must have guided judicial resolutions or judgments during the period studied, it strikes me as possible and interesting to contextualize or explain these determinations by examining the social surroundings, prior judgments, doctrine, commentaries on the case, and ideas and values of the time. With this, we can begin to fill the lacuna mentioned by Rojas Avedaño.

Other topics also must be addressed when studying judicial practices. The respect of procedural deadlines and the rights of defendants and the accused must be considered. Equally important are reflection on the sentencing and analysis of agreement and dissent among criminal court judges, TSJ magistrates, and SCJ ministers. It is also relevant to analyze the performance of the MP agent and defense attorney and the weight their requests or the defendant's confession had on the judges' rulings. Information is available to study these aspects, so historians tread on firmer ground here. The void becomes less deep.

This chapter explores that gap and studies homicide cases. I opted to analyze murders, given their impact on society and because in those cases judges elaborated on the motivations and grounds, while the parties exhausted all instances. Furthermore, documentation is abundant, permitting comparisons of disparate stances of judges.

I conducted a quantitative analysis and qualitative approach. The former yielded few results. Around 1980 distinguished litigators lamented the lack of statistics on the behavior of courts and settlement of disputes.[2] They don't exist. The extant series reveal only the number and gender of those convicted and sentenced for crimes. In the Federal District between 1929 and 1971, around 17,000 individuals were convicted of homicide, and 10,500 were sentenced (see tables 5 and 6).

The number of murder suspects recorded was higher in some years (1930, 1946–52) and lower in others (1953, 1955). In contrast, the number of defendants sentenced gradually increased from 1941. However, if the demographic growth of Mexico City is considered, in both cases, especially in the number of accused, there is a decrease: The percentage of homicide suspects in the city's population declined from 0.91 to 0.006 percent, and those sentenced for that crime dropped from 0.009 to 0.005 percent. This decrease contrasts with the perception and concern of Mexico City residents, who perceived higher crime rates and a growing sense of insecurity.

Table 5. Defendants charged with murder, 1929–71

YEAR	TOTAL	BY GENDER		% OF ALL CRIMINAL DEFENDANTS	% OF THE D.F. POPULATION
		M	F		
1929	385			2.51	
1930	570			2.56	
1931	351			2.66	
1932	369			4.26	
1933	325			3.38	
1934	460			5.73	

YEAR	TOTAL	BY GENDER M	F	% OF ALL CRIMINAL DEFENDANTS	% OF THE D.F. POPULATION
1936	438			7.31	
1937	377			4.86	
1938	486			6.17	
1939	411			6.30	
1940	447			7.03	0.025
1941	467			5.10	
1942	416			4.68	
1946	659	631	28	6.56	
1947	599	569	30	5.61	
1948	585	559	26	4.63	
1949	605	574	31	5.00	
1950	516	497	19	4.67	0.016
1951	511	487	24	4.68	
1952	541	519	22	5.60	
1953	186	178	8	4.81	
1954	304	284	20	4.59	
1955	288	276	12	4.29	
1956	352			4.98	
1957	406	392	14	5.52	
1958	357	345	12	5.43	
1959	402	383	19	5.50	
1960	332	306	26	5.74	0.006
1961	349			6.05	
1962	356			6.41	
1963	355	336	19	6.45	
1964	466	423	43	8.10	
1965	375	357	18	5.82	
1966	384	368	16	5.92	
1967	409	389	20	6.30	

1968	389	377	12	6.15		
1969	420	404	16	6.84		
1970	421	406	15	6.53		0.006
1971	398	389	9	4.75		
Total	16,960	9,449	459	5.73		

Sources: Departamento de Estadística Nacional-Revista, *Estadística Nacional*, 1920 and 1930; Dirección General de Estadística, *Anuario Estadístico*, published throughout the period.

Table 6. Defendants convicted of murder, 1937–71

YEAR	DEFENDANTS CONVICTED OF MURDER	BY GENDER		% OF ALL MURDER DEFENDANTS (BY 5-YEAR PERIODS)	% OF ALL CRIMINAL DEFENDANTS	% OF THE D.F. POPULATION
		M	F			
1937	222			47.89	8.23	
1938	228				9.50	
1939	226				10.33	
1940	173				8.48	0.009
1941	199				8.86	
1942	182				6.89	
1943	180				6.58	
1944	169				7.54	
1945	179				8.27	
1946	214	210	4		9.43	
1947	257	247	10	42.08	12.53	
1948	285	270	15		11.38	
1949	205	198	7		7.75	
1950	221	213	8		7.36	0.007
1951	217	209	8		7.17	
1952	250	242	8	97.66	6.92	
1953	383	366	17		7.06	
1954	324	320	4		6.48	
1955	346	332	14		7.65	
1956	329				7.01	

YEAR	DEFENDANTS CONVICTED OF MURDER	BY GENDER		% Of ALL MURDER DEFENDANTS (BY 5-YEAR PERIODS)	% OF ALL CRIMINAL DEFENDANTS	% OF THE D.F. POPULATION
		M	F			
1957	306	298	8	92.86	6.22	
1958	352	340	12		7.22	
1959	322	317	7		6.47	
1960	380	361	19		7.61	0.007
1961	371				7.87	
1962	419			98.55	8.00	
1963	344	334	10		7.50	
1964	374	356	18		8.47	
1965	447	422	25		8.79	
1966	324	309	15		7.58	
1967	393	374	19	105.64	8.80	
1968	411	395	16		6.50	
1969	425	404	21		6.84	
1970	408	393	15		8.10	0.005
1971	520	507	13		9.37	
Total	10,580	7417	293		7.80	

Source: Dirección General de Estadística, Anuario Estadístico, published throughout the period.

In both cases, mostly men were recorded; women represented only 4.85 percent of defendants charged and 3.95 percent of those convicted.

Finally, those charged with homicide were more likely to be convicted than those charged for other crimes; although murder suspects represented 2.5 to 7.3 percent of the total defendants charged, the convicted represented 6.5 to 12.5 percent (taking the lowest and highest figures of the period). This probability was accentuated with time, verging on 100 percent starting in 1950. However, men and women differed: On average, 78.47 percent of male defendants and 63.83 percent of women defendants were convicted of the crime.

The statistics do not permit additional conclusions and are insufficient for an analysis of judicial practice, but they offer a starting point and frame of reference for a qualitative study.

The high number of murder trials made it impossible to analyze a truly representative sample. Thus I studied a limited number selected based on various criteria. First, I opted to study only famous cases. Although these judicial processes differed from those that did not attract media attention, I chose them for their social impact, the tenacity of the litigators, and the potentially greater availability of documentary sources. Moreover, a central concern of this work is the image of justice, and the press is a leading actor. I agree with the notion of Robert Buffington and Pablo Piccato that all causes célèbres are, by definition, a public account because detectives, suspects, witnesses, and other authors participate in the account.[3] Choosing high-profile trials allowed me to continue exploring the field of representation, tracing ideas and social values that emerged from courts, and comparing the court judgment with the "rulings" of other groups in the community.

The press widely disseminated the cases. In the twentieth century yellow and sensationalistic journalism intensified, continuing a trend begun in the nineteenth century by El Imparcial, founded in 1897, which marked a sea change. The leading dailies, formerly centered on opinions, now focused on news and reporting. They sought to increase their print run and readership. To reduce prices, they used innovative printing presses and attracted the attention of potential consumers by covering shocking events or crimes, offering articles illustrated initially with engravings and later with photographs.[4] Consequently, newspapers like Excélsior, El Universal, and especially La Prensa and El Universal Gráfico (El Universal's afternoon supplement) gave an important space to sensationalistic reporting. In 1966 La Prensa, which boasted the highest circulation, supposedly printed between thirty-five thousand and seventy thousand copies daily.[5]

Magazines had even more readership. These included Magazine de Policía, an Excélsior supplement published between 1944 and 1969 with the motto "To point out the evils of society is to serve it," and Alarma, which appeared in 1963 with a black-and-yellow headline dripping with blood. Its pages "combine the interest in peeping at bad luck with the 'voluptuosity' of the horrifying," wrote Carlos Monsiváis.[6] A year after its first issue, the crime committed by four sisters known as "Las Poquianchis" increased sales to two million copies.

News focused on crime and trials received less attention than during the time of jury trials, when newspapers reported on hearings in broad daily coverage. Nevertheless, they continued reporting on trials and judgments.

Sensationalistic publications brought fame to reporters like Alberto Téllez Vázquez (better known as "El Güero" Téllez), David García Salinas, and Alberto Ramírez de Aguilar, as well as photographers like Adrián Devars Jr., Enrique Metinides, the Casasola brothers, and Enrique Díaz.[7]

Reporters and police were in close communication. El Güero Téllez reminisced that police stations alerted veteran journalists when a crime was committed.[8] Sometimes reporters arrived before detectives. Interestingly, they not only covered the news but also participated in investigating and questioning, conducting inquiries and sharing their results with the police.[9] Reporters left testimonies of their work. Alberto Ramírez de Aguilar did so in his column "Siguiendo pistas" (Following clues) and in the film of the same name. It was not the only movie that re-created this collaboration. In La gota de sangre (The drop of blood), a reporter immediately reaches the room with the corpse, participates in the investigation, exchanges opinions with detectives, and reports his findings.[10] Similarly, in En busca de la muerte (In search of death), the Excélsior reporter is the first at the crime scene and the widow's house and later discovers the criminal.[11] Journalists participating in investigations also left a trail of documents, such as one identifying the suspect in the murder of Jacinta Aznar. This is backed by other examples, such as the participation of reporter José Pérez Moreno in the First Congress of Attorneys General of Mexico, held in 1939.[12]

Radio and TV also broadcast crime news. The media credited other means, creating a sort of cultural circuit. Reporters wrote scripts, and screenwriters represented reporters. Luis Spota depicted himself reporting in the film Con el dedo en el gatillo (Finger on the trigger),[13] while in La gota de sangre, the radio, by publicizing the details of the persecution of a woman who killed her husbands, conditioned the actions of those involved. In Raffles, the TV interview in which the thief announced his escape led to a community-wide reaction, resulting in the capture of the interviewee.[14]

Crimes occupied ample space in the media because by publicizing, re-creating, or exaggerating them, businessmen won readers, listeners, and viewers. Jurists and journalists complained of the use and abuse of this news. El Universal lamented that criminals were made into "teratological heroes, cause for envy of frequent wrongdoers, pampered by psychiatrists and criminology."[15] Similarly, El Universal reproached the "morbid press" that had ceased to write for "healthy and normal" people by giving so much space to covering crime, as if addressing "people of the underworld."[16] El Universal claimed that by making criminals into celebrities, newspapers invited readers to imitate them and "see them glorified on their pages."[17] The BMA called for banning articles on crimes of passion: "Descriptions of these acts in their terse objectivity are necessary and justified in trials or criminalistic office files; but turned into publicity with a multitude of details, in sensationalistic form . . . they can have no other natural purpose than to become schools of criminality and constant incitements to vice."[18] Calls to censor crime journalists were unsuccessful.[19] In defense of reporters, La Prensa contributors alleged that judges and attorneys wanted to silence the journalists to hide their mistakes; the newspaper reported on the unjustified release of two defendants as an example.[20]

Beyond mutual recriminations, police, judges, attorneys, reporters, and photographers clearly coexisted in the world of crime and justice.[21] The media gave access to another actor: society. Most hearings were public, but after the elimination of jury trials, few people attended.[22] According to Carlos Monsiváis, newspapers turned tragedy into performance.[23] They multiplied the number of spectators and, to a degree, the number of judges, because these spectators also "judged." Based on this, it is worth assessing to what extent public opinion could influence judges.

In sum, the weight I have given in this work to representations led me to study high-profile murders. Furthermore, because newspaper information is insufficient, I selected notable cases that could also be analyzed through police, judicial, and prison records or documents drafted by the parties. In general, this explains why court cases predominate in the pre-1947 sample, because records are kept in the Archivo General de la Nación and are more accessible. Similarly, I decided to exclusively analyze two types of murder: those that deserved greater comprehension by legislators and reporters (committed, according to defendants, out of grave fear or in self-defense) and those most heavily punished under the law and in public opinion (those perpetrated during robberies).

I assembled a sample of eight cases, studied using diverse sources. In some trials, two or more individuals were defendants, so I discuss a total of eight men and four women. According to statistics and as seen in judicial records, women defendants were a minority of the total. They are overrepresented in my sample because of my interest in assessing the possible influence of defendant gender and the notion of gender in judicial rulings; furthermore, in trials of women, constant references were made to moral concepts and codes of behavior, providing a rich source for understanding the culture of the time. Four defendants were from privileged sectors, possessing money and influence, while the others were from the middle-class and low-income groups. Considering the social structure and statistics, the former were also overrepresented, which reflects the notoriety they garnered for their crimes.

The sample illustrates and supports impressions or opinions of judicial practice discussed in chapter 3, on the public image of justice. It also makes it possible to delve into general concerns I faced in conducting research. First, regarding the performance of judges and judicial discretion, I point out discrepancies or coincidences in rulings concerning defendants' guilt, circumstances surrounding the crime, and sentencing. This allows me to evaluate whether they were "easy or clear" or "difficult or controversial" cases (based on the classification in my presentation of preliminary questions). I also analyze whether judges imposed light, medium, or severe sentences, in which "light" refers to a sentence between the minimum and the minimum plus one-third contemplated for murder, and "severe" refers to one between the maximum and the maximum minus at least one-third (see table 7).[24]

Table 7. Years in prison for murder under the Criminal Code, 1929–55

	COMMITTED IN A BRAWL	SIMPLE	QUALIFIED (CALIFICADO, COMMITTED WITH PREMEDITATION, ADVANTAGE, SURPRISE OR BETRAYAL)
1929–31	For the aggressor an average sentence of 10, and 6 for the person attacked	8–13	20
1931–51	From half to a sixth of the sentence for simple murder (roughly 4–11)		13–20
1951	4–12		13–30
1955		8–20	20–40

Source: Created by author.

I also reflect on the attention that judges paid to SCJ judicial precedents, which is relevant, given its nineteenth-century origins, as the judicial system had been closed to precedents and had counted on judges' strict adherence to the law. In addition, I note the existence of denunciations on the observance or

lack thereof of essential elements of the justice system (such as judge autonomy and equality under the law) and the rights of the accused and defendants
(including arrest by court order, freedom from solitary confinement and the
use of force, presence of the defense attorney, and meeting procedural deadlines). Additionally, I appraise whether judges in their rulings followed MP
requests or defense arguments in their conclusions. It is important as well to
consider the weight they gave to the defendant's statement and confession and
to complaints lodged by defendants concerning the use of violence to extract
confessions. Finally, I analyze the emergence of social mentalities and ideas in
trials. I also reflect on the coincidence of sentences with public opinion or, as
Armando Z. Ostos indicated in 1941, on their discrepancy. As TSJ president at
that time, he wrote, "On many occasions resolutions are contrary to the feeling
of the collectivity and the truth palpable in the awareness of public opinion."[25]

The remainder of this chapter is divided into three sections focusing on
different reasons given for murder. I begin with the trials of defendants who
argued they had acted in self-defense of person or property. I turn next to murders that occurred during violent disputes, and in the last section, I examine
those committed in cases of robbery or burglary.

IN DEFENSE OF THE INDIVIDUAL, PROPERTY, AND SOCIETY

The 1929 and 1931 Code drafting committees considered violation of the criminal law to produce criminal liability, but they cited exceptions. For instance,
under the 1931 Code, violating a criminal law in self-defense or defense of
honor was free of liability, and acting under a well-founded, "irresistible"
(overwhelming) fear of suffering imminent and serious harm was exempt.
Otherwise, committing a crime when of unsound mind, under complete
intoxication, or at the command of a legitimate superior, in fulfilling a legal
duty, or in the legitimate exercise of a right were excluded. In this section,
I analyze murder cases in which defenders argued having acted under two
of these situations: acting in self-defense or under the fear of imminent and
serious harm. Both contexts are interesting for the study of criminal law, its
application, and its interpretation.

Under the liberal model, through the "social contract," members entrust
the state to preserve their rights; therefore, it monopolizes the legitimate use
of physical violence and prohibits the use of vigilante justice. Nevertheless, in
the absence of authorities, members may need to and are permitted to defend
themselves from harm considered imminent.

The authors of the two Criminal Codes in force between 1929 and 1971 determined that individuals who thwarted a violent, unfounded aggression that put their life, honor, or assets or those of any other person in danger were acting in self-defense (*defensa legítima*). The determination of self-defense required the following conditions: the defendant had not provoked the aggression, had not been able to prevent or escape it, and had not caused greater harm than what he tried to avoid.[26] The 1931 Code drafters added a paragraph about individuals who defended themselves from a stranger who attempted to break into or was already inside their home, in the domicile occupied by their family, in the shop front where goods were stored, or in a home or shop they were legally obligated to defend.[27]

The 1929 and 1931 Code authors did not consider individuals who committed a crime to be criminally liable if they had been filled with a well-founded, serious, overwhelming fear. However, the codes differed. The 1929 drafters referred to the well-founded, overwhelming fear of imminent, serious harm to the person himself or herself, or to antecedents or descendants, spouses, relatives (with kinship up to the fourth degree and affinity to the second), or persons to whom they were connected by love, respect, gratitude, or close friendship. This pertained to cases where the defendant had not caused the danger or was obligated to confront it through his or her professional activity.[28] In contrast, the 1931 drafters spoke of both serious and well-founded, overwhelming fear to a real (they included the requirement that it be real), serious, and imminent harm to their person or assets (including goods) or to the person or assets of anyone else (without limitations). This was if there was no other practicable and less harmful means and if the individual had the legal duty to face the danger because of his or her job or position.[29]

In sum, legislators exempted from criminal liability individuals who acted when their lives were threatened or they believed their lives were threatened, specifying a difference between self-defense (which required the presence of the threat) and grave fear (which required the individual to be convinced of the threat if intimidation was plausible and if prior actions justified their fear). In the first case, the individual had to try to avoid the aggression through other means, employing a rational means in their defense, and not causing greater harm than what they were trying to avoid, whereas these requirements were less present in the second case (absent in the 1929 Code, but the 1931 Code mentioned the possibility of having employed another practicable, less harmful means).

The exceptions mentioned were connected to aspects such as delimiting the state and individual in the social contract (considering the restrictions of the former, legislators expanded the latter's margins of action), the state monopoly over the legitimate use of force (because legislators accepted that in the absence of authorities, private parties may have to resort to violence to prevent harm), the definition of the lawful and the unlawful (since the code drafters considered unlawful acts as lawful if they were committed in defense against unlawful aggression), and the scope of reason (which accommodated the defense of being of unsound mind). Therefore, these exceptions are interesting in the study of criminal and criminal procedural law.

I also consider them relevant for an analysis of judicial practice. Defense attorneys often used the presence of exemptions of criminal liability because they sought the acquittal of their clients. However, it was not easy for litigators to prove defendants had acted in self-defense or from deep fear, nor was it easy for judges to determine whether the events had occurred in this way and, for example, to ascertain whether an overwhelming fear had filled the murderer when killing or whether their life was in imminent danger exactly when committing the murder. It thus was difficult to determine whether the defendant had acted in self-defense or grave fear because the line defining both exceptions was tenuous in the legislation. In these cases, judges had broad latitude for discretion.

This explains the scj justices issuing numerous *tesis* and the publication of magistrate and judge rulings related to the exceptions of self-defense and grave fear, through which they sought to clarify the circumstances that permitted admitting the defenses and their differences. I synthesize the salient points as follows:

A) In the case of self-defense, they adduced that the existence of aggression must have been explicit and prior to or contemporary with the defensive act. For example, a *tesis* from the scj First Chamber formulated in 1934 stated, "If the assault the deceased tried to carry out on the accused had not been initiated, it could not be considered imminent, which the law requires to be exonerated by self-defense; because there is no doubt this does not refer to the simple threat or fear of an aggression, but rather the very assault is going to take place immediately, without any doubt."[30] In various judicial opinions, the simple motion of taking out a weapon was rejected.[31] The TSJ magistrates observed the opinion, for example, of a second-instance ruling issued in 1961: "The fact the deceased had put his hand in the bag does not justify the existence of a risk, because it must be expressed with positive actions."[32]

By reiterating the impossibility of admitting a threatening attitude, "a danger that can be sensed," as the precedent of an action committed in self-defense, some opinions of the SCJ First Chamber referred to an attack that occurred before or at the same time as the act of self-defense. A 1962 *tesis* clarified that imminent danger could not be understood as "what is sensed, the conjectural that might or might not occur," but rather "what we already see vented on us," is "indubitable," and "prompts acting to the instinct of self-preservation."[33] It rejected the possibility of applying the self-defense exclusion if the defendant shot the attacker in the back.[34]

As for accrediting aggression, the value granted to qualified confession (admission of the crime but claiming grounds for exemption from liability or arguing having done so legally) is interesting. In 1945 the First Chamber adduced, "Solely the confession of the accused on which it seeks the self-defense exclusion is insufficient to prove the current, violent, and unjust aggression."[35] Generally, for the self-defense exclusion, it deemed qualified confession must be fully accepted if it was not refuted by other evidence.[36]

Similar considerations were expressed for the grave fear exclusion. Sixth Chamber magistrates granted the confession probative value if isolated (without proof refuting or corroborating it, provided it was probable, persistent, and credible) and, furthermore, if other data supported it.[37] However, as in various opinions issued by the SCJ First Chamber, in this case the requirement for the existence and accreditation of aggression was more lax than for self-defense because the mere presence of a triggering act was admitted, when the accused had previously been assaulted or threatened, which explained the assumption of risk or their mental state.[38] In 1959 the chamber established a difference between fear (*miedo*) and dread (*temor*). It specified that fear implied "a more substantial disturbance than that produced by dread," so fear "required the action present in a real threat," while dread "can occur without that action, independently of it."[39] In 1942 it established in another *tesis*: "Because fear is the anguished disturbance of emotions over risk or harm that warns the imagination of the individual possessed by that emotion, the reality of danger is not necessary for the exclusion to exist, instead the simple subjective representation in the perpetrator."[40] Therefore, in several *tesis*, the authority had determined the need to accredit that threat caused grave fear or "deep disturbance" that made the defendant lose his or her mind.[41] This reflects the growing importance given to expert evidence.

B) The SCJ determined the impossibility of admitting exclusions when the murderer could have been able to prevent the aggression (and could have avoided it) or had provoked it. For example, a *tesis* formulated in 1957 said, "The accused goes to a given place, knowing that a person with whom he had had prior quarrels is there and carrying his gun beforehand; and if this person shoots at the accused and the accused shoots the other causing his death, there is no self-defense, because he anticipated the aggression against his person and accepted the dispute underlying the act."[42] Therefore, various *tesis* established that the individual who had taken the life of another in a fight could not argue he or she had acted in self-defense, and the TSJ observed the criteria described.[43]

C) The SCJ First Chamber rejected the possibility of updating the self-defense exclusion in murder cases if the defendant could have avoided the threat, causing lesser harm than death, or if the repelled threat had not endangered his life. For example, a 1961 *tesis* established the need to take into account the "rational proportion between the harm caused and the good defended" and the need for the means employed to be determined based on "the nature or severity of the aggression," saying that "this will lead in each case to a comparison not only of the instruments used, but also of the personal conditions of the aggressor and the victim."[44] Using the same logic, the codes required the use of rational means of defense. The same was not the case for grave fear. The rationality necessary in self-defense hindered grave fear based on absence of will, conscience, discernment, and reflection. Under this assumption, the First Chamber held that the individual must act unconsciously or with conscience diminished by trauma, under the influence of instincts, "turned into a true robot."[45] Or, as stated in another *tesis*, the fear provoked in the defendant a "psychological phenomenon of inhibition that prevents perfect reasoning and the full use of other mental faculties."[46] According to the TSJ Sixth Chamber, fear could be considered grave and grounds for exemption of criminal liability only when one acted solely under the influence of instincts, dominated by a primary emotion that is "common to men and animals."[47]

Hence, in various opinions, the First Chamber established the difference between self-defense (understood as consciously acting to repel unjust aggression) and grave fear (acting robotically, without reflection, at the impulse of emotions seized by fear).[48] Acting in self-defense was considered a cause of justification and the defendant was imputable ("because the agent has the right to execute it"), whereas grave fear was an excluding factor of criminal liability and the agent was unimputable (acting without will, lacking conditions of imputability).[49] Therefore, it considered the excluding factors of self-defense and grave fear as contradictory and challenged the impossibility of their coexistence in a single act.[50]

D) Finally, the SCJ First Chamber indicated that murderers could not act when the threat had ceased.[51]

Despite the efforts of legislators and ministers to define the characteristics of excluding factors and their scope, in courts self-defense and grave fear continued to influence diverse interpretations and gave rise to controversies. Therefore, cases used to assess judges' margin of interpretation of acts and laws offer the possibility of exploring discrepancies, and these cases offer rich material to explore judicial practices.

In discussing these exemptions from liability, it is illustrative to study the emergence of ideas and social values in courts and, based on this, to assess their impact on actions and decisions of individuals who intervened in the judicial process. Frequently in these matters, references were made to the prevailing conception of gender at the time, for men because self-defense was associated with masculinity (emphasizing courage and daring) and for women because grave fear was justified by reason of their constitution (being regarded as weak, fragile, and emotional).

I explore the processes in which exclusions of self-defense or grave fear were involved based on six trials. Some were brief and others lengthy, because judges could accept the presence of these excluding factors of criminal liability when issuing an order dismissing charges for lack of merit (*auto de libertad*) or confining a suspect to jail (*auto de formal prisión*) or, at the end of the trial, when issuing a ruling. These trials serve as an example of three situations: the death of a stranger entering the defendant's home (Miguel Desentis González), murders resulting from domestic violence (Ana Irma Schultz, Emma Perches Frank, and Soledad Rodríguez Prado, or "Chole la Ranchera"), and killings committed during quarrels (the death of Guty Cárdenas and the murder by Humberto Mariles, discussed in the section "Death While Fighting").

Aggressive Burglar Shot Dead

As established under the Criminal Code, the existence of self-defense is presumed if individuals caused any harm to someone caught breaking into their home or finding the intruder inside, at home where their family was, in the place where their property was kept, or in a shop they were obligated to defend, as long as it was nighttime and the burglar engaged in violence toward persons or objects.[52]

In courts, the first and second paragraphs of this third section of Article 15 lent themselves to diverse interpretations. For example, in 1968 the Fifth Criminal Court condemned a man who had killed an individual trying to break into his house because it deemed that the intruder had harmed neither persons nor goods, and thus the homeowner had not acted in self-defense. However, in the appeal, the TSJ regarded that it was enough that the thief was trying to enter his home, as set out in the first paragraph, because the legislators had not contemplated violence to persons or things; thus it ruled that he had acted in self-defense and acquitted him.[53]

We might imagine that the same principle should apply if the intruder had been inside the home, because the threat to persons or assets was greater; however, under the second paragraph of the third fraction, the admission of exclusion of liability for self-defense was conditioned not only by the time (i.e., nighttime) but also by the use of violence on persons or property. Exemplifying the application of this assumption was an incident known for the fame of the defendant: Miguel Desentis González, who had been a criminal court clerk and MP agent for several years and was a well-known litigator at the time of the crime.

On January 12, 1940, he killed an individual who broke into his home. He testified that in the wee hours of the morning, the noise of his bedroom door had awakened him, and he saw someone peering in. He fumbled for his eyeglasses on the nightstand, then ran to the wardrobe, where he kept a gun. He searched for the intruder and saw him running up the stairs to the rooftop. Hearing the intruder's threats, he shot at him and caught up with him on the roof as the man tried to escape onto the roof of the neighboring house. Assailed with further death threats and what he interpreted as a movement of the man's arm, but unable to see the intruder clearly without his glasses, he shot for a second time. When the wounded man fell on the other side of the neighbor's wall, the defendant called the police. He claimed he had fired out of the belief that he would be attacked and to ensure his children's safety, considering that whoever breaks into a home "is willing to do anything." He added that he only intended to scare the intruder, thinking that at that distance and without his glasses, he wouldn't hit the man. When the police arrived, they found the corpse and objects stolen from the murderer's home on the neighbor's roof.[54]

Newspapers offered different versions of the events. El Universal Gráfico first reported the story and stated only that when Desentis González saw the thief, he had looked for his glasses on the nightstand and found the pistol he used.[55] The next day La Prensa dramatized the situation: "A slight sound alarmed the lawyer, who at that moment thought it wasn't yet time for the housekeeper to arrive, and his doubts were dispelled when unexpectedly the sinister face of a stranger appeared at the door of his bedroom. In a single bound, [he] jumped up and anxiously fumbled for his eyeglasses in the nightstand." The account continued, "Afraid of greater evil, not only [for himself], but also his young daughter who was sleeping a few meters away, he opened a wardrobe and took out a pistol." Equally dramatic was the account describing the scene under the stairway: "The crisp report of a firearm drew a cry of rage from the mouth of the fugitive, who far from daunted then tried to attack the lawyer, who again pulled the trigger, and with sure aim wounded the criminal in the neck."[56]

El Universal Gráfico favored Desentis González by omitting that he had shot a man trying to escape. This account described the murder as a "typical case of self-defense, much more justifiable if one takes into account the miscreant broke into the home and public awareness is rightly fearful of the rise in crime."[57] In contrast, La Prensa let its readers know the investigative agent did not consider it proven that Desentis González had killed in self-defense, because he had shot a fleeing individual.[58] Excélsior, just as had El Universal Gráfico, "absolved" the defendant. It reproduced Desentis González's version, including the detail that the thief had tried to jump on him from the stairway.[59] None of the newspapers published photos of the defendant or his home.

As La Prensa noted, the agent in charge of the investigation considered the self-defense exclusion inapplicable—not for the reason given by the newspaper, but because of the controversy I referred to: It was not proven that the intruder had exercised violence against the persons or things in the house. Consequently, he requested the indictment of Miguel Desentis González.

Newspapers publicized the name of the deceased, José Roa Rodríguez Martínez. El Universal Gráfico maintained that he had passed through the police station nine times, using different names, and had been found guilty of murder and armed robbery.[60] Excélsior went further; after describing him as a "dangerous outlaw," it claimed his criminal history was enough to show that Desentis González's life had been in danger and the accused had acted in self-defense.[61]

On January 14 Desentis González was transferred to Lecumberri Prison and was assigned to the Tenth Court, but the judge recused himself because he was a friend of Desentis González's. Instead, his first clerk, Eduardo Fernández Guerra, acted as judge. The MP agent was José Hernández de la Garza, and the defense attorneys were Antonio de P. Moreno and Emilio Pardo Aspe.[62]

The matter was settled with unusual speed. A few hours after his detention, the defendant gave his preliminary statement. He confirmed what he had said in the borough office and, responding to the MP's questions, clarified that from the stairway and while the intruder was crouching, the man had shouted, "You're dead." And on the rooftop, when the intruder turned around toward Desentis González and made a gesture with his arm, he said to the defendant, "We're fucking you." Desentis González affirmed that at both moments, he had felt like a perfect target because the thief was above him. The MP agent confirmed with the meteorological service that on the day of the crime, the sun had not yet risen at 6:30 in the morning, and the defendant had faulty eyesight.

Hours later, the litigators filed their briefs. The defense maintained that the main element of proof was the defendant's confession and argued that under the *tesis* of the SCJ First Chamber, it had to be taken in its entirety, because no elements contradicted it or made it improbable. Instead, they argued that the proof supported it: The meteorological report confirmed it was nighttime; the police report said the thieves had removed objects; the time the intruder had spent behind bars denoted the danger he represented; the ophthalmologist corroborated that the defendant was nearsighted; the forensic specialist affirmed that bullets had entered the deceased's body from the front; and the testimonies of residents of the neighboring tenement proved that the two accomplices had escaped through there.

The MP agent, Hernández de la Garza, reported that the criteria of the attorney general of the Federal District had been to let the judge, after considering the case records, issue the appropriate ruling. He refrained from making a request and merely expressed an opinion. He considered the last paragraph of the third section of Article 15 to be applicable because the intrusion was committed at night and the intruder had used violence on persons (supported by the existence of his criminal record) and things (confirmed by a broken wardrobe and a briefcase). Furthermore, he noted that the expert report had shown the bullets had entered the front of the deceased's body and also that one of them had a downward path, which contradicted the account of the defendant, who claimed he had fired from below the stairway. The prosecutor recalled that when interrogated on the matter, the defendant had responded that given the way the events had transpired, it was impossible to specify his movements. Despite the explanation, Hernández de la Garza considered the defendant's statement to have continued "suggesting the presumption was true, while no proof contradicted it." Finally, he maintained his opinion concerning the relevance of applying the self-defense exclusion.

The judge ruled the same day, January 15. Hours before the deadline required to issue an *auto de formal prisión* or *auto de libertad*, he affirmed that the proceedings were completed and he already had sufficient elements to rule, commenting that "it was unnecessary to let the analysis of excluding factors of liability to be studied in the judgment to end the case, but rather they can be done at any procedural stage." He ordered Desentis González's release, maintaining that the defendant had acted in self-defense, since the intruder was dangerous and had broken into the defendant's home at night, committing an aggression against the safety of his home, his personal integrity, and that of his children and his belongings.[63] El *Universal Gráfico* applauded the ruling, saying, "It could be deemed a social guarantee."[64]

Nevertheless, two days later, when it seemed the matter had been concluded, the MP agent, claiming he was fulfilling the obligations of his office, asked the judge for a new proceeding: He asked the expert witnesses to determine whether the bullet that entered the deceased's body from above had produced Roa Rodríguez Martínez's death and whether the trajectory contravened Desentis González's confession. To support the filing, he referred to Article 302 of the Criminal Procedure Code, which stated that the release order for lack of merit did not prevent the prosecution from proceeding with new data. He asked that if his request was rejected on the grounds that an order for release for lack of merit was not issued, but rather an order for complete freedom, the appeal must be taken as filed, because it was not deemed appropriate that complete freedom be decided at that procedural stage.

The judge argued that his decision was final. He maintained that the release order for lack of merit was issued when the relevant proof was presented and no certainty existed about the corpus delicti and the criminal liability of the accused, but that had not been the case, because the evidence supported that Desentis González had acted in self-defense. He ruled that the decision could only be revoked by the TSJ and admitted the appeal.[65]

The case was referred to the Seventh Chamber. In April 1940 the magistrates considered that at any stage of the proceedings, having accredited the existence of an exclusion of liability, it was appropriate for the judge to issue the order of absolute freedom, so the grievance argued by the MP was unfounded. Furthermore, they asserted that by determining the exclusion, the judge had based his decision on Hernández de la Garza's own petition (motion filed by the public prosecutor, *pedimento*), among other elements. They spoke of petition, not of opinion, because an MP agent could not be deprived of his functions during the proceeding, so his opinion could not be regarded as personal. Moreover, they affirmed that in the petition, the agent had not requested the release order for lack of merit, but on the contrary, he had expressed his conviction that the defendant had acted in self-defense and had asked the judge to rule on what was lawful, and the judge had ruled absolute freedom. Therefore, they ratified the judge's decision, proceeding with the release of the accused.[66]

Both legal rulings were made swiftly and before the constitutional deadline, procedural laws were respected, and the ruling was extremely mild for the defendant, because his confession was granted full probative value despite the existence of contradictory proof: the expert opinion on the bullet's trajectory.

The judgments were not far from the opinion of journalists, who justified the murder committed by Desentis González based on the victim's criminal record and the danger he posed to the community, terrified of growing crime.

It could be categorized as an "easy or clear" case if the MP agent had not filed an appeal. The actions of the prosecution clashed. The fact that an official with the agent's experience suggested the judge considered the self-defense exclusion (discounting the ballistics report) and was questioned once he had made his decision (giving weight to the expert opinion he already had) lends itself to suspicion. Two hypotheses are possible. First, perhaps the MP agent was following an instruction from his superior, the attorney general, although he disagreed and trusted that the judge once alerted about the bullet's trajectory would not rule to release the defendant. Second, it may be that the MP agent did not seek a conviction, thus paving the way for the judge to justify acquittal, but then appealed to eliminate the objections to the agent's actions or the liability he would have had if he had not noticed the expert opinion, requesting neither clarification nor consideration.

We'll never know, but two particularities should also be noted: the minor importance given to the ballistics report questioning Desentis González's confession and the speed of the ruling. It is impossible not to wonder whether the fact that the accused was a legal professional and might have had friends or influences in the court had any bearing. This possibility is lessened, however, if we heed the controversy this type of matter triggered and especially if we consider how similar cases in the following years resulted in similar rulings.

For example, in 1948 the Fourth Criminal Court determined a man had acted in self-defense when he took the life of an intruder who had awakened him by opening his bedroom door and then hid behind the sofa. The defendant said that while chasing the intruder, the man assaulted him by pushing the armchair at him. Ultimately, the defendant was acquitted, just as was Desentis González. It was a majority vote, since one of the three judges, Vicente Muñoz Castro, issued a dissenting vote. He regarded the defendant's confession implausible and the aggression against the persons living and assets in the home not accredited.

In consonance with the dissent, the MP appealed. TSJ Seventh Chamber magistrates confirmed the ruling by deeming that most of the extant proof corroborated the confession. Moreover, they sustained the requirement in the last line of the third section of Article 14—namely, that the exercise of violence on persons or belongings by the intruder did not have to be "strictly and rigorously noticeable," because "as the fundamental normative concept of the presumption under consideration, inviolability of the home—the foundation of the family and society—must prioritize this concept." They defended their idea with two arguments: Codes of other nations admitted the presence of the intruder in the home as sufficient, and they considered it illogical that in the first paragraph, the 1931 Code drafters justified the harm caused by the aggressor who attempted to break into the home but not once he was already inside.[67] Following the same line is a final judgment issued in 1953 by the SCJ First Chamber, which considered self-defense accredited in the case of a man who injured an intruder whom he happened upon in the patio of his home while the man was trying to break into the house.[68] Therefore, as described, those cases, including that of Miguel Desentis González, generated controversy in courts.

"You're Not a Criminal, You're a Martyr!"
Equally interesting were the trials of women who argued they acted in self-defense or to defend their relatives from the aggression of male relatives.

An initial exploration of the legal archives reveals that many women tried for murder between 1929 and 1971 committed the crimes in their homes and killed relatives. Martha Santillán Esqueda reached the same conclusion in her study of female criminality between 1940 and 1954. She finds that this type of trial represented 47 percent of the total and adds that although it was well argued that they had acted in self-defense and accredited that they had suffered prior aggression at the hands of the victims, almost all of them were judged liable for homicide in quarrels in which they were the victims. She interprets this from the minor importance given to domestic violence, a topic then absent from the political and social agendas, even those of feminists, and barely mentioned by criminal attorneys such as Matilde Rodríguez Cabo and María Elvira Bermúdez, who also understood it as a problem limited to the popular sectors.[69]

My research in judicial archives allows me to share that impression: Most female defendants were considered liable for murder committed in quarrels, although some were acquitted by accepting the exclusion of self-defense, and others were convicted of simple or qualified homicide. Significantly, in their trials, attorneys added grave fear to the self-defense argument. In general, and contrary to what occurred when defending men, attorneys representing female defendants who alleged they had acted in self-defense also argued they had acted out of an uncontrollable fear of their aggressor. The gender stereotype justified that women felt fear, but not men. Women were seen as weak, prone to be fearful (in men, that sentiment could be interpreted as weakness) and irrational, and disposed to feel emotionally upset. Therefore, the argument fit female murder suspects, but not men.

Four well-known cases illustrate these two conclusions. I begin with one in which the exemption was accepted (Ana Irma Schultz) and later discuss two in which it was rejected (Emma Perches Frank and Soledad Rodríguez Prado).[70]

On the night of December 17, 1944, María de los Ángeles Schultz (daughter of a well-known geographer and sister of Guillermo Schultz, discussed below) sought out attorney Antonio de Padua Moreno Torres to tell him some thieves had entered her home and killed her husband. The next morning the attorney notified the Ninth Borough MP, and several policemen went to the house on Mariano Escobedo, the property of a first captain of the Mexican Army, Roberto Sánchez Sordia. In the home, they found his widow and his daughter, Ana Irma Sánchez Schultz, both injured.[71] The fame of the deceased and his wife's family explain the notoriety of the case, which garnered greater attention when it was suggested the murder might have involved well-known state politicians.

The widow and daughter stated they were in the kitchen, when they heard a bang and other noises from the dining room. They ran to the room and saw two unknown subjects fighting with the captain, and they were beaten trying to defend him. Later, one of the men turned off the light, and the other tried to strangle the mother. Then Roberto Sánchez Sordia tried to flee, and the intruders killed him in the hallway. The two women maintained that they were unable to describe the men because the intruders had their backs to them at the beginning and then were in darkness after the lights were off.[72]

The reporters made the story their own. La Prensa added a detail: The women had lost consciousness from the blows.[73] Images of them lying on the ground and with their heads bandaged were published in Excélsior, El Universal, and El Universal Gráfico; the first two included a photo of the deceased in life (fig. 1), and the third, in a sensationalistic tone, included one of his corpse. Furthermore, the articles disseminated the results of the investigation. The body was taken to Juárez Hospital for the autopsy. The Excélsior reporter explained that "the gunpowder burns and tattoo" around the neck wound suggested the victim was shot at close range.[74]

The newspapers also published statements revealing that the deceased had had difficulties with a legislative deputy from San Luis Potosí, was being prosecuted for slandering a high official in the PGJ, had received death threats, and had given orders not to open the door to anyone.[75] La Prensa spread two hypotheses: The killers were members of a gang of car thieves and smugglers apprehended by the captain when he was head of Police and Traffic in Monterrey or they were hit men hired by a former lover.[76] One day later, the newspaper said the thugs had been located and had killed Roberto Sánchez Sordia in revenge for his actions in Tlaxcala.[77]

The case was handled by the deputy chief of the judicial police himself. Examinations performed on María and her daughter showed they had been beaten, but the Expert Service of the PGJ did not find indications that intruders had scaled the bars of the grille or damaged the home's doors, so it questioned their account, also learning that the captain did not have a good relationship with them.[78] They fell under suspicion. According to La Prensa, "Police interrogations became even narrower, firmer, and more tenacious. Finally on Saturday night, after tough questioning, the girl's strength faltered and now crushed, with no way out, almost cornered by the detective she exclaimed amid uncontrollable sobs: Yes, it was I who killed my father, may God punish me, but I did it to save my mom!"[79]

Ana Irma, who was eighteen, confessed on December 23. Newspapers reproduced her account in detail. She claimed that the man whom she had

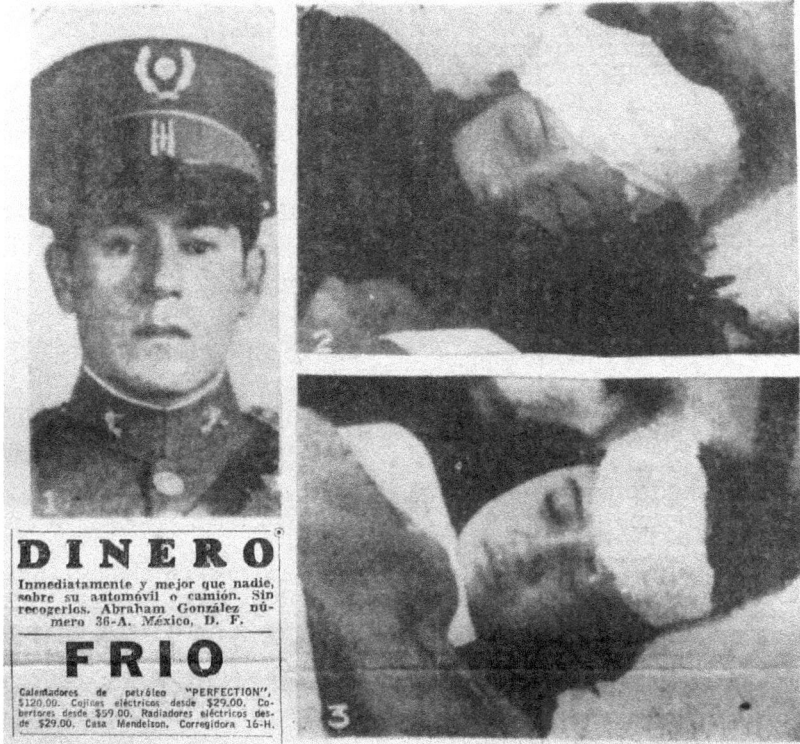

Fig. 1. "Víctimas de un crimen misterioso" (Victims of a mysterious crime). El Universal, December 19, 1944, 1. AGENCIA ©EL UNIVERSAL.

believed was her father (she found out he wasn't while overhearing a conversation in the hospital) often drank and had a violent character. Friction between the captain and her mother was frequent. The day of the crime, both women were listening to the radio when he returned home and chastised them for not having cleaned the dining room. "My father had been drinking that afternoon and seemed deranged. He was not a habitual drunk, but sometimes he drank and anger, rage, madness ensued." The wife began to clean the dining room. He berated her and told her to get out of the house; she refused, saying "she would not go because it went against her honor and if she did so, it would be in a legal manner." He hit her.

In response to her call for help, her daughter ran into the room and cried, "Don't kill my mother, don't hit her!" (according to El Universal) or "Daddy, Daddy, don't hit my mother, let go of her" (according to La Prensa). He responded, "Enough of this mess, I'm going to kill both of you now" (El Universal). The man went to the bedroom and returned with his .45-caliber service weapon, repeating that he would kill them if they didn't leave the room. The daughter, considering her father drunk and with the gun in his hand, ran to a room to find a .32-caliber weapon they had for protection in case of burglary. When she returned, her father had left the pistol on the table and was strangling her mother with a cord. She shot him, and María tried to run away, but he followed his wife to the terrace to hit her. Ana Irma went after them; she remembered only having shot the first time.[80]

María's deposition was slightly different. She asserted that when her daughter entered the dining room to defend her, her husband struck Ana Irma with a bottle of habanero sauce. María took advantage of the confusion to escape, but he caught up with her and pushed her down the stairs. At that moment she heard a shot; although he was injured, he kept strangling her, then she heard a second shot.[81]

Ana Irma Schultz was taken to Lecumberri Prison and brought before Francisco Argüelles, the eleventh judge of the Fourth Criminal Court. The next day, December 24, she gave a preliminary statement, accompanied by her attorneys, her uncle Guillermo Schultz and Antonio de P. Moreno. The judge asked why she had lied in her first statement. She responded that it was out of fear of "offending the memory of her parents and ancestors," but that later, based on an examination of conscience and without anyone advising her, she had decided to tell the truth. She added that she remembered firing the second shot when she saw the captain still beating her mother. The day of the confrontation hearing, she and her mother were in agreement: The second shot had been fired as María de los Ángeles Schultz remembered it, on the stairs to the terrace. Ana Irma asserted that "there was no other alternative than to defend herself and her mother by shooting Captain Sánchez because if not, he would have killed them."[82] The description was dramatized by El Universal: "When I saw the pistol and his enraged mood, I understood imminently he would kill my mother. But I couldn't let that happen, she was my mother, she was hurt, I love her, and it wasn't a matter of letting that crime be committed, something arose within me, I violently understood I had to act without hesitation."[83]

The *La Prensa* writer raised the question journalists ask all murderers: "Are you sorry to have killed your father?" She responded, "Yes sir, very, I tell you from my heart." She clarified that although she already knew he was not her father, "I always loved him as if he were and I treated him as such and respected him."[84]

The papers sympathized with the mother and daughter. *La Prensa* described the former as "a selfless mother, made to sacrifice," and Ana Irma as "an unhappy little woman" who showed "signs of physical distress and great moral suffering."[85] *Excélsior* editorialized, "The young woman is extremely depressed. She speaks slowly, laboriously, and everything indicates she has profoundly felt the death of the man she believed was her father."[86] The images coincided with the texts and showed her suffering, with her face half covered by a black veil. Consequently, they condemned the captain. *El Universal* maintained, "He had an irascible, violent, very brusque and surly character; his military occupation seemed to have had a strong influence on his private life, in which he was authoritarian and extremely profane and rude."[87]

On December 27 the MP agent asked that an *auto de formal prisión* be issued; the judge did so. The defense attorneys filed an *amparo* request for the transgression of rights in constitutional Articles 14, 16, and 19, a violation derived from the *auto*. Second District Judge Juan José González Bustamante heard the case and granted the provisional stay of the requested act. The criminal court judge granted release on bail, and Ana Irma left jail.[88]

Once the trial began, the defense attorneys argued that Ana Irma Schultz had acted in defense of her mother and was driven by the grave fear that she would suffer irreparable harm, which was accredited by expert opinions. Various witnesses said the mother had tried to get a divorce because the captain often beat her and had a violent temper; two of them claimed he had threatened them with his gun. However, relatives of the victim denied the statements and suggested that the widow had committed the crime but the daughter had been blamed so the mother could keep the inheritance. The MP accused the defendant of murder committed in a quarrel in which she has been provoked.[89]

As the trial developed, on April 2, 1945, the Second District judge issued the *amparo* judgment. In various final rulings, he maintained that the SCJ had established that an exemption of liability could be determined at two procedural moments: the *auto de formal prisión* or the ruling. Additionally, contrary to a *tesis* issued by the court, which rejected the possible coexistence of self-defense and grave fear, Judge González Bustamante asserted:

While some argue self-defense precludes grave fear, evidently both figures are complementary, if one considers the relatively pusillanimous, relatively determined temperament of the person repelling the aggression. In the case study it is a minor who refers to the difficulties that happened in the home given the violent character of Captain Sánchez whom she always saw as her father. . . . Disorganized families in which violence and threats slowly undermine their stability cannot but produce in the spirit of minor children who are presential witnesses of those events, a complex fear that begins to grow without having the character of a reverential fear, but rather an underlying morbid fear of the violence they witness.[90]

Moreover, he affirmed that Ana Irma Sánchez Schultz's confession was backed by proof. The deceased "was a man with a violent character accustomed to drinking alcohol," and that day he had ingested it; the murderer had seen him hit her mother and he had struck her; and she believed "being drunk, he was going to fulfill the threat of killing her" so "there was no other alternative than to defend herself and her mother because it was completely certain if she hadn't, he would have killed her." He deemed the self-defense and grave fear exclusions proven, and finally, he granted the *amparo* on the *auto de formal prisión* for her.[91]

Given that no appeal was filed, on April 19, 1945, three months after Ana Irma Sánchez Schultz committed the crime, Judge Francisco Argüelles ordered her release. The swiftness reflects, as in the case of Miguel Desentis González, special consideration toward the defendant. Furthermore, the judges concurred. Thus it was an "easy or clear" case in which the resolution, the defense attorney's conclusion, and the stance of newspapers coincided.

However, the two other women whose trials are described in this section were condemned.

The first is the case of Emma Perches Frank. A tall blonde with green eyes, she participated at age sixteen in the first car races that admitted women, and with this, according to *El Universal Gráfico*, she had given "the whole country" reason to talk. Although she had been victorious in the "whirlwind of motor sports," later she would "fall victim to the whirlwind of life."[92] She was twenty-five when, on June 8, 1933, she appeared at the Sixth Borough of the MP to declare, "I've just killed my husband!"[93] The victim, Fernando Hernández, was a traffic officer. The case became famous because the victim was a policeman and because of the automotive celebrity of the murderer, who also had a brother who was a colonel.

Taken to Lecumberri, she gave her preliminary statement on June 9. She stated that when she met Hernández, she was married, but she considered her marriage null, since the pilot she thought was her husband had already abandoned her because, as it later became clear, he was already married. Alone with her children and in dire economic straits, she began to live with the traffic cop, whom she later married and who, from the start, "began to torment her with jealously, accusing her of alleged past or future misconduct." He beat her and she denounced him. However, the authorities did not intervene. "Desperate from that life, Mrs. Perches proposed divorce to her husband on repeated occasions; but he always answered that rather than divorce, he would kill her and himself," wrote a reporter for El Universal Gráfico.[94]

Emma Perches Frank's account said that, the night before the crime, her husband came home completely drunk. She changed his clothes and put the pistol he carried on a table in the living room; later, he took it when he went out for a drive to clear his head. The next morning, while their children and servant were out and she helped him get dressed, she asked him for a separation because he was often drunk and "they had frequent arguments." He invited her into the living room and said, "We are going to end this once and for all." As he walked toward the table where the gun was, she pounced on the weapon and shot until the gun was empty, fearing for her life, since he had already shot at her on two occasions after an argument. Seeing him dead, she ran to her sister's house.[95]

The reporters, present at the proceeding, reproduced her statement but also participated. "Repentant?" asked a contributor to El Universal Gráfico. "In no way!" she answered. "He made me suffer too much."[96] In general, the journalists expressed compassion. They presented the defendant as a desperate victim of deceit, because the traffic cop had been cheating with a woman who went to the police station and claimed she was his fiancée. Furthermore, El Universal Gráfico alleged that she found herself in a grave situation: Her children "had been taken in by some women workers out of charity," and her sister used to visit her but had just been committed to an insane asylum.[97] They portrayed her as a fragile, defeated woman (fig. 2). According to La Prensa, "Her slender body was shaken by a nervous breakdown, sobs, rather cries, escaped from her throat, and later she threw herself onto the pavement, fainting."[98] El

Universal suggested, "The exhaustion of the above-mentioned lady is terrible. She weeps in silence and remains long hours without uttering a word."[99]

On June 12 Perches Frank was formally detained. She was tried by the Eighth Criminal Court, composed of Luis Garrido, Raúl Carrancá y Trujillo, and Federico Dosamantes. José María Gutiérrez defended her; he argued that Perches Frank had acted under tremendous pressure because she knew the deceased could attack her. He compared her case to another notorious trial, that of "Mano de Águila" (Eagle Hand), an individual who had recently been acquitted for shooting a military man, and affirmed, "He was released taking into account he fired, just as Emma, for fear of dying at the hands of the military man; how was it possible not to admit a woman had experienced the same fear when in the presence of an overexcited, armed man who had promised to kill her?"[100] The servant ratified Perches Frank's statement and affirmed the husband had arrived drunk and was violent. The defense attorney invoked the exemptions of liability of grave fear and self-defense, and as subsidiary, excess in self-defense.

The MP agent did not concur with that possibility; instead, he invoked the investigation carried out by judicial police. Professor Benjamín Martínez, head of the office in charge of forensic investigation, concluded that the deceased had received the first bullet when he was trying to get up from the chair where he was seated, the second as he was falling back after the impact of the first bullet, and the third when he fell to the floor. The experts appointed by the prosecution presented a corroborating report, indicating the victim was seated when Perches Frank had fired.[101] Moreover, colleagues from the deceased's workplace attested to his good behavior, affirming that "he didn't drink and he was of blameless conduct and affectionate in his interactions."[102] Other witnesses observed that he was very much in love with his wife and they quarreled because she was never at home. A police headquarters identification service background sheet that recorded the prior arrest of Perches Frank for outrageous conduct was exhibited. One witness maintained that Hernández had told him his wife had vowed to kill him and that her first husband said he was leaving Mexico because "he was going to end up in court any day because of her." So the MP accused her of simple murder.

The judges denied that the self-defense exemption could be applied, as they concluded one of the requirements was the existence of an actual aggression, which they deemed had not occurred. They granted full probative value to the prosecution's expert reports, which showed the deceased had been shot

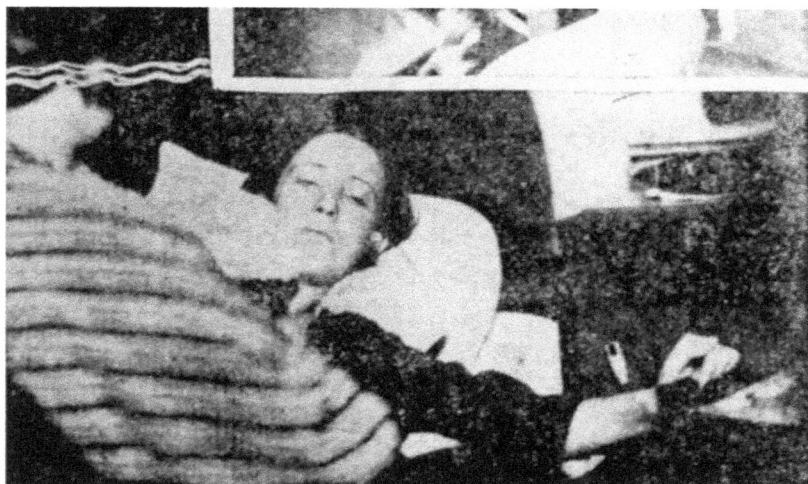

Fig. 2. "Emma Perches se desmaya" (Emma Perches faints). *La Prensa*, June 11, 1933, 1. Material provided by the Fototeca, Hemeroteca y Biblioteca Mario Vázquez Raña / Organización Editorial Mexicana S.A. de C.V.

while seated. Furthermore, they considered that although the threat could have existed, the defendant could have avoided harm because she was near the exit. They also refuted the claim that she had acted in fear: First, they did not believe in the existence of a threat and prior shooting incidents, as they doubted a traffic officer would have missed if he had shot at her. Second, they did not deem accredited the "relatively weak nature of Mrs. Perches," who had practiced shooting firearms and been a race car driver, "activities requiring presence of mind and command of nerves," adding that the biopsychological report showed her to be a normal person. In the June 14, 1934, ruling, they unanimously found her guilty of simple murder and sentenced her to nine years in prison.[103]

The defendant appealed, and the TSJ Seventh Chamber confirmed the decision.[104] She filed for an *amparo*, received by the First Chamber. Her attorney, José María Gutiérrez, argued that constitutional Articles 14 and 16 had been violated and that a penalty that did not fit the case had been applied. He contended that Fernando Hernández had made Emma Perches an "object of ongoing cruel treatment" and on various occasions had wanted to kill her. Finally, after a serious attempt to kill her, the defendant had duly defended herself, taking his life. He added that there was no probative element that contradicted the qualified confession of the accused, who stated she had acted in self-defense driven by grave fear. On the contrary, elements supporting her confession had not been considered: the impacts of the bullets that Fernando Hernández had shot at Emma Perches and the multiple statements that attested to the type of life the victim had given her, with his continual mistreatment, death threats, and murder attempts, "circumstances that subjectively and objectively had engendered fear about grave and imminent harm such as the loss of life in the accused." In conclusion, he held the judgment had not been duly substantiated.

The First Chamber dismissed the statements regarding Hernández's conduct and held that to admit the exemption, it was indispensable to accredit that by performing the act, the actor was materially obligated to do so, which was not accredited. Instead, the chamber affirmed that the ballistics report showed the contrary. In addition, it asserted, from the plaintiff's statements, that he was not armed during the shooting, but she had a pistol, was an expert in firearm use, and was familiar with danger "because on one occasion she took part in car races winning second place." The chamber was certain there could be no self-defense or grave fear because the defendant could have avoided the acts. It formulated the following *tesis*:

> The exemption of self-defense does not exist, although the accused affirms when she told her husband they should divorce, he told her he agreed, at that moment the matter would end and she tried to go to where the weapon was where the events transpired and found a pistol; with which she killed her husband, because that would not have happened if there had been aggression, unless it had been imminent, violent, and unjust; even more so if the accused grabbed the gun, as already indicated, and was expert in handling firearms, and experienced in all sorts of danger.[105]

Finally, on October 9, 1936, the ministers unanimously rejected the protection of federal justice.[106] I do not know how much time Perches Frank remained in prison, but in 1945 she had been released and filed an injunction against her dismissal as a multilingual police office in the Department of the Federal District commissioned to the Secret Services of that office, protection that was granted to her.[107]

Clearly, she was no ordinary woman, having participated in activities and areas customarily banned to women, as her judges insisted repeatedly. They assumed she could not have been afraid, a possibility that reporters indeed admitted (here a gulf separates the ruling and the press's opinion). If that option had been accepted, it might have led to a different ruling (although the fact the victim had been a policeman might not have helped). Deadlines and procedural law were respected. It could be considered an "easy or clear" case with no dissent among the judges.

The conviction of Soledad Rodríguez Prado, better known as Chole la Ranchera, was more severe. The "beautiful rancher," a tall, thickset, tawny-skinned woman with ordinary features, exhibited poise, fortitude, and cynicism, according to La Prensa.[108] She submitted an account of her life to the newspaper a few days after the murder. "The lie can be clear in an instant, the brightness of a match quickly extinguished before the stream of blinding and dazzling light of truth," but she offered to tell the "truth, that which is and always will be." She yearned, "I hope I will be understood and the cleanliness of the mirror of my life again will shine, erasing the stain that hateful slander has marked on its polished surface."[109] The daily devoted the front page to her and reproduced her handwritten words, giving veracity to the account (fig. 3).

Rodríguez Prado recounted that she was the daughter of the overseers of a hacienda near Zamora, Michoacán. She grew up in a family of women: "From a young age, we learned to handle the rope, ride horseback, and shoot without fear. Pistols were toys for us. Nevertheless, my mother did not overlook my education. She taught me to have faith in God and to be good."[110] At seventeen she moved with her family to Zamora, where she met Alfonso Rodríguez, in whom, she said, "I found a good man, but only good." Perhaps for that reason, and marginalized by her own husband, she fell in love with hacienda owner and journalist Ignacio "Nacho" Quiroz Ramírez, with whom she had a daughter. The romance was tumultuous: "If adultery were brave, it would be passable, but it is inevitably cowardly. Lying, or at least remaining silent to conceal the truth, is the axiom of those who deceive. I fell into what I hated the most."[111]

With time, the husband grew suspicious, and she decided to leave her latest lover, but he sent her husband the letters she had written to him, so she was forced to leave her husband and went to Mexico City with her daughter.[112] "They say women who fail in their conjugal duties are cursed by heaven. Then I must be cursed," she wrote. Indeed, life in the capital was tough for her. Nacho, a correspondent for various Zamora newspapers, joined her, and they lived in the Hotel Casa Blanca. He did not mind spending money and

NO SOY CRIMINAL; SOY UNA MÁRTIR

Fig. 3. "No soy criminal; soy una mártir" (I'm not a criminal; I'm a martyr). *La Prensa*, May 9, 1943, front page. Material provided by the Fototeca, Hemeroteca y Biblioteca Mario Vázquez Raña / Organización Editorial Mexicana S.A. de C.V.

fulfilled all her whims, but she paid by putting up with his jealous rages: "At the theater, the movies, if any man looked at me it was enough to arouse his senile jealousy. . . . I withstood his volatile character, which gave me unbearable moments or sweet parentheses. But ultimately, it was insufferable. He saw a rival in any man, and in me, an insatiable woman who gave herself to the first passerby."[113]

One of these scenes led to tragedy. In the wee hours of May 3 Hotel Casa Blanca employees heard shots and called the police. The journalist died shortly before reaching the hospital. He had a pointblank shot to the head. Soledad confessed she had killed him because he had fired two shots at her before.[114]

The news published in dailies attracted public attention as a murder of passion involving a well-known figure, Ignacio Quiroz Ramírez. Newspaper images show the killer and victim. The *La Prensa* article also includes an image of the daughter, heightening the drama of the account (fig. 4).[115] Even more sensationalistic is a photo published the same day by *El Universal Gráfico* showing the killer accompanied by Quiroz Ramírez's corpse.[116]

Hours after the tragedy, elegantly attired, Rodríguez Prado surrendered to the authorities. The next day she was taken before the first judge, Ángel Escalante. Her defense attorney was José María Gutiérrez, who had also represented Emma Perches de Frank.

In her preparatory statement, Rodríguez Prado reaffirmed what she had told investigative agents: She had fired after Quiroz Ramírez had. She described how, after one of their frequent arguments, he got into bed, while she remained in the rocking chair near the door. "Even lying down, he kept insulting me, calling me the harshest and cruelest names. The argument became unbearable. The cup of my patience overflowed. In a fit of madness, Nacho grabbed his pistol from the nightstand and fired two shots at me." The bullets passed near her daughter, and this gave her the strength to run to the bed, grapple with him, wrest the gun from him, and point it at his forehead. "I fired and killed him in a moment of overwhelming fear, indescribable panic."[117]

She testified for court officials and reporters. The *La Prensa* correspondent asked the same question as earlier, "Are you sorry for your crime?" and received a similar answer: "Yes, because this is very lamentable; but no, because I know I was in danger. If I had died, my little girl would have been left defenseless." The reporter then asked, "What do you think was the cause of the tragedy?" Without hesitation, she said, "Jealousy. He was extremely jealous. He wanted to kill me, and I killed him."[118]

"His jealousy killed him; his jealousy weaponized my arm." That was her defense. She affirmed, "If God had allowed him to speak before dying," he would have confirmed what she testified. In the account of her life and her crime, she remembered, "The bullets that cut Nacho's life short still ring in my ears. I'm sorry all the time. They are my obsession, my delirium. I still have the impression in my retina of his blazing eyes looking at me and that convulsively moved my hand to kill him. I still can't escape my fright, nor do I know what perverse spirit spoke from deep in the abysses of my heart." She claimed, "I killed, that's true, but I did so in self-defense," and added,

TRAGEDIA EN EL "CASA BLANCA".—La nota ro-
ja del día en la Metrópoli la dió el Hotel "Casa Blanca":
protagonistas, una mujer de tipo ranchero y un hombre entrado en edad, periodista. Ella lo mató sin que ex-
plique por qué le disparó. Nuestras gráficas muestran
en la parte superior al Sr. Ignacio Quiroz Ramírez, co-
rresponsal en Zamora de varios periódicos, muerto por
Soledad Rodríguez, quien aparece en la parte baja.

EL CERI
gráfica a
mera señ
niendo en
go Rodríp
calles del
quien ya
delito, se;
el día de

Fig. 4. "Tragedia en el 'Casa Blanca'" (Tragedy in the "Casa Blanca"). *La Prensa*,
May 4, 1934, 1. Material provided by the Fototeca, Hemeroteca y Biblioteca Mario
Vázquez Raña / Organización Editorial Mexicana S.A. de C.V.

"My conscience does not accuse me of having acted deliberately and tells me,
you're not a criminal, you're a martyr!"[119]

On May 4 the events were reconstructed. *La Prensa* published the details of
the experts' examination of the wall behind the rocking chair and their doubts
about the murderer's account because investigators suggested she had shot
the victim while he was asleep (fig. 5).[120] Newspapers condemned her before
the judges. *El Universal Gráfico* stated that without a doubt, it was premeditated
murder.[121] *La Prensa* suggested she could have killed her lover while he was

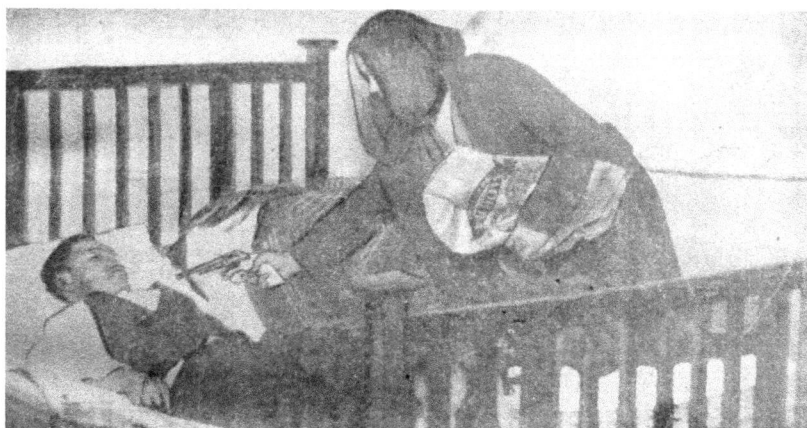

Fig. 5. Crime reconstruction of the killing of Ignacio Quiroz Ramírez. *La Prensa*, May 5, 1934, 1. Material provided by the Fototeca, Hemeroteca y Biblioteca Mario Vázquez Raña / Organización Editorial Mexicana S.A. de C.V.

asleep, and the illustrator drew an executioner coldly and calculatingly executing a defenseless man.[122] Reporters didn't like her. They described her as a "tigress," "strong woman," and "fierce rancher."[123]

Within the deadline indicated by law, on May 7 Judge Ángel Escalante ordered her confinement.[124] The trial was assigned to the First Criminal Court. Besides Escalante, its judges were Jesús Zavala and Antonio Fernández Vera. The prosecutor was Miguel Desentis González, and the attorneys were José María Gutiérrez and a public defender, Raúl Banuet.

The MP contended that Rodríguez Prado had killed her lover because of his jealousy (based on her alleged confession to hotel employees, who claimed that she had told them the cause had been jealousy, referring to his feelings) and had shot him while he was sleeping (according to the prosecution's ballistic experts and the medical examiner, the place on the wall with holes indicated they had been made by a person who was standing and not lying down in bed, and the projectile that killed the journalist had entered his body at the nape of his neck and not from the front). He accused her of having committed a qualified murder characterized by premeditation, advantage, surprise, and betrayal and called for a thirteen- to twenty-year sentence.[125]

Her defense attorney, José María Gutiérrez, requested that she be considered solely liable for murder in a quarrel in which she was provoked. Faced with the expert reports, Rodríguez Prado admitted she had fired one of the two bullets in the wall. She claimed that everything had occurred as she described it, but fearing the authorities would not believe her, she thought it would be better to testify that he had fired the gun on more than one occasion. She added that while in bed, he threatened to kill her. The psychiatric report requested by the defense from Alfonso Quiroz Cuarón and José Sol described her as schizophrenic, suggestible and prey to a paranoia syndrome.[126]

On July 21, 1935, the judges unanimously convicted her of qualified murder and sentenced her to seventeen years in prison.[127]

Despite the defendant's account, her defense attorney did not request that the exemptions of self-defense and grave fear be considered. He asked that the case be considered a quarrel, but the judges and the MP maintained that a quarrel could not have occurred. Furthermore, they believed the crime had been committed with premeditation, surprise, and advantage, so they dismissed the possibility of convicting her of simple murder. They issued a sentence for qualified homicide.

Rodríguez Prado appealed, and the TSJ Sixth Chamber heard the case. Her defense attorney, Luis Carpintero, argued that the criminal court judges had not considered the defendant's personality (known only "through the fantasies the popular mind had forged") nor that of the deceased (whose violent and aggressive character made it possible to understand the defendant's fear). He requested that they consider various testimonies. His witnesses described Soledad Rodríguez Prado as a good, honorable woman who had met the journalist through economic hardship, when her husband sent her to get loans and negotiate payment terms, because besides being a journalist, Quiroz Ramírez was a wealthy hacienda owner who held the lands the murderer's husband was renting. At the same time, they described Quiroz Ramírez as "mentally deranged" and "intractable, deranged, and evil-hearted."[128]

Rodríguez Prado asked to be heard in justice and that a date be set for the hearing, which was postponed because of the defense attorney's health. Meanwhile, she became the leader of female inmates in cellblocks of distinction (independent one-room cells with a kitchen and shower) who were being sent to cellblock E (with cells shared by several women) under the argument that the "tough female man-killers" caused shameful scenes. She argued that they were being forced out to sell the space to "well-heeled women," and they were allowed to stay in their cells.[129] Her daughter Celia accompanied her in prison.

In October 1935 she named a new defender, Jorge Guerra Leal. The hearing was conducted on October 7. The attorney argued that Chole la Ranchera had acted in self-defense out of grave fear and called for her acquittal. His arguments can be grouped into three themes:

A) He held that the sentence was not duly grounded in law and fact and had been rendered without the support of a meticulous study of the defendant. He described it as a sentence typical of "jurists from years ago," but completely at odds with "our revolutionary law," and suggested that Judge Escalante had not even had contact with Rodríguez Prado, "given the practice of some judges of entrusting their clerks to conduct proceedings, from the preliminary statement until the time to rule, [when] they take the file compiled by clerks to finally study it."

B) He insisted on considering the prior events and history of Rodríguez Prado's life. She came from a humble family and could only study to the third year of primary school. During her marriage, she faced economic hardship, and her husband used her as a messenger, exposing her to the "flirting, amorous requirements, persecution, and harassment" of the wealthy hacienda owner, which were "increasingly more insistent and shameless." He had put her in a quandary: preserve her honor but sacrifice the ideal of economic independence, because turning him down implied they would lose the rented lands, or lose her honor but secure the money needed for planting. Her final decision was not easy, and the journalist used all his weapons to seduce her (because she was, as the experts claimed, a weak, suggestible woman with no will), and after he succeeded, he betrayed her, revealing the affair to her husband (as witnesses attested, he was an "evil, dangerous man," who spared nothing to get what he wanted, becoming the master and absolute lord of "Chole" by provoking the rejection of her husband).

C) He noted that while political and civil law marked differences between men and women (the product of men's fear of women and their desire to keep women tutored, subdued, and in a position of inferiority), criminal law started with equality, which was not equitable. Drawing inspiration from writer Sor Juana, he asked that men accept the liability they had over their actions and asked, "If we induce them [women] to evil, how can we expect them to do good?" He affirmed that women are more prone to good than to evil, saying, "When she commits a crime, [or] better said, when she courageously and resolutely defends herself, it is because her patience has been tried and has already decided to rise up against the scoundrel who won her heart, outraged and forced her, causing the tragedy." In other words, he turned the victim into the perpetrator—and more generally, male victims into the perpetrators of their own deaths. To illustrate the trend of women performing good, he related that none of the female defendants acquitted by jury trial for having killed their husbands or lovers in the 1920s had reoffended. By speaking of acquittals, he was basing his request on earlier judicial practices or custom. He concluded that on account of equity, the judges must judge female defendants "as gentlemen in the broad, noble meaning of this word."[130]

The magistrates considered Rodríguez Prado's version implausible because she had confessed that one of the two shots to the wall had not been fired by the deceased; witnesses affirmed that the three shots had been almost simultaneous, so time would not have allowed him to shoot first before she wrested the gun from him, killed him, and then fired the last shot from the rocking chair; and he had stood up to see her moving toward the bed. Finally, they deemed that even if her account were admitted, she had fired when already in possession of the gun, so the threat had ceased. Therefore, on January 25, 1936, unanimously they ratified the first-instance sentence.[131]

Rodríguez Prado filed an *amparo* claim and was again represented by Guerra Leal. The defense attorney held that constitutional Article 14 had been violated because the provisions corresponding to the case—namely, exemption of criminal liability consisting of self-defense and the state of need derived from grave fear or well-grounded, uncontrollable fear of imminent harm—had not been applied. He reiterated that personality studies had not been given proper value, adding two arguments: He contended that once she had the weapon, the victim had made a violent movement to try to recover it, forcing her to shoot. He also alleged that the ballistic report contained errors because when reconstructing the events, the experts had fired with a gun different from the original while the door was closed. He requested that the First Chamber ministers consider the lack of qualifiers from not admitting the defendant had acted in self-defense or out of grave fear. The ministers, heeding the ballistics report and the witness statements on the time between shots, unanimously considered the defendant's account implausible, and on September 5, 1936, they denied the protection of federal justice, ratifying the conviction.[132]

The judges coincided and adopted the MP's position, refusing to give any weight to the confession. They issued a severe sentence, agreeing with the assessment of journalists. Judicially, there was respect of judicial deadlines and procedural laws. Thus it was an "easy or clear" case.

The convicted woman appointed another defense attorney, José Menéndez Fernández, known as "El Hombre del Corbatón." By then the case was closed, but a pardon or change in the place of imprisonment could still be obtained. Awaiting the ruling of the nation's president, Chole la Ranchera remained in the penitentiary, but her daughter was no longer allowed to be there because of her age. Therefore, when the pardon was denied in 1940, she asked to be moved to Islas Marías because there she could be with her daughter.[133]

She was taken to the federal penal colony in April of that year. In the group composed of 162 convicts, the famed María Elena Blanco was also traveling there. The event captured the attention of journalists, who opined that "an intensely sentimental, painful, cruel tone" had been given to the "wretched" Soledad and her child.[134] *Excélsior* reported that the deputy chief of security had offered to take care of the child, but she refused, saying her daughter was "her whole life and [she] could not be apart from her."[135] In November 1942 Rodríguez Prado was confined in the Morelia Penitentiary, had served eight years of prison, and was possibly preparing her parole.[136]

In sum, in the cases of all three women, at some point in their trials, in addition to claiming self-defense, their attorneys contended that they experienced grave fear, an argument employed more frequently in defense of women than of men. Although it cannot be said that this was the factor that swayed the judges, because there were other probative elements in all the cases, a correspondence between journalists' opinions and judges' judgments can be noted, as well as a certain relationship between the degree of moral transgression of women defendants and their criminal convictions.

DEATH WHILE FIGHTING

For individuals who argued they had acted in self-defense or to defend a third party, just as the coexistence between self-defense and grave fear was denied, the coexistence of both exemptions of criminal liability with quarrels was also rejected. However, it was not easy to determine whether defendants had acted to defend themselves from unwanted and unprovoked aggression or had voluntarily participated in a fight that ended with the opponent's death. This was the context of two cases that gained notoriety, the first for the identity of the deceased, singer-songwriter Guty Cárdenas, and the second for that of the killer, Olympic rider Humberto Mariles.

A Singer Was Silenced

On April 5, 1932, celebrated singer-songwriter Guty Cárdenas (Augusto Alejandro Cárdenas Pinelo) lost his life in Salón Bach, on Calle Madero.[137] He was at the peak of his artistic career, having just returned from successfully touring the United States. His fame made his death front-page news: "All meeting places are filled with comments related to the killing of the above-mentioned composer," asserted *La Prensa*.[138]

Witnesses issued statements that were contradictory on many points, but they coincided in identifying a Spaniard, Ángel Peláez Villa, as the killer responsible for his death. After a few hours, it was possible to reconstruct what happened.

Guty Cárdenas had arrived at Salón Bach accompanied by his friend Rosa Madrigal and an entertainment impresario, Eduardo Gálvez Torre; another singer, Arnulfo Larios, joined them, along with two Spanish shoe store owners, Ángel and José Peláez, and a flamenco singer, Jaime Carbonell, known as "El Mallorquín."

"You're no good at that," José Peláez said to Guty when he was singing a Spanish song with El Mallorquín. Days later, José Peláez testified that the Mexican singer had been "unbearable"; he had insulted many people and offered one man 5 pesos to let him destroy the man's sombrero. He recounted that Guty's annoyance grew as people enthusiastically applauded Carbonell's performances and not his own because "he was so drunk he couldn't sing."[139] The Yucatec singer felt offended and challenged José to "arm wrestling" or "finger wrestling." Then the fight started. José's brother Ángel drew a pistol and chambered a round. The dispute was interrupted and the groups separated, the three Spaniards going to the counter and the others to a private room. Under the pretext of going to the restroom, Guty left his friends and approached the brothers, perhaps to challenge José again. The fight erupted anew, and José smashed a bottle in Guty's face. Injured and staggering, Guty drew a pistol and shot twice, wounding José, who collapsed. In response, Ángel fired five times, one bullet accidentally hitting El Mallorquín in the arm, but three others met their mark. Guty died instantly when a bullet struck his heart. It was shortly after 11:30 p.m.[140] A police agent arrived on the scene and disarmed Ángel, who was trying to flee.[141] He was taken to the borough office and his brother to the hospital.

Later, Benjamín Martínez, head of the Criminalistics and Identification Lab at Police Headquarters, arrived. In his report to the head of Investigation and Safety of the Secret Police, he acknowledged his report was faulty because, as he maintained, "during my investigation I ran into multiple difficulties, including, primarily: the site of the event was not preserved, and access was open to all."[142] There were plenty of reporters, who interrogated those present. El Universal Gráfico published photos of the protagonists, as did La Prensa, which also included photos of the deceased (figs. 6 and 7).

Although witnesses identified Ángel Peláez Villa as the shooter, he denied firing and claimed that when his brother fell, he had bent down to help him and heard the shots.[143] Earlier, when the Excélsior reporter questioned him at the crime scene, he stated that he had seen his brother grab the bottle, and at that moment, someone shot José and attacked Guty.[144] At the insistence of the investigating agent, he responded, "Either I'm not explaining myself well or you don't want to understand me; I've told you repeatedly how it happened, and you try to say something else."[145] That night, the paraffin test to check for gunshot residue was done on the Spaniards and the deceased; all came back positive.

Cárdenas was buried in the Spanish Cemetery. "Long ago, perhaps since the burial of poet Amado Nervo, there has been no more sincere demonstration of grief for an artist in Mexico as there was yesterday for the young composer Guty Cárdenas," lamented La Prensa.[146] Journalists, musicians, and performers silently paraded by the casket, and the burial on Thursday was a true expression of popular mourning, reported Magazine de Policía.[147] Indeed, high officials from Yucatán attended alongside famed singers, who sang "Un rayito de Sol," "Nunca," and other well-known compositions by the deceased.[148]

Ángel Peláez Villa was assigned to Eighth Criminal Court judge Joaquín César. The same day as the funeral, April 7, he confessed: "I had to shoot Guty Cárdenas, because I thought he had killed my brother José and he kept firing."[149] He maintained that the singer, pistol in hand, had approached the group and shot his brother, who struck Guty with the bottle to defend himself; that is, José struck Guty after the singer had fired once without hitting his mark. However, although injured, the singer continued shooting. Therefore, the defendant had to use the weapon he had drawn when he saw his adver-

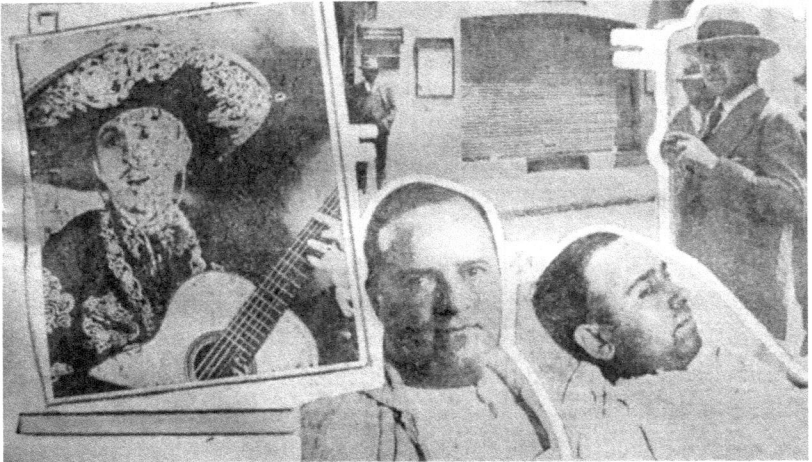

Fig. 6. Guty Cárdenas, José Peláez Villa, and Ángel Peláez Villa. El Universal Gráfico, April 6, 1. AGENCIA ©EL UNIVERSAL.

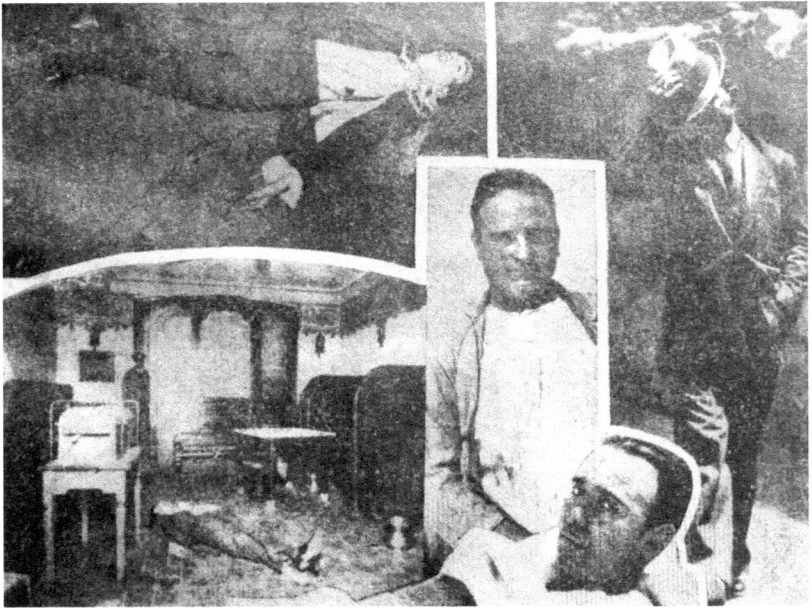

Fig. 7. Protagonists and crime scene. La Prensa, April 7, 1932, 1. Material provided by the Fototeca, Hemeroteca y Biblioteca Mario Vázquez Raña / Organización Editorial Mexicana S.A. de C.V.

sary was armed. In sum, he claimed he had acted to defend his brother's life and his own.[150]

The grief-stricken public sent letters to newspapers demanding weapon possession be banned, but constitutional Article 10 permitted it; carrying guns outside the home was allowed until 1971. *La Prensa* summed it up: "There is no reason, we're told, for a musician, a shopkeeper, and generally any person who does not belong to the police to always carry a gun hanging from his belt."[151]

On April 9, based on the statements of Ángel Peláez Villa and the witnesses, the judge issued the *auto de formal prisión* for the defendant.[152] The case was assigned to the Third Criminal Court, composed of Joaquín César, Ernesto G. Garza, and Eduardo Hernández Garibay. The last named judge recused himself and was replaced by Eduardo Gómez Gallardo Suárez Teruel.[153] In the end, José de la Hoz Chaubert also formed part of the tribunal.

The confrontation of testimonies revealed that Guty Cárdenas had fired before being struck with the bottle.[154] On May 5 José Peláez Villa died from his wound. MP agent Miguel Desentis González considered Ángel liable for the crimes of homicide and injury committed in a fight, in which he was the aggressor and instigator, and for illegally carrying a weapon. His defense attorney, Darío Pastrana, argued that he had acted to defend his brother, wounded Jaime Carbonell out of recklessness, was unable to prevent the resulting harm, and carried the gun rightfully under the Constitution.[155]

On September 19, 1932, with a majority of votes, the criminal court judges ruled that Ángel Peláez Villa had acted to defend his brother and acquitted him of the other two crimes, injuries and carrying a weapon. Contrary to the MP's contention, the two judges who voted in the majority—Gómez Gallardo and de la Hoz Chaubert—considered Cárdenas Pinelo to have instigated the quarrel because "he had drunk too much," and "overwrought by the alcohol, in that setting so prone to fights and disagreements over the most pointless causes" and "in the distinctive recklessness of all drunks," he had followed José Peláez to the bar. They averred that the defendant had not even participated in the fight because he fired when it was over and one of the adversaries, his brother, was already defenseless on the floor. Finally, they justified his intervention: "The defendant's defensive reaction is evident and was proportional to the attack, given the circumstance he could not hesitate to defend his brother." They then asked, "How could he remain unaffected, indifferent, idle, when seeing his brother, such a loved one, was going to be killed by an adversary who already aimed his weapon at him?" Finally, they concluded, "This would reveal an absolute lack of valor and love that would be condemned by everyone."[156]

By justifying Ángel's intervention in defense of his brother, judges alluded to the prevailing codes of ethics and conduct of the time. Condemning drunkenness and linking alcohol consumption to committing criminal acts were common in those years, when governmental campaigns against alcoholism gained momentum (justified based on the supposed damage drinking caused to consumers' health and behavior), in addition to ordering the review and closure of nightclubs and spaces considered harmful.[157] In parallel, the judges exalted masculine courage, which was nothing new because bravery has been an attribute continually valued in men. Furthermore, they highlighted family affection, again not new, although the significance given to the family might have been reinforced at that time out of concern over the family institution (stemming from concern over the rising entry of women into professional life and the workforce) and the weakening of religious morality (an effect of the anticlericalism of revolutionary governments). The criminal court judges justified their decision based on the general acceptance of those models, maintaining that a lack of valor and brotherly love on the part of Ángel Peláez Villa would have been condemned by everyone. In other words, they suggested their judgment was in consonance with society's judgment.

This exempted him from liability related to the murder. They also considered him excluded from liability for injuries because he had fired to defend his brother's life, and this included the consequences of the shots (involuntarily injuring the flamenco singer). Finally, they deemed that carrying the gun was not a violation of the law because the possession of weapons was contemplated in constitutional Article 10. Judge Ernesto Garza issued a dissenting judgment. He coincided with his colleagues by not considering Peláez Villa liable for the crime of injuries and bearing a weapon, but he diverged in deeming him liable for murder committed in a quarrel, coinciding with the MP agent. He maintained that Peláez Villa had indeed intervened in the dispute, which was not over when he fired, and he argued that legitimate defense could not be confused with intervention in a fight to help an adversary. He asserted that the killer should be given a sentence of eight years in prison.[158] However, he made no reference to a SCJ *tesis* in which the First Chamber rejected admitting the exclusion of self-defense when the defendant had participated in a fight.[159]

In sum, by a majority vote, the Third Criminal Court determined Peláez Villa had acted in defense of his brother's life.[160] The MP appealed. The TSJ

Fifth Chamber judged the trial. With a majority of votes, on September 5, 1933, the magistrates revoked the ruling that the Third Criminal Court had issued almost a year earlier, and they adopted as their judgment the dissenting vote of judge Ernesto Garza, considering Peláez Villa liable for the crime of homicide in a quarrel, provoked by his opponent. Moreover, although they confirmed the acquittal for the crimes of carrying a weapon and injuries, they rejected the argument that he had acted in defense of his brother's life because they believed it had been a quarrel, incompatible with the exemption for the possibility he had of avoiding it and thus preventing the outcome. They accepted that although he had been the aggressor, he had been provoked:

> Augusto Cárdenas Pinelo was the instigator and for the same reason rationally and humanly it should be established Ángel Peláez Villa attacked Augusto Cárdenas Pinelo provoked by the shot he fired at his brother José, because although Ángel would have foreseen the quarrel, although he did nothing to prevent it and although it could have been prevented, it is entirely in accordance with reason and human nature that upon seeing his brother wounded and Cárdenas in an attitude of continuing firing, that he intervene in such a quarrel to render Cárdenas useless in continuing to harm his brother.[161]

They gave him four years of prison, with the possibility of earlier release.[162] Later, Peláez Villa filed an amparo. He was represented by Emilio Pardo Aspe, who argued that to the detriment of his client, constitutional Article 14 had been violated, as the magistrates had erroneously applied the Criminal Code article referring to quarrels and overlooked Article 15 of the same code, referring to the exemption for self-defense (defensa legítima). In addition, the attorney considered various articles of the Criminal Procedure Code to have been violated, including the regulations related to proof, because the testimonies of unsuitable witnesses known for slander and bias had been religiously respected; moreover, the judges had not adequately considered the ballistics report, which sufficed to accredit the exemption of self-defense.

Returning to the imprecise application of criminal law, the defense attorney contended that by considering it could not have been an act Peláez Villa committed to defend his brother's life because it had been a quarrel, the magistrates had incurred various errors. The first was by considering there had been a quarrel (because the chamber had established that criminal law experts defined a quarrel as the express or tacit concert of two persons to settle their differences in a fight, but later they admitted it involved three persons, departing from the definition they themselves had given and also from behavior defined by law as a crime, which did not begin with the agreement of wills or from a verbal dispute, but rather from a physical fight). The second was in assuming that by simply leaving the establishment, the Spaniards could have avoided the aggression (because they could not have foreseen it, since Guty Cárdenas had already left, and they would have had no reason to suppose he would return). The third, and most important, was in not contemplating that the murder had been committed when the fight ended (because the brothers had defended themselves from the shots when the fight was over, even when José Peláez Villa was already motionless on the floor, and thus the defendant had defended his brother by firing and had not been involved in a quarrel). He asserted that his client had intervened not to participate in a fight, but to defend his brother from an aggression after a quarrel had ended, and the judges had admitted it into their legal argumentations (considerandos) by establishing that Ángel Peláez Villa had intervened when he saw his brother wounded and Guty Cárdenas ready to fire again, and that he had done so to prevent Cárdenas from continuing to do harm.

The M P agent recommended the amparo be granted because he agreed Article 14 had been violated, since the ruling chamber had dismissed the exclusion of liability in favor of the accused. He claimed that the chamber had admitted that by intervening, Peláez Villa had acted not with the intention of fighting or seeking revenge, but in legitimate defense of his brother. That is, there was notable inconsistency between the criteria upheld by the chamber in this legal argumentation and their judgment in which they considered the defendant criminally liable for murder.

Four years had passed since Ángel Peláez Villa had been remanded; he had served his sentence, and surely he was out of prison. Therefore, the ministers were not in a rush to rule. Two years passed before the matter was heard on January 21, 1938. Based on the testimonies, they asserted that there was a first quarrel but also a second, because Guty Cárdenas had fired after being hit with the bottle, not before. They maintained that for self-defense to be operative, the aggression had to be unfair, but if there was a quarrel, this was not the case. They contended that whoever intervened in a quarrel to help a participant cooperated to sway the solution of the conflict in his favor, not to make up for his incompetence in repelling an unjust attack. That is, they believed the intervention of a third party was justified when he noticed the presumed victim was powerless to defend himself, and this would have occurred only if Ángel had entered the establishment at the moment when his brother was already motionless and Guty was shooting at him, without knowledge of the antecedents of the attack. On the contrary, they affirmed, he intervened when he realized the quarrel was unfavorable for his brother, and thus he was not acting in his brother's defense. Finally, they considered the contradiction the ruling authority had committed: By accrediting his defense as the instigator in the quarrel and rejecting the application of the exemption, it had omitted the statement of the very chamber in the sense that it considered the murder had been committed in a quarrel to attenuate the defendant's punishment, because otherwise it would have ruled simple or qualified homicide. Consequently, in the judgment issued on January 21, 1938, the First Chamber justices denied the *amparo*.[163] The delay in the ruling attests to the backlog.

As seen in this case, when considerations like masculinity and family carried so much weight, both ideas about self-defense and the circumstances had to be present to admit this exemption. The matter was highly controversial: There were discrepancies between the findings of the MP agent and first-instance judges, two of the first-instance judges and second-instance magistrates, the federal MP agent and SCJ ministers, and finally, one minister and his colleagues. It is worth asking whether, in these disagreements, the identity of the victim or the grief of society over the loss of the singer had any bearing.

The Fallen Rider

Nor was this matter easily resolved.

On August 14, 1964, Humberto Mariles, a general and Olympic equestrian champion, was driving his Peugeot on Mexico City's Anillo Periférico (ring road) when a Chevrolet changed lanes and cut him off. The second vehicle was driven by Jesús Velázquez, a construction worker then working on a building in Chapultepec Forest. For almost three kilometers (close to two miles), they pursued each other, yelling and hurling insults, then stopped near the construction site. In this account, the two participants in the incident coincided. Another point was indisputable: Minutes later, the builder, seriously wounded, was taken to the Red Cross hospital. However, there is no certainty regarding what happened after the two vehicles stopped and when the wounded man reached the hospital, because the accounts of those involved and witnesses differed.[164]

The first version of events was presented by two forest caretakers, a police-man, and a worker. One of the forest watchmen asserted that he had seen the construction worker get out of his Chevrolet and go to the storerooms, chased by a serviceman uttering "unrepeatable words." He also maintained, just as the second guard did, that the general had fired at the other man, who "sought refuge," and after shooting, he had hit the man in the head as the other tried to protect himself. Finally, another construction worker stated that he had gone to help his boss, who was on the ground, and the general had struck him too. In sum, according to the witnesses, Velázquez had gotten out of his car to hide, and Mariles followed him, gun in hand, insulting him, and at about five meters (sixteen feet), shot him in the back and then beat him.

They added that as they tried to lead the aggressor to the authorities, he responded, "I'm General Mariles!" He was not taken to the borough office; he accompanied the wounded man to the Red Cross hospital. Dr. Carlos Moreno, head of the emergency ward, received the victim and allowed Mariles to remain in the emergency room. The general asked the elderly policeman who was following him to stop and said, "I give you my word of honor, as a military man, I'm not going to flee." When the MP agent withdrew to the hospital door, the general entered the restroom and escaped through the window—like "a common criminal," in the words of La Prensa.[165] It was sug-gested the policemen guarding him allowed him to flee in complicity with Dr. Moreno, who was his friend and owed debts to the fugitive, so the doctor's arrest was ordered. Moreno secured an *amparo* and stated he was friends with the general because they shared an interest in horses; he claimed the general had expressed his intention to take care of the wounded man, but the doctor was unaware he was the aggressor. The MP agent also filed an *amparo* against arrest; he admitted his friendship with the accused but denied helping him flee. Mariles had loyal friends, who denied their participation in the escape but not their ties with him.

In the days that followed, newspapers let their imagination run wild on two facets of a single event: a traffic incident with a fatal outcome and the general's disappearance. Of the cases addressed in this book, this was the one that got the most publicity for Mariles's fame and the way the events occurred, because Jesús Velázquez was at death's door in the hospital for days, and the murderer was on the run for months.

"The truth is no policeman had specific orders to arrest Mariles, nor is there the desire to see him behind bars," asserted La Prensa.[166] The police did not immediately look for Mariles; the arrest warrant was issued two days after the tragedy. By that time, his attorney, Adolfo Aguilar y Quevedo, had filed an *amparo* against the arrest, in which the general claimed Velázquez had threatened him with a trowel, and he had fired in self-defense. It was the first time he gave his version. First District Judge Eduardo Ferrer Mac-Gregor set bail at 1,000 pesos and granted a temporary suspension of the arrest order for seventy-two hours; in that time frame, the accused had to appear before the MP.[167]

After surgery, Jesús Velázquez testified before investigators and reporters. The bullet had entered his back and affected major organs, so he spoke "slowly and softly, complaining of sharp pain." When he entered the hospital, he claimed all he remembered was that he'd had a traffic incident with General Mariles, who had shot him. Following the operation, his account was more detailed, and he coincided with the eyewitnesses. He maintained that he had accidentally cut off the Peugeot, its driver chased him, and he could see the man was angry and armed, so he went to his workplace to find a hiding place; however, when he got out of his car, he was hit first by the bullet and then by his pursuer, who struck him with the butt of his pistol, saying "no one mocks him" and "he demanded respect with or without his uniform."[168]

The reporters took the victim's side and publicized his version, which left no room for the aggressor's self-defense plea. They emphasized that the crime had been committed with advantage, because Mariles had shot a fleeing, unarmed man in the back. It was a cowardly crime followed by an equally cowardly escape, the reporters insinuated. The photos conveyed the same image. For instance, the photographic composition published in La Prensa on August 19 suggests the arrogant, provocative defendant seeming to challenge his victim, of slighter build, defenseless, and bedridden (fig. 8).

The prosecutor was María de los Ángeles Mancera, who, according to El Universal Gráfico, was known for the "rectitude of her actions."[169] La Prensa expressed the same opinion, claiming it would not be easy for the murderer to "extricate himself from the matter," because Mancera would be as "combative as in other sensational cases that have reached her."[170] In this panorama, the minister of national defense declared the general must be treated like any other criminal, adding that he had retired from the army over a conflict regarding National Equestrian Association lands.[171] On August 20, 1964, the prosecutor considered the investigation complete, and there were enough elements to accredit the probable guilt of Mariles. For that crime, the code contemplated less than five years of prison, so he could get bail.[172]

Fig. 8. "Con inaudita saña lo atacó Mariles" (Mariles attacked him with unprecedented fury). *La Prensa*, August 19, 1964, back page. Material provided by the Fototeca, Hemeroteca y Biblioteca Mario Vázquez Raña / Organización Editorial Mexicana S.A. de C.V.

The case was heard by Ninth Criminal Court judge Rafael Pérez Palma. After the seventy-two hours granted to Mariles ended, he did not appear to testify, so the temporary suspension of the arrest warrant was terminated. The police went to the airport because rumors had spread that the accused would escape to New York.[173] He was sought as liable for the assault, but Jesús Velázquez's death turned him into a fugitive for murder. The head of the Forensic Medicine Service had no doubt as to the cause of Velázquez's death on August 23: The bullet entering his back had injured a lung. The autopsy also revealed various contusions and abrasions to his head and the backs of his hands, produced by a blunt weapon.[174] *Excélsior* assured that the prosecutor had enough evidence to accuse Mariles of murder, and given the minimum eight-year sentence for this crime, he could not be released on bail.[175]

The first effect of the news was solidarity with his widow and nine children. *Excélsior* received donations from individuals and groups, and Federal District mayor Ernesto P. Uruchurtu gave the widow the deceased's severance pay as a city employee and announced his intention to provide permanent support for her children.[176] A second effect was skepticism over the impartiality of the officials who would oversee the case and criticism of the murderer, despite his having been and continuing to be a national sports hero.

Humberto Mariles had an upward trajectory in the army. The son of a lieutenant colonel, he began his military career in 1927. As second captain, in 1938 he entered the equestrian corps, two years later being promoted to first captain. From then on, through presidential decrees and his sporting merits, he went up in rank, appointed brigadier specializing in horseback riding in 1952 and ratified by the Senate eight years later.[177] He was part of the military hierarchy and interacted with several Mexican presidents: Lázaro Cárdenas, Manuel Ávila Camacho, and Miguel Alemán. For years he dominated Mexican horsemanship. As the director of the National Equestrian team and leader of the National Equestrian Association, he received its subsidy, assets, and lands.[178] And this was all because of his athletic triumphs. According to his attorney, in international competitions he won 1,168 individual first prizes and 864 team awards.[179] He earned medals, riding Arete, at the 1948 Olympiads in London. When he returned, he was recognized by the president, named a colonel, and acclaimed by the multitudes.

"My efforts were always aimed at dignifying Mexico, my homeland, the army, and my family. I think I've been fortunate because I've seen such efforts crowned by the accomplishment of my objective," he affirmed in 1965.[180] Nevertheless, he was not beloved by the community. After the Chapultepec incident, testimonies were published on his prior misdemeanors and offenses, arrogance, and acts of impunity. La Prensa reported that traffic agents had ticketed him on one occasion, and not only did he avoid paying the fine but he also managed to get the officers fired. Other policemen maintained they had been struck by the general when they detained him for violating traffic regulations.[181] National Equestrian Association members asserted that they had to change clubs to protect themselves, and sports columnists affirmed they had been assaulted by the horseman after publishing unfavorable articles.[182] One reporter contended that Mariles mistreated his subordinates and that during a competition, he hit a soldier with a whip when the man made a mistake in setting up an obstacle.[183] His police file (reporters claimed he had faced trials for slander, threats, and injury) and his military file (according to Excélsior and La Prensa, riddled with offenses) came to light.[184] El Universal Gráfico questioned whether he was a general because the Senate had not ratified him and suggested that his discharge from the army had been from insubordination and usurpation of land belonging to the National Equestrian Association.[185]

In sum, journalists displayed animosity toward Mariles (possibly influenced by solidarity with sports reporters).

Similarly, based on his history of impunity, they expressed concern over the treatment Mariles had and would receive. They questioned the legitimacy of the temporary suspension of the arrest order issued by the district judge. La Prensa claimed that in that lapse, Secret Service agents had located him in a luxurious restaurant but had to leave with their "tails between their legs" because Mariles "with a broad smile showed them the *amparo*."[186] In his column Zodiaco, Fabián Moreno concluded that for the "laughable" sum of 1,000 pesos, he had obtained "the right to laugh at Justice, at our ailing Justice [system] that is the object of all sorts of mockery."[187]

Journalists also expressed doubts about the efforts to capture him. The judicial police joined the Secret Service and put up posters requesting the community's cooperation (an unprecedented act, according to El Universal Gráfico).[188] They searched the fugitive's properties and sought him in the homes of friends, members of the political elite (former President Miguel Alemán and the widow of former President Manuel Ávila Camacho), and public figures (such as broadcaster Paco Malgesto).[189] The search was fruitless, and it was suggested he had left the country.[190] Officials' statements left reporters unconvinced. In the words of an El Universal Gráfico writer, "If justice is properly served, the general must be detained by agents of the judicial police, who know perfectly well where to find him."[191] Humorists and illustrators were not far behind.[192] Sucesos para todos devoted a Day of the Dead poem to him:

> Treacherously, in cold blood,
> he killed a Christian one afternoon,
> fleeing, happy and healthy,
> thanks to the police.
>
> For his excellent aim
> and killing people
> without even taking a breath,
> it was scathingly said
> he was a beast at shooting.[193]

Jurists and citizens were also skeptical. BMA President Manuel G. Escobedo believed that Mariles's friends helped him mock justice.[194] La Prensa readers called for his capture and criticized the Secret Service.[195] The military man was nicknamed "Matariles," a word play on his name and the verb "to kill."[196]

Papers warned of the consequences of these doubts. *Excélsior* asserted that "easy escapes and mockeries of justice and the law" by "a powerful criminal based on his cronyism with new or old politicians" would make people believe the only way to protect themselves was the law of the jungle.[197] El *Universal Gráfico* declared, "Now, more than ever, he must be apprehended. The public in the capital, who no longer believe in justice, demand it to regain confidence in our laws that were apparently made to safeguard the interests of the wealthy and influential."[198]

Mariles was a fugitive for ten months, until June 1965. Every so often, rumors spread of his surrender. For example, the magazine *Mañana* announced that he would appear to "defend himself with the support of the law, instead of remaining hidden, an ugly thing for a general."[199] *La Prensa* echoed news from the *Edinburg (TX) Daily Review*, which reported that he was hiding in Texas and would return to show Velázquez's death had been accidental and to participate in the 1968 Olympiads. Attorney Aguilar y Quevedo confirmed that his client intended to appear "like any other ordinary person," without using influences.[200] *La Prensa* devoted front-page coverage to doubting his "humility" and intention (fig. 9).

The next day Mariles was apprehended in his attorney's home. It is unclear whether he surrendered and called the authorities (as he claimed); he was thinking of appearing in the borough office later, but the police got him up early (the prevailing account, because it was in the interest of both parties); or he was not considering surrendering, but the police trapped him (as police affirmed at the beginning). According to the police version—defended by *Excélsior* and disseminated by *La Prensa*—an agent heard a family servant saying on the telephone the fugitive would visit his attorney the next day or he was hiding in his home.[201] It was different from Mariles's version. The medalist maintained he had called the attorney general to surrender. El *Universal Gráfico* spread the news, but with nuances, reporting that he had called journalists and the police to set up "a *mise-en-scène* to seek a 'palliative' to the crime and a minimum sentence for the rider."[202]

Both apprehended and apprehenders made concessions. The Federal District attorney general contended that the military man had called him to express his intention to surrender, but just in case, the police had intercepted him.[203] Meanwhile, Mariles admitted that the police had "been close to trapping

Fig. 9. "Regresó Mariles" (Mariles returned). La Prensa, June 13, 1965, front page. Material provided by the Fototeca, Hemeroteca y Biblioteca Mario Vázquez Raña / Organización Editorial Mexicana S.A. de C.V.

him."[204] He suggested he was planning to surrender, going by his defense attorney's home, and had been surprised by the agents.[205] Ultimately, the circumstances of the capture-surrender are unclear, but evidently the conditions were negotiated. Reporters arrived quickly, which was in everyone's interest: The police and the fugitive would score points if their version was accepted by readers, and for Mariles the presence of the media ensured his rights were respected.

The attorney general appeared at the attorney's residence. Surrounded by his lawyers in the garden, Mariles gave an interview to the newspapers and television. He claimed that "twenty thousand circumstances" had prevented him from appearing before the court, including chronic mastoiditis. He maintained that he had surrendered for his family's peace of mind, "to redeem himself before society," to "repair the damage done to the nation," and to save his honor and that of the army. In consideration of his background as a military man and athlete, he asked the people to allow him to explain; he asked the authorities to judge him as a "common, ordinary man," ignoring his rank and sporting merits. Again, journalists questioned the accused's sincerity. La Prensa published a photo of the despondent military man, wiping his tears, but the caption reads, "He was crying like a woman, which he could not justify as a man." It questioned how a man could claim shooting another man in the back was an accident. They disqualified his masculinity, yet did not assign feminine weakness to him, and asserted that his pain was feigned.

Before boarding the patrol car, Mariles emotionally bade farewell to his family. The scene was captured by La Prensa (fig. 10). The photo caption writer warned viewers not to be moved: If the general's daughters were moved by his farewell, how much more were his victim's fatherless children suffering? The photo included a similar warning because it showed him hugging his wife, alluding to a privilege the widow was deprived of. Political cartoonists contributed as well: "Humberto Mariles will appear before the authorities to be judged and prepare for the Olympiads. But we know there will be no competition for shooting your fellow man," wrote a Jueves de Excélsior collaborator.[206]

The accused was taken to the PGJ, where reporters were waiting for him. After granting an interview, he made his first statement before the MP in the presence of attorneys, friends, journalists, and curious onlookers. He interrupted his statement to "greet, hug, and exchange words with his friends."[207] The legal machinery was moving (fig. 11), but the general did not seem to surrender to his judge. He declared he had not escaped; had gone to the hospital to ask Dr. Carlos Moreno, a "childhood friend," to give the victim the best attention; and when the surgery was over, had left by the emergency entrance because he needed to receive some Venezuelan horsemen.[208] La Prensa questioned this because its reporters had been at that entrance but had not

LA PRENSA
el periódico que dice lo que otros callan

90 CENTAVOS | MEXICO, D. F., LUNES 14 DE JUNIO DE 1965 | AÑO XXXVII | NUMERO 13,696

MARILES SE ENTREGO

(PAGINA DOS Y CENTRALES)

Daño Irreparable En tanto que Patricia y Alicia Mariles pudieron ayer abrazar a su padre, el inculpado de homicidio Humberto Mariles, en otro lugar nueve inocentes criaturas no podrán tener cerca de ellas ni un instante a su padre, Jesús Velázquez Méndez, pues la pistola del exolímpico destrozó para siempre el hogar de un honrado trabajador y dejó en la orfandad a una numerosa familia. Ahora a un crimen alevoso le llamarán "accidente", pero para los huérfanos su situación no tiene nada de accidental. (Información en la página dos). Foto de Rodolfo Martínez.

Fig. 10. "Mariles se entregó" (Mariles turned himself in). *La Prensa*, June 14, 1965, front page. Material provided by the Fototeca, Hemeroteca y Biblioteca Mario Vázquez Raña / Organización Editorial Mexicana S.A. de C.V.

seen him.[209] When he concluded, Mariles was assigned to the Ninth Criminal Court; at the doors to Lecumberri Prison, its director, Carlos Martín del Campo, also a general, awaited him.[210]

The judge, Rafael Pérez Palma, heard his testimony on June 15. The prosecution was represented by agent Enrique Soto y Paz and the head of MP agents,

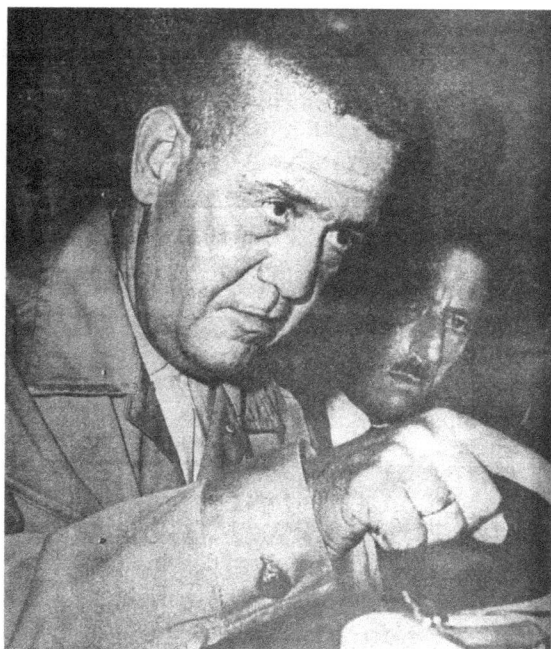

Fig. 11. "Maquinaria judicial en marcha" (Judicial machinery in motion). *La Prensa*, June 15, 1965, back page. Material provided by the Fototeca, Hemeroteca y Biblioteca Mario Vázquez Raña / Organización Editorial Mexicana S.A. de C.V.

José María Nava Huicochea. Also present were four defense attorneys and a throng of acquaintances and unknown observers. For two hours, Mariles gave his testimony. In tears, he lamented that an unintentional tragedy had occurred; he did not ask for leniency but for a law-abiding trial. He recounted that he was driving on the Periférico side lanes when a vehicle came alongside him and the driver shouted, "Good-for-nothing general, get outa the way." He thought it strange the driver knew his military rank and later called him by his name, which made him think someone had sent the man. He kept driving, but the man he now knew was Jesús Velázquez cut him off in his car, forcing him to stop as he watched Velázquez approach with a trowel. "I only had time to pull out the gun and hit him in the head with my right hand, but far from shrinking, he became furious and continued attacking with greater force." The defendant claimed he fired to intimidate the other man, without intending to harm Velázquez. "If my intention had been to kill him, I would have emptied the gun." At that moment, he added, no one was present who could back up what he said, because the first policeman arrived when it was over; therefore, the witness testimonies were false. He also maintained that the ballistics experts had lied.

In the second place, he argued that the builder was a dangerous individual: Evidence proved Velázquez was known to drive drunk, and days before, the man had shot at a family. In addition, he reiterated the explanation he had given the day before about his prolonged absence, insisted he had been ill, and said he feared not being judged impartially, because he had been slandered by journalists, and the events in Chapultepec had already been altered by "low-level employees embedded in police offices and strangers who intervened to alter the investigation." They all intended to destroy him. Then he described various other incidents, including the eviction of the National Equestrian Association from its venue and the mysterious death of several jumping horses. In sum, he considered the incident that caused Velázquez's death to have been orchestrated or at least exploited by his enemies.[211]

His defense attorneys presented evidence to prove Mariles's statements, and his comrades-in-arms defended him. Six division generals, headed by Gilberto R. Limón, requested that the National Defense Ministry transfer him from Lecumberri to the Military Social Rehabilitation Center, but Defense Minister Marcelino García Barragán rejected the possibility and clarified that it was a crime for the Federal District judicial authorities.[212] The generals backed down and said they respected the judges' authority. Nevertheless, others stood by their statements. For the army to have one of its members in an ordinary prison was an insult, and they offered up a fact: In the military prison, 75 percent of the prisoners were confined for common law offenses, and when necessary, they were moved to the civil court. Mariles's stay in Lecumberri put this tradition at risk. The visit of another general, Adolfo León Osorio y Agüero, who shortly before was acquitted of a crime, thanks to Aguilar y Quevedo's defense, triggered special commotion.[213] The matter was an important one. Until 1855 members of the army were judged by military courts even if they committed a common law offense; the Juárez Law marked the end of military jurisdiction, and military courts survived to hear violations of military regulations committed by its members. Nevertheless, the privileges of the military persisted, one of them being the prison in which they had to await their trial. Visits of military men and politicians to Lecumberri might have exerted pressure on the judge, as well as influencing journalists and public opinion. Newspapers continued publishing news on the economic hardship of the bereaved.[214]

On June 18 the judge issued the *auto de formal prisión*. He considered the defendant's possible guilt to be based on the testimony of the general, the victim, and witnesses (the two guards, an auxiliary policeman at the crime scene, and the master builder's helper). The defense attorney requested that the following be added to the record: the medical certificate revealing Velázquez had ingested alcohol, the expert opinion that the bullet had entered from above to below, and the qualified confession of his client contending he had acted in self-defense.[215]

The formal indictment did not diminish suspicion of the general's privileges. Journalists denounced the visits he received in prison and irregularities interpreted as a prelude to his admission to the military hospital: a transfer to the infirmary, justified by the mastoiditis, and "moral depression, along with a nervous breakdown." When he left, he was taken to the wing for "distinguished" inmates.[216] They were also skeptical of the trial. La Prensa described the judge as "weak or partial" (fig. 12) and listed errors, such as allowing the defendant to greet his friends and speak at length of his riding glories, while the El Universal Gráfico announced that "credible sources" had revealed Mariles would be released in six months.[217] The authorities denied the rumors. After studying the case, the Federal District attorney general concluded that the defendant had not acted in self-defense; instead, Mariles had committed a murder with advantage, and he asked the MP agent to follow this criterion, clarifying that no consideration would be given to "Olympic trophies" and "strict compliance with the law" would be overseen. The agent, Enrique Soto y Paz, who replaced María de los Ángeles Mancera stated the same. For his part, Judge Rafael Pérez Palma declared that he knew society was watching and "the prestige of justice" was in his hands.[218]

The Olympic medalist was tried in the Third Criminal Court, composed of the examining magistrate, Pérez Palma, who was later replaced by José Alfonso Everardo Álvarez; Roberto Campos Cos; and Enrique Ríos Hidalgo. Nineteen months elapsed from the detention to the final decision.[219]

The MP agent, María de los Ángeles Mancera, based on the version given by the victim and witnesses, maintained that when Velázquez realized his pursuer was armed, he stopped shortly before Mariles at the construction site, seeking refuge and a place to hide; he ran to some storerooms downhill, where the general shot him in the back, and once he was wounded and on the ground, Mariles struck him with the butt of the pistol. She asserted that the builder died from the wound because all abdominal injuries produce inflammation of the peritoneum (membrane covering the abdominal viscera), which explained the later complications.

Juez Débil o Parcial es el de Mariles; Temor de una "Sorpresa"

(PAGINA DOS)

LA PRENSA
el periódico que dice lo que otros callan

Gritos y Sordera

En tanto que los abogados se trenzaban en una discusión que no pudo ser dominada por el juez, el reo Humberto Mariles se ponía una mano en la oreja, como si no oyera bien la voz de la justicia que le declaraba bien preso. Los licenciados que se gritaron a más y mejor fueron —arriba— Adolfo Aguilar y Quevedo, defensor del homicida, a la derecha, y Antonio Huerta González Roa, representante de la familia de la víctima de Mariles. (Información en la página 2). Fotos de Malaquias Ramírez.

Fig. 12. "Juez débil o parcial es el de Mariles" (Mariles's judge is weak or biased). *La Prensa*, June 19, 1965, back page. Material provided by the Fototeca, Hemeroteca y Biblioteca Mario Vázquez Raña / Organización Editorial Mexicana S.A. de C.V.

The defense attorneys supported Mariles's qualified confession and argued the following. First, Velázquez had provoked the incident: After cutting off the defendant, the builder had pursued and insulted him; blocked the road, forcing him to stop; then got out of the Chevrolet to strike him with a trowel. Second, to defend himself, Mariles had only hit the victim in the head with his gun, and when he saw that did not stop the man, he fired (at a short distance because they were fighting face-to-face). Third, when Mariles saw his opponent wounded, he took him to the Red Cross hospital to get the best medical attention possible and waited until the end of his surgery to leave the hospital (without fleeing). And fourth, the surgeons had not detected one of the bullet holes and did not properly treat the injuries, which caused the generalized peritonitis leading to his death.

Two matters must be clarified: the circumstances surrounding the commission of the crime and the cause of Jesús Velázquez's death. The parties presented expert opinions, and given their disparity, the judge requested the intervention of third-party experts. The most important aspects addressed were the following:

A) **Personalities of those involved**: It was important to assess if one of the men could have avoided the clash. Defense expert witnesses concluded that Jesús Velázquez Méndez was a person with a low cultural level; of disorderly character and lacking moral restraint, which translated into disorderly and anarchic family life, procreating children, cohabiting with different women at the same time; he was an alcoholic and intoxication provoked the reaction of pathological inebriation in his personality, with intense and aggressive fighting urges, which led him to various quarrels. The prosecution's expert coincided with this assessment, maintaining that the builder did not express an interest in his life and displayed a major tendency to aggression. Meanwhile, the third-party expert described his conduct as bellicose and aggressive, especially in traffic incidents, and asserted that he often consumed intoxicating beverages. Furthermore, the experts all agreed that he was drunk on the day of the incident. None of the expert witnesses—either those for the prosecution or the third-party experts—examined the accusations of despotism and violence attributed to the general.

Based on the preceding, the defense considered it implausible to suppose the builder in the incident had acted completely differently from his customary behavior, just as it was implausible to think the general, whose antecedents and personality were not destructive and antisocial, suddenly acted contrary to a life exemplarily dedicated to ethical values, and to fire his gun without motive to kill someone fleeing from him, avoiding the conflict.

b) **Shooting distance and bullet trajectory**: Experts in medicine, criminalistics, and physics and mathematics concurred that the bullet entered from the back of the body and traveled from below to above. It was important to demonstrate the angle of the bullet, because the prosecution claimed that Mariles had shot his victim in the back while he was fleeing, and therefore the bullet had entered from above to below, whereas the defense maintained that it had been a fight. Consultants for the defense accepted that the bullet entered from below to above and argued that Mariles was standing beside his car door and Velázquez struck him from the upper part of the sidewalk. Prosecution witnesses found it difficult to justify how and why, if the builder was running down a slope, the bullet had entered from below to above, but they offered two hypotheses: Velázquez had slipped and was face down when he received the impact, or he was running with his thorax angled forward. As for the distance, the prosecution witnesses concluded that Mariles had fired from more than a meter (as the witnesses maintained), for otherwise the builder's clothes would have had gunpowder traces. However, the prosecution's experts claimed the bullet had been shot at a brief distance, because if it had been between one and five meters (as these witnesses calculated), the projectile would have crossed his body, but it had not.

c) **Cause of death**: It was necessary to determine whether Velázquez died because of complications inherent to the wounds produced by the bullet or whether he could have been saved had it not been for medical negligence; in the latter case, Mariles would be liable for the original wound but not the death. Experts for the prosecution alleged the former: Velázquez died from these complications (generalized peritonitis and pulmonary edema) because all wounds penetrating the abdomen can trigger peritonitis. In contrast, the defense attributed death to the poor quality of material to suture the wound they detected and asserted that the fate of the wound would have been different if the doctors had realized the bullet had produced two holes in the stomach and not just one, a bullet hole they did not see because it would have been necessary for the surgeons to make a surgical cut for exploratory purposes. The judge requested a third-party expert opinion, but his study was inconclusive.

In addition to the expert witnesses, the parties offered testimonies. For the prosecution, these were essential because, besides Velázquez's testimony, they had the accounts of the four eyewitnesses: the two Chapultepec Forest guards, the auxiliary policeman, and the builder's helper, who in the three-hour confrontation hearing stood by their statements. The defense objected to their testimonies. Their objection to that of Velázquez was that in his first statement, he had said only that he had a traffic incident with General Mariles, but later, he gave a more detailed statement, and the prosecution's experts considered it impossible he would have remembered such details. And those of the prosecution witnesses presented so many contradictions it seemed each of them had witnessed a different event. The defense insisted on the validity of Mariles's qualified confession, although the prosecution objected to it. Moreover, the defense presented testimonies of former Mexican presidents, ministers of state, authorities of foreign countries, priests, high-ranking military men and ordinary soldiers, and riding and sports teammates, who praised Humberto Mariles's sporting achievements and exemplary family life, in addition to declarations of Velázquez's immorality. They continued alleging that the incident, and especially the testimonies and experts for the prosecution, were part of a plan to harm the general, a long-standing victim of "political and military persecution."[220]

A year after the incident, Mariles declared that he had faith in justice and lamented that the society he had served all his life judged him harshly; he asked reporters to tell the truth to prevent public opinion from forming a different idea of the facts.[221] Journalists continued showing animosity. For instance, El Universal Gráfico questioned the praise of Mariles by his friends and warned justice could be "twisted" from corruption.[222]

At the end of the hearing, the prosecutor concluded that the defendant had committed murder with unfair advantage. According to Criminal Code Article 316, "advantage" is when the criminal was physically stronger than the victim or the victim was unarmed, when the defendant was superior in the weapons used or had greater skill in using them, when means were used that weakened the victim, or when the victim was unarmed or fallen and the other armed or standing. According to María de los Ángeles Mancera, these elements had been present: Mariles had greater physical strength, was armed, and his life was not threatened, for he had fired at a distance while his opponent was fleeing. She requested that he be sentenced to thirty years in prison (for qualified murder in Article 320, the code contemplated between twenty and forty years).

In contrast, the defense attorneys asserted that Mariles had acted in self-defense and asked for his acquittal. Since the self-defense exemption was not admitted, they asked as an alternative to consider that the builder's death had resulted from postsurgery complications, so the defendant was liable for only the original wound.[223]

On November 10, 1966, months after the constitutional deadline had passed, the Third Criminal Court ruled. One week earlier, the judges declared they had not yet studied the completed file sent by the Ninth Judge in charge of the instruction stage of the process and the draft judgment, José Alfonso Everardo Álvarez. The strangest part, according to some newspapers, was that one of them, Roberto Campos Cos, declared the same thing hours before the ruling was issued. According to *Excélsior* and *El Universal Gráfico*, Everardo Álvarez submitted the ruling draft to his colleagues at lunchtime, and in the afternoon, the matter was resolved.[224]

At the sentencing, the judges established that Mariles had education and sporting accomplishments; however, "the deceased was a person with little instruction and education, whose moral quality was accredited by the circumstance that although married, he had marital life with other women, whom he was accustomed to beating, constant drinking, and was argumentative."[225] It is understood they were referring to the temperament and violent antecedents, especially tied to other traffic incidents (because it made it possible to imagine his potential reaction at the event judged), but it was hardly surprising they issued a purely ethical judgment, alluding to a "moral quality" stemming from his marital relations.

In addition, they determined that Mariles had not acted in self-defense, nor had he killed in a quarrel, because the fight ended when the builder fled, and expert reports on the distance at which the shot had been fired and the fact that the bullet entered from his back, as well as the testimonies of the deceased and eyewitnesses, did not permit updating the self-defense exemption. Nevertheless, they did not believe it was qualified murder. They considered that advantage had to be examined from two viewpoints: objectively (the agent of the crime had to be in superior condition to the victim) and subjectively (the agent had to have awareness of his superiority). In other words, the presence of the above-mentioned elements in Criminal Code Article 316 was insufficient; instead, it was necessary for the defendant to have been aware of his advantage. It concluded that Mariles did not have this, because "after having felt offended, he was outraged and acted suddenly without awareness of the victim's inferiority." They alluded to various scj *tesis*, which denied the possibility of configuring advantage if the aggressor had no awareness of his superiority.[226] At that time, in various SCJ rulings, reference was made to this point. One of them, in 1939, was contrary to the logic of the Third Criminal Court, stating that it was not indispensable for the aggressor to reflect on the victim's situation of inferiority; the superiority of the offender sufficed.[227] Nevertheless, the rest of the *tesis* I located followed the same line as the ruling of the first-instance judges.[228]

To recap, the Third Criminal Court members did not consider it evident that Mariles had been aware of his advantage, to postulate in criminal matters "so that a qualification can be held to exist it had to be unquestionably proven and if there is doubt of its existence, for the application of the principle of being the most favorable for the defendant, it must be excluded."[229] Hence he was not found liable of qualified homicide. Finally, it denied the possibility of applying Article 305 of the code, because for this, they contended, it would have been necessary to establish that the wound caused by the bullet had not endangered the victim's life. Found liable for simple murder, he was sentenced to ten years in prison (the Criminal Code contemplated between eight and twenty years). The sentence was merciful.

The MP agent declared that she would appeal because the fact Mariles had shot a man trying to flee in the back had not been considered. The general professed that from the moment Judge Everardo Álvarez had taken over the Ninth Court, he heard the judge was determined to harm him and had pressured his two court colleagues to sign the ruling without having studied the case in depth. His attorneys insisted the same: The ruling had been hastily voted because, according to their estimates, the judges only had the file in view for half an hour. They affirmed that one of the judges was not even in the courtroom at that time.[230] Hence Mariles went back to what he had said earlier: He suggested it was all orchestrated by someone above the judges and even the TSJ magistrates, but he clarified he did not believe it was the nation's president. In a later interview, to congratulate the TSJ magistrates, he expressed his confidence that they would properly assess the evidence. He also wanted to win over the journalists, asserting that he bore no resentment because they had transmitted the information from official sources.[231]

The journalists' opinion on the sentence was not homogeneous. Some were in favor. *El Universal Gráfico* assured that "for the majority of attorneys," it was "the closest to the law that could be ruled."[232] *La Prensa* held the same in its headline: "Mariles was sentenced to 10 years with fair compliance with the law."[233] Days later, *Impacto* columnist Bill Llano described the judges' decision as "barely logical and . . . looks lenient" but also as "another symptom things are improving in Mexico," because before, idols, the influential, and wealthy escaped "justice," and Mariles "is an example of those three conditions."[234] However, in contrast, Fabián Morales, in his Zodiaco column, considered that "justice had taken a wrong step" and reminded readers ten years did not compare with the thirty requested by the prosecution.[235] Indeed, the prevailing impression was that the judges had not favored either side by adopting a medium term, and therefore, they had not been bought or pressured.

The TSJ Seventh Chamber heard the appeal and, on August 11, 1967, sentenced Mariles to twenty years in prison (the minimum for qualified murder in the Criminal Code).[236]

Arguments and Magistrates' Considerations

- *Grievances expressed by the defense:*
- Failed assessment of the evidence because magistrates had not conferred efficacy to evidence that had it and instead had given it to information that lacked it (contradictory statements of prosecution witnesses and the victim's second statement). Also, expert reports showed that the projectile had affected vital organs and the abdominal wounds produced peritonitis without any proof demonstrating that the generalization of the peritoneal infection had resulted from a botched surgical intervention.
- Noncompliance with the law and SCJ *tesis* establishing confessions should have full evidentiary value if they were not undermined by any evidence.
- Failure to apply the Criminal Code articles because of the denial of the self-defense exclusion or a quarrel.

- *Grievances expressed by the MP:*
- Lack of awareness of the danger represented by Mariles, revealed by prior antecedents, his response to being cut off, and his cruelty in striking the master builder when he was wounded and on the ground.
- Failure to apply the Criminal Code articles related to the murder committed with the qualification of advantage, because the defendant's superiority was proven (with the victim's and witnesses' testimonies and ballistics reports) and sufficient advantage had existed, without the need to reflect on the victim's inferiority.

- *Considerations in sentencing:*
- The defendant's guilt was demonstrated by his confession and the testimonies, and the validity of the deceased's second statement was accepted.
- Defense expert reports indicated the shot had been fired from the back at a distance greater than one meter, and they were closely related to other proof.
- The evidence contravened the defendant's statement and supported the prosecution witnesses' testimony.
- The magistrates deemed the claim admissible. They noted the difference between relative advantage (under Criminal Code Article 316, when the defendant acted with advantage but had run the risk of being killed or wounded) and absolute advantage (under Article 317, when the defendant had advantage but had not run a risk). In the adjudicated case, they considered that the second had occurred, the defendant with his "exacerbated displeasure" over the incident had provoked the clash, and noticed the victim "was not armed and was in fact fleeing," and without running any risk, the defendant had fired "with total advantage."

The medalist regarded it as an "absurd and unjust" decision and asserted that he was not a murderer because he had acted in self-defense and, an element not previously mentioned, had been defending his honor. "I would like to see one of those magistrates withstand, for almost an hour, the impertinence of a stranger who insults them, to see if with everything and their magistracy they not act as I did."[237] Two columnists from the magazine *Impacto* shared his indignation. Roberto Blanco Moheno claimed the Third Criminal Court judges had issued a "relatively just" decision as "a sentence for murder in a quarrel" could be, but the TSJ magistrates had abused their powers "to vent their rage on a prisoner and give a disproportionate, overly harsh sentence." He did not ask that the defendant be pardoned and described the impunity of personal position and ties of the influential as unacceptable, but he did ask that Mariles be judged as any other man, believing that the general's fame had harmed him and the judges had "used a heavy hand" to cover up other errors.[238] Columba Domínguez was more radical. Referring to Mariles, she claimed, "An honest, hardworking man, an exemplary Mexican, like thousands of others, he is suffering unjust imprisonment merely because he was the victim of unfair aggression against his dignity, honor, and life."[239]

After hearing the sentence, Humberto Mariles announced he would request the protection of federal justice. In December 1967 his attorneys presented the grounds for violation, which they published months later with an introduction by the Olympic champion. "This book contains the history of injustice," declared Mariles in a widely disseminated text, published in magazines like *Jueves de Excélsior* and *Impacto*.[240] He claimed to be respectful of the law: "A traitor, coward, or felon has nor never will come from the Heróico Colegio Militar. To be its son is to be loyal, and that loyalty is expressed above all in the profound, sincere conviction that respect and compliance with our Constitution is the only basis on which all of us together can build a Mexico that is greater, more respected, more worthy, more beautiful with each day." He expressed confidence in its due application: "How could I, then, not have faith in the justice of my fatherland, on which that Constitution is based?" And alluding to his training, he maintained he had acted in defense of his life and its honor.[241]

The *amparo* was admitted on January 17, 1968. Four of the grounds for violation—the first, second, third, and fifth—were virtually the same as the grievance presented in the appeal.[242] Here I discuss two central questions. The scj First Chamber coincided with the magistrates by deeming that the first-instance judges had indeed carefully studied the expert reports and rejected the possibility of considering—months after the incident, without examining the wound, and based on theoretical hypotheses—that some injuries had not been detected. Otherwise, the chamber could not imagine it had been murder in self-defense or even a quarrel because of the fact that the shot had entered the victim's back. As for the qualification of advantage, the chamber coincided: By getting out of his car, Mariles, with an "impulsive temperament," was very angry at being cut off and the exchange of offensive words, and in an uninterrupted sequence, he chased the builder and shot the man; thus it was not possible to accredit that he was fully aware of the need to protect himself from any danger. On March 14, 1969, by four unanimous votes, the chamber granted the *amparo* for the sole effect that the authority responsible would render void the appealed judgment and issue a new judgment eliminating the advantage qualification, leaving in place the first-instance punishment of ten years of prison for simple homicide.[243]

The tsj Seventh Chamber issued the new verdict on April 20, 1969. Months had elapsed since Mariles was arrested, so he would not serve ten years of prison but barely eight (minus the months of parole). Informed of the sentence, and after thanking his friends for their support, the general appeared resigned, but he reiterated that "as a man and a soldier," he had acted in self-defense of his honor.[244]

In early May he was transferred to Santa Martha Acatitla.[245] He spent six years in this prison because he was awarded the right to parole. When released on June 14, 1971, the prisoners sang "Las golondrinas" (a traditional farewell song), the guards presented arms and played the bugle, and the official in charge declared, "We hope you give us another gold medal at the Munich Olympics." It was a triumphant exit. The first thing he did was to visit the presidential residence of Los Pinos to deliver a letter of gratitude to Luis Echeverría. Then he went to the cemetery to thank former President Manuel Ávila Camacho. Various public figures organized celebrations in his honor. Mariles claimed to have job offers in the United States and Canada, but he expressed his desire to remain in Mexico and train a team for the Olympics.[246] One year later his participation was announced in the parade commemorating the Revolution, held annually on November 20.[247]

No one ever imagined the rider would soon encounter another obstacle. On November 28, 1972, he was arrested in Paris with five suitcases containing 60 kilos (132 pounds) of heroin valued at U.S.$15 million. Seven other alleged members of a ring smuggling drugs from Europe to the United States through Latin America were arrested. Mariles's participation was key because it was assumed that, since he had a diplomatic passport and his baggage was not checked, he could pass customs. He claimed his innocence and argued that he was transporting the suitcases as a favor for some friends, saying, "I didn't even look at what was inside because I'm not curious."[248] His attorneys again spoke of a trap: The government had sent him unexpectedly and unjustifiably to Paris; someone had planned everything.[249] Mexican newspapers didn't miss a beat and started a new onslaught. They referred to the earlier case and claimed he had started drug trafficking in prison, and for some time the Federal Police and Federal Bureau of Investigation (FBI) were carefully monitoring him.[250] Humberto Mariles was taken to La Santé Prison, facing a sentence of ten to twenty years in prison. He never got to trial. On December 6, 1972, he was found dead in his cell. Speculations and rumors mentioned suicide, stroke, or assassination. The autopsy did not dispel doubts. The Olympic champion's remains arrived in Mexico on December 9, and he was given a wake with the attendance of figures in politics, the army, and sports.[251]

Humberto Mariles was a controversial personage. His trial was equally controversial. Of all the cases studied here, it generated the most talk of influence peddling and even corruption. His trial clearly falls into the category of "difficult or controversial" cases, because the first- and second-instance judges of local jurisdiction disagreed, and so did the SCJ ministers. The prosecution did not agree with the first judgment, the defense disagreed with all the rulings, the second sentence received no support, and the final judgment imposed a middle stance like the first, which also left considerable dissatisfaction.

ROBBERY AND DEATH

In the late 1920s the country was regaining political stability; the creation of the Partido Nacional Revolucionario heralded a new age and the peaceful alternation of power. However, the memory of a city occupied by revolutionary factions that, to preserve order, had resorted to emergency laws, summary trials, and executions was still fresh. The police had been debilitated, and gun possession was widespread. As in the United States, gangs of elegantly attired and well-armed individuals arose. This had repercussions in the following decades. Robberies, which had rarely been committed with violence in the past, involved increasingly greater force and less ingenuity.

Murders connected with robbery sparked concern and indignation. Society could explain or justify other types of homicide, but it drastically condemned those resulting from greed. Criminal Code penalties for homicide varied with time; qualified homicide merited thirty to twenty years of prison (Article 320) in the 1930s, when the punishment for robbery ranged from two to ten years imprisonment, depending on the value of stolen property. Up to three years were added if the homicide was committed with violence and three more years if committed in a home or by a worker against his boss, a house guest, or dinner guest, among other considerations (Articles 370–74, 381). Murders committed during a robbery had to be punished under the hypothetical case of accumulation, in which penalties were the sum of the sentences for each crime; therefore, they approached the maximum limit permitted by law.[252]

The severity of legislators and judges was accompanied by equally harsh judgments on the part of society, reflected in community statements and reporters' opinions. Examples are the trials of two gangs that killed the victim they robbed, one consisting of Alberto Gallegos and his two accomplices, the other of Gonzalo Ortiz Ordaz, María Elena Blanco, and two underlings. In the first case, the killers were men and the victim a woman; in the second, a couple victimized a man. The differences bring up reflections on the weight of gender in the treatment of the defendants. In addition, one of Gallegos's accomplices was categorized as Indigenous, so racial prejudices emerged as well.

"Buffoonery with Tragic Aspects"

On February 23, 1932, a street sweeper notified authorities that the lights in the home of Jacinta Aznar, at Insurgentes no. 17, had been on for more than a month and a strong odor was coming from the door. Accompanied by reporters and photographers, the police found the owner's half-burned body covered by a bedspread.[253] The stench was so overpowering they had to wear gas masks. That same afternoon El Universal Gráfico published images of the deceased's home and of her, alive and dead. The next day the paper gave a full-page spread to the news (fig. 13). Albeit similar, the photographic composition had two differences: She appeared full-length, and forensic expert Benjamín Martínez, whose presence indicated the investigation had begun, was included on a smaller scale. The crime became infamous. Journalist Manuel Espejel Álvarez claimed it served as a pretext for "reportorial fantasy," and newspapers permitted the participation of readers. "Everyone turned out to be close friends of 'Chinta' and were familiar with unpublished details."[254]

Neither the photos nor the testimonies made Jacinta Aznar y González Gutiérrez seem likable. Excélsior described her as "one of the outstanding beauties of Mexico." At death she was forty-five. A devout Catholic, she came from a well-heeled, notable family from Yucatán and "suffered a sort of delirium of grandeur." She studied in the best schools in Mexico and abroad, including universities like Cambridge and the Sorbonne, and spoke English, French, and Italian. She inherited money and properties in Mérida and lived off their rents, even though several houses were mortgaged. She rubbed shoulders with politicians, diplomats, and artists, and rumor had it she was a spy for the Germans in World War I, a friend of dictator Primo de Rivera, and lover of the king of Spain. She enjoyed traveling and going to movies, the theater, and Sanborns, but her bad temper distanced her from family and friends; she often fired domestic workers "because she couldn't stand them." The last letter she wrote was addressed to Miguel de Unamuno, whom she reproached for criticizing monarch Alfonso XIII.[255]

Others, like Manuel Espejel y Álvarez and Xavier Sorondo, were blunter in their characterization. The first, La Prensa contributor and editor of the book in which Gallegos described his crime, wrote of the victim, "She entered the less flowery, but flatter, path of disillusioned, moody, neurasthenic woman

Fig. 13. "Espeluznante crimen" (Chilling crime). El Universal Gráfico, February 23, 1932, front page. AGENCIA ©EL UNIVERSAL.

who distances herself from her relatives and friends because she did not want to answer indiscreet questions, who quarrels for futile reasons with the servants and people whose services she needs." He remarked on her solitude and disillusionment: "She left her house, without any accompaniment, and returned the same, alone and bored, with that irritation of the old maid who had been unable to realize her dream in life."[256] The second, an Excélsior columnist, described her as a spinster who looked older than she was, with an "irascible and unpredictable" temperament, isolated even from her family and willing to withstand the "material encumbrances" of a house over the company of servants. He added that she was an independent woman, who would not tolerate constraints and who behaved in society "with the same intemperance as a general with his troops on the battlefield." He made veiled allusions to gender and ultimately explicitly said she came and went with masculine freedom.[257]

In the novel Ensayo de un crimen (Rehearsal for a crime), written almost ten years later, Rodolfo Usigli presents a similar image. Jacinta Aznar inspired the character of Patricia Terrazas, who stirred a profound desire in the protagonist, Roberto de la Cruz, to kill her. In a few lines, Usigli details the appearance and personality of the woman from Chihuahua (unlike Jacinta Aznar, who was from Yucatán): "She could be forty, maybe forty-five, although a closer examination produced the vertigo of the unfathomable, and it felt like, under the pancake makeup that covered her face, Patricia Terrazas might have been a thousand." Her headwear "seemed plucked from a nineteenth-century family museum and to smell of mothballs," especially her alarming hats, which "elicited that mistrust of wonder blended with mockery and inquiry." Usigli also needed a few words to outline her personality: She presented herself with "the accented and shrill singsong of her grating voice," her delirium of grandeur always on display, as she bragged about her ties with kings of Spain. She had no friends. "I don't have live-in servants because I can't stand them. I live alone with my memories and my hopes," she confessed to Roberto de la Cruz.[258] With simpler costumes, but a similar attitude, she is represented in Luis Buñuel's film based on the novel and filmed in 1955, Ensayo de un crimen (The criminal life of Archibaldo de la Cruz). The vulgarity comes through in her conduct more than her appearance.

Initial inquiries revealed that the crime was committed on January 22, the date of the newspaper found in her bedroom, while those from the next day and thereafter were piled up outside the front door. It was also known that the victim had succumbed to blows to her head. Neighbors and acquaintances attested to her character and made veiled suggestions she was a lesbian. Finally, a promising clue emerged: a handwritten note signed on January 19 by Alberto Gallegos Sánchez, a photography lighting technician who had gone by Aznar's house and, not finding her, left a note saying he would come back the next day.[259]

For days the police followed him. Surprisingly, Gallegos called the police chief and offered information on the crime. According to Excélsior, the photographer, "of natural and astute intelligence," must have realized he was being shadowed by policemen and "understood he was lost, that they suspected him, and only a stroke of true astuteness could save him."[260] He stated that he had met Jacinta Aznar at the post office; she liked the photos he showed her at the cashier's and requested his service. She had him go to her house. When he arrived, she was with a man, Paco "El Elegante." She asked the photographer for some blowups, and when he returned hours later to deliver them, no one opened the door, so he left the note the police found. The next day Gallegos opened the door and saw Jacinta Aznar sprawled on the floor, asking for water for some pills. He went for a glass and found her dead when he returned; when he got closer, he became stained with her blood. He fled. Fear had prevented him from calling the police, together with the visit and threats of El Elegante.[261]

Journalists found his account unconvincing. They believed Paco could not have killed Jacinta Aznar while Gallegos went for water, and if he had struck her earlier, Gallegos would have noticed, and she would not have been able to speak or drink water. Also, the date on the note (January 19) did not coincide with when the photographer claimed he left it (January 22). They suspected he had killed the wealthy woman and later returned to her house to move the body (which would explain the bedspreads found tied in a bundle), but he did not do so because the body was beginning to decompose. The reporter offered other clues: He assumed Gallegos had taken expensive jewelry, as the deceased had costume jewelry but also some genuine pieces. The matter of the key was especially intriguing because it was unclear how the alleged killer had obtained it.[262]

Reporters actively participated in the investigation and made conjectures. Espejel Álvarez claimed "they had snuck into the cells," and by talking to the accused, "they heard from his lips the lesson learned, noting tremendous contradictions in his account."[263] One political cartoon, published on March 12 in *Excélsior*, rendered Jacinta as a skull, leaving no doubt as to the press's reaction.

On February 27 Alberto Gallegos was arrested. After the arrest, the investigation seemed to be stalled. However, newspapers kept receiving letters and news from readers. Some considered Gallegos capable of killing for money: One asserted that the photographer offered to kill his brother-in-law for 200 pesos. Another heard him speak of "a rich old lady" with whom he'd had a romance and asked him, "Are you going to inherit?" Gallegos responded, "A heavy blow is enough."[264]

On March 3 the photographer was accused and made his preliminary statement in front of the judge. The courtroom could not accommodate all the onlookers. According to *La Prensa*, among others, there were clerks and employees of the tribunal and pretty girls who didn't want to miss out on the spectacle. Also present was legendary José Menéndez (El Hombre del Corbatón) and a fortune teller who promised to announce, with the help of his crystal ball, whether the accused was guilty or innocent.[265] Complying with the constitutional deadline, on March 5 the judge issued the *auto de formal prisión*. "I hope in the course of the investigations I manage to overturn all the accusations and prove I am innocent," Gallegos declared.[266]

Pedro Alberto Gallegos Sánchez, known as "El Conde Federico" (Count Federico), was thirty, single, tall, slim, with light-brown skin, and as he described himself, "eloquent." Born in Amecameca, State of Mexico, his father, the town mayor and "one of the richest local merchants," had satisfied all his whims. After the Revolution broke out, he and his family moved to Mexico City because their property was taken from them. They bought clothing stalls in covered markets, and Alberto ran one of them. Later, he decided to go to the United States, where he met a woman; he claimed he was arrested because he lived with her in various states without marrying her and thus had violated the Mann Law (passed in 1910 to curtail the exploitation of white women by prohibiting transporting them from one state to another for "immoral purposes"). After serving his sentence, he was deported. Back in Mexico City, he got a job in a photography laboratory as a sales agent promoting large-scale, well-lit portraits, which he illuminated.[267]

From the start, journalists saddled Gallegos with the death of Jacinta Aznar. *El Universal Gráfico* and *La Prensa* considered his "temperament extremely erotic," with a "hidden fascination for atrocious savagery," and alleged that his "perverse urges" prevented him from escaping the impulse that women aroused in him.[268] The first paper recommended he be given a psychoanalytic test and "classified among instinctive sexual perverts, without any idealism, who only satisfied their animality, with the absolute totality in pleasure." In a tone reminiscent of Cesare Lombroso, it claimed he possessed "the evil and innate wildness of primitive man."[269] In Sorondo's words, he represented criminals who were as dangerous as a hungry tiger and possessed "sadistic inclinations" but at moments acted with "abnormal tenderness" and possessed a "sentimentality that makes them cry like children seeking maternal protection."[270] *Excélsior* noted the transition from coldness and cynicism to tears or repentance, such as in the description of his entry into the crime scene: "He could not conceal his emotion, although seconds later and being, as he is, a man of resources, was calm and smiling."[271]

In sum, the photographer was presented as the incarnation of the true type of Lombroso's criminal, cynical, lying, phony, whiny, bloody, cruel, and with a powerful mental capacity for crime, an alert intelligence for criminality, a strong will, and enormous control of nerves. Catalina D'Erzell described him in Excélsior as a hardened criminal, who carried the burden of a corpse without any need to confess: "The cynicism, hypocrisy, lies are new crimes that pile up on his crime. In his brain and soul, there is more putrefaction than in the mutilated body of his victim."[272]

Medical examiners assigned by the MP found in Gallegos "stigmas of degeneration" and an excessive development of his face that made him macrocephalic. They described him as a healthy and normal individual, intelligent but lacking culture, with perfect use of reason and memory, capable of controlling emotions and impressions, of "extremely sexual" temperament, and who probably consumed drugs.[273]

Roberto de la Cruz, protagonist of the novel Ensayo de un crimen, met José Asturias (Alberto Gallegos) on the day of the death of Patricia Terrazas (Jacinta Aznar). Having planned the perfect crime, Roberto went to her apartment to kill her. He was about to open the door with the key she had given him when he saw someone leaving. He described the man as tall and vulgar, with an "enormous and hairy" hand, "big ears and a long, simian face with strangely unpleasant features."[274]

The homicide caused profound concern in society. Júbilo reported in his column Acotaciones del Momento in El Universal Gráfico that he had returned after several days of vacation, and the papers awaiting him made him think "Mexico City was in a bloody deluge," adding, "Frankly the impression is strong, and you don't need to be fainthearted to shudder with fear. The atmosphere is saturated with crime. The newspapers, mirrors of public conscience, speak of nothing else. The people, the same. People must realize they are murderable."[275] Contributor don Catarino concluded in another section of the same daily: "The passion with which all social classes in the Republic follow the trial of the sensational murder are unprecedented in the history of crime in Mexico."[276] Such was the proliferation of news that one newspaper spoke of an exploitation of scandal, sensationalism, and morbid interest in dailies and of a betrayal of the trust of parents who allowed issues to enter their homes.[277]

They spoke of endemic and each day more alarming criminality, which prompted fear among capital dwellers for their lives and property. The attorney general denied a rise in crimes but admitted that cruelty in committing them had increased.[278] Finally, there were calls for harsher laws and the adoption of the death penalty, which had been abolished in 1929, only three years earlier.[279] For jurists, journalists, and citizens, it was "severe and hateful" or a "sad necessity," but essential for its efficacy and the state of Mexican prisons.[280] According to Pedro Gringoire, it was theoretically possible to suppress the death penalty in a "stage of social, judicial, and criminal evolution, which we haven't yet reached"; therefore, "by introducing that abolition into our code, legislators put the dome before the foundations."[281] It was suggested the adoption had the support of Congress. Voices against it were weak.[282]

Significantly, talk focused on a certain type of criminals. Columnist RIP-RIP considered the difference to mark the type of victim or motive. He regarded those who deserved capital punishment as those who terminated the lives of old people or women or who killed to rob and used "means denouncing the absolute lack of any sense of morality."[283] According to Xavier Sorondo, the difference straddled both the possibility of reforming the killer and the need to eliminate a degenerate and dangerous killer (close to the description of Lombroso's innate criminal).[284] Some authors pointed to the need to adjust law and practice. A La Prensa editorialist contended that ley fuga (guards killing a prisoner to prevent his escape) had become an aspiration of a society aware of prison failures and that saw the use of violence on criminals who had acted violently as a natural consequence.[285] Manuel González Ramírez maintained that Mexicans "romantically" intended to resolve their problems with the law, but they often were living "on the fringes of the precept"; hence abolitionists should know that "with or without a prohibitive law," criminals would be executed when "deemed necessary." In his opinion, it was not a legislative problem, but a cultural matter.[286] Sorondo coincided with the idea that, in any case, criminals were executed, but he warned that ley fuga did not have the same impact as execution from a court sentence because it made "the official executioner into a low-life thug who attacks his defenseless victim," who in turn became a "brave man whose blood must be avenged."[287]

The use of metal pipes as weapons also drew attention at this time, in contrast to the long-standing concern over the proliferation of firearms after the Revolution. A political cartoon by Ernesto García Cabral in Excélsior suggests this, showing a man buying a pipe instead of a gun. In his column, Júbilo referred to the identification of the Mexican with his gun, which he was using as an object to influence others, like an amulet or even a decoration. The gun's use was widespread, showing it was sufficient to "accredit their nationality." Continuing the irony, he held that the pipe represented an evolution, perhaps "downward," but clearly a change regarding the revolutionary period's "delirious love" for guns and, in this sense, "a firm step toward the real calm following bellicose agitation."[288]

The investigation ended with Gallegos's arrest. According to Manuel Espejel Álvarez, irregularities had been committed, especially overlooking what the defendant had said about Paco.[289] The accused was charged with intentional homicide, robbery, and damage to the property of others. The proceeding was headed by Juan Antonio Fernández Vera, second judge of the First Criminal Court. Initially, the prosecutor was Juan López Moctezuma, but he was replaced by Luis Gonzaga Corona Redondo. The defendants had various attorneys: the head of the Public Defender's Office, Guillermo Schultz, as well as Raúl Banuet and Eduardo Mac-Gregor. Additionally, given that criminal law allowed the appointment of representatives without a law degree, and perhaps to be able to have contact with his mother in prison, Gallegos named her as his attorney.

When the instruction phase began, the judge ordered a second reconstruction of the crime, which generated more expectation than the first. Benjamín Martínez dominated the scene.[290] The defendant arrived surrounded by policemen, responsible for safeguarding him from "the people's ire."[291] Reporters and photographers portrayed the crime scene for readers and spectators (fig. 14).

The judge and police were as certain of the photographer's guilt as they were of the existence of accomplices. Soon it was discovered that El Elegante existed, and he was Paco Alvear, count of La Cortina, who had visited the victim before returning to Madrid. His possible intervention in the crime was ruled out, and the list of suspects was reduced to two: the building's caretaker (mozo) Eugenio Montiel and a work colleague of Gallegos's, Juan Sánchez Trinidad. The former was described by Excélsior as an individual of medium height, dark-skinned, "ruddy," and "pure Indigenous type," of the humble class, with hirsute hair and a short "shower" of mustache hairs. El Universal Gráfico presented him as a "totally ignorant, small-town bricklayer."[292]

In his statement and in the confrontation hearing, Montiel admitted the defendant had offered him money to keep quiet about seeing him enter the house, and he accepted it but asked him to wait until January 22, his day off. However, the photographer did not wait and came back the same day. Montiel

Fig. 14. "La casa del crimen" (The house of crime). El Universal Gráfico, March 10, 1932, front page. AGENCIA ©EL UNIVERSAL.

stated that he saw Gallegos knock on Aznar's door, accompanied by Sánchez Trinidad, and when she opened the door, the photographer hit her. "I shouted at them not to hurt her; but the tall guy (Gallegos) sent me away with an insult, and the short guy (Sánchez) pointed a gun at me and told me to keep quiet, otherwise he'd shoot me." He said they took the valuables, and when they left, they threatened him again and gave him 200 pesos, which he used to buy the turkeys he served at his wedding. He gave his reason for confessing as "the weight on my conscience; I wanted to get rid of that remorse."[293] La Prensa reported that according to Montiel, before leaving, the killers raped the victim; this aroused "a shiver of indignation."[294]

The alleged accomplice, Juan Sánchez Trinidad, known as "El Pelón" (Baldie), was the only one who had spoken well of Gallegos after his arrest. He believed the photographer was innocent because "he treated everyone well and only had the weakness of being liked by women he flattered." He didn't mess with his buddy, and journalists didn't mess with him. They described Sánchez Trinidad as an insignificant man, short, skinny, pale, who looked consumptive and feeble, with a wide forehead, round bulging eyes, and a small mustache. Photographers were more generous with him; not only did they capture him frontally, seated, dressed in a suit, but they also included his wedding picture, marrying a young woman dressed in white (even if it was not as recent as Montiel's, whose wedding was not included). Based on the images, it seemed strange a man like this could have participated in the crime. Xavier Sorondo described him as a rodent (small, of soft and courteous speech and measured gestures) who seemed to be a civilized fellow incapable of breaking the law.[295] El Pelón denied his participation, and in the confrontation hearing, he claimed Montiel was lying: "He's mistaken, he's confusing me with someone else; it's not true."[296]

Montiel and Sánchez Trinidad appeared before the judge on March 15. Not even a day had passed when the latter retracted his initial statement and blamed Gallegos. He maintained that he had accompanied the photographer to leave the photos, but upon arriving, Gallegos struck the victim and he was hypnotized by fear; according to El Universal Gráfico, when he finished his declaration, filled with fear, he begged to be locked up far from the killer.[297] La Prensa offered another version: When Gallegos heard his colleague's "sincere confession," he covered his face with his hands and collapsed.[298] On March 18 the judge issued the auto de formal prisión for the alleged accomplices in the murder of Jacinta Aznar.[299]

After Sánchez Trinidad confessed, Gallegos offered to tell the truth in exchange for money. He claimed the subdirector of Belem Prison had persuaded him to confess and stop two innocent people from being charged with the crime. His version of the encounters with Jacinta Aznar, his first visit and that of January 21, was the same, but the account of what happened the next day was different. Paco ceased to exist. Gallegos revealed that while he was waiting to be paid for the blowups, he saw some diamond earrings, a ring, and a necklace. "The cursed idea of robbery took hold of me, feeling something horrible," he said. He took the jewelry; she surprised him and went to the balcony to call for help. He covered her mouth, and in the scuffle, she was hit by the piano. She screamed even more, and he struck her with a wooden rolling pin. Then he cleaned up a bit, looked for more jewelry and money, and left. "What I did was in a moment of madness, fear, and I will never be able to explain how I committed that crime."[300]

In response, Sánchez Trinidad changed his statement. He said he had remained in the entrance hall because Gallegos left him there. He had heard the photographer chatting with Jacinta Aznar, followed by a struggle and more noise, so he left the house. In this new version, he was no longer a direct but an indirect witness.[301]

Two days later the trial took a different turn, described by *Excélsior* as "buffoonery with tragic aspects." The photographer denied what was said in his letter and maintained that he had written it not to confess his guilt, but to prove his innocence. He did so theatrically; he took the text, passed a matched across the back side, and the following words appeared: "Everything I declare here is false, I am innocent."[302] According to *La Prensa*, the public at the hearing could not believe it and described the defendant as a "comical," crazy, "unmitigated fraud." It was necessary, concluded the reporter, to give him a medical exam.[303] *El Universal Gráfico* had another explanation: Gallegos declared he alone was liable so his accomplices would not need to identify him as the main actor and withdraw their statements, as Sánchez Trinidad had done.[304] But Montiel did not do the same; instead, he expanded his statement, claiming he had indeed participated in looting.[305]

A new change in testimonies led *Excélsior* to indignation, now describing the buffoonery as "the trial of liars."[306] Montiel contended that he did not know Gallegos and presented witnesses who claimed he had stopped working at Aznar's house before the murder, and between January 17 and 22 he was doing construction work.[307] In an ironic tone, the reporter pointed out that believing these last statements—Montiel doing construction work, Sán-chez in the waiting room, and Gallegos innocent—would have people think the victim had committed suicide by hitting herself with a pipe.[308] Political cartoons soon appeared. *Excélsior* published one showing a little girl who preferred reading about Gallegos to other stories, since, in her words, this story is more fantastic.

In early April the psychological report came out. The prosecutor's expert concluded that Gallegos was a microcephalic individual (with a reduced cra-nial cavity) but normal physically and mentally. He had an athletic body, great intelligence, and an astounding memory but lacked emotions. In a tone sim-ilar to that of journalists, the expert maintained that Gallegos had an elevated sex drive.[309] As for Montiel, just like the journalists, he affirmed that the man was coarse and ignorant, and he also held that Montiel presented signs of chronic alcoholism and degeneration, in concordance with what was thought of Indigenous people.[310] In the late nineteenth and early twentieth centuries diverse authors believed the *pueblo bajo*, or Indigenous race, presented signs of degeneration. Degeneration theory held that alcoholism and malnutrition weakened individuals and that the propensity to alcoholism and illness was inherited, resulting in an ever more pathologically decrepit race, both phys-ically and morally.

The defendants' statements kept changing. Montiel retracted what he had said days earlier. *El Universal Gráfico* opined that everyone wanted the same end: lying to confuse justice and "to become heroes in a judicial error, instead of the role of murderers which is their truth."[311] However, in contrast to the existing evidence of Gallegos's alleged accomplices, the proof against the photographer was considerable and varied. The owner of a pawnshop claimed Gallegos sold him the jewelry. It was also said he had committed other murders, and a judge in Córdoba sent the records of an investigation on a photographer's death.[312]

Three months after the trial began, the file was placed before the parties to the litigation, who had ten days to present evidence.[313] Before the deadline, Gallegos, in his memoirs, changed his version of the facts. He claimed he met Aznar on a streetcar and showed her his photos, and she asked him to do a job for her. He began to flatter her to get more work, and when he realized she was single and had money, he decided to woo her. They spent the night together. Days later, in the street, a man approached them; she told Gallegos the man was her cousin Paco and asked him to pretend not to know her. Hours later, the photographer went to visit her, and when he didn't find her home, he wrote a message as if it were a work visit. When he returned, the same man was there. Gallegos and Aznar pretended to negotiate the price of photos. As Paco said goodbye, she went to the door with him, and on the way, they argued; he asked her for money and to sign some papers.

The next day, January 22, she confessed that Paco wasn't her cousin, but rather the father of a son she'd had in Europe, a hustler who was now threatening her because he couldn't accept her being with another man. The doorbell rang and it was Paco. Jacinta asked him to wait in the garage. He heard them quarrel and then the visitor left. He entered the dining room, where everything was knocked over and she was dying, so he fled to avoid being blamed. To his surprise, later Montiel and Sánchez falsely accused him.[314]

The defense attorneys alleged that they had tried to "put the criminal on the path of truth, which could have been more favorable than that of lies and farces," but they gave up because this was impossible to achieve.[315] A public defender, Alfonso J. Cruz, was appointed.[316]

For Gallegos, the MP agent requested twenty-nine years and eight months of prison for the punishment of thirteen to twenty years that corresponded to qualified murder (committed with premeditation, treachery, and advantage) plus robbery. This was close to the maximum sentencing limit for prison, which was thirty years. As for Montiel, the agent did not regard him as the perpetrator of the murder, but rather as an accomplice (who participated by helping the perpetrator commit the crime) and requested a sentence of twenty years. In contrast, he considered Sánchez Trinidad as having only been an accessory (encubridor, who, after committing a crime and without having participated, received the product of the crime or hid it), for which the Criminal Code contemplated between fifteen days and two years of prison (Article 400). The defense attorneys proclaimed the innocence of their clients and called for acquittal.[317]

The hearing was held on December 14 and 15, 1932. The First Criminal Court was also composed of Ángel Escalante and Jesús Zavala. As in the days of juries, crowds attended to see the defendant and hear the allegations; the police should have prevented the crowd from entering, permitting access only to the group that fit in the courtroom.[318] The prosecutors were Carlos Franco Sodi and Miguel Desentis González. Diverse figures paraded through the defense. A woman, Gloria Mejía Fernández Pentanes, represented Sánchez Trinidad. Needless to say, women had a short career in the courtroom; only four years earlier, a female attorney had represented a defendant for the first time, at least in a public trial. Montiel was defended by Luis Noyola, and Gallegos by Alfonso J. Cruz. (Gallegos intended to hire Raúl Carrancá y Trujillo, but he declined because of his friendship with Aznar.)

The hearing opened with the reading of the file; then the attorneys participated. Prosecutor Desentis González began by apologizing to the public, whom he feared were disappointed because the end of the jury trial "deprived the speaker of all literary and elegant ornament, to leave cut-and-dried language without rhetoric in its place." In a tone reminiscent of the positivist school, with his use of terms from the natural sciences for the explanation of social phenomena and comparison of society to a living being, he disclosed, "Society in the instinct of preservation deduces those who harm it." Then he delved into the matter. He began with the accusation against Gallegos and Montiel and listed the evidence that proved they had been in Jacinta Aznar's house on the day of her death. He referred to Montiel as a wily Indigenous man, words also used by *Excélsior*, which reveal the racial prejudice and longstanding conviction that members of the Indigenous race, by nature and heritage, were liars and untrustworthy. When he got to Sánchez Trinidad, he asserted that there was insufficient evidence to condemn him as a perpetrator (Sánchez Trinidad had confessed only that he had accompanied his friend Gallegos to the victim's house, and Montiel's statement was the sole evidence against him). Therefore, he was accused of concealment (*encubrimiento*).[319]

Then it was the defense's turn. Luis Noyola, Montiel's attorney, maintained that his confession had been obtained with torture and that the contradictions demonstrated he had not been in the room. He asked the judges to act as the jury had: They never condemned an innocent man, and given the risk of doing so, they preferred to acquit a defendant. Gloria Mejía Fernández based her defense on Sánchez Trinidad's weakness: "He is an emaciated man, without will, who is useless; and Gallegos, the strong man, could not accept a doll like him as an accomplice." She added, "Criminals only admit people who can be useful to them, and Sánchez wasn't." Furthermore, she claimed that the testimonies of guilt had been obtained by force and supported her client's last version. Later, she took advantage of her situation as a woman and asked for compassion toward the defendant's mother. She began by admitting her audacity in facing a tribunal composed of men experienced in criminal law: "Here, sirs, where I feel I am surrounded by wise men, I think I am smaller; nevertheless, in the name of a woman's and mother's tears, which at these moments are spilling there in Oaxaca, for this man who is innocent, I ask for clemency for him and I trust that you, lord judges, will acquit this poor wretch and will not condemn someone who has not been guilty." Therefore, unlike Desentis González, she was not resigned to abandoning the strategy and style of jury trials, and thus she did not disappoint the public in attendance.

Then it was the turn of Alfonso J. Cruz, Gallegos's defense attorney, who requested clemency. He described the suffering his client had endured since being arrested, and in Gallegos's name, he asked for the forgiveness of society and the officials for the successive "fanciful statements" issued because of poor advice and "all imaginable tortures." Therefore, with the argument of torture, he discarded the first statements and relied on the last version, maintaining his client's innocence.[320] He was neither the first nor the last to argue that the confession had been extracted by force.

The defendants maintained their innocence. Interest was already focused on those who would receive the longest sentences: Gallegos and Montiel. Sánchez Trinidad had ceased to attract attention and did not even win a place in the gallery of portraits; only the first two were photographed behind bars, concerned about their fate. They insisted on the falseness of the confession. Montiel described the circumstances under which it had been forced out of him. Gallegos held that he had received threats of being hung by his thumbs until death or tied up with his intestines. They introduced doubt in the judges because the only evidence against them was their own statements and the accusations of their supposed partners in crime or torment. In the end, Gallegos Sánchez addressed his judges: "You'll acquit me because I swear again, I didn't kill that lady, nor did I need to kill [her]."[321] The newspapers made their position clear, as illustrated by a political cartoon showing Gallegos, with his hands dripping blood, declaring, "I swear to God and my beloved parents that I didn't kill Miss Aznar."[322]

The First Criminal Court issued a sentence on January 12, 1933. It condemned Gallegos to twenty-two years of prison (twenty for homicide, two for robbery), Montiel to eighteen years and six months (for co-perpetration in homicide and robbery), and Sánchez to two years (the maximum for concealment).

There was unanimity only on Gallegos; in the cases of the other two defendants, Judge Ángel Escalante issued a dissenting vote. He believed they must be acquitted. In accordance with the police investigation, he noted that the crime had been committed on January 22 and estimated it had occurred between ten and twelve in the day, as indicated by the remains of breakfast found in the kitchen and the house clothes worn by Jacinta Aznar. Also in accord with investigation results, he considered that the victim had received the first blow from the back and had died immediately. This made it clear Montiel had lied in his confession, because he claimed the crime had been committed at night and he had heard Aznar utter some words before dying. Therefore, the confession was implausible, and the defendant also stated it had been extracted with torture. The absence of the servant on the day of the crime, continued Escalante, was accredited by the statements of the witnesses who assured they had only seen him on January 8, the only day he worked for Aznar, as well as of those who avowed that he had worked with them on a construction site far away on the day of the crime and before that. Therefore, in the judge's opinion, there was no complete certainty of Montiel's participation, and under Article 247 of the Procedure Code ("in case of doubt [the defendant] must be acquitted"), he declared acquittal.

He basically contended the same in the case of Sánchez Trinidad. After assessing the evidence and facts, he came to a logical conclusion: Since there was insufficient evidence of the defendant's guilt as perpetrator, the solution was not to accuse him of concealment to thus ensure punishment for at least a lesser crime. The judge asserted that if his presence at the crime had been established, he should have been accused as a co-perpetrator and not as a concealer, and if the belief was that he was not there, he should not have been accused of anything because "he couldn't cover up what he didn't hear or know."[323]

According to *Excélsior*, the Gallegos sentence caused indignation in the community, which considered it too merciful and held that if capital punishment were still in force, he surely would have received the death penalty.[324]

The condemned men filed appeals. Gallegos referred to his good behavior in prison, arguing that he was peaceful, disciplined, and obedient; read and wrote letters for the illiterate; and helped his fellow inmates write their legal texts and gave them classes in English, mechanics, and photography. He also claimed there was no evidence against him and blamed the false accusations on journalists trying to attract readers. Nevertheless, in February 1933 the TSJ Fifth Chamber confirmed the sentence issued by the criminal court.[325] Apparently, Count Federico was the only one who remained in prison, because Montiel's sentence had been reversed, and by that time Sánchez Trinidad was almost finished serving his sentence.[326]

The photographer was to be sent to Islas Marías. To avoid enforcement of the sentence, his mother and legal representative filed an appeal. It argued the violation of constitutional Articles 14, 16, and 20 and held that there was insufficient evidence to convict him and that given any doubt, he should have been acquitted.[327] While he awaited the resolution, the debate over the death penalty gained importance. In favor of it, Don Catarino wrote, "The only death penalty that must be abolished is that of peaceful, respectable, and useful persons to society, who live in terror, fearing falling prey to the cleverly wielded pipe blows of troglodyte citizens."[328] The community continued to agree, as evidenced in the results of a new survey published by La Prensa.[329] However, jurists such as Francisco de Paula Herrasti, Emilio Pardo Aspe, and others were opposed and asserted that the statistics did not show a reduction in criminality in the nations where and periods when capital punishment had been suspended.[330] Conversely, a columnist declared that "the individual who kills blinded by rage; he who murders driven by bitterness" was less hateful than the criminal law representative who coldly suppressed lives. "Society is then crushed by two weapons: that of the caveman criminal or that of the code," he concluded.[331]

In this context, before the ruling of the Supreme Court had arrived, Gallegos was transferred to Islas Marías on August 24, 1933. Therefore, the claimed violation (acto reclamado) awaiting the decision of the ministers was not suspended. He continued to maintain his innocence. He complained to journalists about what he saw as a falsehood in their reporting: He had not wept when he was notified that he would be sent to the penal colony. "Here I am, calm, fearless, and ready for what will come." He only, as he expressed it to his fellow inmates, feared the ley fuga, which had been applied to Luis Romero Carrasco one year earlier.[332]

He asked reporters to take his photo and give him a copy. He was accompanied by Roberto Alexander Hernández, a famous thief known as the Mexican Raffles, who was also being taken to the penal colony. When Gallegos got the photograph, he dedicated it to the police chief: "A photo of my last day, because maybe they'll kill me tomorrow" (fig. 15). His fear became a reality. Two days later, on his way to the penal colony, in Teoloyucan, State of Mexico, a guard shot him. According to the military report, Gallegos tried to escape.[333] The press widely covered the event. Rodolfo Usigli revisited its content in Ensayo de un crimen: On the journey, José Asturias (Alberto Gallegos) asked permission to get out at a station to walk a bit; he tried to escape, and a soldier shot him, "fulfilling his duty."[334]

Many thought Gallegos had been executed. It was said he had not tried to flee because, with Romero Carrasco's death in mind, he had already expressed his fear to the press and the police chief. A doctor's daughter who had left the station claimed that when she heard the shot and saw the stiff body, she knew he had been dead for hours. Others alleged he was found face up; therefore, he had not been shot in the neck as he was fleeing.[335]

For El Universal Gráfico, it was the end everyone expected: "Today Alberto Gallegos paid with his life for the crime he committed."[336] The newspaper's position was to be expected. Months earlier, before the application of the ley fuga to Romero Carrasco, another collaborator wrote, "Nothing has been lost." He maintained that the "general criterion" did not at all regret the killing of criminals with such antecedents and hoped their deaths served to stop the crime wave.[337]

Others condemned the death. A group of around forty workers went to the La Prensa offices to demand punishment for those responsible for the homicide and suggested it was a setup; they were not against the reinstitution of the death penalty, but they did oppose its application outside the law under the pretext of the ley fuga.[338] They were not the only parties to invoke this argument. La Prensa empathized with the protesters. It admitted it had been the paper with the strongest "ideological tenacity," and its "journalistic breadth" had supported the reinstitution of the death penalty, but it condemned the illegal death because "done behind the law's back, it loses all force of moral sanction."[339] Raúl Carrancá y Trujillo asserted that by abolishing the death penalty—which he considered useless, immoral, barbaric, and antiscientific—the state limited itself and was forced not to apply capital punishment. But in practice, the state apparently did not accept that limitation, and thus it was preferable that the death penalty be introduced into the Criminal Code.[340] These ideas inspired Rodolfo Usigli to have one of his characters announce, "It would be more decorous to execute a killer with the legal apparatus than to apply the ley fuga."[341]

Gallegos's trial is interesting and has multiple nuances. There was a clear overlap between judges and public opinion.

The press's verdict was immediate: Reporters attributed the murder to him from the time of his arrest and did not hesitate to blame him for other deaths, whether planned or carried out. They also blamed him for other things, such as criticizing him for seducing minors, since his honor and that of their families were at stake; although honor had lost importance after the Revolution, it had not ceased to matter. He was an almost perfect

Fig. 15. Alberto Gallegos and Raffles. *La Prensa*, August 23, 1933, 2. Material provided by the Fototeca, Hemeroteca y Biblioteca Mario Vázquez Raña / Organización Editorial Mexicana S.A. de C.V.

killer; therefore, it didn't matter that his victim wasn't perfect. (Jacinta Aznar broke with expected feminine attributes and behavior, was rude, mistreated her servants, and might have been a lesbian.) Apparently, there were echoes in the community. *Excélsior* maintained, "Society itself has condemned Gallegos and partners, so the judgment of the First Criminal Court will come as no surprise." According to *El Universal Gráfico*, "countless people," mostly women, wrote to the judge asking for a "harsh sentence" for the criminal.[342] The participation of reporters, their importance in the investigation phase, and the scope of their opinions were noteworthy.

Judicial proceedings were longer and more complex. The first thing that stands out is the defendants' changing statements: Gallegos changed his version six times, and Sánchez Trinidad and Montiel changed theirs three times. In all cases, they incriminated themselves in the initial statements and declared their innocence in the last. All of them attributed their confessions to torture. If they are to be believed, their rights had been violated and a common practice in the inquisitorial system had returned, which admitted torture to obtain confessions, regarded as the leading and most trustworthy evidence. The defendants could have lied in accusing the police of torturing them, but they would not have done so if they thought no one would believe them; on the contrary, they knew they could create doubts in the minds of the judges and in public opinion, and this is important. As mentioned earlier, various witnesses of the time denounced the use of force to extract confessions. In fact, in his novel, Usigli imagines this is how the confession of José Asturias (Alberto Gallegos) was extracted when Rodolfo de la Cruz, spooked over the transfer to Islas Marías, stopped incriminating himself and the penitentiary director "helped by two officials, harassed Asturias, threatened him, menaced him with a whip, a pistol, and a promise of 'ley fuga.'"[343] The fact that what was said by the defendants was credible is another example of the public's mistrust of the police and the belief that laws were not always applied and rights were not always respected. Not many months had passed since Plutarco Elías Calles had held that it was necessary to move from a country of caudillos to a country of institutions; he did not also say a country of laws, but it was implicit. Would the displacement of caudillos be accompanied by the end of abuses by authorities? Would the creation of the Partido Nacional Revolucionario and presidential rule mean greater respect and strict adherence to legality? It should have been so. Hence the accusation of Gallegos and his accomplices reaffirmed the need for change, but it also questioned the path that had been taken, an important task or evil omen for the newly arrived president, Abelardo Rodríguez.

Other than accusations of torture, the law was respected: The time limits were met in the local courts between detention and the initial statement, and between this and the court order to hold the defendant in custody; constitutional time limits for the end of the trial, which was reasonably short, were not exceeded; and procedural regulations were observed. The defendants had defense attorneys and made full use of all resources. In their allegations, they maintained their innocence, doing so by refuting confessions, contributing evidence, and demanding acquittal in the case of reasonable doubt. They also sought the public's compassion, which arose over Sánchez Trinidad's weakness, Montiel's ignorance and crudeness, and Gallegos's mother's suffering, as well as his own suffering and torment. Therefore, although the prosecution was resigned to fulfilling the new rules of the game, defense attorneys were not; they sought to pull heartstrings, if not of the professional judges, at least of public opinion.

Thus it was a trial without controversies but with controversial sentences (and a dissenting vote). The disagreements among judges stand out, not regarding Gallegos's guilt, but regarding that of Montiel and Sánchez Trinidad. Their divergence concerning Montiel began even before the ruling was made. The MP accused him of concealment, but the journalists did not agree; they did not interpret this as a desperate act to save the lack of evidence, but as the result of "excessive sentimentalism" by the MP agent.[344] Hence they did not question accusing a possibly innocent defendant of concealment, but rather they accused him of concealment of a possible homicide. However, the questioning of judge Ángel Escalante, who in his dissenting vote advocated the release of the supposed accomplices and, most importantly, gave credence to the accusations of torture and questioned the validity of the confessions. Thus even judicial officials distrusted the police. The disagreement among the judges continued (apparently the TSJ magistrates revoked the sentence of Montiel and acquitted him). There are different opinions and resolutions of judges of first and second instance, which makes it possible to classify this trial as a "difficult or controversial" case.

Another point of the trial merits attention: With the *amparo* admitted, not only was the remission of Gallegos to Islas Marías suspended but also the decision arrived almost twenty years later. The claim was admitted in 1933, but the matter was never reviewed until 1950, and the judgment was issued in 1952. With the death certificate, the request was considered appropriate, but the decision was made to dismiss the trial "for the obvious and perfectly known fact that Gallegos Sánchez had died, the press of this capital and the whole nation having published the news of his death."[345] This calls into question the effectiveness of the *amparo* and obviously illustrates the backlog in the SCJ.

In Gallegos's trial, the outcome also deserves comment. The questionable application of the *ley fuga* suggested a planned or ordered execution. It was not the first time. I referred earlier to the case of Romero Carrasco. At around the same time, Daniel Flores, condemned for an attempted attack on President Pascual Ortiz Rubio, was found dead in his cell. There was fertile ground for distrust, on this occasion of the government or military agents. Gallegos himself began to sow mistrust the day before his departure; after his death, various witnesses continued planting it.

Doubt—indeed, the acceptance of a planned death—demands reflection on two points: the (dis)agreement regarding the punishment and the (dis)agreement on its execution. According to predominant opinion, the photographer deserved death, and the abolition of the death penalty was condemned. *Excélsior* affirmed, "The new Criminal Code suspended the death penalty, which should have been applied to this vile killer."[346] One of its writers, Catalina D'Erzell, declared, "All Mexico today yearns for the death penalty, and even for that police inspector who fakes the suicide of killers. Beings like Gallegos and Romero Carrasco should not be in this world. They are dead consciences, in which the miracle of resurrection cannot be verified. Before them, all punishments, all efforts at vindication will fail."[347]

Even Gallegos agreed with capital punishment. After the killing of Romero Carrasco, a journalist told him people just shrugged their shoulders because they believed he did not deserve to live and asked him his opinion. Gallegos proclaimed that he was in favor, but only for "criminals resistant to all rehabilitation and who are a grave danger to society."[348]

Therefore, society agreed with the judges who ruled Gallegos guilty but disagreed with the legislators who abolished capital punishment. However, it should be asked whether, in the words of Catalina D'Erzell, those who "yearn[ed] for the death penalty" also missed policemen who faked suicides of killers or, following the reporter who interviewed Gallegos, whether everyone shrugged when the *ley fuga* was applied. This was not the case with Gallegos. Many claimed to prefer capital punishment to the killing of inmates. At that time, an important sector of the capital associated the *ley fuga* with the age of Porfirio Díaz and not with the revolutionary regime, not with a state that aspired to become one governed by the rule of law and a Mexico that yearned for peace, security, demilitarization, institutionalization, and legality.

"With a Soul of Steel, and a Smile on Her Lips"

Four years after Jacinta Aznar's death, another crime shook the capital: A man had been killed during a robbery, jeweler and real estate broker Francisco Javier Silva.[349]

His body was found on May 21, 1936, in the town of Magdalena, State of Mexico. Hours earlier, a report had been filed over his disappearance. Those who filed the report had left him at the door of his house at night, and the next morning they found out he had not slept there. The case was entrusted to the secret police. The agents soon found a lead. They asked Silva's friends

Fig. 16. "Cómo fue encontrado el cadáver de Francisco Javier Silva" (How Francisco Javier Silva's body was found). *La Prensa*, May 22, 1936, 1. Material provided by the Fototeca, Hemeroteca y Biblioteca Mario Vázquez Raña / Organización Editorial Mexicana S.A. de C.V.

to accompany them to the place where the cadaver was discovered. The corpse was tied with wire, his face so disfigured from beatings he was unidentifiable, but his clothing and ID left no room for doubt.[350] Reporters were there and produced a photocomposition, like that of Jacinta Aznar, showing a portrait of Silva in life and his corpse (fig. 16).

Francisco Javier Silva was fifty years old and had a comfortable life, but no great fortune. The murderers had taken him on the old road to Texcoco, going through the town of Magdalena around 2:30 a.m. They had parked at a lonely spot and beaten him to death; they wanted to bury him, but the ground was so hard they could only partially cover him. It was believed the motive had not been robbery; two of the dead man's rings had been removed but not a valuable tiepin, and only a sugar bowl and watch were missing from his house. Furthermore, a senator claimed Silva had asked him days before to use his influence for the police to intervene because the jeweler was being blackmailed by his ex-lover, a beautiful cabaret entertainer, María Elena Blanco.

Silva's housekeeper testified that he had installed Blanco in his house, and she proclaimed herself "lady and mistress." He bought her lots of fine silk lingerie, dresses, hats, perfumes, and cosmetics. However, "the honeymoon only lasted fifteen days." One morning when the housekeeper served breakfast, her employer told her to gather the used clothing (not the new pieces or the gifts) and put them in Blanco's suitcases because the entertainer would be moving, and "if the señora returned, not to let her in." A day later, a man came looking for Blanco. The next day she returned with Silva, but when he found out the man had gone to look for her, they quarreled; the scene repeated, then the unknown man returned to ask about her. Things got worse when Silva ran into him. That night he threw his lover out. She disappeared for a while, but the night before the crime, she reappeared. Silva sent her away, saying, "This isn't an inn."[351]

The police searched for her. Her real name was Esperanza García Márquez Sánchez Guerrero, but she went by María Elena Blanco. The newspapers played an important role in capturing her. They publicized her description in different cities, and finally, on June 9, after eighteen days, she was found in Guadalajara, where she was sharing a hovel with Gonzalo Ortiz Ordaz (fig. 17).[352]

María Elena did not speak of the crime but instead told the newspapers of her life. She claimed to deeply love Gonzalo Ortiz, even though he earned a meager salary as an archivist at the Beneficencia Pública (Public Charity) and had lied to her that he was an engineer. Later, she met Francisco Javier Silva, whom she left because he was extremely jealous and constantly recriminating her, making a scene if she greeted an acquaintance on the street. One of the men who made him jealous was the owner of the Cine Ermita, who was courting her. After a fight, she went with the movie theater owner, who set her up in a better house. However, she missed Gonzalo Ortiz, so she returned to him. "I never loved anyone the way I now love Gonzalo," she professed. "All those guys who bowed to my slightest whim and gave me, within their means, money, jewelry, clothes, and treated me very well were a bunch of weak characters."[353]

In another statement to *Excélsior*, she claimed her two previous husbands were proper, "but much less than Gonzalo, who besides being a complete gentleman is a fine, cultivated man." She admitted he had beaten her; nevertheless, she reiterated, "I love him more than the others."[354] Journalists closely followed the case. Her love was clear. She denied that she and, more fervently, her love participated in the crime: "'The night of the crime, Gonzalo was by

Fig. 17. María Elena Blanco and Gonzalo Ortiz. *La Prensa*, June 12, 1. Material provided by the Fototeca, Hemeroteca y Biblioteca Mario Vázquez Raña / Organización Editorial Mexicana S.A. de C.V.

my side, and we were not apart for a moment. He didn't leave my arms for a moment!' . . . And so continued the woman's defense of the man she adores: perverse and murderous; but, for her, all love and passion."[355]

Gonzalo Ortiz Ordaz confessed a day earlier. On June 15, after five days in a detention cell, he requested an interview with the Security Commissions head, who invited witnesses and journalists to confirm the statement was voluntary. Again, the importance of journalists is noteworthy as witnesses to the way the defendant gave his statement. Dressed in the torn and dirty clothes he was wearing in Guadalajara to throw off the police, the accused said he had looked for Silva with the intention of avenging María Elena, because he was overcome by anger at hearing many of the offensive words Silva had said to her, which she had repeated to him "in intimacy." The next day he added that the love itself had hurt him because he found out she had lived with the other man.

The day of the beating, he took a gun and two friends, Luis Magaña Velasco and Oscar Bazet Hermosillo. He asserted that María Elena had stayed in the hotel, with an eye ailment. They went to the jeweler's house and waited for him at the door. When they saw him arrive, Ortiz said to him, "I want you to give me an explanation about María Elena." They forced him into the car, and as they drove through the Roma and Del Valle neighborhoods, they continued to insult Silva. Ortiz affirmed that he was satisfied when they returned to the victim's house, but his accomplices were not. They got out of the car and entered the house. Returning to the car, they then took Silva into the house, and the second time they came out, they brought the owner out with his hands tied with a wire. They headed to the highway, without fearing the police because Magaña had a secret agent ID. Then they stopped and started to beat Silva. Ortiz claimed that he tried to defend him, but his friends said they had to kill him so he "wouldn't sing" and "bring everyone to disgrace." Bazet continued beating him, while Magaña found a huge rock and dropped it on his head. They threw the body in a hollow and covered it with dirt and branches. They spent the night in the car, and the next morning Ortiz picked up María Elena, who was unaware of what transpired, and they went for a holiday in Guanajuato.[356] He had also defended his woman.

The statement did not convince the agents and journalists. They didn't believe the defendant had only wished to teach the victim a lesson because if that were the case, he wouldn't have needed to take accomplices and weapons. Nor did they believe he would have been satisfied by merely insulting his love rival, while his friends, who had nothing to do with the man, brutally beat him. They were certain the motive was robbery, and they thought María Elena had participated because a woman's shoeprint was found in the car.[357]

They called on her to corroborate the events. She went out to the patio to speak with the same group of policemen and reporters who had interviewed her lover. She was also wearing the clothing that served as a disguise, but she had washed them several times and mended them, her hair was done, and unlike her lover, she did not smell and had a pleasant appearance. The police asked her to confess, but she stuck to her story: She had been in the hotel, her lover had not left, and he never carried a gun.[358]

Ortiz and Blanco filed for an *amparo* before the First District judge when they had been detained for more than seventy-two hours without resolving their legal situation; the term stipulated in the Constitution had been violated. They claimed they had suffered isolation, mistreatment, and torture. The judge allowed the lawsuit and requested information.[359]

After the confession, on June 17 Gonzalo was sent to Lecumberri and brought before a judge. María Elena remained in the detention cell. She had two pieces of evidence against her: She had been Silva's lover and had connected him with Ortiz, and her footprint was in the car. The supposed accomplices, Bazet and Magaña Velasco, were fugitives. Little is known of the first; he had been a faithful soldier of Pancho Villa, had a bad record, and was said to be "fierce in crime." Much more is known of the second; not only did he have a record but he also had contacts, friends, and relatives in the police force. He had driven the car, with legislative license plates, transporting the men who had killed Fernando Capdeville in September 1927; he escaped punishment because of a series of irregularities committed during the investigation, and once he was released, his file disappeared. From then on, he was protected by powerful people and had a special police agent ID.[360]

The case took a turn when Magaña's sister appeared with her statement. According to her version, three days before the crime, María Elena, Gonzalo, and Oscar had asked her to get a car and two guns because they wanted to scare and beat Silva. The day of the events, María Elena lured him to the car; they forced him in and drove to the highway, where Gonzalo and Oscar tied him up and beat him to death. The victim begged for mercy: "Mari, tell them to stop, I'll give you whatever you ask for!" While she mocked him, Oscar struck him with a nightstick, and Gonzalo stabbed him and finished the job, throwing an enormous stone on his head. It all happened so quickly there was no time to pull out the gun and stop them. Later, she heard the criminals had met several times to plan the hit, and from the start, they planned to kill him because María Elena wanted to avenge his rejection.

This testimony was published in newspapers. The police showed it to María Elena, who rushed to give her version and deny what Magaña had said. She declared before the police on June 18, after spending more than a week in the detention cell. She maintained that when Gonzalo found out she had lived with Silva, he was enraged and told her he was going to beat the man and sought out two criminals, Bazet and Magaña. She begged him not to do it, but she was only able to witness the beating because she wanted to prevent him from participating and to protect him. His accomplices wanted Silva to give them 20,000 pesos. Silva claimed he didn't have the money, so they beat

Fig. 18. María Elena Blanco's confession. *La Prensa*, June 19, 1936, 5. Material provided by the Fototeca, Hemeroteca y Biblioteca Mario Vázquez Raña / Organización Editorial Mexicana S.A. de C.V.

him. Gonzalo objected and reminded them they only had to beat Silva up, but because Gonzalo was unarmed, he couldn't do anything. Francisco Javier implored María Elena, "Save me, you're the only one who can help me." She confronted Magaña and Bazet, but when they threatened to kill her, she said to Francisco Javier with tears in her eyes, "Forgive me, but if I save you, they'll kill me too." They headed to Puebla. Bazet said they had to kill him because he would identify them to the police.[361] A photocomposition was published (fig. 18). The editors opted to include the two defendants, and not just María Elena, to underscore her complicity. In the images, both look expressionless and calm. The headline, "María Elena, seated before journalists, during her 'agitated confession,'" does not correspond to the visual.

The next day, June 19, María Elena entered Lecumberri, where Gonzalo was waiting for her and gave her a long hug.[362] She was brought before the judge. That day a new photocomposition was published in which she plays a relatively central role in the images but lacks agency, which is held by the officials surrounding her (standing, while she is seated) or leading her to prison (fig. 19). The newspapers spread news of her statement in addition to Gonzalo's retraction, claiming he had been tortured into giving his statement.[363]

On June 20 the judge issued the *auto de formal prisión* for Gonzalo. Two days later, on June 22, María Elena also retracted her statement. She declared that she and her lover were innocent and she had been tortured to testify: "I have been tortured; indescribable torture prevented me from freely and spontaneously giving my statements, so those that have been established until now are absolutely ineffective. I do not ratify a single word in the statements, because they contain substantial falsehoods, resulting from the suffering I have been subjected to." She took refuge in the second subsection of constitutional Article 20 (which established that no one can be compelled to testify against themselves) to demand her confession be dismissed, and she reserved the right to declare when she considered it pertinent. In conclusion, she expressed two convictions: First, public opinion would not be unfavorable when the truth came out, and the press would do them justice. Second, her fundamental rights would be respected because President Cárdenas would not permit shameful acts like those committed by past leaders to be perpetrated. She considered that the judge was also a representative of "that tendency toward an absolute respect for the law."[364]

On June 23 the judge issued the *auto de formal prisión* for María Elena.[365] Blanco and Ortiz were accused of kidnapping, homicide, and crimes related to the person of Francisco Javier Silva. She was called to the defendant's cage in the courtroom, and when she heard the notification for the first time, she lost her composure and hysterically screamed, "If you want to make me a victim, here I am ready to die before you touch a hair of Gonzalo, my great love, my only passion."[366]

María Elena was born in Guadalajara, probably in 1915, although she did not reveal her age. To escape poverty, she had immigrated to the United States. According to *Excélsior*, she was deported for "bad conduct" because "she committed thousands of scandals in the cabarets of Los Angeles and worked as a dancer in an entertainment troupe."[367] In Ciudad Juárez she married

YO CONFESADO

DIJO MARIA ELENA CON UNA SONRISA EN LOS LABIOS QUE DESTILABA INMENSA AMARGURA

INFORMACION EN PAGINA TRES

MARIA ELENA, "LA VAMPIRESA", quien ya se encuentra alojada en una de la celdas de la Penitenciaría, a disposición del Juez que instruya el proceso por el asesinat del comisionista Francisco Javier Silva, ratificó y aun amplió ayer su primera declara ción ante la Procuraduría del Distrito Federal.—Aquí vemos a esta extraña, desconcer tante y bella mujer, durante las diligencias en la Procuraduría y cuando era sacada d los separos de la Sexta Delegación.

Fig. 19. "María Elena, 'La Vampiresa'" (María Elena, the vampiress). *La Prensa*, June 20, 1936, 1. Material provided by the Fototeca, Hemeroteca y Biblioteca Mario Vázquez Raña / Organización Editorial Mexicana S.A. de C.V.

Jesús Saldaña, with whom she had a daughter, who was taken away by her mother-in-law. She had various lovers before marrying a second time, but she fled after only nine days and ended up in a bordello, where she learned to smoke marijuana, a drug she could never give up.[368] She was tall and fair-skinned, with black curly hair, large eyes, long eyelashes, a haughty bearing, and notable beauty. She was always well groomed, never without makeup or unkempt. "Men categorized her among women for whom they'd commit any foolishness; women envied her and saw her as a dangerous rival," claimed *Magazine de Policía*.[369] According to the newspapers, her charms earned her the kindness of the penitentiary director and privileges. But she did not obtain the favor of journalists, who usually called her a "vamp." *La Prensa* also branded her as "cynical," "heartless," and a "cruel executioner."[370] *El Universal Gráfico* dubbed her a "gold digger par excellence."[371] Meanwhile, *Excélsior* described her as a woman "strong to every test, with a soul of steel, and a smile on her lips."[372] Thus she incarnated the fear of opportunistic, unscrupulous women, man-eaters, and female emancipation.

In contrast, Gonzalo Ortiz Ordaz was a man lacking any charm. Born in Pachuca, he was now twenty-six, with no physical or mental afflictions or family history of serious pathologies, except for his father, who suffered a "mental illness." He finished high school and the first year of engineering studies; however, according to *Excélsior*, he had a "mediocre intellect."[373] He earned the animosity of newspapers, who referred to him as Ortiz, without his first name or second surname, or simply as the "grim criminal." *El Universal Gráfico* held that he had lived off women, had committed another crime, and was proud to have escaped the authorities' attention of a crime perhaps related, according to *Excélsior*, to his own father.[374]

The trial began in that environment. The judge overseeing the proceeding was Jesús González Insunza, eighteenth judge of the Sixth Criminal Court. The MP agent was Francisco Díaz Martínez, later replaced by Carlos Pasquel. Ortiz Ordaz had various attorneys and was finally represented by David Pastrana Jaimes, who according to *Excélsior*, "had had the bad luck of losing all his cases."[375] María Elena Blanco appointed the public defender Armando Z. Ostos, but he declined because he was friends with the deceased. Given the defendant's refusal to appoint another attorney, claiming "she could only trust him," the judge appointed the head of the Public Defenders' Office, José Gracia Medrano. Later, she appointed Bernabé López Patrón and finally

David Pastrana Jaimes. Oscar Bazet's attorney was Ramiro Estrada, then a public defender.

Journalists and photographers joined the proceedings. The statements of María Elena and Gonzalo were rife with contradictions: She had first said she found out about the crime in newspapers but later ratified what her lover said, claiming she learned of it the next morning in the hotel. Moreover, first she denied knowing Magaña and Bazet and said she thought they were Gonzalo's driver and helper; then, in her hysterical statement in the trial, she admitted knowing that Gonzalo had hired them to beat Silva up (agreeing with Gonzalo). The confrontation hearing was inconclusive, but it allowed the lovers to agree on their testimony; when María Elena answered, she looked at Gonzalo as if to ask, "Right?" For his part, he remained silent when the judged asked and agreed when she did.[376]

To Magaña's testimony was added that of Bazet, who was detained on June 26. Bazet stated that the day before the crime, he had met Magaña, who came with Gonzalo, whom he didn't know. "We'll stop being poor. There's seventy thousand pesos in a stockbroker's strongbox," they told him. The offer was tempting. "I was having a rough time; my wife was going to give birth and I didn't have a penny," Bazet said. The night of the crime, they met; María Elena accompanied them. His account was like those of the others, but he claimed Magaña killed Silva.[377]

Desperate to save Gonzalo, María Elena took the blame. She said she had hired Oscar and Luis to beat Silva without her lover's knowledge, never imagining they would kill him, and she tried to stop it. She declared that Gonzalo had confessed under torture and to save her. She claimed that now she was telling the truth; her earlier statement had been a lie extracted under torture, as they had mistreated her for nine days when she was in the detention cell.[378] *Excélsior* did not believe her and compared her to Gallegos, who had kept changing his testimony.[379]

Excélsior reported that "many students from the Law Department, as well as a throng of curious onlookers, mainly women, out of a certain morbid interest in seeing the female killer" attended the confrontation hearing.[380] María Elena stuck to her story. She denied that her motive was robbery and pointed out that she'd had many opportunities to take the money while she was living with Francisco Javier. Her motive was revenge and to prevent Gonzalo from killing the victim, but a scare and a beating were enough for revenge. Looking at Oscar, she accused, "You and Magaña killed him, Gonzalo wasn't with us,

Gonzalo is innocent; if he has incriminated himself, it's to defend me, because he loves me so much. I cooked up 'the beating' because I didn't want him to get his hands dirty. And I went with you and tried to stop the killing; that's how you jabbed me with the knife you were carrying."[381] The confrontation produced nothing new. As for throwing the stone, Oscar blamed Gonzalo, Gonzalo blamed Oscar, and María Elena blamed Luis.

On July 2 Bazet was formally detained.[382] For *La Prensa*, the case was clear: The attack had been planned well in advance, María Elena had seduced Francisco Javier to find out where he kept the money, she had not left Gonzalo, and her affair with the jeweler was part of the plan.[383] A letter from María Elena to her mother in English, to prevent anyone else from reading it, was made known. In it, she stated that Gonzalo was guilty: "My heart is broken because he is Silva's killer," and "I don't want to leave prison to share every day with him."[384]

At the end of the year the defendants filed for an *amparo*. María Elena's attorney, Bernabé López Patrón, claimed the act of the eighteenth judge violated constitutional Articles 14, 16, and 19 by issuing the *auto de formal prisión*. The district judge dismissed the request, arguing that the defendant had accepted the act by filing the appeal against it. The defense attorney, dissatisfied with the ruling, presented an *amparo* demand.[385]

The year 1937 saw the acceptance of the *amparo* and a change in María Elena. She ended her relationship with Gonzalo and blamed him for the crime, claiming she had not done so before out of fear because she felt a "morbid love" for him. She asserted that Silva had always been very kind to her and she didn't need to steal from him because he would have given her anything she needed. She requested that the hotel administrator and maid testify, as that night she had not gone out but was recovering from being struck in the eye, and a public charity doctor checked her. She also asked that Silva's servants testify: They could confirm she managed the house as she pleased and had keys to everything, meaning she could have taken anything she wanted.[386] A new confrontation hearing was held, and María Elena and Gonzalo agreed, while Oscar denied their testimony.[387]

Days later, according to *La Prensa*, the scj denied Ortiz Ordaz the appeal against the decision of the district judge who had initially refused to grant an *amparo* against his *auto de formal prisión*.[388] The case of María Elena Blanco was different, however, and on April 29, 1937, the same court revoked the district judge's resolution and ordered the court to enter her claim for the same purpose.[389]

Almost a year after the trial began, in mid-May 1937, the file was made available to the parties.[390] In June María Elena requested a reconstruction of the crime.[391] Judge Inzunza initially did not agree but later authorized it. A crowd gathered outside Silva's house, and when the suspects arrived, they shouted at them, "Thieves! Murderers! Kill them! Hang them!" In contrast, a contemptuous silence met Oscar. It had been clear "to the people, the vamp and the man of the big sideburns are profoundly antipathic to them."[392] It was the last court proceeding. Prosecutor Carlos Pasquel asked for thirty years for María Elena Blanco and Gonzalo Ortiz Ordaz for kidnapping, robbery, criminal association, first-degree homicide (with aggravating circumstances of premeditation, perfidy, advantage, and cruelty). According to the Criminal Code, for qualified homicide the sentence was thirteen to twenty years of prison; for robbery of more than 500 pesos, up to two years; and for kidnapping, twenty years. Because they had committed various crimes in a single event, the highest punishment (twenty years) had to be applied plus the rest, but up to a limit of thirty years. Considering he had voluntarily turned himself in and confessed, for Oscar Bazet the prosecutor requested between twenty and twenty-five years.[393]

The attorney of Gonzalo and María Elena, David Pastrana Jaimes, declared that they were innocent because Gonzalo had not injured the victim and María Elena had not even been present.[394] In contrast, Ramiro Estrada, Oscar Bazet's defense attorney, accepted the guilt of his client, calling for benevolence for his confession and his help in proving the guilt of the other defendants.[395] The hearing was held on November 13, in the absence of the defendants. María Elena's defense attorney, Pastrana Jaimes, didn't budge. He accused the press of slandering his client, whom, according to *Excélsior*, he portrayed as an "innocent, pure, unstained victim who should be taken to the altars."[396] He maintained that only Bazet's testimony was against her and could not be accepted as evidence; the statements of the hotel employees, who claimed she had not left the building, and the medical examiner who cured her eye, which was so badly injured she could not go "from here to there in committing a crime," proved that she could not have been present at the murder.[397] He concluded, "María Elena is a great sinner of love, and precisely for the overwhelming passion she felt for her man, Gonzalo Ortiz Ordaz, she let herself get involved in the scandalous killing."[398]

The Sixth Criminal Court was composed, in addition to Insunza, of Rafael Matos Escobedo and Ignacio Pérez Vargas. They had to issue a sentence before fifteen days. In his judgment draft, Insunza contemplated the same penalty as the MP, thirty years, for Gonzalo and María Elena. However, unlike the prosecutor, he proposed for Bazet a sentence of five to ten years for attenuating circumstances that worked in his favor: having voluntarily turned himself in and confessed, being the only defendant to declare the truth, and helping clarify the crime.[399] The sentence, issued on February 7, 1938, was similar to the draft in the cases of Ortiz Ordaz and Blanco: he received thirty years of prison and she, twenty-eight years and eight months.[400] However, in Bazet's case, judges Pérez Vargas and Matos Escobedo differed from Insunza and were close to the MP petition, so by majority, the criminal court imposed twenty-two years and eight months. Despite her despondency, María Elena hid her age, but she could not overlook it. It hurt her to think of how old she would be when released: "It means my twenty years and the thirty they give me are fifty; therefore, I will be released when I'm fifty. Why aren't they more chivalrous with me?"[401] Magaña was not found, according to reporter El Güero Téllez, for a "false sense of friendship and comradeship" with the colleagues of his father, a Secret Service commandant, protected him.[402]

The convicted defendants filed an appeal. While they were waiting for the resolution, the love of María Elena and Gonzalo blossomed. They wanted to get married in April 1938. Permission was denied because it had not been a year since her divorce from her second husband. In September Gonzalo was killed by another convict in the carpentry workshop, but the motive was unclear. Journalists expressed no indignation. The title of a La Prensa article expressed a prevailing idea: "He who kills by iron dies by iron!" In the opening words of the article, the writer asserted Ortiz Ordaz had met "someone who in one way or another became the avenging hand of the unfortunate old man" (turning Francisco Javier Silva into an old man gave greater weight to his death).[403] Just as years before in the case of Alberto Gallegos, a convict had died in custody under suspicious circumstances.

María Elena promised to follow him in death but was unable to attend the funeral because permission was denied. She didn't take long to recover. Three months later she was engaged to her first boyfriend, a professor from Texas.[404] Interviewed by La Prensa, she presented herself as a decent woman, a pure, naive, innocent heroine. She claimed that although she continued to love Gonzalo, her old flame inspired a "good love" in her. She explained that he felt responsible for her fate: If he had married her in Los Angeles, she would be living happy and calm there. She said she warned him, "I'm no good for you, you outside and me inside!" Nevertheless, he moved "heaven and earth" to have her sentence commuted.[405] In vain, he sought a sentence reduction or pardon, and failing that, he also failed in his attempt to marry her. María Elena canceled the wedding and announced she would not wed merely for the illusion of feeling married: Her groom had to get her out of the terrifying prison.[406]

Mental instability followed love. María Elena was not an easy prisoner. Problems arose from the start, when she refused to leave her cell to attend proceedings. According to La Prensa, not having "the life she wanted to have" gave her a strong sense of punishment.[407] As time passed, she became aggressive and injured several inmates, including Mother Conchita, so she was constantly locked up in a punishment cell. Magazine de Policía explained, "She felt she died with her beloved. There was nothing else for her in the world. No hope lifted her heart. She got sick. She almost went mad. She quickly lost weight. She became, at last, a human rag."[408] A doctor stated she suffered from "severe mental disturbances" and had to be taken to the Castañeda (mental hospital), but the TSJ deemed it was not secure, so she was moved to a special department in the penitentiary.[409]

On June 16, 1939, the TSJ Eighth Chamber confirmed the criminal court's judgment.[410] While she was waiting for the Supreme Court ruling, María Elena became the girlfriend of killer Jorge Laffit Guerra. She was in love again when, on April 1, 1940, she was denied the protection of federal justice.[411] "I hope in God and justice that I shall return soon from the Pacific," she said when she left for Islas Marías on April 20. "She looked calm, although saddened," declared an Excélsior writer. Before leaving, she hugged the photographers.[412]

She continued to be the subject of speculation and myths. It was said she sporadically received "thick rolls of American bills" sent by her beloved Texan. It was imagined she was living like a great wealthy lady, bejeweled, venerated, and surrounded by admirers and lovers. Three months after she reached the island, an inmate who was now the postal administrator of the islands became her fourth and perhaps last husband.[413] But not her last man. According to Excélsior, she had gotten various inmates to serve her, fanning her "with enormous fans, while she, lying in a hammock, sleeps or reads like a new Cleopatra," so she was known as the Queen.[414]

Just as in the Gallegos case, multiple changes were made in the testimonies; to justify them, the defendants claimed to have confessed under torture. This could speak of a police system far from respecting rights or, at least, the trust of defendants that their testimonies would be believable and, therefore, a distrust in the police. Equally far from the respect of rights and legality was the length of time the suspects were detained before being presented to the MP and between their arrests and the *auto de formal prisión*s, both exceeding constitutional limits.

As in the Gallegos case, there was dissent among the criminal court judges, not with respect to the main defendants, María Elena and Gonzalo, but regarding an accomplice, Bazet. In the first case, the decision was "easy and clear"; in the last (Bazet), it wasn't. The judges' sentencing of the three was severe. Also, society considered that they deserved longer sentences than what the judges could give. The people who crowded the courtroom during the defendants' appearances continued to think some criminals deserved death, including the hangman's noose—a public death with torture. Newspapers abstained from supporting this idea (as they had done years earlier during Gallegos's trial), but they reported it. Not surprisingly, society accepted Gonzalo's murder. Indeed, public dissent could exist with legislators on the ban on capital punishment, but not with judges on the sentence applied to murderers.

FINAL REFLECTIONS

Eight famed murder trials are a minimal sample, considering the number of homicide trials between 1929 and 1971, even if we focus exclusively on celebrated cases. Furthermore, the cases that captured the press's attention have different features than those that did not interest them: The judges were perhaps more scrupulous because they were under close scrutiny; the litigators worked hard and elaborated on their allegations because victory generated money and earned them points in their career; some cases were noteworthy because of the fame of defendants, who probably received privileged treatment; and finally, reporters gave detailed accounts of the investigation and trial, opening the door to public participation and the influence of public opinion on judges' decisions. Also, it is important to remember that in my sample, profiles of some defendants are overrepresented, particularly members of privileged classes and women.

Nevertheless, the qualitative study of these matters produced relevant results, which could be obtained only through a meticulous analysis of a small number of trials. It permitted observation and ratification of tendencies, practices, or problems denounced in diverse publications of the time by jurists, litigators, defendants, reporters, and citizens, including the following: lengthening procedural time limits and backlog; failure of collegiality, violation of immediacy and delegation of functions; violation of defendants' rights, specifically, the use of force or isolation to obtain confessions; and the weight of influences or corruption.

A) **Lengthening procedural deadlines and backlog:** The trials studied reveal the existence of judicial backlog, especially in federal justice. However, also in local justice, a gradual extension of judicial processes is evident and exacerbated in the final years of the period studied. Examples of the consequences of the backlog are the matters of Ángel Peláez Villa, whose *amparo* request was resolved almost four and a half years after it had been filed and when he had served his sentence, and Alberto Gallegos, whose resolution was issued almost twenty years late, when he was already dead as a consequence of the act he sought to suspend, the transfer to Islas Marías. On the one hand, as for procedural deadlines marked by the Constitution, in general, the most immediate were respected (that is, the time between the arrest and the preliminary statement or between the arrest and the formal order for release, or *auto de formal prisión*). However, the deadlines were shamelessly violated in the case of María Elena Blanco and Gonzalo Ortiz Ordaz, who remained in police holding cells for more than ten days. Those accused of murder committed during a robbery also had to wait longer than other defendants for the judgment and sentence, in contrast to the length of trials for other types of homicide. Also worth noting is the swift resolution of matters involving members of privileged groups, such as those of Miguel Desentis González and Ana Irma Sánchez Schultz. On the other hand, trials lasted longer over the years, which could have resulted from the disproportion between the population and courts and the overload of court workloads.

B) **Failure of collegiality, violation of immediacy, and delegation of functions:** In two trials analyzed, I found evidence of denunciations. As for collegiality, the defense attorneys for Humberto Mariles, along with some journalists, maintained that two of the judges on the Third Criminal Court barely had time to see their colleague's draft, which they accepted without prior study. As for failure to comply with immediacy and the delegation of functions, the defense attorney of Soledad Rodríguez (Chole la Ranchera) claimed that the judge had never met his client and that this was common.

C) **Violation of rights, specifically, use of force or isolation to obtain confessions:** Those accused of murder committed during a robbery claimed that their confessions before investigating agents had been induced after days of isolation (the documents indicate they had remained arrested longer than permissible) and with violence. In those cases, the discovery of the victims' bodies led to the investigation, and the identities of the murderers were unknown, so the defendants' complaints were credible given the need of law enforcement to find the criminals, but also because denunciations of this kind were made by jurists of the time.

D) **Weight of influences or corruption**: Complaints about these problems arose in the case of Humberto Mariles, when they were openly suggested—or feared—by jurists and journalists.

Qualitative analysis made it possible for me to fulfill some of the research concerns cited in the book's introduction, specifically, assessing aspects such as the margin of judicial discretion, the defendants' agreement or dissent, and based on this, the proportion of "easy or clear" relative to "difficult or controversial" cases in my sample, the performance of the parties and their weight in judicial decisions, the emergence of social ideas and values in the courts, and the role of reporters and correspondence with or distance from judicial decisions with respect to the opinions expressed by newspapers. My conclusions are as follows:

A) **Margin of judicial discretion and proportion of "easy or clear" relative to "difficult or controversial" cases**: In the eight cases analyzed, twelve individuals were tried, and dissent arose among judges to varying degrees. In that of Ángel Peláez Villa and Humberto Mariles, the judges clearly disagreed. Within the sample, "difficult or controversial" cases prevailed. This attests to the margin for the interpretation of facts, evidence, and laws by judges, a margin then no longer questioned. Furthermore, by approaching judicial practices, I observed repeated references to judicial precedent and SCJ *tesis*. Just like legislators and journalists, judges were more understanding with defendants who acted, or argued that they acted, in self-defense or out of grave fear than those who killed during a robbery, who were given harsher sentences and fall within this category. They were also severe with women motivated by greed, as with María Elena Blanco and, to a degree, Soledad Rodríguez Prado, who could have been seen as leaving her husband and killing out of ambition.

B) **Acts of procedural parties and their weight in judicial decisions**: A trend evident from the time is the force of the MP agent's petition. In ten of the twelve cases, the criminal court attended the plaintiff's petition; on only one occasion did they respond to the defendant's position (Ángel Peláez Villa), and on another occasion, they did not respond to either of the two (Humberto Mariles). I also noted increasing weight given to expert witnesses in trials and their reports in judgments.

c) **Emergence of society's ideas and values in courts:** Differences related to gender stand out. There are two important points. First, the argument of grave fear was used in the cases of women, but it was absent in those of men who killed under similar circumstances because fear was not given weight with men but was assumed with women. Second, there was greater questioning of the claim of self-defense by women seen to be morally transgressive (like Chole la Ranchera) than by those who fit the model of acceptable conduct before the crime. In general, judges were more understanding with women who, before killing, fit the desired model (Ana Irma Sánchez Schultz) and less so with those who had transgressed ethical and behavioral codes (María Elena Blanco, Soledad Rodríguez Prado, and Emma Perches Frank).

D) **Role of reporters and correspondence of judicial decisions with the newspapers' opinion:** Journalists immediately appeared at crime scenes and participated in inquiries and statements, interrogating witnesses and the accused. They played an important part in describing the criminals. In all cases, I note a correspondence between judges' rulings and opinions expressed in newspapers.

6. THE SUPPRESSION
OF CRIMINAL COURTS

According to the preamble to the 1970 initiative of reforms to the Criminal Procedure Common Code, "Among the most important reforms in the present initiative is the suppression of criminal courts, thus hereafter criminal justice will be administered solely by unitary courts. The need for greater speed in the administration of justice and the increase of agencies in charge of administering it have been considered, such as the desirability that the full process develops before a single judge to better meet procedural immediacy requirements and encourage more appropriate individualization of the punishment."[1]

The proposal to suppress first-instance collegial courts and the arguments supporting it are part of this initiative presented by senators in 1970, shortly after President Luis Echeverría referred the draft of the Law that Establishes the Minimum Regulations for the Social Rehabilitation of Convicts (Ley que Establece las Normas Mínimas para la Readaptación Social de Sentenciados) to the Mexican Congress.

The late 1960s saw crisis and disenchantment. The 1968 student movement and governmental reaction emblematized the crisis and marked a watershed in political history. Students from diverse universities spearheaded a protest, expanding their petitions to include social demands and respect for fundamental rights. They won the support of the middle class and public opinion. Shortly before the Olympiads began, hundreds of students were killed or jailed at a mass protest in the Plaza of Tlatelolco.[2]

The economy had slowed, and exports fell as imports and public debt increased. The Mexican president's power and image deteriorated, as opposition parties won support. Social protest was on the rise, such as the guerrilla movement in Guerrero and Morelos and student, teacher, doctor, and truck driver strikes and protests in Mexico City. Works appeared denouncing inequality, such as Luis Buñuel's 1950 film *Los olvidados* and Oscar Lewis's 1964 book *Los hijos de Sánchez (The Children of Sánchez)*. A cultural sea change swept Mexico. Women embraced professional and educational circles (in

1970 economically active women represented 16.4 percent of the population), as well as social and student movements. They continued fighting for their rights, and in 1964 the National Union of Mexican Women (Unión Nacional de Mujeres Mexicanas) was created.[3] Moral precepts were questioned, sexual freedom was defended, and use of the pill was on the rise.[4] Rock and roll and the hippie movement shaped the younger generation; long hair and miniskirts reflected the rupture.[5]

In 1970 the nation's capital saw reforms. With the forced resignation of Ernesto Uruchurtu, opposition to subway construction ended, and urban expansion continued. The urban sprawl invaded the Federal District (or Mexico City, terms now used interchangeably), which was divided into sixteen delegations.[6] Neighborhood councils representing each borough were created and expanded citizen participation.[7]

Gustavo Díaz Ordaz governed the country from 1964 to 1970. The Partido Revolucionario Institucional candidate for his successor was Luis Echeverría. According to Soledad Loaeza, during his electoral campaign and when assuming the presidency, Echeverría presented himself as open to democratization (distancing himself from Díaz Ordaz's policies and repression of the student movement) and a promoter of social policies. Once in office, he sought to rebuild relations between government and society, advancing political and social reforms.[8] These years witnessed the bill to improve penitentiaries and respect for prisoners' rights. Various senators believed it was time for broader criminal reform, not only addressing the penitentiary problem but also updating the Criminal Codes and the Organic Law for Tribunals. Committee members responsible for adjudicating the senators' initiative called on experts for opinions. Other jurists opined in the press. The debate aired ideas concerning collegiality and the justice system in general. In this chapter, I examine the Senate's proposal, other opinions, and the reform that terminated criminal courts.

THE INITIATIVE'S PROPOSED CHANGES

Backers of the initiative continued to hold that justice must be administered by professional judges and did not deviate from the general principles of the current justice system.[9] Nevertheless, the proposed changes were significant. The foremost change was the suppression of first-instance collegial justice, replacing it with unitary justice, administered by one judge overseeing the phases of the judicial process. They justified the change based on the need to speed up the resolution of cases and bring the judge closer to the defendant. They also argued that whereas criminal courts (Cortes Penales) were collegial courts, the rest of the Federal District criminal courts were unitary, and it was important to standardize them.[10]

OPINIONS

The initiative was sent to two joint committees: the Justice Committee and Legislative Studies Committee.[11] Enrique Olivares Santana, chairman of the Senate Main Committee (Gran Comisión del Senado), publicly declared that the reform was of "such social preponderance" it was important to hear the "experts'" opinions.[12] The proposal was submitted to the consideration of judicial officials and jurists, who were representatives of academic institutions and attorney associations.

The consultation was conducted on two tracks and overseen not only by senators but also by deputies who were committee members and would later examine the initiative. The legislators visited SCJ ministers and TSJ magistrates.[13] In public hearings in January, they heard the opinions of distinguished jurists; members of the Academia Mexicana de Ciencias Penales, Sergio García Ramírez, Victoria Adato, Olga Islas de González Mariscal, Ricardo Franco Guzmán, Alfonso Quiroz Cuarón, Javier Piña y Palacios, Francisco Argüelles, Gustavo Malo Camacho, and Raúl F. Cárdenas; BMA President Francisco Javier Gaxiola; and well-known litigators Adolfo Aguilar y Quevedo, Andrés Iglesias Baillet, Víctor Velázquez, and Jorge Mario Magallón Ibarra. The initiative drew the interest of numerous jurists, who expressed their opinions in newspapers.[14]

Although some experts limited their opinions to the initiative, others took the opportunity to express their ideas on the justice system and the administration of justice. For instance, Franco Guzmán called for the creation of a National Commission of Criminal Studies to conduct a profound analysis of criminal law legislation, during which the legal initiative should be suspended.[15] Iglesias Baillet also defended major legislative reform, championing the unification of the country's Procedure Codes.[16]

In contrast, Aguilar y Quevedo argued that the efficacy of justice depended "more on budgets and judges than good will."[17] He and other experts, exiled Basque intellectual Ramón de Ertze Garamendi, González Bustamante, and Ranferi Gómez Díaz y Valencia Solís, targeted the need to increase the budget to augment the number of courts and officials' salaries.[18] Members of the BMA and other associations likewise asserted that justice could improve only with budgetary autonomy and better salaries for judicial officials.[19]

Aguilar y Quevedo also referred to judicial appointments. José Ángel Ceniceros and Gómez Díaz concurred; the latter recommended an increase in court staff and the presence of upright, trained, and honest judges, chosen for "their probity, strength of character, and independence."[20] Iglesias Baillet believed that most justice could not continue to be composed of negative elements and that unitary judges must be selected with rigorous criteria "because the application of justice in the future will depend on their honesty and capacity."[21] Solís Quiroga deemed the "total revision of the apparatus of the administration of justice" indispensable, necessary "to purge it of vices, corruption, and inadequate personnel."[22] Pedro Mucharraz, an attorney once imprisoned, maintained he never saw his accuser and barely saw the judge and public defender, whom he referred to as an irresponsible document signer in describing courts as "markets to the highest bidder."[23] Froylán López Narváez concluded that the judiciary had little autonomy, and in courts "business and irregularity often dominate the fates of men and property."[24] As a solution, Ignacio Medina Lima proposed creating the judicial career.[25] Argüelles supported this idea, saying, "The Criminal Code is not a panacea resolving the problem of crime in one fell swoop."[26] Judges in favor, Isidoro Asús Catalán and Gladys María Cristina García, mentioned the insecurity criminal court judges faced.[27] Solís Quiroga proposed an agency to provide auxiliary scientific and technical services to judges for expert guidance.[28] Velázquez suggested opening an office of experts independent of the Department of the Federal District.[29]

In addition, there were calls for applying the laws that sanctioned judges and judicial officials guilty of misconduct in performing their duties. Adato insisted this law should be applied not only to judges but also to MP agents, and Gaxiola extended it to defense attorneys.[30] In this vein, it seemed strange to Ceniceros that since December 1932, when he was deputy federal attorney general (under Attorney General Emilio Portes Gil and President Abelardo Rodríguez), there had been no request to remove any official.[31]

The subject of jury trials arose in this context. Chapter 2 described the debates surrounding jury trials. Opinions had not changed in the years preceding the presentation of the initiative, but in the late 1960s criticism prevailed. Quiroz Cuarón was against reinstatement of jury trials, especially given the possibility of their possible restoration: "The institution of the jury is an alarming factory of arbitrary verdicts of innocence, which produce impunity with its inevitable consequences of social disillusionment."[32] Years earlier, Héctor Solís Quiroga had referred to jury trials as "emotionally and femininely fickle," anachronistic, and inclined to acquit defendants.[33] Meanwhile, Garrido denied that a few people chosen randomly to be on a jury could represent "popular sentiment" and contended that the task of judging must fall to well-trained judges because trust could not be vested in simply anyone.[34] Ignacio Burgoa claimed that verdicts resulted from "the conscience and variable mood of its members" and therefore were uncertain and deviated from the law.[35]

Few voices defended jury trials. In the mid-1960s jurist José Antonio Llamosa García described the jury as a "symbol of human dignity" and the "conquest of freedom before the strict slavery of Positive Law and the coldness of its texts."[36] In 1970 Luis Quintanilla claimed the court had to be reestablished with greater powers because, thanks to the educational policy of revolutionary governments, the Mexican people were now prepared, and qualified jurors were available.[37]

The rest of this section considers the points contained in the senators' initiative, particularly the suppression of criminal courts. Experts spoke of the advantages and disadvantages of collegial courts, specifically of criminal courts and their performance. After the reform was adopted, García Ramírez examined the pros of collegial versus monocratic justice. Concerning the former, he referred to the sum of judges' ideas and experiences, a greater possibility of impartiality and judicial independence, and thus a strengthening of defendants' rights. As for the latter, he cited strengthening the judge's responsibility, simplifying judicial organization, speeding up proceedings, and better developing principles of orality, concentration, and immediacy.[38]

Shortly before the initiative was passed, González Bustamante, referring exclusively to first-instance justice, explained the disadvantages of collegial courts. He characterized criminal courts as a form of institution copied from abroad and said José Almaraz had made a serious mistake in transplanting it in Mexico. He contended that given the existence of second-instance collegial courts, there was no justification for first-instance tribunals. In his opinion, on this level, it led to delays and hindered "the normal and expeditious handling of business" because records sent by the examining judges sat on their colleagues' desks. He added that it impeded respect for the principle of immediacy because the judges not in charge of the instruction phase did not know the defendant, which was not the case when the judge intervened unitarily. Finally, he averred that unitary judges assumed a greater respon-

sibility and endeavored for the law to be correctly applied to avoid misjudg-
ments on their part.[39]

Years earlier, Manuel Rivera Vázquez had argued that a collegial tribunal
was optimal to consider, in "light of the wisdom of its members," possible
violations of the law in prior judicial rulings, but he declared his opposition
to collegial justice in first-instance tribunals. Far from intending judges to
be passive entities uniformly applying the law, he indicated that because
of diverse factors influencing each judge's perception (capacity, honesty,
enlightenment, knowledge of life, and humankind), it was difficult for the
three judges to coincide on the circumstances surrounding the crime and the
criminal and for their opinions to be identical. He concluded that "the nuances
and disharmony of diverse criteria" would lead to disharmony in the court.[40]

Significantly, the suppression of criminal courts was backed by all the
experts participating in the debate, who justified it based on the following
arguments:

A) **Simplification and unification of judicial organization**. García Ramírez
held that "there was no reason to support the diversity of judicial bodies in
the districts of the Federal District," and it was worth unifying them because
the other courts were unitary.[41]

B) **Greater speed in case resolutions**. Quiroz Cuarón claimed, "The advantage is evident of the suppression of criminal courts, whereby the process
will continue fully under a single judge. It will considerably augment the flow
in the administration of justice." He backed his statements with numbers:
There were five alleged criminals for every thousand inhabitants in the capital,
each of the criminal courts had more than 5,000 defendants, but if unitary
courts were created, each would have 1,785 cases. The swiftness in handling
cases would increase threefold, and judges could devote more time to study
each case.[42] Malo Camacho assured that the reform would solve one of the
worst problems in justice: insufficient speed in judicial proceedings.[43] García
Ramírez, Gaxiola, and public defender Eduardo Aburto Portillo agreed with
them.[44] *Novedades* explained, "The aim of the new system is to speed up the
administration of justice."[45]

C) **Respect for the principle of immediacy**. Velázquez claimed that eight
or nine of every ten defendants did not know their judges because tribunal
officials conducted the proceedings; he called for terminating the delegation
of functions and regarded it easier to eradicate this practice in unitary courts.
Malo Camacho, Adato, Cárdenas, del Castillo, Aguilar y Quevedo, and Igle-

sias Baillet considered the development of the process before a single judge would promote immediacy and the proper individualization of the sentence.[46] Héctor Calderón, head of MP agents, predicted it would stimulate "morality, concentration, and immediacy."[47] García Ramírez maintained that although a bifunctional judge could lose impartiality in ruling, he could have a better understanding of the defendant.[48]

D) **Strengthening the accusatory system.** According to García Ramírez, unitary courts enhanced the necessary aid of the defense, and the oral presentation of conclusions would permit hearings from declining further, because they were not always held, and when they were, all three judges were not present, having "been replaced by a formal appearance, useless paperwork, and vain ratifications." He added that the compulsory presence of defense attorneys at hearings ended the defendant's defenselessness, and oral support of the conclusions granted importance to the hearing and emphasized its orality.[49]

E) **Reduced corruption.** It is possible to believe collegial courts favored controlling judges' actions and their honesty, but at that moment it was an isolated opinion, and there were contrary thoughts. For example, *Novedades* contended that "extant judicial paths and specifically those connected to those criminal courts" were not working, and "they favored those who distorted justice on the paths of their particular convenience."[50]

Ultimately, agreement existed on abolishing criminal courts or first-instance collegial justice.

THE REFORMS

In the February 9, 1971, session, the joint Justice and Legislative Studies Committees presented their report and proposal for reforms to the Criminal Procedure Code. In the next day's session, Senator Ignacio Maciel Salcedo gave the general presentation of the initiative.[51]

The matter was briefly debated by members of the committees that oversaw the report; with their agreement, his proposal was approved. Without further ado, they proceeded to vote. The Criminal Procedure Code reforms were unanimously approved by 51 votes.[52] They held the first reading of the joint committees' report on the initiatives to reform the Organic Law of Tribunals of the Federal District and unanimously approved it on February 16.[53]

The proposed decree to reform the Criminal Procedure Code was then sent to the Chamber of Deputies for approval. It was debated in the February 17, 1971, session. At that time the deputies were focused on agrarian reform, and they paid little attention to reforming the Criminal Procedure Code. The project was unanimously passed, broadly and in detail, with 156 votes.[54] In the February 18 session, they held the first and second reading of the Organic Law of Tribunals, which was also unanimously passed.[55]

The decree reforming the Criminal Procedure Code was published in the *Diario Oficial* on March 19, 1971.[56] It entered into force on June 16 the same year. That day, the judges on the formerly collegial criminal courts became judges of the twenty-one existing unitary tribunals, and four new ones were created, for a total of twenty-five.[57] TSJ President Emilio César Pasos thanked the judges because the change meant sacrificing their summer vacations; he expressed his satisfaction over the reforms and his congratulations for the advent of a "more humane" justice.[58] Thus criminal courts ceased to operate in Mexico City.

FINAL REFLECTIONS

The 1971 reform was intended to strengthen a justice system appropriate for a liberal or democratic state governed by rule of law. It did not alter the planned path. By suppressing criminal courts, legislators sought to respect the principle of immediacy and resolve the backlog.

Although these problems were repeatedly denounced, the delegation of functions, sway of influences, and corruption were also criticized in the early twentieth century. Some experts suggested the suppression of collegial courts would put an end to these issues because unitary judges would bear full responsibility for their resolutions.

However, other experts thought none of these problems could be resolved with the 1971 reform because they deemed it incomplete. They contended that the deficiencies in the administration of justice could not be overcome with minor adjustments, and the challenge called for a profound overhaul of criminal law. They also believed that to resolve matters such as insufficient personnel and the inefficacy of judges, it was necessary to increase the number of courts, change the appointment procedure, create a professional judicial career, and raise salaries. For this, more resources had to be allocated to justice. Aguilar y Quevedo asserted that the problem with justice was of an administrative order because the insufficient budget hindered "the exercise and enforcement of law in courts," along with matters that went beyond changing the law and involved the effective application of laws.[59] Adato argued, "Justice has developed around a series of fictions, simulations clothed in legality."[60]

It was necessary to ensure law was observed by officials and judges, and if not, the corresponding law must be applied.

To recap, the suppression of collegial courts in first-instance justice and replacing them with unitary tribunals brought about an important change in the judicial system. However, the foundations of the model of justice did not change. For instance, justice continued to be administered by judges trained in law and appointed by higher judges and was closed to citizen participation. Trials were still essentially written, and MP agents had considerable weight. Furthermore, as authors of the time stated, the 1971 reform did not address the problems that plagued justice because that would have required budgetary changes, other legal reforms, and putting old and new laws into practice. As García Ramírez postulated, the suppression of criminal courts was part of a broader three-part plan: criminal, procedural, and penitentiary. In his words, "The occasion that triggered broader, substantial modifications was the law establishing the minimum rules for the social rehabilitation of convicts." Therefore, he believed, it was not the procedural aspect that underwent major changes.[61]

CONCLUSION

In the 1917 Constitution, Mexico emerged as a liberal, democratic state ruled by law. This Constitution and the codes and laws promulgated in the following decades contemplated a justice system with this state model governed by specific principles: autonomy of judges, who had to be attorneys with degrees and prior experience; equality of defendants under the law and in courts; respect for suspects' and defendants' rights; strict observance of substantive and procedural laws in trials; rationalization of judicial discretion and individualization of sentencing based on an understanding of the defendant; free-of-charge, public, and transparent trials; equilibrium between parties in trials; and broad defense.

In an environment conducive to legal change and a climate of institutionalization and professionalization, the framers of the 1929 Code eliminated trial by jury, given the belief that professional judges were in a better position to discern the distinctive characteristics of the defendant. Moreover, they thought collegial courts would permit the elimination of arbitrariness and control the margin of discretion. Their clear sympathy for the positivist school and their flirtation with organic determinism drew criticism and generated tension evident in the code, stemming from the desire of its drafters not to violate the principle of equality consecrated in the Constitution, while accommodating the consideration of each defendant's specific traits.

The 1931 Code drafters found equilibrium. Although the 1929 code was repealed, some proposals, such as the creation of the criminal courts, survived. These codes, as did the laws or reforms issued between 1931 and 1971, sought to preserve and strengthen the elements of a system aimed at defending the rights, freedoms, and goods of Mexico City's inhabitants. In this field, Mexican legislation of the time was at the cutting edge worldwide and included demands made by international agencies and treaties. In essence, it also had the ingredients today regarded as indispensable for speaking of a justice system appropriate for a liberal, democratic legal state.

These principles were included in legislation; therefore, their observance by judges, judicial officials, and the police would permit the existence in practice of the justice system and state model, whereas their inobservance would lead to the converse. To understand police and judicial practices, I turned to testimonies from the time and, to a lesser degree, to homicide trials. In the years when criminal courts operated, jurists, intellectuals, screenwriters, and journalists both praised and criticized the actions and practices of administrative authorities, legislators, judges, litigators, and the police. In fact, critical observations predominated.

Some complained of the meager budget assigned to courts, claiming that the lack of economic resources prevented them from fulfilling their duty and that low salaries tested officials' honesty. Others denounced the existence of partisanship and cronyism in judicial appointments, which indebted the appointees to their benefactors and could influence their future actions or resolutions. Still others spoke of influence peddling, corruption, absenteeism, delegation of functions, and breaches of the immediacy requirement and the foundations of collegial justice by judges or labeled the police as inefficient and accused them of violating defendants' rights and even of committing crimes. These denunciations suggest that judicial laws were violated in practice.

Based on these things, jurists and journalists asserted that the postrevolutionary government had broken one of the main promises of the armed movement: satisfying the Mexican people's hunger and thirst for justice (from Justo Sierra's words quoted in chapter 3). Hence they claimed the revolutionary state had not fulfilled its commitment. Beyond that, and addressing the authorities' inability to protect the safety and property of citizens, they pointed out the state (without adjectives) had failed. Furthermore, repeatedly citing the violation of procedural rights and due process in general by judges and the police, as well as the violation of laws governing justice, the unequal application of the law and the lack of judges' independence would preclude fully speaking of a state governed by the rule of law. Going beyond and in response to the inability of authorities to protect the citizens' legal good demonstrated that the state had simply failed.

The criticism surely affected the suppression of criminal courts and the adoption of unitary courts. The 1971 reform drew on the arguments made, gained force in the framework of a broader legislative change, and fed on a general sensation of political crisis and social disillusionment.

In sum, between 1929 and 1971 justice had a tarnished image.

Exploring practices offers a more nuanced and colorful image. For example, judges' profiles suggest that partisanship and cronyism persisted in some appointments; however, it is less perceptible in the second part of the period because judicial careers became longer, allowing judges to gain experience and independence. In the same vein, although the trials studied exemplify problems denounced by witnesses of the time (police abuses, isolation or torture to compel confessions, backlogs and lengthening procedural time limits, the absence of public defenders, judges delegating functions, corruption, or the role of influences), they also illustrate the observance of essential principles of the model of justice and attest to good procedural practices. Obviously, the situations varied not only depending on the time but also depending on different types of judges, officials, and police involved.

Thus the analysis of trials permits refining, dimensioning, and nuancing the conclusions of witnesses at the time concerning the observance (or lack thereof) of fundamental rights and laws in judicial and police practices. It also enables us to explore other aspects of the process and address other research concerns. The first is assessing the proportion of "difficult or controversial" versus "easy or clear" cases. In my sample, the former were more numerous than the latter. There were reiterated discrepancies among judges regarding the defendants' criminal liability and the circumstances under which crimes were committed. Although this could be explained by considering that the sample covered high-profile cases, in other trials, judges perhaps examined the draft judgments proposed by the examining judges in less depth (as testimonies suggest). Another interesting matter seen in case records is the importance first- and second-instance judges gave to *tesis* based on their growing importance granted by legislators.

The possibility of understanding the performance of procedural parties is significant as well. Defense attorneys played a leading role in high-profile cases, in which, according to accounts of the time, their acts differed from those of most trials. MP agents also had enormous weight, as seen in the amount of attention judges gave to their petitions, and their petitions were of major importance in judges' decisions, which was recurrent and widespread.

Finally, exploring judicial experiences permitted addressing another fundamental core of this work: journalists' influence on society's ideas and ethical conceptions (or their impact on public opinion), the influence of public opinion on judgments and the performance of authorities and judges, and to close the circle, the influence of judgments on the community's ideas and values.

Responding to the interest and demand of readers, listeners, and viewers, sensationalistic magazines and supplements, journalistic articles, radio news, and films proliferated in postrevolutionary Mexico. Journalists, broadcasters, and screenwriters not only described and re-created crimes but also strengthened or gathered ideas, opinions, and visions of the crime, good and evil, prohibited and permitted, moral and amoral. In other words, journalists, broadcasters, and screenwriters shaped ethical notions and customs of readers, listeners, and viewers, or at least influenced their opinions and assessments of the crimes and justice in general and of each criminal and trial in particular. They played a key role in influencing public opinion.

It was not possible to determine whether this public opinion was a factor in the way trials or judgments played out. What I can say is that in the cases analyzed, judgments were close to the press's opinions of the criminals, and the community supported these. For instance, criminals who received the greatest public condemnation, such as María Elena Blanco and Gonzalo Ortiz Ordaz, received harsh sentences. In fact, Ortiz Ordaz and Alberto Gallegos died or were killed in custody under mysterious circumstances. Finally, judicial rulings disseminated by the press reinforced opinions and prior values of readers, listeners, and viewers.

In the movie La otra (The other one) María and Magdalena (both played by Dolores del Río) embody two extremes, the first representing positive values (decent, sincere, honorable, capable of loving), and the second, negative values (hypocritical, vain, disloyal, cold, and opportunistic). Out of greed, Magdalena marries the man loved by her twin sister. Later, María falls in love with a policeman, but her misery leads her to kill Magdalena to take her place. When her brother-in-law dies, the path of good would have given her an unexpected reward: The deceased leaves her an inheritance she could have enjoyed in the detective's company. However, the path of evil she took brings a cruel punishment: Her sister's lover blackmails her because both had poisoned the husband. María loses her fortune and is punished for the murder committed by Magdalena, but she is actually suffering the consequences of killing Magdalena, abandoning her fiancé, and leaving the path of good.[1] Hence the outcome brings viewers a moral lesson. The harsh sentences given to women like Chole la Ranchera and María Elena Blanco perhaps also transmitted a similar message to the community.

Dolores del Río, Chole la Ranchera, and María Elena Blanco died many years ago, and some have disappeared from the collective memory. However, their stories and the history of justice described here have not lost their power. The bases of the justice system and judicial institutions, practices, and negotiation mechanisms from 1929 to 1971, as well as the problems and solutions, ideas and values, persisted in the decades that followed and continue to this day. Remaining challenges include reducing violence and criminality, combating impunity, achieving an effective and trustworthy justice system, and increasing citizens' trust in the administration and enforcement of justice. History has no clear edges or radical cuts; it lives in the present and heralds the future.

ACKNOWLEDGMENTS

I am indebted to the University of Nebraska Press for its willingness to publish this work and specifically to the Confluencias series editors, Susie Porter, Diana Montaño, and María Muñoz. I am also grateful to the Instituto de Investigaciones Históricas of the UNAM, my research center for almost thirty years.

In the original Spanish publication of this work, I thanked institutions, colleagues, and friends important in my professional growth and the development of my work; I reiterate my appreciation to all of them. My gratitude also goes to Sergio García Ramírez and José Ramón Cossío Díaz for their forewords and especially to García Ramírez for serving as my advisor in the Department of Law at the UNAM for the dissertation that gave rise to this book. I take this opportunity to acknowledge my colleagues in the Permanent Law and Justice History Seminar and the Permanent Sociocultural History of Crime and Transgression Seminar for our enriching interactions for more than twenty years.

I thank my friends and colleagues for their support in the translation process and those who gave me ideas in reviews of the work in Spanish. Although I cannot mention all of them, I would like to acknowledge Claudia Agostoni, José Antonio Caballero, Marcela Corvera, Norman Macdonald, Rafael Estrada, Graciela Flores Flores, James A. Garza, Daniela Marino, Mariana Masera, Pablo Mijangos, Pablo Piccato, Diego Pulido, Odette Rojas Sosa, Gemma Santamaría, Martha Santillán, and Gisela von Wobeser.

I am grateful to Victor Macías-González for suggesting I publish this book in English, Debra Nagao for the careful translation, Emily Casillas for her editorial support, UNP for its meticulous editorial supervision and design, and Eric Esteban del Castillo for preparing the index. I also thank William Suarez-Potts, Ricardo Salvatore, and Timothy M. James for their comments on the manuscript and their support in translating legal terms into English.

The first edition of this book, published in Spanish, was dedicated to my children, María and Leonardo. This new version was possible thanks to their closeness and that of Leonardo López Luján.

APPENDIX A

MAGISTRATES APPOINTED TO THE TSJ

In this appendix, the prosecutors of the Local Prosecutor's Office (Ministerio Público) are abbreviated as MP agents, the Supreme Court is abbreviated as SCJ, and the Supreme Justice Tribunal is abbreviated as TSJ.

MAGISTRATES APPOINTED IN 1928

Former Magistrate

Adolfo Valles Baca (magistrate between 1911 and 1915):
MP agent, public defender, criminal judge during Díaz administration, later federal attorney general

SINCE 1919

Eleuterio Martínez
José Espinosa y López Portillo: MP agent
Julián Ramírez Martínez
Sabino M. Olea y Leyva: litigator during and after the Revolution

SINCE 1922

Juan de la Cruz García

SINCE 1923

Carlos Echeverría: magistrate in Sinaloa, general in the Revolution, commander and governor of Tepic
Clemente Castellanos
Everardo Gallardo Canseco: various positions in courts during Díaz administration, federal MP agent and district judge, correctional and criminal judge in D.F.
Joaquín Lanz Galera: deputy at the Constitutional Convention, federal deputy
Luis Ramírez Corzo
Vicente Santos Guajardo: criminal judge during or after the Revolution

New Magistrates

Adalberto Galeano Sierra: interim governor and senator, magistrate and attorney general in Campeche

Alfonso Teja Zabre: court clerk before the Revolution,
later civil judge, public defender, MP agent
Alfredo Ortega
Carlos Lauro Ángeles: MP agent in the State of Mexico, judge
in Michoacán, federal deputy and judge in the capital
Francisco Castañeda
José M. Ortiz Tirado: public defender and MP agent
José Ortiz Rodríguez
Matías Ochoa
Miguel Castillo Tielemans
Rafael Santos Alonso

MAGISTRATES APPOINTED IN 1934

Former Magistrates

SINCE 1925

Clemente Castellanos

SINCE 1928

Adalberto Galeana Sierra
Alfredo Ortega
Carlos L. Ángeles
Filiberto Viveros
José Ortiz Rodríguez
Matías Ochoa

New Magistrates

WITH PRIOR EXPERIENCE IN COURTS

Abelardo Medina y Díaz: judge
José Trinidad Sánchez Benítez: judge
Luis Díaz Infante: judge
Luis G. Corona: political background and judicial career
Luis Pintado: judge
Platón Herrera Ostos: judge
Rafael Gual Vidal: judge
Rafael Martínez Mendoza: political background and judicial career
Teófilo Olea y Leyva: political background and
judicial career in military courts

WITH NO PRIOR EXPERIENCE IN COURTS

Alberto Coria: federal deputy
Carlos Soto Guevara: federal deputy
Eliseo Rosales y Cadena

Enrique Pérez Arce: revolutionary participant, deputy, governor of Sinaloa
Ignacio Herrera Tejeda: revolutionary participant
Manuel M. Moreno: federal deputy
Miguel Alemán Valdés: deputy, senator
Norberto de la Rosa
Valentín Rincón

MAGISTRATES APPOINTED TO FILL VACANCIES BETWEEN 1940 AND 1943

With Prior Judicial Experience

Daniel Salazar
Ernesto Aguilar Álvarez: judge and TSJ magistrate in Veracruz
Horacio Alemán
Luis Cataño Morlet
Marino Castillo Nájera
Raúl Carrancá y Trujillo
Salvador Mondragón Guerra: judge and TSJ chamber clerk
Victoriano Anguiano: MP agent, former deputy,
    and Partido Popular founder

With Prior Political Careers

Eduardo Arrioja Insunza: deputy
Gustavo Cárdenas Huerta: Partido Revolucionario Institucional secretary
Víctor Alfonso Maldonado: deputy
Wilfrido Cruz: secretary to the governor of Oaxaca, deputy,
    senator, Partido Nacional Revolucionario general secretary

MAGISTRATES APPOINTED IN 1944

New Magistrates

Alberto Bremauntz
Armando Z. Ostos: deputy from Tamaulipas, later litigator
Eduardo Arrioja Insunza
Efraín Aranda Osorio
Ernesto Aguilar Álvarez: civil judge and magistrate in Veracruz
Francisco de Sales Valero
Gonzalo Martínez de Escobar
Ignacio Villalobos Jiménez: civil judge and magistrate
    in Jalisco, MP agent, and judge in Mexico City
Jesús Z. Nucamendi
Rafael Rosales Gómez: judge

Salomón González Blanco: senator, also magistrate
in Tabasco and SCJ minister
Salvador Mondragón Guerra: judge and TSJ clerk
Victoriano Anguiano Equihua: deputy for Michoacán and Partido
Popular founder, later federal MP agent and judge

Ratified Magistrates

SINCE 1928

Adalberto Galeano Sierra
José Ortiz Rodríguez
Matías Ochoa

SINCE 1934

Enrique Pérez Arce
Valentín Rincón

SINCE 1940

Daniel Salazar Hurtado
Gustavo Cárdenas Huerta
Horacio Alemán
Luis Cataño Morlet
Miguel Medina Hermosillo
Raúl Carrancá y Trujillo
Wilfrido Cruz

MAGISTRATES APPOINTED IN 1951

New Magistrates

Alfredo Briseño
Celestino Porte Petit: magistrate in Veracruz and Mexico City, MP
agent, member of the Criminal Code Drafting Committee
Edmundo Elorduy Delgado: judge
Eduardo Mac-Gregor Romero: criminal court judge
Emilio César Pasos: criminal court judge
Enrique A. Enríquez: Constitutionalist Army colonel, deputy in the
Constitutional Congress, MP agent and judge in military courts
Francisco Salcedo Casas: magistrate in Veracruz
Gabriel Gómez Mendoza
Genaro Ruiz de Chávez: criminal court judge
Godofredo Beltrán
José Castillo Larrañaga: district judge in
Tamaulipas, MP agent, court clerk
José Valentín Medina Ochoa: magistrate in Jalisco

Leonardo Pasquel

Mario Cazarín

Pedro Zorrilla

Ratified Magistrates

SERVED FOR MANY YEARS

Adalberto Galeano Sierra (since 1928)

Platón Herrera Ostos (since 1934)

SINCE 1944

Alberto Bremauntz

Ernesto Aguilar Álvarez

Ignacio Villalobos Jiménez

Rafael Rosales Gómez

Salvador Mondragón Guerra

Victoriano Anguiano Equihua

SINCE 1947

Aguilar y Maya

Alberto R. Vela

Francisco de Sales Valero

Miguel Lavalle Urbina

MAGISTRATES APPOINTED IN 1957

New Magistrates

Alberto González Blanco: criminal judge

Aulo Gelio Lara Erosa: criminal judge

Donato Miranda Fonseca: deputy, minister of planning and
budget and presidential candidate, judge and magistrate

Eduardo L. Bienvenú Herrera

Gregorio Merino Bastar

José Víctor Cervantes Aguilera

Pedro Guerrero Martínez: deputy, administrative positions,
MP agent, head of public defenders, attorney general

Tito Ortega Sánchez: deputy and senator

Ratified Magistrates

SERVED FOR MANY YEARS

Adalberto Galeano Sierra: appointed in 1928

Alberto Bremauntz: appointed in 1944

Godofredo Beltrán: appointed in 1947

Gonzalo Martínez de Escobar: appointed in 1940

Ignacio Villalobos Jiménez: appointed in 1944
Miguel Lavalle Urbina: appointed in 1947
Platón Herrera Ostos: appointed in 1934

Eduardo Mac-Gregor Romero
Emilio César Pasos
Enrique A. Enríquez
Francisco De Sales Valero
José Castillo Larrañaga
José Valentín Medina Ochoa
Julio Sánchez Vargas
Salcedo Casas Porte-Petit

Gloria León Orantes

MAGISTRATES APPOINTED IN 1963

New Magistrates

Alberto Sánchez Cortés: criminal court judge
Ernesto Hernández Páez
Guillermo Colín Sánchez: MP agent, judge, attorney
   general of the State of Mexico, litigator, presidentially
   appointed positions and political background
Javier Ordoñez Farrera: supernumerary magistrate
Juan C. Gorráez Maldonado: governor of Querétaro
María Luisa Santillán
Rafael Ojeda Guerra: supernumerary magistrate
Raúl Ortiz Urquidi: district judge, secretary of study and accounting
   in the SCJ, Legal Office head of the President's Office,
   presidentially appointed positions and political background
René González de la Vega: supernumerary magistrate
Salvador Martínez Rojas: criminal court judge

Ratified Magistrates

SERVED FOR MANY YEARS

Celestino Porte Petit: appointed in 1951
Eduardo Mac-Gregor Romero: appointed in 1951
Emilio César Pasos: appointed in 1951
Gloria León Orantes: appointed in 1954
Godofredo Beltrán: appointed in 1947
José Castillo Larrañaga: appointed in 1951

José Valentín Medina Ochoa: appointed in 1951
Julio Sánchez Vargas: appointed in 1951

Alberto González Blanco
Aulo Gelio Lara Erosa
Eduardo L. Bienvenú Herrera
Gregorio Merino Bastar
Ignacio Calderón Álvarez: supernumerary magistrate
José Víctor Cervantes Aguilera
Luis G. Saloma: supernumerary magistrate
Pascual Flores Guillén: supernumerary magistrate
Tito Ortega Sánchez

MAGISTRATES APPOINTED IN 1968

New Magistrates

Abel Treviño Rodríguez
Alfredo Beltrán Arreola
Antonio Taracena Alpuín
Roberto Galeano Pérez: civil judge

Ratified Magistrates

SERVED FOR MANY YEARS

Celestino Porte Petit: appointed in 1951
Eduardo Mac-Gregor Romero: appointed in 1951
Emilio César Pasos: appointed in 1951
Gloria León Orantes: appointed in 1954
Godofredo Beltrán: appointed in 1951
Ignacio Calderón Álvarez: appointed in 1957
José Valentín Medina Ochoa: appointed in 1951
José Víctor Cervantes Aguilera: appointed in 1957
María Luisa Santillán: appointed in 1954
Pascual Flores Guillén: appointed in 1957
Tito Ortega Sánchez: appointed in 1957

SINCE 1963

Alberto Sánchez Cortés
Ernesto Hernández Páez
Javier Ordoñez Farrera: supernumerary magistrate
Juan C. Gorráez Maldonado
Rafael Ojeda Guerra
Salvador Martínez Rojas

APPENDIX B

JUDGES APPOINTED TO THE CRIMINAL COURTS

JUDGES APPOINTED IN 1928

First Court

Ángel Escalante: with prior experience
Ernesto G. Garza: with prior experience
Ramiro Estrada: with prior experience

Second Court

Eduardo Hernández Garibay: with no prior experience in courts
Jesús Zavala: with no prior experience in courts
Juan Antonio Fernández Vera: with no prior experience in courts

Third Court

José de la Hoz Chaubert: with prior experience
Mariano Fernández de Córdova: with prior experience
Miguel Lavalle: with prior experience

JUDGES APPOINTED IN 1931

First Court

Ángel Escalante: former criminal court judge
Jesús Zavala: former criminal court judge
Juan Antonio Fernández Vera: former criminal court judge

Second Court

Mariano Fernández de Córdova: former criminal court judge
Miguel Lavalle: former criminal court judge
Ramiro Estrada: former criminal court judge

Third Court

Eduardo Hernández Garibay: former criminal court judge
Ernesto G. Garza: former criminal court judge
Humberto Esquivel Medina: newly appointed

Fourth Court

Fernando Castaño: newly appointed

Francisco González de la Vega: newly appointed
Juan López Moctezuma: newly appointed

Fifth Court

Alberto Régulo Vela: former correctional court judge
Hermilo López Sánchez: former correctional court judge
Platón Herrera Ostos: former correctional court judge

Sixth Court

Clotario Margalli González: former correctional court judge
José Hernández de la Garza: former correctional court judge
Rafael Matos Escobedo: former correctional court judge

Seventh Court

Enrique Arévalo y Valle: former correctional court judge
Genaro Ruiz de Chávez: former correctional court judge
Práxedis de la Peña: former correctional court judge

Eighth Court

Federico Dosamantes: newly appointed
Luis Garrido: newly appointed
Raúl Carrancá y Trujillo: newly appointed

JUDGES APPOINTED IN 1934

First Court

Adolfo Montoya
Antonio Espinosa Rodríguez: member of the council in Mexico City
Juan José González Bustamante

Second Court

Darío Pastrana Jaimes: judge, defense attorney
Gregorio Ayala Calderón: judicial positions in
    Michoacán, magistrate in Nayarit
Hilario Hermosillo: deputy and interim governor of San Luis Potosí

Third Court

Enrique Toscano
José Jiménez Sierra
Raúl Jaimes

Fourth Court

Carlos Ramírez Arronte
Ricardo Abarca
Vicente Muñoz Castro

Fifth Court

Alberto R. Vela: ratified judge, deputy, government minister in Oaxaca

Isaac Olivé

José Espinosa y López Portillo: MP agent, TSJ magister

Sixth Court

Ignacio Pérez Vargas: defense attorney

Jesús González Insunza

Rafael Matos Escobedo: ratified judge

JUDGES APPOINTED BETWEEN 1940 AND 1943

New Judges

Alberto González Blanco: court clerk

Alfonso Martínez Sotomayor

Carlos Morales

Clemente Castellanos: magistrate

Eduardo Fernández Guerra: court clerk, interim judge

Eduardo Hurtado Aubry: interim governor of Campeche

Emilio César Pasos

Fausto Galván Campos: court clerk

Genaro Ruiz de Chávez: criminal and correctional judge

Gilberto Suárez Arvizu: government secretary in Sonora

José Luis Gutiérrez y Gutiérrez: MP agent,
    government secretary in State of Mexico

José Trinidad Sánchez Benítez: magistrate

Lorenzo Reynoso Padilla: judge in Colima and Jalisco

Manuel Avilés

Refugio Rocha Alva

Ratified Judges

Alberto R. Vela

Ignacio Pérez Vargas

José Espinosa y López Portillo

Juan José González Bustamante

Rafael Matos Escobedo

Vicente Muñoz Castro

JUDGES APPOINTED IN 1944

New Judges

Arturo Prior Martínez

Aulio Gelio Lara Erosa: interim criminal judge, court clerk

Carlos Espeleta Torrijos: MP agent, TSJ interim magistrate
Eduardo Mac-Gregor: public defender
Ernesto Meixueiro Hernández: MP agent
Francisco Argüelles Espinosa: court clerk, secretary
    of study and accounts in the SCJ
Ignacio Calderón Álvarez
Jaime Blanco
Luis Gonzaga Saloma
Luis H. Monroy: magistrate of Federal Fiscal Tribunal and TSJ
María Teresa Puente
Mario G. Escalante: secretary of study and accounts in the SCJ
Ramón Franco Romero
Salvador Castañeda del Villar

Ratified Judges

SINCE 1934

Vicente Muñoz Castro

SINCE 1940

Alberto González Blanc
Alfonso Martínez Sotomayor
Fausto Galván Campos
Genaro Ruiz de Chávez
Gilberto Suárez Arvizu
Lorenzo Reynoso Padilla

JUDGES APPOINTED IN 1951

New Judges

Alberto Sánchez Cortés: public defender,
    attorney general, TSJ magistrate in Veracruz
Clotario Margalli Lara
Eduardo Urzaiz Jiménez
Ignacio Acosta Fuentes
José Martínez Lozano: head of MP agents
Mario Guillermo Rebolledo Fernández: former MP agent,
    judge, attorney general, interim governor of Veracruz
Pablo Roberto Desentis
Porfirio Díaz Sibaja: former MP agent

Ratified Judges

SINCE 1940

Alberto González Blanco
Alfonso Martínez Sotomayor
Lorenzao Reynoso Padilla

SINCE 1944

Aulio Gelio Lara Erosa
Carlos Espeleta Torrijos
Ignacio Calderón Álvarez
Luis Gonzaga Saloma Córdova
Mario G. Escalante
Ramón Franco Romero
Salvador Castañeda del Villar

JUDGES APPOINTED IN 1957

New Judges

Antonio F. Reyes Rivera
Clemente Valdez
David Lomelín Pastor
Eulalio Aguirre Bárcena
Héctor Terán Torres
Mariano Castillo Mena
Roberto Campos Cos
Salvador Martínez Rojas

Ratified Judges

SINCE 1944

Carlos Espeleta Torrijos
Ramón Franco Romero
Salvador Castañeda del Villar

SINCE 1951

Alberto Sánchez Cortés
Eduardo Urzaiz Jiménez

NOTES

I. PRELIMINARY QUESTIONS

1. Terms taken from Lorente, *De justicia de jueces.*
2. Elías Calles, "Discurso de apertura de las sesiones del Congreso de la Unión" and "Informe presidencial," *Diario de Debates de la Cámara de Diputados* (hereafter *Diario de Debates*), Legislatura XXXIII, Periodo Ordinario, diario 6, September 1, 1928.
3. Rodríguez Kuri, "Ciudad oficial," 418–19.
4. The boroughs at this time were Guadalupe Hidalgo, Azcapotzalco, Ixtacalco, General Anaya, Coyoacán, San Ángel, La Magdalena Contreras, Cuajimalpa, Tlalpan, Ixtapalapa, Xochimilco, Milpa Alta, and Tláhuac.
5. Rodríguez Kuri, "Ciudad oficial," 424.
6. Miranda Pacheco, *La creación*, 53–95; Davis, *El Leviatán*, 101–17; Sánchez-Mejorada Fernández, "Los elementos jurídicos," 248–49.
7. Zapata, "Población y sociedad," 254–61; Unikel, *El desarrollo*, 250.
8. Padilla, *Después de Zapata*, 21–33.
9. The boroughs now were Azcapotzalco, Gustavo A. Madero (formerly Guadalupe Hidalgo), Iztacalco, Cuajimalpa, Álvaro Obregón (formerly San Ángel), Coyoacán, Iztapalapa, Magdalena Contreras, Tlalpan, Xochimilco, Tláhuac, and Milpa Alta.
10. Rodríguez Kuri, "Ciudad oficial," 429–30.
11. Rodríguez Kuri, "Ciudad oficial," 438–42; Davis, *El Leviatán*, 157; Sánchez-Mejorada Fernández, "Los elementos jurídicos," 253.
12. Davis, *El Leviatán*, 154–83, 203–17; Zapata, "Población y sociedad," 258–61.
13. For instance, Kandell, "Mexico's Megalopolis" or Sánchez Ruiz, *La Ciudad de México.*
14. The same tendency is reflected in national statistics. See Piccato, *History of Infamy*, 271–77.
15. The distance can be explained by various factors, including unreported or undiscovered crimes. See Piccato, "Una perspectiva histórica."
16. Quiroz Cuarón, "La criminalidad evoluciona."
17. "Mayor rigor," 61.
18. García Ramírez, "Quehacer," 23–24.
19. For studies on homicide of the time, see Núñez Cetina, "El homicidio"; Núñez Cetina, "Reforma y justicia." On the impact of the Gregorio Cárdenas case, see Ríos Molina, *Memorias de un loco.*

20. See the collection published by Editorial Diana in 1996 (between them, Luna, *La nota roja, 1930–1939*, and Brocca, *La nota roja, 1960–1969*); De Mauleón, *El tiempo repentino*; Fernández Reyes, *Crimen y suspenso*.
21. See Pulido Llano, *El mapa rojo*, 15–24.
22. Quoted in González Rodríguez, "La avenida," 169.
23. See Rojas Sosa, "La ciudad"; Rojas Sosa, "El bajo mundo"; Rojas Sosa, "Una amenaza."
24. Caporal Pérez et al., *Diagnóstico*, 75–105; Santillán Esqueda, "Mujeres *non sanctas*."
25. Pulido Llano, *El mapa rojo*, 154–55.
26. *Anuario Estadístico de los Estados Unidos Mexicanos* (annual publication of the Dirección General de Estadística del Distrito Federal); Rojas Sosa, "La ciudad," 65.
27. José Agustín, *Tragicomedia mexicana*, 97, 137; Monsiváis, "Círculos de perdición," 6; Jiménez, *Sitios de rompe*; Medina Caracheo and Vargas Ocaña, "La vida nocturna."
28. José Agustín, *Tragicomedia mexicana*, 94.
29. Santillán Esqueda, *Delincuencia femenina*, 18–28; Santillán Esqueda, "Mujeres delincuentes," 392–97, 413–14; Santillán Esqueda, "Infanticidas"; Santillán Esqueda, "'La descuartizadora"; Núñez Cetina, "Reforma social."
30. Santillán Esqueda, *Delincuencia femenina*, 18.
31. Monsiváis, Prólogo, 32–35; Vaughan, Introducción, 45; Santillán Esqueda, "Posrevolución y participación," 158–66.
32. Santillán Esqueda, "Posrevolución y participación," 153–57; Santillán Esqueda, "Mujeres y leyes," 128–36.
33. Figures in Santillán Esqueda, *Delincuencia femenina*, 19–21; Santillán Esqueda, "Discursos de redomesticación," 108. Assessment of qualitative change in Porter, "Espacios burocráticos."
34. Maza Pesqueira and Santillán Esqueda, "Movilización," 205–9.
35. Infante Vargas, "Por nuestro género," 80; Santillán Esqueda, "Posrevolución y participación," 178–82.
36. Santillán Esqueda, "Discursos de redomesticación."
37. A. Zavala, "De Santa"; Santillán Esqueda, "El discurso tradicionalista."
38. Rubenstein, "La guerra."
39. "Indicadores de población del área metropolitana," FAQC, sobre 2.
40. Pérez Montfort, "La cultura," 293–94. On radios, see Piccato, "Altibajos," 240–41.
41. De los Reyes, *Sucedió en Jalisco*, 143–205.
42. Fernández Reyes, *Crimen y suspenso*, 67.
43. Agüero, "Las categorías"; Fioravanti, "Estado y constitución," 17–22; Garriga, "Orden jurídico"; Grossi, *Mitología jurídica*, 24–29.
44. Fioravanti, "Estado y constitución," 16–29.

45. For example, Luigi Ferrajoli differentiates formal democracy (based on the principle of popular sovereignty and granting the people the power to legislate, so that political and civil rights are present) and substantial democracy (which supposes limits to the state's power and establishes the preponderance of human rights). *Democracia*, 80–82. Larry Diamond also marks a difference between electoral and liberal democracies, suggesting the former can coexist with practices that violate human rights. *Spirit*, 21–26.
46. García Ramírez, "Los sistemas," 5.
47. García Ramírez, *Los derechos humanos*, 13. See also García Ramírez, *Panorama*, 1–13.
48. García Ramírez, *Panorama*, 15–26.
49. Diamond, *Spirit*, 22.
50. Gudiño Pelayo, "El papel"; Concha, "Hacia una justicia."
51. García Ramírez, "La reforma jurídica," 61; García Ramírez, *El sistema penal*, 29; García Ramírez, *Panorama*, 18.
52. Ernst, "Independencia judicial," 235.
53. Calamandrei, *Proceso y democracia*, 87, 91–102.
54. Bobbio, *El futuro*, 36–38, 94–118.
55. García Ramírez, *Panorama*, 87.
56. Whitehead, *Democratization*, 1–5, 6–35.
57. Kalifa, *Crimen y cultura*, 12.
58. Monsiváis, *Los mil*, 39.
59. Piccato, *History of Infamy*, 5–6, 64–66, 99, 102.
60. Santillán Esqueda, *Delincuencia femenina*, 50–63; Santillán Esqueda, "Mujeres delincuentes."
61. Tuñón Pablos, "Cine," 94.
62. Piccato, "El significado," 58.
63. García Ramírez, *Los reformadores*, 117–88.
64. Calamandrei, *Proceso y democracia*, 43.
65. Guastini, *Estudios*, 13–14.
66. Vernengo, "Interpretación," 255.
67. Nieto, *El arbitrio*, 47, 81–91, 103–6, 203–70 (207n).
68. Fix-Zamudio and Cossío Díaz, *El poder judicial*, 46–47.
69. Prieto Sanchís, *Ideología*, 54.
70. Cuellar Vázquez, "Los jueces."
71. Cardozo, *La función judicial*, 2–3.
72. For example, Herbert Hart speaks of difficult cases where the law does not provide a solution and judges must exercise their discretion. *Post scríptum al concepto*, 54, 56. In contrast, Ricardo Guastini highlights a difference between normative/regulatory formulations that do not require interpretation and others with an unclear or debatable meaning. *Estudios*, 3–5, 16–18.
73. Ezquiaga Ganuzas, "Función legislativa," 51.

74. I reached this conclusion in a study on the Porfirio Díaz administration, "Las flores del mal." Others who have expressed the same idea are Corona Azanza, "He dominado"; Rivera Reynaldos, "Criminales"; Rivera Reynaldos, "Crímenes pasionales"; Santillán Esqueda, *Delincuencia femenina*, 295–314; Santillán Esqueda, "Narrativas," 172–84; Vidales Quintero, *Legalidad*, 264–73.

75. Salvatore, *Subalternos*, 19, 216–17, 260–61.

76. García Ramírez, "Los sistemas," 76.

77. Speckman Guerra, "Digna flor"; Piccato, *History of Infamy*, 77–78, 94; Piccato, "Todo homicidio," 638–39; Piccato, "El significado," 71–72.

78. García Ramírez, *Los reformadores*, 29–33.

79. Del Arenal, *El Derecho*, 10.

80. Jueces México (M03447–M03447), Juicios México (M02524–M02524), Jurado Popular México (M03458–M03458), Jurados México (M03455–M03455), Justicia México (M03419– M03422), and Justicia Administración de México (M02357– M02363).

81. Piccato, *History of Infamy*, 69.

82. Burkholder, "El periódico"; Burkholder, "Construyendo."

83. Piccato, *History of Infamy*, 69–73.

84. Burkholder, "Construyendo," 91; José Carreño Carlón, "Un modelo histórico de la relación entre prensa y poder en México en el siglo XX," Revista Mexicana de Comunicación, March 1, 2000, http:// mexicanadecomunicacion.com.mx/rmc/2000/03/01/un-modelo-historico -de-la-relacion-entre-prensa-y-poder-en-mexico-en-el-siglo-xx/.

85. Arno Burkholder, "La prensa Mexicana de la Segunda mitad del siglo XX: Una pequeña revision," accessed May 2018, https://www.septien.mx/wp -content/uploads/2015/10/repensar-historia-prensa.pdf.

86. Monsiváis, "Señor Presidente," 132–38.

87. "La reforma integral de unos códigos es urgente," El Universal, May 14, 1968.

88. Piccato, "El significado," 76; Piccato, "Murders of Nota Roja," 196–98; Piccato, *History of Infamy*, 63–64.

2. THE DESIGN OF JUSTICE

1. Criminal Procedure Code (Código de Procedimientos Penales, hereafter CPP), 1894, arts. 46, 48, 427, 436, 478–501, 512–42.

2. See Suarez-Potts, *Making of Law*, 5.

3. The 1857 Constitution entrusted the SCJ with resolving disputes over laws or acts of authorities violating constitutional rights and required sentences to deal with specific individuals even when more than one was affected (arts. 101, 102). The 1869 law rejected the *amparo* for judicial dealings, but in practice, the SCJ admitted it. Cossío Díaz, "El juicio de amparo." In general, admission in criminal matters was accepted because certain interpretations

of the law were deemed permissible in civil law. Jones, *Estudio*; Rabasa, *El artículo*, 14; Vallarta, "Inteligencia." For the characteristics of the *amparo* suit, see Baker, *Judicial Review in Mexico*, 37.

4. Buffington, *Criminales y ciudadanos*, 61–100; Speckman Guerra, *Crimen y castigo*, 93–110; Urías Horcasitas, *Indígena y criminal*, 145–66.

5. Urueta, "Delito y delincuentes," 271.

6. Martínez, "El jurado," no. 35, 1–2; Sodi, *El jurado*, 393–419.

7. Sodi, *El jurado*.

8. Speckman Guerra, "El jurado"; Piccato, *History of Infamy*, 21–23.

9. For example, Serralde, *La organización judicial*, 73; the Unión Liberal project, *Diario de Debates*, Legislatura XVI, tomo III, 219–23, 447–513.

10. Report of the first head of the Constitutionalist Army to the Constitutional Congress. Carranza's report and project, opinions, debates, and voting on the articles are in Marván Laborde, *Nueva edición*.

11. Project of Reforms to the Constitution of 1857 (hereafter Proyecto), January 5, 1917, dictamen, 35th and 37th sessions, January 8 and 10, 1917.

12. Proyecto, December 20, 1916, dictamen, 18th and 19th sessions, December 20 and 21, 1916.

13. Proyecto, December 20 and 27, 1916, and January 10, 1917, dictamens, 21st, 24th, and 38th sessions, December 23 and 27, 1916, and January 11 and 13, 1917.

14. Proyecto, December 22, 1916, dictamen, 26th session, December 29, 1916.

15. Proyecto, December 19, 1916, dictamen, 27th and 29th sessions, January 2 and 4, 1917.

16. Proyecto, December 30, 1916, and January 10, 1917, dictamens, 27th, 31st, and 40th sessions, January 2, 5, and 15, 1917.

17. Proyecto, art. 73-VI, XXV, XXVI, January 8, 1917, dictamen, 14th, 47th, and 54th sessions, January 15, 17, and 21, 1917.

18. Report read by the first head of the Constitutionalist Army; Proyecto, December 30, 1916, and January 10, 1917, dictamens, 27th, 31st, and 40th sessions, January 2, 5, and 15, 1917.

19. Proyecto, December 19, 1916, dictamen, 27th and 29th sessions, January 2 and 4, 1917.

20. "Convocatoria para el primer concurso que abre la Secretaría de Justicia con el objeto de formar nuevos códigos para el Distrito y territorios federales," published on several days in the *Diario Oficial*, including June 2, 1915.

21. Laws on the organization of tribunals of 1919, 1922, and 1928.

22. Macedo, "El Código Penal," 7; Macedo, "Algunas ideas."

23. Decree of Congress of the Union Authorizing the Executive to Reform the Criminal Code (Código Penal, hereafter CP), CPP, Civil, Civil Procedure, Commercial, Federal Criminal Procedure and Federal Civil Procedure Codes, January 7, 1926.

24. Mendoza, "El nuevo código," 302, 305. See also notes in the first section (hereafter PS) of El Universal: Alberto Casamadrid, "Conferencias sobre la filosofía del nuevo Código Penal," February 7, 1929, 5; "Otra reforma: La del Código Penal," January 5, 1929, 1, 10; "Más que el daño se penará la intención," February 1, 1929, 1, 6; "En qué teoría se inspira el proyecto del Código Penal," February 3, 1929, 1, 11; "Las observaciones al nuevo Código Penal," February 5, 1929, 1, 10; "Conferencias sobre la filosofía del nuevo Código Penal," February 7, 1929, 5.

25. Almaraz, Exposición, 12–13, 18.

26. Almaraz, Exposición, 18–19, 46.

27. Almaraz, Exposición, 52, 53.

28. Almaraz, Exposición, 19–20, 24, 48, 49.

29. CP 1929, arts. 47–55, 64–67, 175–76, 194–95. For the justification, see Almaraz, Exposición, 96–98, 101.

30. Almaraz, Exposición, 149, 150.

31. Almaraz, "New Mexican Penal Principles," 538–39.

32. "Principales novedades del Código Penal," El Universal, February 27, 1929, PS, 1.

33. Almaraz, Exposición, 157.

34. "Las observaciones al nuevo Código Penal," Excélsior, February 5, 1929, PS, 1, 10.

35. Chico Goerne, "La metafísica del delincuente y los ensueños legislativos del nuevo Código Penal," Excélsior, April 30, 1929, PS, 5.

36. Mendoza, "El nuevo código," 305; Almaraz, Exposición, 25.

37. "Algo más sobre el Jurado Popular," Excélsior, August 28, 1929, PS, 5.

38. Olea y Leyva, "Proyecto," 10.

39. "La rehabilitación del jurado," El Universal, April 29, 1929; "No hay que prostituir el jurado," El Universal, May 11, 1929; "La rehabilitación o el hundimiento del jurado," El Universal, August 7, 1929.

40. On suppression, see Speckman Guerra, "Crónica."

41. CPP 1929, art. 26.

42. CPP, arts. 10, 26. There were three other judicial districts: San Ángel (boroughs of San Ángel, Magdalena Contreras, Cuajimalpa), Coyoacán (Coyoacán, Tlalpan, General Anaya), and Xochimilco (Xochimilco, Milpa Alta, Tláhuac).

43. CPP 1929, arts. 32, 35.

44. 1917 Constitution (hereafter CPM), art. 73-VI; Ley Orgánica de los Tribunales (hereafter LOT) 1928, arts. 14, 15, 21.

45. Leyes orgánicas del Ministerio Público de 1929, arts. 22–23, 34–37, and 1954, arts. 24–26, 33–38.

46. Reglamento Orgánico de la Policía Preventiva del D.F., September 22, 1939; Reglamento de la Policía Preventiva, November 12, 1941, arts. 83, 159–64.

47. CPP 1929, arts. 292–99, 440–43.

48. CPM 1917, art. 20-IX; CPP 1929, arts. 276–83.

49. CPM 1917, arts. 19–20; CPP 1929, arts. 284–91, 533.

50. CPP 1929, arts. 307–85, 415–30.

51. If the defense did not present the document, it was tacitly regarded as an assumption of the conclusion of not guilty, but the consequence of the lack of presentation of conclusions by the MP was not contemplated, in which event the process was paralyzed.

52. García Ramírez, "Los sistemas," 85.

53. CPP 1929, art. 444.

54. García Ramírez, "Los sistemas," 89, 94.

55. Ley Orgánica del Ministerio Público 1929, art. 47.

56. CPP 1929, arts. 170–75, 445.

57. CPM 1917, art. 20-VIII.

58. If the appeal was denied, a motion for review of appeal denial could be filed, and the TSJ would determine whether the appeal was admissible. CPP 1929, arts. 305–6, 530–35, 546–53.

59. CPP 1929, arts. 536–45.

60. CPM 1917, art. 107-II, III; Ley de amparo 1919, arts. 30, 93–94, 109.

61. Ley de amparo 1919, arts. 3, 5, 11–12.

62. CPM 1917, art. 107-III; Ley de amparo 1919, art. 51.

63. If the lawsuit did not contain the requirements, the Supreme Court was to indicate the omissions and grant the plaintiff three days to correct the defects; otherwise the appeal was dropped. Ley de amparo 1919, arts. 103–4.

64. CPP 1917, art. 107-IX.

65. As José María Serna de la Garza explains, a tesis is the criterion (only one for each tesis) maintained by the court and passed through a drafting process that implies extracting from the ruling the point of law that can be considered a law formulated by the court. It is not an extract, does not contain specific information, and must be written in a clear, understandable way without the need to resort to the legal decision. "Concept of Jurisprudencia," 141.

66. Leyes de amparo 1919, arts. 147–49, and 1935, art. 193. See also Suarez-Potts, Making of Law, 6.

67. Abarca, El derecho, 31, 33.

68. March 17, 1944, circular in Carrancá y Trujillo, Un año, 14–15.

69. "Un criterio uniforme en la jurisprudencia," Excélsior, March 21, 1944, PS, 3; "Terminará el caos en todos los tribunales," El Universal, March 20, 1944, 9.

70. "Algunas opiniones." See also Almaraz, Exposición, 189–98; "Las críticas para el nuevo Código Penal," Excélsior, October 18, 1929, PS, 1.

71. Mendoza, "El nuevo código," 299.

72. González de la Vega, La reforma, 21.

73. Carrancá y Trujillo, Derecho, 79.

74. Teja Zabre, "Las nuevas orientaciones," 54–55; de la Cueva, "Razón e historia," 50–51.
75. Ceniceros, "El nuevo código," 13; Ceniceros, "La escuela positiva," 203; Garrido, "La doctrina," 240; González de la Vega, *Derecho penal*, 254–55.
76. Rivera Silva, "El positivismo," 567.
77. Carrancá y Trujillo, *Derecho penal*, 77; Carrancá y Trujillo, "La legislación penal mexicana," 301; Garrido, *Ensayos*, 29; González de la Vega, "Fue necesario derogar"; González de la Vega, *La reforma*, 20; González de la Vega, *Derecho penal*, 254.
78. Antonio Ramos Pedrueza, "La agonía del jurado popular," *Excélsior*, December 7, 1929, PS, 5.
79. Olivé, "La nueva ley orgánica," 37–40.
80. Armando Z. Ostos published several articles, all of them titled "El jurado popular," in *El Universal*, October 9, 16, 20, 1931, and notes in *Breves comentarios*, 27–41.
81. "La administración de justicia no ha mejorado," *El Nacional Revolucionario*, July 9, 1930, 3.
82. "Una vanidad mexicana y el Código Penal," *Excélsior*, November 25, 1929, PS, 5.
83. Garrido, *Ensayos*, 29.
84. Ceniceros, *El nuevo código*, 79–81.
85. José Almaraz, "La polémica alrededor del Código Penal," *El Nacional Revolucionario*, September 11, 1930, 3, 5.
86. *Diario de Debates*, Legislatura XXXIV, año I, periodo ordinario, no. 37, December 8, 1930; Decreto que Faculta al Ejecutivo Federal para Expedir los Códigos Penal y de Procedimientos Penales, January 31, 1930.
87. Teja Zabre, "Exposición." The text is included in some editions of the code; I refer to the 1936 Botas edition.
88. García Ramírez, "La Academia Mexicana," 764–95.
89. For example, "Anteproyecto de Código Penal."
90. In *El Nacional Revolucionario*: "Está listo el Código Penal," April 20, 1931, 1; "Opinión de González Bustamante," June 11, 1931, 3, 8; "Erróneamente se juzga al nuevo Código Penal" and "La nueva legislación penal," August 19, 1931, 6.
91. Teja Zabre, "Exposición," 8, 13; Ceniceros, *El nuevo código*, 25, 35–36.
92. Carnevale, "Una tercera escuela."
93. Ceniceros, "La escuela positiva," 204, 210; Ceniceros, "El Código Penal," 256–57.
94. Teja Zabre, "Exposición," 28–31; Teja Zabre, "Doctrina," 340–41; Ceniceros, *El nuevo código*, 77–78.
95. Garrido's response to the inaugural speech to the AMCP delivered by Celestino Porte Petit. Porte Petit, "El Código Penal."

96. Teja Zabre, "Exposición," 13–15.
97. CP 1931, arts. 7, 52. For the drafters' justification, see Ceniceros, "La escuela positiva," 204; Ceniceros, "El Código Penal," 256–57; Ceniceros and Garrido, *La ley penal*, 38.
98. Ceniceros, *El nuevo código*, 91.
99. Ceniceros, *El nuevo código*, 97–99.
100. Porte Petit, "El Código Penal," 154.
101. Ceniceros, *El nuevo código*, 98.
102. CP 1931, arts. 51, 52, 74; Ceniceros, *El código*, 91–99; Ceniceros, "El Código Penal," 257–58; Ceniceros and Garrido, *La ley penal*, 151.
103. Teja Zabre, "Exposición," 23.
104. Ceniceros, *El nuevo código*, 92.
105. Teja Zabre, "Exposición," 21.
106. Ceniceros, *El nuevo código*, 92.
107. Teja Zabre, "Exposición," 23–24.
108. CPP 1931, arts. 10, 631.
109. CPP 1931, art. 636. For causes of responsibility, see arts. 225–27.
110. CPP 1931, art. 135. For evidence, see arts. 135–261.
111. The confession was considered full proof only if it was made before the judicial police who conducted the initial inquiries or the trial judge, by subjects over the age of fourteen with full knowledge, and if it was credible in comparison with other evidence presented at the trial. Similarly, only the following were considered full proof: inspection at the location (*prueba ocular*), the coinciding testimonies of two or more witnesses, public documents (issued by officials, notaries, or parish priests), and private documents if the author judicially recognized them. Rivera Silva, *El procedimiento*, 166–244.
112. García Ramírez, *Justicia penal*, 84–86.
113. CPP 1931, arts. 326, 416, 423, 425.
114. CPP 1931, art. 317.
115. CPP 1931, arts. 318, 325–27, 427.
116. Reinstatement could be requested if the judge accompanied by the clerk or MP agent had not attended the trial, if they had not carried out the proceedings requested by the litigants, if the accused had not been able to obtain a defense attorney, if the cause of the accusation or the accuser's name was not known, or if the parties had not been permitted to withdraw or modify existing supervening conclusions. CPP 1931, arts. 430–31.
117. Ceniceros, *Un discurso*, 9.
118. Carrancá y Trujillo, "La legislación penal vigente," 39–40; González de la Vega, "La evolución," 10228–29.
119. Ceniceros, *Un discurso*, 9.
120. Garrido, *Ensayos*, 29.

121. Almaraz, *Algunos errores*, 21.
122. Ostos, *Breves comentarios*, includes a compilation of *El Universal* articles from October 1931.
123. Porte Petit, *Exposición*, 9.
124. Porte Petit, "El Código Penal."
125. American Declaration of the Rights and Duties of Man, May 2, 1948, arts. 2, 25–26.
126. Universal Declaration of Human Rights, December 10, 1948, arts. 9–11.
127. Convention for the Protection of Human Rights and Fundamental Freedoms (European Convention), November 4, 1950, arts. 5–7, 19.
128. Amended charter, art. 112.
129. American Convention on Human Rights (Pact of San José), November 22, 1969.
130. Manuel Ávila Camacho, speech, June 2, 1941, reproduced in "El Presidente de la República."
131. Carrancá y Trujillo, "La injusta igualdad."
132. Teja Zabre, *Hacia una criminología*, 10–11, 26–27.
133. S. Zavala, "Nuestros legisladores," 117–19.
134. Eduardo Zaffaroni, "El indígena frente al derecho penal," typescript, Fondo Alfonso Quiroz Cuarón (FAQC), sobre 77, expediente 2.
135. Ben David, "Remaking."
136. As Ben David demonstrated in "Remaking," the Peruvian code of 1924 gave special treatment to Indigenous criminals and considered the existence of ethnic categories.
137. Ben David, "Remaking," 26–28, 38–39.
138. Zayas Lezama et al., "Necesidad."
139. Medina Osalde, "Ponencia," 744.
140. Medina Osalde, "Ponencia," esp. 741; Hernández Islas, "Necesidad."
141. Hernández Islas, "Necesidad," 747.
142. "Primera Convención," 762–63.
143. Ceniceros et al., "Las razas indígenas."
144. Almaraz, *Algunos errores*, 34–36.
145. Porte Petit, "El Código Penal," 157–70; Porte Petit, *Evolución legislativa penal*, 97.
146. Quiroz Cuarón and Savido, "El juez penal."
147. Proyecto de reformas de 1934, Exposición de motivos del Título Primero, cap. I: Responsabilidad.
148. Proyecto de reformas de 1934, Exposición de motivos del Título Cuarto, cap. V: Perdón judicial, arts. 97–100.
149. Vela, "Perdón judicial," 118–19.
150. See Porte Petit, *Exposición*, 9; Garrido, *Ensayos*, 147–48.
151. Arilla Bas, "Breve ensayo," 398–99.
152. Machorro Narváez, *El anteproyecto*, 8–9, 36.

153. See "La restauración del jurado popular," *El Nacional Revolucionario*, August 10, 1932, PS, 3.
154. "¿Cómo debe reestablecerse el jurado?," *El Universal*, December 9, 1937, PS, 3, 4; "El restablecimiento del jurado popular," *El Universal*, September 1, 1938, PS, 1, 14; "No se restablecerá el jurado popular," *Excélsior*, October 25, 1938, PS, 1, 8.
155. "El jurado popular," *Criminalia*, April 1939.
156. "Posible restauración del jurado popular," *El Universal*, July 14, 1941, PS, 1, 5.
157. De Pina, "El jurado," 454.
158. "¿Qué opina usted de que se reimplante el jurado popular?," *Novedades*, August 8, 1941, PS, 7.
159. "¿Cómo debe reestablecerse el jurado?"; "El jurado popular," *El Universal*, March 16, 1940, PS, 3.
160. "El jurado popular debe restablecerse," *La Prensa*, October 3, 1940, 11; Ramírez, "El restablecimiento," 15; "Acción estudiantil a favor de que se restablezca el jurado popular en México," *Excélsior*, August 5, 1940, PS, 1, 9; "Restauración del jurado," *El Universal*, August 5, 1940, 9.
161. "¿Qué opina?"
162. Ramírez, "El restablecimiento," 15; "El jurado popular debe restablecerse."
163. Pardo Aspe, "Mariachis y juzgadores," 453–58.
164. "¿Debe ser restablecido el Jurado Popular?," *Excélsior*, November 28, 1939, PS, 5; survey results published in *Criminalia*, "¿Qué opina?"; Pallares, "El jurado popular," 5.
165. Antonio Ruiz Cabañas, "Todo es según el color con que se le mira," *La Prensa*, August 13, 1941, 12.
166. "Tribuna de la opinión libre," *Excélsior*, November 28, 1939, PS, 5.
167. Ruiz Cabañas, "Todo es según el color"; Carlos Franco Sodi, "Funcionarios y jurado popular," *El Universal*, April 12, 1940, PS, 3, 4.
168. "¿Qué opina?," 20.
169. Ruiz Cabañas, "Todo es según el color."
170. On Ostos's opinion, see articles published in *El Universal* in 1931, included in Ostos, *Breves comentarios*, 31–41.
171. "El jurado popular en el sistema judicial," *El Universal*, August 15, 1941, PS, 1, 14.
172. See "Posible restauración"; "El tribunal va a tratar sobre el desaparecido jurado popular," *La Prensa*, July 24, 1941, 4; "Corriente en pro de la restitución del jurado popular," *El Nacional Revolucionario*, August 6, 1941, 8; "El jurado popular ha vuelto a ser discutido," *Excélsior*, August 11, 1941, 14; "Rechazarán los senadores el proyecto del Jurado Popular," *Excélsior*, August 9, 1941, PS, 1, 13; "Todo es según el color." On support for juries, see "Acción estudiantil"; "Restauración del jurado," *El Universal*, August 5, 1941, PS, 1, 12.

173. González de la Vega, "Las Cortes Penales."
174. Rivera Vázquez, "El arbitrio," 5.
175. Franco Sodi, "El anteproyecto," 226.
176. "El nuevo código," *La Justicia*, April 1949.
177. The Senate's decision was hailed in *Criminalia* ("El jurado popular") and *Novedades* ("El peligro del jurado," August 11, 1941, PS, 5).
178. The criminal code remained untouched until 1938. According to Francisco Argüelles, from then until 1956 a reform was made every eleven months. "Las modificaciones," 629. Rafael Ruiz Harrell notes that between 1931 and 1999 seventy decrees with 689 changes were promulgated. The pace of reform was not constant; between 1931 and 1982 an average of 4.6 articles were reformed per year, while between 1983 and 1999 the average was 29.5 (*Código penal histórico*, 7).
179. LOT 1932, arts. 4–49; LOT 1968, art. 46.
180. CPP 1929, art. 26.
181. CPP 1931, art. 630; LOT 1932, art. 87.
182. "Los Orígenes de las Deficiencias Judiciales," *El Universal*, April 15, 1942, 9.
183. Manuel Rivera Silva, "La administración de justicia," *Excélsior*, December 4, 1942, PS, 4, 11; Franco Sodi, "Esa justicia señor regente," *Excélsior*, December 13, 1943, PS, 3, 4.
184. "Editoriales," *La Prensa*, December 10, 1940, 11.
185. Sodi de Pallares, "Manifiestas injusticias con la justicia en México," *El Universal*, April 2, 1942, 9; Villarreal, "Está muriendo de inanición el Poder Judicial de nuestro país," *Excélsior*, April 8, 1942, segunda sección (hereafter SS), 1, 6.
186. "La administración de justicia" (*La Justicia*); García, "Los abogados," 92; opinion of BMA members in Bremauntz, *Por una justicia*, 201.
187. Decree of December 23, 1948.
188. "El rezago judicial"; Alcalá-Zamora y Castillo, "Algunas observaciones," 29; "Independencia total del poder judicial (Moreno Tagle)," *La Prensa*, December 19, 1954, 3, 14; BMA committee in Bremauntz, *Por una justicia*, 202.
189. "Memorando," 25; *La administración de justicia*, 2–4, 6, 9–11, 13–14.
190. "La justicia en México" (Ramos Praslow), *Excélsior*, July 26, 1966, PS, 1, 12, 14; *La administración de justicia*, 14–15; Domínguez del Río, *La administración*, 31, 70–71; "La justicia en la balanza de la justicia," *Novedades*, January 2, 1966, PS, 20, "El problema de la justicia," *El Universal*, June 4, 1965, PS, 3 and SS, 20, 23; "La justicia en México" (Escobedo), *Excélsior*, August 2, 1966, PS, 1, 14.
191. Decree of December 23, 1948; LOT 1968, art. 70.
192. For the 1932 estimate I used the 1930 base population of the Federal District, for 1935 the average population of 1930 and 1940, for 1956 the average population of 1960 and 1970, and for 1970 that year's census (fifth, sixth, seventh, eighth, and ninth general censuses, INEGI).

193. CPM 1917, art. 73-VI; LOT 1928, arts. 14, 15, 21; LOT 1932, 12, 13, 16; LOT 1968, arts. 11, 12, 16.

194. Lázaro Cárdenas's Initiative to Reform Articles 73, 94, 95, and 97 of the Constitution. *Diario de Debates*, Legislatura XXXVI, año I, Período Ordinario, diario 11, September 12, 1934, session.

195. *Diario de Debates*, año I, Período Ordinario, diario 29, November 28, 1934, session.

196. Reforma a los Artículos Constitucionales 94, 95-I, II, 73-VI, December 15, 1934; Decreto que Reforma la Ley Orgánica del Ministerio Público del Distrito y Territorios Federales, December 31, 1934.

197. Fernández del Castillo, "Nuestra realidad," 132–34.

198. BMA, El problema, 13–16; "La administración de justicia," *Jus*, 316–17.

199. *Diario de Debates*, Legislatura XXXVIII, año I, Período Ordinario, diario 41, December 30, 1940, session.

200. Ávila Camacho, "Discurso pronunciado en el acto inaugural del Palacio Federal del Poder Judicial," June 2, 1941, in *Igualdad democrática*, 13–20.

201. Carrancá y Trujillo, *Un año*, 5.

202. Salazar Hurtado, "La inamovilidad."

203. "Una justicia mejor," *El Universal*, April 15, 1942, 9.

204. "Editoriales," *La Prensa*, December 21, 1940, 11.

205. Letter to Ávila Camacho from SCJ ministers, December 10, 1943, in "Documentos para la historia."

206. *Diario de Debates*, Legislatura XXXIX, año I, Período Ordinario, diario 32, December 22, 1943.

207. "La nueva administración de justicia," *El Universal*, November 4, 1944, 9.

208. "La organización judicial," *El Universal*, October 10–12, 1944, 10, 9, and 9, respectively.

209. "La inamovilidad judicial" (1948) and "Las reformas judiciales" (1951); "De poder a poder," *El Universal*, July 12, 1944, 9.

210. "Justicia paralizada," *Excélsior*, January 7, 1944, PS, 4.

211. Initiative for constitutional reforms formulated by the Mexican President's Office, in *Diario de Debates*, Legislatura XLI, año II, Período Ordinario, diario 18, November 1, 1950, session.

212. *Diario de Debates*, Legislatura XLI, año II, Período Ordinario, diario 24, November 21, 1950, session.

213. *Diario de Debates*, Legislatura XLI, año II, Período Ordinario, diario 32, December 21, 1950, session, and December 30, 1950, decree.

214. Flores García, "Algunos problemas." Fernández del Castillo coincided in 1939 ("Nuestra realidad," 130); Octavio Trigo in 1942 ("Por una justicia mejor," *El Universal*, April 11, 9); attorneys surveyed by *La Nación* and Porte Petit in 1950 ("La Nación señala siete puntos concretos para lograr una recta y eficaz administración de justicia," December 26, 1942, and "Anteproyecto

de código," 329); Bremauntz, representatives of attorney associations and schools, and Juan Gutiérrez Lascuráin, president of the Partido Acción Nacional, in 1955 (Por una justicia, 87–99, 193, and La administración de justicia, 14–15); Virgilio Domínguez, BMA president in 1963 (La administración de justicia, 70–71); and Excélsior editorialists in 1969 ("Inamovilidad judicial," March 26, PS, 6).

215. Flores García, "Algunos problemas."

216. Alcalá-Zamora y Castillo, "Algunas observaciones," 29–30.

217. Almaraz and Vela in 1934 ("La especialización," 42–43, and "Funcionarios de carrera," 42); the BMA in 1940 (El problema, 22–23); Octavio Trigo, Francisco Serralde, and Manuel Rivera Silva in 1942 ("Por una justicia mejor," 9); "La administración de justicia," El Universal, February 22 and 28, 9; and "La administración de justicia," Excélsior, December 4, PS, 4, 11; La Justicia in 1948 and 1949 ("La inamovilidad judicial" and "La carrera judicial"); Porte Petit in 1950 ("Anteproyecto," 329); Vela in 1953 ("Carrera judicial," 333–35); Alberto Bremauntz, Alberto Lumbreras of the Partido Obrero Campesino Mexicano, Vicente Lombardo Toledano of the Partido Popular, and Manuel Terrazas of the Partido Comunista Mexicano in 1955 (Bremauntz, Por una justicia, 191–200, 285–95); Javier Gaxiola, Antonio Pérez Verdía, and Trinidad García in 1957 (La administración de justicia, 14–15); Leopoldo Aguilar in 1959 ("La justicia del orden," 15); Flores García in 1960 ("Crónica del Primer Congreso," 19); Domínguez del Río in 1963 and 1968 (La administración de justicia, 61, 70, 71, 110); and Excélsior in 1966 ("Justicia y técnica," August 16, PS, 6).

218. Statements in Armando Arévalo García, "La justicia en la balanza de la justicia," Novedades, January 2, 1965, PS, 20. Other supporters included Fernández del Castillo in 1948 ("El proyecto de ley," 9510); Ramos Bilderbeck in 1961 ("Por una secretaría"); and journalists Villarreal in 1942 ("A qué se debe la impunidad de los delitos," Excélsior, November 1, SS, 1, 11) and Ricardo Iturbe González in 1965 ("Corrupción Judicial, he ahí el problema," El Universal, December 19, PS, 1, 23).

219. On approval, see Diario de Debates, Legislatura XXXV, año I, Período Ordinario, diario 48, December 28, 1932, session; Legislatura XLVII, año II, Período Ordinario, diario 24, November 28, 1968, session; Legislatura XLVII, año II, Período Ordinario, diario 27, December 10, 1968, session; Legislatura XLVII, año II, Período Ordinario, diario 29, December 27, 1968, session.

220. "Felicitan."

3. THE PUBLIC IMAGE OF JUSTICE

1. Editorial, Excélsior, December 15, 1943. In this chapter, I revisit concepts of Tarello, Cultura jurídica, 181–82.

2. "Consignan los magistrados del tribunal un artículo publicado por un abogado," *Excélsior*, August 25, 1940, SS, 15. See also Carlos Soto Guevara, "La administración de justicia," *El Universal*, June 2, 1940, PS, 3, 7.

3. Trigo, "Por una justicia mejor," *El Universal*, April 6, 1942, PS, 1, 6; "En favor de una verdadera justicia," *El Universal*, April 8, 1942, PS, 3. Articles were published throughout the year.

4. See *Excélsior* PS ("La justicia en paños menores," December 5, 1942, 1, 7; "Memorial de la Cámara de Senadores," December 10, 1942, 1, 12; "La pugna entre el Senado y el Tribunal llega a los Diputados," December 11, 1942, 1, 10; "El Tribunal Superior acusa al Senado de ligereza," December 11, 1942, 1, 15; "Es beneficiosa la controversia sobre los jueces," December 12, 1942, 7); *El Universal* (Franco Sodi, "Senado, justicia y escándalo," December 14, 1942, 3, 8); *El Nacional Revolucionario* ("Punto final en una controversia," December 11, 1942, PS, 1, 6).

5. Ceniceros, "De la prensa," 374.

6. "Jueces y legisladores," *Excélsior*, November 25, 1967, PS, 7A, 8A.

7. "¿Ha sido usted una de tantas víctimas de la justicia?," *La Prensa*, December 15, 1942, 3. On the results, see "La encuesta relámpago," *La Prensa*, November 30, 1942, 29; "Siguen denunciándose las inmoralidades de la justicia," *La Prensa*, December 17, 1942, 12, 22; "Copiosa cooperación de los lectores de *La Prensa* a la obra cien veces patriótica de lograr que en México impere la justicia," *La Prensa*, December 21, 1942, 29.

8. "¿Cómo quisiera usted que fuera la administración de la justicia?," *Novedades*, December 14, 1942, PS, 9.

9. Opinions in *Novedades* were repeated by other publications. For example, the BMA disseminated its members' opinions in *La administración de justicia*.

10. Prats published seven interviews in the *Excélsior* PS: "La justicia en México," with Ignacio Ramos Praslow, July 26, 1A, 12A, 14A; Gustavo R. Velasco, July 27, 1A, 11A; Víctor Manuel Ortega, July 29, 1A, 12A, 25A; Raúl Cervantes Ahumada, July 30, 1A, 15A, 17A; Armando R. Ostos, July 31, 1A, 14A, 16A; Ignacio Trinidad García, August 1, 1A, 18A, 19A; Manuel G. Escobedo, August 2, 1A, 14A.

11. "Justicia y sociedad," "Seguridad de la justicia," and "Las dos políticas," *La Prensa*, December 21, 1940, 12.

12. "La función judicial," *La Justicia*, 10285.

13. Juan Gutiérrez Lascuráin, president of the National Action Party (Partido Acción Nacional), in Bremauntz, *Por una justicia*, 192.

14. "Necesidad de justicia," *Excélsior*, January 19, 1942, PS, 4.

15. "La reforma judicial," *El Universal*, December 10, 1966, PS, 1, 15, SS, A26.

16. "La CTM contra la Suprema Corte," *Novedades*, March 12, 1941, PS, 5.

17. "Notas de México," *Excélsior*, September 12, 1942, PS, 4, 7.

18. "Nueva justicia," *El Universal*, October 9, 1940, PS, 3, 7.

19. "Propósito plausible," *Excélsior*, June 19, 1941, PS, 4.
20. García, "Los abogados," 79; "La justicia en México," *Excélsior*, August 1, 1966, PS, 1A, 18A, 19A.
21. "Notas de México," *Excélsior*, September 12, 1942, PS, 4, 7.
22. "Depuración," *El Universal*, May 13, 1965, PS, 3.
23. Ávila Camacho, "Discurso," June 2, 1941, in *Igualdad democrática*, 13–20, esp. 18; "Se proyectan trascendentales reformas en el ramo judicial," *El Nacional*, December 26, 1964, PS, 1, 7.
24. Luis Garrido, "El problema de la justicia," *Excélsior*, December 13, 1963, PS, 3, SS A23.
25. "Para la historia," *El Nacional Revolucionario*, January 25, 1942, PS, 3.
26. González de la Vega, *La reforma*, 44. The same idea is in Carrancá y Trujillo, "Historia," 223.
27. "Justicia y técnica," *Excélsior*, August 16, 1966, PS, 6A.
28. Bremauntz, *Por una justicia*, 135.
29. "Memorando," 26.
30. Trigo, "Por una justicia mejor," 3, 6.
31. Villarreal, "Está muriendo de inanición."
32. Bremauntz, *Por una justicia*, 137.
33. "Factores diversos detienen la administración de justicia," *El Universal*, September 12, 1965, PS, 7.
34. Bremauntz, *Por una justicia*, 130.
35. Bremauntz, *Por una justicia*, 132–33.
36. "La administración de justicia," *La Justicia*.
37. Bremauntz, *Por una justicia*, 196, 133–35.
38. "Evolución del Ministerio Público," *El Nacional*, April 1, 1942, PS, 1, 8.
39. Villarreal, "Reina una anarquía completa en la administración de justicia," *Excélsior*, November 15, 1942, SS, 1, 5; "Cementerio de la justicia," *Excélsior*, November 22, 1942, PS, 10, 12.
40. Cárdenas, "El Ministerio Público," 10.
41. "Crimen sin castigo," *Novedades*, June 1, 1966, PS, 1, 8.
42. "La moralización de la justicia," *El Universal*, July 9, 1940, PS, 3.
43. Puig, *El ideal*, 5.
44. "Física y moralmente hay que sanear las delegaciones," *El Universal*, June 3, 1940, PS, 1, 15.
45. Trigo, "Por una justicia mejor," 3, 6.
46. Villarreal, "Está muriendo de inanición."
47. García, "Los abogados," 93. See also Alcalá-Zamora y Castillo, "Algunas observaciones," 29; Pedro Zorrilla in Bremauntz, *Por una justicia*, 132; "Sobre la justicia"; BMA president Virgilio Domínguez, "Los once puntos de la Barra Mexicana," in Domínguez del Río, *La administración*, 70–71; and

the opinion of political party leaders Alberto Lumbreras and Vicente Lombardo Toledano in Bremauntz, *Por una justicia*, 132.

48. Aguilar, "La justicia del orden," 14. Also in "Memorando," 25.

49. Cárdenas, "El Ministerio Público," 10; "La administración de justicia," *Novedades*, January 13, 1966, PS, 4.

50. Bremauntz, *Por una justicia*, 202.

51. Carrancá y Trujillo, "Allá van leyes," 28.

52. "La otra imagen," *Excélsior*, October 31, 1968, PS, 6A, 10A.

53. "Los orígenes de las deficiencias judiciales," *El Universal*, April 15, 1942, 9.

54. See "Lacras de la justicia según el presidente del Tribunal Superior," *Excélsior*, October 23, 1942, PS, 13; Rivera Silva, "La administración de justicia," *Excélsior*, December 4, 1942, PS, 4, 11; Trigo, "Por una justicia mejor," 3, 6; Sodi de Pallares, "Manifiestas injusticias"; "Siete puntos concretos para lograr una recta y eficaz administración de justicia," *La Nación*, December 26, 1942; "El rezago judicial"; "Independencia total del poder judicial" (Moreno Tagle), *La Prensa*, December 19, 1954, 3, 14; opinions of Toledano, Lumbreras, and Gómez Mont in Bremauntz, *Por una justicia*, 191–200, 130; *La administración de justicia*, 2, 4, 6, 9, 13; "Memorando," 25; "Los once puntos de la Barra Mexicana," in Domínguez del Río, *La administración*, 70–71; "La justicia en México (Ortega)," *Excélsior*, July 29, 1966, PS, 1A, 12A, 25A; "Justicia y técnica," *Excélsior*, August 16, 1966, PS, 6A; "Con mejores salarios sí habrá justicia pronta y expedita," *El Universal*, August 26, 1968, PS, 1, 6.

55. "La administración de justicia," *Novedades*.

56. "Justicia mexicana (Ostos)," *Excélsior*, July 31, 1966, PS, 1A, 14A, 16A; Alfonso Trueba, "La otra imagen," *Excélsior*, October 31, 1968, PS, 6A, 10A; Bremauntz, *Por una justicia*, 136.

57. Trigo, "Por una justicia mejor," 3, 6.

58. "A qué se debe la impunidad de los delitos," *Excélsior*, November 1, 1942, SS, I, II.

59. BMA, *El problema*, 16–17.

60. See text by Trinidad García in 1948 ("Los abogados," 92), Alcalá-Zamora y Castillo in 1950 ("Algunas observaciones," 29); Bremauntz and BMA members in 1955 (Bremauntz, *Por una justicia*, 135, 202); Escobedo and Fernández del Castillo in 1957 (*La administración de justicia*, 2, 4, 6, 9, 13); Pozo in 1966 ("La administración de justicia," *Novedades*); and Ostos (*Excélsior*, July 31, PS, 1A, 14A, 16A).

61. Bremauntz, *Por una justicia*, 132.

62. "Calendario," *El Universal*, June 16, 1966, PS, 2, 19.

63. Alcalá-Zamora y Castillo, "Algunas observaciones," 29.

64. "La justicia pide justicia," *Excélsior*, November 9–11, 1965, PS, 5, 18A; PS, 5, 16A; and PS, 5A, respectively.

65. "La administración de justicia," *Novedades*.
66. Trigo, "Por una justicia mejor," 3, 6. See also Bremauntz, *Por una justicia*, 135, or his editorial "Justicia limpia y expedita," *Novedades*, December 10, 1964, PS, 4.
67. "La federalización de la justicia," *El Universal*, August 10, 1935, PS, 3, 8.
68. "Esa justicia señor regente," *El Universal*, December 13, 1943, PS, 3, 4. Others coincided: Salazar Hurtado, "Lacras de la justicia"; Serralde, "La organización judicial," *El Universal*, April 25, 1945, PS, 3, 6; Trueba, "Justicia corrompida," *Excélsior*, November 3, 1964, PS, 6A; and Senator Alfonso Guerra, "La justicia en la balanza de la justicia," *Novedades*, December 28, 1965, PS, 1, 10.
69. Ricardo Garibay, "Administración de justicia y policía," *Excélsior*, January 6, 1971, PS, 7A.
70. Mendieta y Núñez, *La administración*, 139, 217.
71. C. P. A., "Contra la justicia venal y los muchos cuerpos policiacos," *Novedades*, April 29, 1965, PS, 1, 11; "Justicia limpia y expedita," *Novedades*, December 10, 1964, PS, 4.
72. Quiroz Cuarón, "Crisis," 319.
73. The critiques were not new. See, for the 1920s, Pulido Esteva, "Los negocios," 20–26; Pulido Esteva, "El caso Quintana," 318–20; Ponce Hernández, "La gestión," 93–108.
74. Carrancá y Trujillo, "Sobre el valor," 464.
75. Alfonso Quiroz Cuarón, "Ni técnica ni recursos," *Excélsior*, November 25, 1967, PS, 7A.
76. Reaching a similar conclusión, Piccato pointed out that private detectives were more respected than the police. *History of Infamy*, 78, 195–96.
77. Garrido, *Ensayos*, 58.
78. Cárdenas, "El Ministerio Público," 7.
79. Moreno Tagle, *Román Lugo*, 14.
80. Trueba, *Justicia*, 37–44.
81. "Crimen sin castigo," *Novedades*, June 1, 1966, PS, 1, 8.
82. "Cementerio de la justicia," *Excélsior*, November 22, 1942, PS, 10, 12; Cárdenas, "El Ministerio Público," 7; "Justicia limpia y expedita."
83. "Inexplicable actitud de un fiscal," *La Prensa*, June 5, 1936, 2, 17; "La pésima actuación de los funcionarios de la octava delegación," *La Prensa*, July 29, 1936, 2, 18.
84. "Impunidad barata," *El Universal*, October 6, 1967, PS, 3.
85. "Únicamente los pobres van a las cárceles," *Excélsior*, November 8, 1942, SS, 1, 12.
86. Mario Rojas Avendaño, "Juzgando a los juzgadores," pt. 2, *Excélsior*, April 20, 1966, PS, 5A, 16A.
87. "Crimen sin castigo," *Novedades*, June 1, 1966, PS, 1, 8.

88. "Tríptico," *La Prensa*, June 1, 1954, 9, 24.

89. Moreno Tagle, *Román Lugo*, 14–15.

90. "Justicia limpia y expedita"; Gilberto Keith, "Justicia imposible," *Excélsior*, April 17, 1969, PS, 7A, 8A.

91. Carrancá y Trujillo, "Sobre el valor," 462.

92. "La prueba de confesión en materia penal," *El Nacional Revolucionario*, February 9, 1931, PS, 3, 5.

93. Colín Sánchez, *Función social*, 21.

94. "Justicia limpia y expedita."

95. Trueba, *Justicia*, 41–42. See also "Tribunales humanizados. Justicia para pobres," *Excélsior*, February 1969, PS, 6A, 8A.

96. See "Consigna el Procurador los tormentos policiacos," *La Prensa*, June 13, 1952, 10; "El famoso pseudochacal fue golpeado con saña," *La Prensa*, June 14, 1952, 2, 6; "Pavoroso relato de los tormentos a detenidos," *La Prensa*, June 17, 1952, 2, 34.

97. Lizardi Ramos, "Tres males y una sola enfermedad," *Excélsior*, December 16, 1942, PS, 4, 11; "¿Debe moralizarse la justicia en México?," *La Prensa*, November 30, 1942, 29; "La justicia en paños menores," *Excélsior*, December 5, 1942, PS, 1, 7; "Pisotean en lugar de impartir justicia," *La Prensa*, May 20, 1952, 26.

98. "Grandes inmoralidades han sido descubiertas en las demarcaciones de policía," *El Nacional Revolucionario*, March 4, 1930, SS, 1, 4.

99. Garrido, *Ensayos*, 52.

100. "Los propios agentes exhiben las inmoralidades policiacas," *La Prensa*, June 19, 1952, 2, 12.

101. "Siguen disfrutando los chambistas," *El Universal*, February 5, 1966, PS, 2, SS, A26.

102. "La administración de justicia común," *El Universal*, April 18, 1969, PS, 3, 9.

103. "En procura de justicia," *Excélsior*, December 4, 1970, A8.

104. Antonio Helú published stories in newspapers and founded the magazine *Selecciones policíacas y de misterio* (1946–57). He also wrote plays and screenplays, such as *La obligación de asesinar* [The obligation to assassinate], which he directed in 1937 and had the same name as the collection of stories, as well as *El asesino X* [Killer X] and *El medallón del crimen* [The crime medallion], directed by Juan Bustillo Oro in 1955 and 1956, respectively.

105. According to Piccato, it was widely accepted that justice was only occasionally achieved and sometimes beyond government institutions. *History of Infamy*, 1.

106. Directed in 1952 by Adolfo Fernández Bustamante, who wrote the screenplay.

107. Filmed in 1957, directed by Sergio Véjar, with screenplay by Ramón Obon, Luis Manrique, and Manuel Canseco.

108. Premiered in 1947, directed by Ismael Rodríguez, with screenplay by Carlos González Dueñas.
109. Directed by Julián Soler, with screenplay by Fernando Morales Ortiz and Mauricio Magdaleno.
110. Directed in 1960 by Zacarías Gómez Urquiza, with screenplay by Alberto Ramírez de Aguilar and Carlos Ravelo.
111. In yet another film, El Suavecito, directed in 1950 by Fernando Méndez, a criminal secures the acquittal of an innocent victim.
112. Directed in 1951 by Ernesto Cortázar, with screenplay by Cortázar and Jaime Luis Contreras.
113. Directed in 1946 by Roberto Gavaldón, based on a story by José Revueltas and Roberto Gavaldón.
114. Premiered in 1948, directed and produced by Raúl de Anda, inspired by the Juan García storyline.
115. Directed in 1952 by Emilio Gómez Muriel, based on the storyline of Max Aub and Mauricio Magdaleno.
116. Other films also serve as examples, including Virgen de medianoche [Midnight virgin] (1941), directed by Alejandro Galindo, and Donde el círculo termina [Where the circle ends] (1955), directed by Alfredo Crevenna.
117. Directed in 1958 by Luis Spota.
118. Directed in 1959 by Arturo Martínez, with screenplay by Raúl de Anda.
119. "Mayor atención en las delegaciones y reorganización del sistema de detención anuncia el Procurador del Distrito," El Nacional, December 13, 1970, PS, 8.
120. "Evolución del Ministerio Público," El Nacional, April 1, 1942, PS, 1, 8; Cantón, "Crimen sin castigo," Novedades, June 1, 1966, PS, 1, 8.
121. "Ni técnica ni recursos."
122. Ceniceros, "Policía de olfato," 331.
123. "Justicia limpia y expedita"; "Tríptico: Policía, Problema, Tiempo," La Prensa, June 1, 1954, 9, 24.
124. Piña y Palacios, "Ponencia," 37; González Bustamante, "Función investigadora," 43; Cantón, "Crimen sin castigo."
125. Pérez Moreno, "Creación de escuelas," 739.
126. Quiroz Cuarón, "Crisis," 319; Quiroz Cuarón, "La justicia," 548; "Ni técnica ni recursos."
127. For example, Attorney General Ornelas, General Police Chief Manuel Núñez, and head of the Investigations Department Orencio Ramírez Horta, "Una moralización eficaz en todo el Ministerio Público," La Prensa, April 5, 1940, 2, 15; Sergio García Ramírez (later appointed attorney general in 1970) "En procura de justicia," Excélsior, December 4, 1940, A8.
128. "Mayor atención en las delegaciones."
129. Ceniceros, "Realidades policiacas," 397.

130. "De la prensa diaria," originally published in *Excélsior*, "¿Qué va a hacer el gobierno para atender el anhelo popular de una mejor justicia?," December 30, 1942, PS, 4, 13; Arévalo Macías, "Más que una revisión," 583–84; José Ángel Ceniceros, "Lacras administrativas y corrupción judicial," *El Universal*, September 5, 1966, PS, 3, SS, B19; Ceniceros, "Programa para mejorar la administración de Justicia," *El Universal*, February 19, 1968, PS, 3, 15; Colín Sánchez, *Función social*, 21.

131. "Contra la justicia venal y los muchos cuerpos policiacos," *Novedades*, April 29, 1965, PS, 1, 11; Cárdenas, "El Ministerio Público"; "Justicia limpia y expedita."

132. Serralde, "La organización judicial," pt. 6, *El Universal*, July 3, 1940, PS, 3.

133. González Bustamante, *Principios de derecho*, 184; "Presos sin defensa," *Excélsior*, September 19, 1942, SS, 1.

134. Gómez Mont, "La justicia de los pobres," *El Universal*, pt. 1, December 1, 1967, PS, 3, 16, and pt. 2, December 6, 1967, PS, 3, 27 and SS, A28.

135. "Presos procesados en juzgados de la Primera Corte Penal se quejan de sus defensores," *El Universal Gráfico*, February 11, 1964, 16.

136. Tuñón Pablos, "Cine," 114.

137. Gómez Mont, "La justicia de los pobres."

138. Carrancá y Trujillo, *Un año*, 13.

139. "La venda en los ojos y los pesos de la ley," *Excélsior*, January 14, 1966, PS, 6A, 10A; Ceniceros, "Lacras administrativas."

140. BMA, *El problema*, 20–21.

141. Manuel Buendía, "La justicia sólo les sirve a los poderosos," *La Prensa*, December 30, 1954, 3, 31.

142. "El problema de la justicia," *El Universal*, June 4, 1965, PS, 3, SS, 20, 23.

143. "¿No son peores algunos abogados que ciertos malos jueces?," *El Nacional*, August 26, 1965, PS, 9.

144. "La administración de justicia," *Novedades*.

145. González Franco, "El Procurador de Justicia," 11068; Ortiz Alarcón, "Justicia al servicio del pueblo," *El Nacional*, November 30, 1967, PS, 3; "¿Cómo quisiera usted?"; "Cayó ya uno de los coyotes judiciales," *El Nacional Revolucionario*, May 15, 1931, SS, 1, 6; Villarreal, "Por fin habrá justicia en los tribunales del orden común," *Excélsior*, December 13, 1942, SS, 1, 12.

146. "Otra fuente de inmoralidad," *Excélsior*, February 3, 1940, PS, Editorials, 5.

147. Villarreal, "Una banda de estranguladores de la justicia," *Excélsior*, October 15, 1942, SS, 1, 12; "Únicamente los pobres."

148. "Un grave síntoma de relajamiento social," *Excélsior*, May 20, 1939, PS, 5.

149. Menéndez, *Memorias*.

150. Mellado, *Belem*, 200–201.

151. Menéndez, *Memorias*, 95.

152. Monsiváis, *Los mil*, 44.

153. García Robles, *La bala perdida*, 35–36.
154. Directed by Adolfo Fernández Bustamante, screenplay by Fernández Bustamante and Paulino Masip.
155. Directed by Chano Urueta, who also participated in the screenplay.
156. Directed by Rafael Baledón, with screenplay by José María Fernández Usáin.
157. "El problema de la justicia," *Excélsior*; "Administración de justicia, sana, pronta y expedita," *El Universal*, October 21, 1942, PS, 1, 5.
158. "Contra los coyotes de tribunales," *El Nacional Revolucionario*, May 14, 1931, PS, 1; Villarreal, "Por fin habrá justicia."
159. "La venda en los ojos y los pesos de la ley," *Excélsior*, January 14, 1966, PS, 6A, 10A.
160. Alfonso Noriega, "El problema empieza con el abogado," *Excélsior*, July 30, 1966, 1, 10.
161. Portes Gil, *Autobiografía*, 449–66.
162. Carrancá y Trujillo, *Un año*, 5.
163. "La nueva administración de justicia," *El Universal*, November 4, 1944, PS, 3, 7.
164. Bremauntz, *Por una justicia*, 51, 66.
165. Fernández del Castillo, "Nuestra realidad," 130.
166. "Justicia," *El Universal*, December 14, 1940, PS, 3.
167. "La inamovilidad en el Poder Judicial," 5753. Expressing similar ideas were District Judge González Bustamante ("Todo es según el color," *La Prensa*, September 8, 1941, 10, 22); jurists or attorneys like Moreno Sánchez ("La judicatura como profesión," *El Universal*, October 21, 1940, PS, 3, 10), Castillo Larrañaga ("Los funcionarios judiciales," *El Universal*, October 19, 1940, PS, 3), Gurría Urgell ("La justicia en México," *El Universal*, November 1, 1940, PS, 3, 5), Ostos ("Todo es según el color," *La Prensa*, March 1, 1941, 11), Abarca (*El derecho*, 115), and Rivera Silva ("La administración de justicia"); and journalist Villarreal ("Como se improvisan jueces penales," *Excélsior*, March 3, 1942, SS, 1, 3).
168. "La justicia desorganizada," "Tinterillos y chicaneros," and "Los títulos colorados," *La Prensa*, December 16, 1942, 8.
169. "Sensación por una iniciativa," *Excélsior*, March 13, 1941, PS, 15; "Exhibirán sus títulos todos los magistrados," *Excélsior*, December 16, 1942, PS, 1; "Depuración de la administración de justicia antes de la inamovilidad," *La Prensa*, December 16, 1942, 3, 23.
170. Bremauntz, *Por una justicia*, 193, 195.
171. "Puro interés bastardo mueve a la judicatura" (Ocampo), *La Prensa*, December 26, 1954, 3, 6; Bremauntz, *Por una justicia*, 71; Domínguez del Río, *La administración*, 33–39; Garrido, "El problema de la justicia"; "El problema de la justicia," *El Universal*, June 4, 1965, PS, 3 and SS, 20, 23; "La justicia en la balanza de la justicia," *Novedades*, January 2, 1965, PS, 20.

172. Héctor Solís Quiroga, "Mejorar la administración de Justicia," *El Universal*, December 29, 1965, PS, 2 and SS, 20.
173. José Ortiz Rodríguez, "El cuartelazo en el Tribunal de Justicia," *El Nacional Revolucionario*, September 19, 1930, PS, 1, 8.
174. Manuel Ávila Camacho, "Modificación de la vida jurídica de nuestro país," *Excélsior*, December 23, PS, 1, 14.
175. Editorial, *Excélsior*, December 25, 1944.
176. "Justicia," "Justicia y presupuesto," and "Los datos olvidados," *La Prensa*, December 10, 1940, 10; Ostos's statement of February 20, 1941, in El Universal ("Una justicia más expedita," PS, 1, 4) and El Nacional ("Providencias a los jueces," PS, 1A, 5A); "Problemas de la justicia"; "El rezago judicial."
177. Villarreal, "Está muriendo de inanición"; Villarreal, "Reina una anarquía."
178. "Todo progresa, menos la aplicación de justicia," *Novedades*, November 12, 1964, PS, 1, 13.
179. "Una justicia más expedita," *El Universal*, February 20, 1941, PS, 1, 4; "Providencias a los jueces," *El Nacional*, February 20, 1941, PS, 1A, 5A.
180. The same opinion was expressed by editorialists in "Problemas de la justicia," *La Justicia*, and "Error, ineptitud y corrupción judiciales," *Sucesos para todos*, February 22, 1969, 11, as well as by law professor Dolores Heduán Virues, "Debe empezar desde abajo la reorganización de la justicia," *Novedades*, April 12, 1966, PS, 10.
181. Villarreal, "Reina una anarquía"; *La administración de justicia*, 3.
182. "Incuria," *La Prensa*, June 10, 1954, 2, 11.
183. "El problema de la justicia," *El Universal*.
184. "La organización judicial," *El Universal*, October 30, 1942, PS, 3, 11; García, "Los abogados," 93; *La administración de justicia*, 12.
185. BMA, El problema, 13; Bremauntz, Por una justicia, 202; "La organización judicial," *El Universal*, October 30, 1942, PS, 3, 11; *La administración de justicia*, 12; "Irregularidades judiciales," *El Universal*, March 26, 1968, PS, 3.
186. Rojas Avendaño, "Juzgando a los juzgadores," pt. 1, *Excélsior*, April 19, 1966, PS, 5A, 15A.
187. "La justicia se levanta tarde," *El Universal*, July 13, 1936, PS, 1, 5; BMA, El problema, 12, 19; González Bustamante, "El procedimiento penal," *El Universal*, May 12, 1941, PS, 2, 20, 23; García, "Los abogados," 91–92.
188. Garrido, "El problema de la justicia," *El Universal*.
189. BMA, El problema, 12, 19; "La justicia se levanta tarde," *El Universal*, July 13, 1936, PS, 1, 5.
190. Carlos Soto Guevara, "La administración de justicia," *El Universal*, June 2, 1940, PS, 3, 7; García, "Los abogados," 91–92; Aguilar, "La justicia del orden," 12; "Justicia," "Justicia y presupuesto," and "Los datos olvidados," *La Prensa*.
191. Velasco and Gaxiola, *La administración de justicia*, 7, 14; Domínguez Carrascosa, "Nuestra administración de injusticia," *Excélsior*, September 24, 1966,

PS, 6A, 8A; Domínguez Carrascosa, "Abusos del litigante," *Excélsior*, October 14, 1966, PS, 6A, 8A; Aguilar y Quevedo, "Justicia, meta suprema," *Excélsior*, December 7, 1966, PS, 7A, 14A.

192. "Justicia," "Justicia y presupuesto," and "Los datos olvidados," *La Prensa*.

193. Ceniceros, "Corruptores," 73.

194. Marxófilo, "La administración de justicia no ha mejorado," *El Nacional Revolucionario*, August 11, 1930, PS, 3.

195. For instance, "Pugna entre jueces y defensores de oficio," *El Nacional Revolucionario*, May 23, 1931, SS, 1; "La justicia se levanta tarde," *El Universal*, July 13, 1936, PS, 1, 5; Eduardo Pallares's interviews with attorneys in "Irregularidades judiciales."

196. Ernesto Basulto, "Fue, es y será," *Universal Gráfico*, May 28, 1942, 6, 17.

197. BMA, *El problema*, 12.

198. Claudio Medina Osalde, "Justicia," *El Universal*, December 14, 1940, PS, 3. Nevertheless, judges had their defenders. See Manuel Andrade ("Con excepción de tres, los demás jueces no son malos," *El Nacional Revolucionario*, August 1, 1931, 9); José María Lozano and Víctor Velázquez ("Los jueces de lo penal son los más capacitados," *El Nacional Revolucionario*, May 22, 1932, SS, 1); Armando Ostos ("El TSJ procurará que los jueces malos sean sancionados, pero para los buenos espera y exige respeto," *La Prensa*, April 6, 1942, 11, 18); Sánchez Vargas (Rojas Avendaño, "Juzgando a los juzgadores," pt. 2).

199. "La justicia se levanta tarde," *El Universal*, July 13, 1936, PS, 1, 5.

200. "Pedirán la consignación del juez García López," *La Prensa*, August 4, 1961, 22, 38.

201. Quevedo y Zubieta, "Vidrios y secretarios rotos," *El Nacional Revolucionario*, June 11, 1931, PS, 3, 8. Armando R. Ostos, "Justicia mexicana," *Excélsior*, July 31, 1966, PS, 1A, 14A, 16A, coincided with this idea.

202. Trueba, *Justicia*, 37–44.

203. "Escrito presentado a la Barra Mexicana," BMA, *El problema*, 6.

204. De Pina, *Código de Procedimientos*, 100–102.

205. Arilla Bas, "Necesidad," 51.

206. Domínguez del Río, *La administración*.

207. "Descrédito total del jurado popular," *El Universal*, May 4, 1965, PS, 1, 19.

208. "Error, ineptitud y corrupción."

209. Marxófilo, "La administración de justicia."

210. Sodi de Pallares, "Manifiestas injusticias."

211. *La administración de justicia*, 3.

212. "Justicia limpia y expedita."

213. "Escrito presentado a la Barra Mexicana," in BMA, *El problema*, 6.

214. Trueba, *Justicia*, 37–44.

215. Matos Escobedo, "Control constitucional," 223:8062–65, 225:8206–10.

216. "La acción penal no es propiedad del Ministerio Público," *El Informador*, April 2, 1943, 3.
217. Alcalá-Zamora y Castillo, *Síntesis*, 525.
218. Franco Sodi, "El anteproyecto," 235.
219. "Errores de justicia," *Excélsior*, April 8, 1966, PS, 6A.
220. "Los orígenes de las deficiencias judiciales," *El Universal*, April 15, 1942, 9.
221. "Errores de justicia," *Excélsior*, April 8, 1966, PS, 6A.
222. Rojas Avendaño, "Juzgando a los juzgadores," pt. 1.
223. Rojas Avendaño, "Juzgando a los juzgadores," pt. 3, *Excélsior*, April 21, 1966, PS, 4A.
224. Alejandro Campos Bravo, "La prófuga," *El Nacional Revolucionario*, August 4, 1929, SS, 6.
225. Fernández del Castillo in BMA, *El problema*, 6.
226. "Justicia de mano izquierda," *Excélsior*, December 14, 1942, PS, 4.
227. "Un grave síntoma."
228. Héctor Solís Quiroga, "Mejorar la administración de Justicia."
229. "La administración de justicia," *El Universal*, June 2, 1940, PS, 3, 7.
230. "Lacras de la justicia"; "Depuración en el ramo penal," *El Nacional*, June 30, 1942, PS, 1, 8.
231. Portes Gil, *Autobiografía*, 459–61.
232. "La judicatura como profesión," *El Universal*, October 21, 1940, PS, 3, 10.
233. "Cómo se improvisan jueces penales," *Excélsior*, March 3, 1942, SS, 1, 3.
234. "Los funcionarios judiciales," *El Universal*, October 19, 1940, PS, 3.
235. "La justicia en México," *El Universal*, November 1, 1940, PS, 3, 5.
236. "Por el ojo de la llave," *El Universal*, November 26, 1940, PS, 3.
237. "Al buen juez," *El Universal*, December 11, 1940, PS, 3.
238. "Justicia de mano izquierda,"4.
239. "Necesidad de justicia," *Excélsior*, January 19, 1942, PS, 4.
240. Bremauntz, *Por una justicia*, 78; BMA, *El problema*, 13; Ceniceros, "Lacras administrativas"; Garrido, "Descrédito total del jurado popular," *El Universal*, May 4, 1965, PS, 1, 19; Trinidad García, "La justicia en México," *Excélsior*, August 1, 1966, PS, 1A, 18A, 19A; Villarreal, "Prácticamente rara vez se administra justicia en nuestro país," *Excélsior*, December 18, 1942, SS, 1, 5; Froylán López Narváez, "Justicia de los setentas," *Excélsior*, September 25, 1970, A7; "La CTM contra la Suprema Corte," *Novedades*, March 12, 1941, PS, 5.
241. "La justicia en México," *Excélsior*, July 30, 1966, PS, 1A, 15A, 17A. Others coincided: Serralde ("La administración de justicia," *El Universal*, February 28, 1942, PS, 3), Moreno Tagle ("Clamor unánime para que aplique pena de muerte," *La Prensa*, December 19, 1954, 3, 14), and José Ángel Ceniceros ("Conceptos sobre organización judicial," *Universal Gráfico*, March 11, 1942, 3, 14).

242. Solís Quiroga, "Juzgados y cárceles," El Universal, March 16, 1967, PS, 3; Solís Quiroga, "Mejorar la administración de justicia."
243. Gonzalo de la Parra, "Justicia Mexicana," El Universal, February 16, 1940, PS, 3.
244. Mendieta y Núñez, La administración, 139, 217. For postrevolutionary corruption, see Gómez Estrada, "Elite de Estado."
245. Portes Gil, Autobiografía, 463–66.
246. "Escrito," in BMA, El problema, 5.
247. "La organización judicial," El Universal, June 7, 1940, PS, 3.
248. "La justicia en paños menores," Excélsior, December 5, 1942, PS, 1, 7.
249. "En México se trafica con la justicia," La Prensa, December 29, 1954, 3, 33.
250. "La justicia en México," Excélsior, July 26, 1966, PS, 1A, 12A, 14A.
251. Pirra-Purra, "La justicia polka," El Nacional Revolucionario, February 20, 1930, PS, 3, 5; Franco Sodi, "Se vende la justicia," El Universal, June 8, 1940, PS, 3; Ceniceros, "Corruptores," 74; Ceniceros, "La revisión," 311; "El problema de la justicia en México," El Universal, May 2, 1965, PS, 1, 16; Ceniceros, "Programa para mejorar"; La administración de justicia, 8; "El problema de la justicia," El Universal, June 4, 1965, PS, 3; "La justicia en México," Excélsior, August 1, 1966, PS, 1A, 18A, 19A; Solís Quiroga, "Juzgados y cárceles"; "Trueba," Justicia, 11–23.
252. Soto Guevara, "La administración de justicia," El Universal, June 2, 1940, PS, 3, 7; "Togas manchadas," Excélsior, June 5, 1940, PS, 5; Miguel Bueno, "El bataclán de la justicia," El Universal, April 29, 1969, PS, 2.
253. Andrade, "Con excepción de tres, los demás jueces no son malos," El Nacional Revolucionario, August 1, 1931, 9; "Los jueces de lo penal son los más capacitados," El Nacional Revolucionario, May 22, 1932, SS, 1.
254. "Datos concretos de las acusaciones," Excélsior, June 7, 1940, PS, 13.
255. "Rehabilitación de la Procuraduría," El Universal, February 15, 1968, PS, 3.
256. "La justicia por dentro," Excélsior, August 5, 1966, PS, 7A.
257. For TSJ presidents' intentions or declarations, see Ortiz Rodríguez, "El cuartelazo"; "El Lic. Ostos declara que procurará que los jueces malos sean sancionados, pero que para los buenos espera y exige respeto," La Prensa, April 6, 1942, 11, 18; Franco Sodi, "Escepticismo," 4; "Todo progresa." For the magistrates' statement, see "Todo es según el color," La Prensa, September 8, 1941, 10, 22.
258. They were pointed out by Domínguez del Río, La administración, 59; Garrido, "La justicia en la balanza de la justicia," Novedades, January 2, 1966, PS, 20; Solís Quiroga, "Mejorar la administración de Justicia."
259. Mendieta y Núñez, La administración, 329–30.
260. "Memorando," 25. Another group of attorneys expressed the same opinion; see Pallares, "Irregularidades judiciales."

261. This was affirmed by BMA, *El problema*, 13; *El Universal*, "La organización judicial," October 30, 1942, PS, 3, 11; Pérez Verdía, *La administración de justicia*, 2, 13; Trueba, "Justicia corrompida"; Solís Quiroga, "Mejorar la administración de Justicia," *El Universal*; and attorneys' groups, "Irregularidades judiciales."

262. "Causa hondo malestar la corrupción de la justicia," *El Universal Gráfico*, December 12, 1938, 3, 18.

263. "Demanda rectitud a jueces penales," *Excélsior*, April 19, 1966. PS, 1, 11.

264. Ceniceros, "Corruptores," 74.

265. "La venalidad judicial debe denunciarla el público," *La Prensa*, December 26, 1954, 10, 26.

266. "La justicia en México," *Excélsior*, July 30, 1966, PS, 1A, 15A, 17A.

267. Bremauntz, *Por una justicia*, 285–95.

268. Villarreal, "Una banda de estranguladores"; "Justicia mexicana," *Excélsior*, July 31, 1966, PS, 1A, 14A, 16A.

269. "Inamovilidad judicial," *Excélsior*, March 26, 1969, PS, 6A.

270. "Los que pagan por pecar," *El Nacional*, November 25, 1967, PS, 3.

271. García Ramírez, "Quehacer," 26–27.

272. Lizardi Ramos, "Tres males."

273. "Entre abogados y jueces," *Excélsior*, January 25, 1966, PS, 7A.

274. "Justicia," "Justicia y presupuesto," and "Los datos olvidados," *La Prensa*; BMA, *El problema*, 12; *La administración de justicia*, 2, 13.

275. Domínguez del Río, *La administración*, 145.

276. "Justicia corrompida," *Excélsior*, November 3, 1964, PS, 6A.

277. "El problema de la justicia," *El Universal*, June 4, 1965, PS, 3 and SS, 20, 23.

278. "Error, ineptitud y corrupción."

279. "Por el ojo de la llave," *El Universal*, November 26, 1940, PS, 3.

280. "Causa hondo malestar la corrupción de la justicia," *El Universal Gráfico*, December 12, 1938, 3, 14.

281. Domínguez del Río, *La administración*, 58.

282. Marxófilo, "La libertad bajo fianza y los obreros pobres," *El Nacional Revolucionario*, June 24, 1930, PS, 3; Salvador Ponce de León, "Actualidades," *El Universal*, February 22, 1944, PS, 3, 4.

283. "Fue, es y será," *Universal Gráfico*, May 28, 1942, 6, 17.

284. "Únicamente los pobres."

285. "Incalificables abusos se cometen por los jueces calificadores en las Delegaciones," *La Prensa*, December 16, 1942, 12.

286. "Tribunales humanizados," *Excélsior*, February 13, 1969, PS, 6A, 8A.

287. "Error, ineptitud y corrupción."

288. "En México la justicia es una mercancía," *Excélsior*, December 16, 1970, PS, 1A, 16A, 34A, 35A. See also Guillermo Jordán, "Justicia," December 5, 1970,

PS, 6A, 9A; Alejandro Avilés, "Problema de todos," December 17, 1970, PS, 6A, 8A; Alfonso Trueba, "La justicia," December 22, 1970, PS, 7A, 11A.

289. See "Censuras por fijar fianzas ridículas," *Excélsior*, December 15, 1965, PS, 1A, 29A; "Denuncia la Cámara inmoralidades judiciales," *El Universal*, December 15, 1965, PS, 1, 20, SS, 33.

290. López Portillo, "Justicia y justicia social," *El Universal*, December 2, 1967, PS, 2, 15.

291. Bremauntz, *Por una justicia*, 196, 199.

292. "La vara de la justicia es garrote vil para los pobres," *La Prensa*, December 25, 1942, 17.

293. "La liquidación de los señores feudales," *El Universal*, May 6, 1942, PS, 3.

294. "Necesidad de justicia," *Excélsior*, January 19, 1942, PS, 4.

295. "Notas de México," *Excélsior*, September 12, 1942, PS, 4, 7.

296. "Justicia a medias para 5 millones de almas," *Excélsior*, June 2, 1960, PS, 1, 10.

297. "La justicia sólo les sirve a los poderosos," *La Prensa*, December 30, 1954, 3, 31.

298. "La encuesta relámpago," *La Prensa*, November 30, 1942, 29.

299. Keith, "Justicia imposible."

300. Raquel Cervera, "El reportero preguntón," *Novedades*, December 14, 1942, PS, 9; and a citizen surveyed, in "Por el ojo de la llave," *El Universal*, November 5, 1942, PS, 3.

301. Bremauntz, *Por una justicia*, 191–200.

302. "Iniciativa del barrista"; Ramos Bilderbeck, "Por una secretaría"; Martínez Báez, "Estudio histórico"; Gaxiola, "Sobre la creación"; Couto, "Sobre la imperiosa."

303. *La administración de justicia*, 8, 10, 13; Garrido, "El problema de la justicia," *Excélsior*; "El problema de la justicia en México," *El Universal*, May 2, 1965, PS, 1, 16. Coinciding opinions were José Castillo Larrañaga representing the Attorneys' Union ("Los funcionarios judiciales," *El Universal*, October 19, 1940, PS, 3); UNAM professors ("Nueva era de justicia en nuestro país," *Excélsior*, September 30, 1940, PS, 1, 11; "Un problema de ética profesional," October 4, 1940, PS, 3); Bremauntz (*Por una justicia*, 285–95); Raúl Cervantes Ahumada (Aguilar, "La justicia del orden"; "La justicia en México," *Excélsior*, July 30, 1966, PS, 1A, 15A, 17A); Trinidad García ("La justicia en México," *Excélsior*, August 1, 1966, PS, 1A, 18A, 19A).

304. Attendees of the International Congress of Criminology in Palermo, Penal and Penitentiary Congress in Berlin, World Congress of Criminology in Rome, Inter-American Congress of Criminology in Buenos Aires, and Pan-American Congress in Lima (all held in the 1930s and early 1940s). See Ceniceros, "El Congreso"; Quiroz Cuarón, paper presented around 1960 at the III *Congreso Interamericano del Ministerio Público*, in FAQC, sobre 55, documento 11. An example of a *Criminalia* article is Francoz R., "El antiguo."

305. Pardo, "El criterio médico," 9.
306. Almaraz, "La especialización," 41.
307. Garrido, "El nuevo juez"; Carrancá y Trujillo, *Derecho penal*, ii, 47; Carrancá y Trujillo, *Teoría del juez*, 25–28; Carrancá y Trujillo, *Métodos*, 27, 32. See also González Bustamante, *Principios de derecho*, 186; Abarca, *El derecho*, 115; Ceniceros, "El Congreso"; Lugo, "Estudio," 25; García Ramírez, "Comentario," 146–47; Quiroz Cuarón, "La criminalidad en la República," 146.
308. González de la Vega, "La especialización"; Domínguez del Río, *La administración*, 62; Garrido, "El problema de la justicia," *Excélsior*.
309. Fernández del Castillo, "Nuestra realidad," 130; González de la Vega, "J. M. Ortiz."
310. See Garrido, "El problema de la justicia," *El Universal*; "La justicia en la balanza de la justicia," *Novedades*, January 2, 1966. PS, 20; Joaquín Baca Aguirre, "Más que nuevas leyes, justicia," *El Universal*, August 8, 1942, PS, 3; Porte Petit, "Anteproyecto," 329; Elorduy, "Los delitos," 79; Portes Gil, "En México se trafica con la justicia," *La Prensa*, December 29, 1954, 3, 33; Javier Cervantes y Anaya and Xavier Olea Muñoz, "El servilismo es otra lacra de la justicia," *La Prensa*, December 28, 1954, 2, 23; BMA members (Bremauntz, *Por una justicia*, 204–5), Cervantes y Anaya and Fernández del Castillo (*La administración de justicia*, 7, 8, 10, 13), Lara Barragán ("Piden más tribunales y menos pseudoabogados," *El Universal*, December 21, 1965, PS, 1, 14), Ceniceros ("Lacras administrativas"), and Domínguez del Río (*La administración*, 61, 110).
311. "Puro interés bastardo."
312. "El problema de la justicia," *El Universal*, June 4, 1965, PS, 3 and SS, 20, 23.
313. "Notas de México," *Excélsior*, September 12, 1942, PS, 4, 7.
314. "Serpentinas," *La Prensa*, December 16, 1942, 9.
315. Bremauntz, *Por una justicia*, 6, 7, 67.
316. Domínguez del Río, *La administración*, 85–86.
317. Ortiz Alarcón, "Justicia al servicio del pueblo," *El Nacional*, November 30, 1967, PS, 3.
318. Ortiz Rodríguez, "El cuartelazo."
319. BMA, *El problema*, 11.
320. "La moralización de la justicia," *El Universal*, July 9, 1940, PS, 3.
321. Baca Aguirre, "Más que nuevas leyes, justicia," *El Universal*, August 8, 1942, PS, 3.
322. "Memorando," 25.
323. Portes Gil, *Autobiografía*, 462-63.
324. "Justicia a medias," *Excélsior*, January 14, 1966, PS, 7A.
325. "Corrupción Judicial," *El Universal*, December 19, 1965, PS, 1, 23.
326. "La justicia en la balanza de la justicia," *Novedades*, January 2, 1966, PS, 20.
327. Elorduy, "Los delitos," 80.

328. Garibay, "Administración de justicia y policía."

329. "Bajo el impulso de las inmoralidades se tambalea la balanza de la Diosa Themis," La Prensa, August 25, 1940, 4, 20; "Triunfo rotundo" and "Honorable presidente," La Prensa, August 27, 1940, 10.

330. The results were published in 1942 in "Total depuración de la justicia mexicana," Excélsior, April 7, ss, 1, 6; "Acuerdo del Pleno ayer," El Universal, April 7, ss, 1, 8; "Se abrió ya una investigación sobre las injusticias de la justicia que ha venido denunciando la prensa," La Prensa, April 7, 3, 5; "Declaraciones del Presidente del Tribunal de Justicia," El Universal, April 8, ss, 1, 8; "Depuración de la justicia," Excélsior, April 8, ps, 4; "Visita a los presos para activar más sus procesos," Excélsior, April 8, ss, 1 and last; "Injustos cargos para los jueces," El Universal, April 8, ss, 1 and last; "Suma y sigue," La Prensa, April 9, 9, 26; "Es falso que el Tribunal Superior abandone a reos," Excélsior, April 10, ss, 1 and last.

331. Ortiz Rodríguez, "El cuartelazo"; "El Lic. Ostos declara"; Franco Sodi, "Escepticismo," 4; "Todo progresa"; "Todo es según el color," La Prensa, September 8, 1941, 10, 22.

332. The former occupied the post from January to July 1940, the latter from December 1940 to September 1941. For their requests, see "Cooperación del público," El Universal, February 10, 1940, ps, 1, 14; "La justicia necesita la orientación y la crítica de la prensa," La Prensa, December 2, 1940, 2, 23.

333. "Física y moralmente."

334. Quiroz Cuarón, "La criminalidad evoluciona," 153.

335. Bremauntz, Por una justicia, 130–31.

336. Arévalo Macías, "Más que una revisión," 582.

337. "Cementerio de la Justicia," Excélsior, November 22, 1942, ps, 10, 12.

338. "Una justicia mejor," El Universal, April 15, 1942, ps, 3; La administración de justicia, 7; López Narváez, "Justicia de los setentas."

339. "Lenta y cara," Excélsior, September 28, 1966, ps, 6A, 8A.

340. Esquivel Medina, "El polvo," 47.

341. "La reforma judicial," Novedades, January 11, 1965, ps, 4.

342. "La justicia en la balanza de la justicia," Novedades, January 2, 1966, ps, 20; Garrido, "El problema de la justicia," Excélsior.

343. Colín Sánchez, Función social, 18–19.

344. "Nueva justicia," El Universal, October 9, 1940, ps, 3, 7.

345. "Notas de México," Excélsior, September 12, 1942, ps, 4, 7.

346. Raúl Carrancá y Trujillo, "Meridiano de México," Excélsior, July 13, 1968, ps, 6A, 8A; Keith, "Justicia," Excélsior, September 10, 1968, ps, 7A.

347. "¿Dónde está la justicia?," Novedades, August 1, 1942, ps, 4.

348. "Justicia a medias para 5 millones de almas," Excélsior, June 2, 1960, ps, 1, 10.

349. "La vara de la justicia es garrote vil para los pobres," La Prensa, December 25, 1942, 17.

350. "Nueva justicia," *El Universal*, October 9, 1940, PS, 3, 7.
351. "Justicia de mano izquierda," 4, 7.
352. "Revisión de leyes," *Excélsior*, May 13, 1968, PS, 6A, 31A.
353. "Las leyes y la realidad," *El Universal*, February 27, 1965, PS, 3 and SS, 20.
354. *La administración de justicia*, 7.
355. Bremauntz, *Por una justicia*, 286.
356. Garrido, "La justicia desvalida."
357. "Esa justicia señor regente."
358. Domínguez Carrascosa, "Restructuración," 7.
359. "Meridiano de México," *Excélsior*, July 31, 1965, PS, 6A, 8A.
360. "La justicia en México," *Excélsior*, July 27, 1966, PS, 1A, 11A.
361. "Justicia," "Justicia y presupuesto," and "Los datos olvidados," *La Prensa*.

4. JUDGES' APPOINTMENTS AND PROFILES

1. CP 1917, art. 73-VI; LOT 1928, arts. 14–21, 25, 68, 77, 83; LOT 1932, arts. 12–18, 27, 64, 92; LOT 1968, arts. 11–16, 25, 52, 75.
2. For biographical data on judges and references, see the appendix in Speckman Guerra, *En tela de juicio*, 577–639.
3. Portes Gil, *Autobiografía*, 459–61.
4. Portes Gil, *Autobiografía*, 460.
5. "Ventaja del nuevo código de lo penal," *Excélsior*, September 18, 1931, SS, 1.
6. *Diario de Debates*, Legislatura XXXVI, año I, Periodo Ordinario, diario 34, December 26, 1934, session.
7. *Diario de Debates*, Legislatura XXXIX, año I, Periodo Ordinario, diario 11, September 3, 1943, session.
8. Antonio Armendáriz, "La nueva administración de justicia," *El Universal*, November 13, 1940, PS, 3, 12.
9. *Diario de Debates*, Legislatura XXXVI, año II, Periodo Ordinario, diario 5, September 22, 1944, session.
10. *Diario de Debates*, Legislatura XL, año II, Periodo Ordinario, Diario 3, September 2, 1947, session.
11. Ricardo Abarca, "La nueva administración de justicia," *El Universal*, November 4, 1944, PS, 9, 13; Carrancá y Trujillo, *Un año*, 5.
12. *Diario de Debates*, Legislatura XLI, año II, Comisión Permanente, Diario 46, March 16, 1951, session.
13. Elorduy, "Los delitos," 80.
14. Bremauntz, *Por una justicia*, 51, 66.
15. *Diario de Debates*, Legislatura XLIII, año II, Comisión Permanente, diario 45, March 15, 1957, session.
16. *Diario de Debates*, Legislatura XLV, año II, Comisión Permanente, diario 52, March 14, 1963, session.
17. Domínguez del Río, *La administración*, 33–39.

18. *Diario de Debates*, Legislatura XLVII, año II, Periodo Ordinario, diario 15, October 18, 1968, session.

19. *Diario de Debates*, Legislatura XLVII, año II, Comisión Permanente, diario 10, March 13, 1969, session. See also "Protestaron a sus cargos los nuevos Magistrados del Tribunal Superior," El Nacional, March 14, 1969, 8; "Toman posesión hoy jueces y magistrados," El Nacional, March 17, 1969, 7; "Tomarán posesión cinco Magistrados," Excélsior, March 14, 1969, PS, 29A; "Reeligieron en el Tribunal Superior al lic. César Pasos," Excélsior, March 18, 1969, 24A; "Pasos sugiere un cambio constitucional," Excélsior, March 25, 1969, 1; "La función de impartir justicia exige un estricto cumplimiento del deber," El Nacional, April 16, 1969, 6.

20. I do not have the complete list, but these included Rafael Murillo Aguilar, Juan José González Suárez, Rafael Pérez Palma, and Antonio I. Quirazo.

21. Four were MP agents (Rafael Millán Martínez, Enrique Navarro Sánchez, Juan Vernis Wunenburger, and Armando Quirasco, apparently recent graduates). Information is lacking on the prior history of the other three (Heriberto Díaz Muñoz, Raymundo Huesca Juárez, and Isidoro Asús Catalán).

22. The organization mentions Eva Esteva McMaster, Enriqueta Laguna Arcos, Marilú Amezcua Huerta, and Victoria Adato Green. "Lucharán las abogadas por llegar a ser jueces," Excélsior, March 16, 1969, 8A.

23. Clemente Castellanos (1925–44), Alfredo Ortega (1928–44), Valentín Rincón (1934–51), Enrique Pérez Arce (1934–49), Vicente Muñoz Castro (1934–51), Alfonso Martínez Sotomayor (1940–57), Lorenzo Reynoso Padilla (1940–57), Francisco de Sales Valero (1944–63), Carlos Espeleta Torrijos (1944–63), Alberto Bremauntz Martínez (1944–63), Ignacio Villalobos Jiménez (1944–63), María Lavalle Urbina (1947–63), Eduardo Urzaiz Jiménez (1951–69), José Víctor Cervantes Aguilera (1957–75), Gloria León Orantes (1957–75), Tito Ortega Sánchez (1957–75), María Luisa Santillán (1957–75), and Pascual Flores Guillén (1957–75).

24. Matías Ochoa (1928–51), José Ortiz Rodríguez (1928–51), Genaro Ruiz de Chávez (1931–54), Alberto González Blanco (1940–63), Ramón Franco Romero (1944–67), Julio Sánchez Vargas (1946–67), José Valentín Medina Ochoa (1951–75), Celestino Porte Petit (1951–75), Alberto Sánchez Cortés (1951–75), Godolfredo Beltrán (1951–75), and Héctor Terán Torres (1957–81).

25. Alberto Régulo Vela Rodríguez (1931–44, 1946–63), Salvador Castañeda del Villar (1944–69), and Luis Gonzaga Saloma Córdova (1944–69).

26. Adalberto Galeana Sierra (1928–63), Platón Herrera Ostos (1931–63), Aulio gelio Lara Erosa (1934–68), Emilio César Pasos (1940–44 and 1951–75), Ignacio Calderón Álvarez (1944–81), and Eduardo Mac-Gregor Romero (1944–76).

5. JUDICIAL PRACTICES AND NOTORIOUS HOMICIDES

1. Rojas Avendaño, "Juzgando a los juzgadores," pt. 2.
2. Fix-Zamudio, "La administración," 145–46; Ovalle Favela, *Temas*, 7–12; García Cordero, *La administración de justicia*, 285–95.
3. Buffington and Piccato, "Tales," 27; Piccato, *History of Infamy*, 5–6.
4. Del Castillo, "El surgimiento de la prensa" and "El surgimiento del reportaje"; Lombardo, *De la opinión*.
5. Piccato, "Murders of Nota Roja," 203–4; Piccato, *History of Infamy*, 67.
6. Monsiváis, *Los mil*, 42.
7. On photographers, see Piccato, *History of Infamy*, 78–79. On Enrique Díaz specifically, see Monroy Nasr, *Historias*.
8. Garmabella, *¡Reportero de policía!*, 28.
9. Speckman Guerra, "Digna flor," 374–75, 379. On the reporter-police connection, see Piccato, *History of Infamy*, 77–78, 94; Piccato, "Todo homicidio," 638–39.
10. Filmed in 1949, written and directed by Chano Urueta.
11. Filmed in 1960, directed by Zacarías Gómez Urquiza with script by Alberto Ramírez de Aguilar and Carlos Ravelo.
12. Pérez Moreno, "Creación de escuelas."
13. Directed by Spota and Adolfo Torres Portillo in 1958.
14. Filmed in 1958, directed by Alejandro Galindo.
15. "La criminalidad y la ciencia," *El Universal*, October 21, 1942, 9.
16. "La apología del crimen en los periódicos," *El Universal*, March 20, 1932, PS, 3.
17. Raúl Carrancá y Trujillo, "Meridiano de México," *El Universal*, January 13, 1968.
18. "Gestión de la Barra Mexicana"; see also Raúl Carrancá y Trujillo, "Meridiano de México," *El Universal*, January 13, 1968.
19. Meade, "From Sex Strangler," 361–65; Piccato, *History of Infamy*, 76; Santillán Esqueda, *Delincuencia femenina*, 55.
20. "Inexplicable actitud de un fiscal," *La Prensa*, June 5, 1936, 2.
21. Speckman Guerra, "Digna flor," 397.
22. Hearings were public except in cases deemed crimes against morality. Individuals older than fourteen could witness the hearings as long as their heads were uncovered and they remained silent and showed respect (CPP 1931, arts. 59–60).
23. Carlos Monsiváis, "Fuegos de nota roja," *Nexos*, August 1992, http://redaccion.nexos.com.mx/?p=1697012.
24. When classifying the sentences, I used criteria like that of Martha Santillán Esqueda, who divides them into low, medium, and high punishment (*Delincuencia femenina*, 305, table).

25. "La descuartizadora de la colonia Roma," *Excélsior*, April 29, 1941, SS, 1.

26. CP 1929, art. 45-III; CP 1931, art. 15-III.

27. CP 1931, art. 15-III.

28. CP 1929, art. 45-III.

29. CP 1931, art. 15-IV.

30. December 16, 1934, AP 2594/34, *Semanario Judicial de la Federación* (hereafter SJF), Quinta época, tomo XLII, 3545. The abbreviation AP refers to direct *amparo*.

31. Speckman Guerra, *En tela de juicio*, 303–4.

32. *Anales de Jurisprudencia*, 1961, tomo CVIII, 219–24.

33. The reiteration of criteria gave rise to judicial precedent: *Legítima defensa*, jurisprudencia penal, SJF, Sexta época, Apéndice de 2011, tomo 3 penal–primera parte SCJN–sección sustantivo, tesis 163, 151.

34. For example, May 11, 1946, AP 8877/45, SJF, Quinta época, tomo LXXXVIII, 1693; and *ejecutoria* (final judgment) of July 7, 1960, AP 6524/51, SJF, Sexta época, Segunda parte del tomo XXXVII, 128.

35. January 10, 1945, AP 7496/44, SJF, Quinta época, tomo LXXXIII, 361.

36. For the reference to the opinion, see Speckman Guerra, *En tela de juicio*, 307–8. The TSJ respected the criteria. See *Anales de Jurisprudencia*, 1949, tomo LXIII, 117–64; 1963, tomo CXV, 1963, 291–97.

37. *Anales de Jurisprudencia*, 1955, tomo LXXXV, 311–20.

38. Speckman Guerra, *En tela de juicio*, 309.

39. July 16, 1959, final judgment, AP 3364/58, SJF, Sexta época, Segunda parte del tomo XXV, 78.

40. March 5, 1942, final judgment, amparo en revisión 7127/41, SJF, Quinta época, tomo LXXI, 3703.

41. See Speckman Guerra, *En tela de juicio*, 310.

42. August 11, 1937, final judgment, AP 1508/37, SJF, Quinta época, tomo LIII, 1631.

43. Jurisprudencia penal, Apéndice de 2011, tomo III–penal primera parte–SCJN–sección sustantivo, tesis 168, 153; and April 2, 1951, final judgment, AP 9772/50, SJF, Quinta época, tomo CVIII, 9. For rulings by the TSJ, see *Anales de Jurisprudencia*, tomo CXVI, 271–81; Speckman Guerra, *En tela de juicio*, 315.

44. November 22, 1961, final judgment, AP 7801/60, SJF, Sexta época, Segunda parte del tomo LIII, 40.

45. December 7, 1946, AP 7768/46, SJF, Quinta época, tomo XC, 2614. See Speckman Guerra, *En tela de juicio*, 316.

46. February 6, 1942, AP 8706/41, SJF, Quinta época, tomo LXXI, 1996.

47. *Anales de Jurisprudencia*, 1955, tomo LXXXV, 311–20.

48. June 10, 1954, AP 6041/51, SJF, Quinta época, tomo CXX, 1189.

49. November 19, 1938, AP 6240/38, SJF, Quinta época, tomo LVIII, 2205.

50. SJF, Quinta época, Apéndice de 1995, Tesis 899, tomo II–parte HO, 571; SJF, Sexta época, Apéndice de 1995, tesis 219, tomo II–parte SCJN, 125.
51. See Speckman Guerra, *En tela de juicio*, 318.
52. CP 1931, art. 15-III. See Carrancá y Trujillo, "Sobre las presunciones."
53. *Anales de Jurisprudencia*, 1968, tomo CXXX, 211–18.
54. Desentis case record, AGN, Galería 6, Fondo Tribunal Superior de Justicia (FTSJ), año 1940, caja 333, expediente 31.
55. "El Lic. Miguel Desentis dio muerte a un ratero," *El Universal Gráfico*, January 12, 1940, 3.
56. "Agresivo ladrón muerto a balazos por el conocido abogado Miguel Desentis," *La Prensa*, January 13, 1940, 4.
57. "El Lic. Miguel Desentis."
58. "No está probado que el hampón a quien mató el licenciado Desentis haya violentado la casa de éste," *La Prensa*, January 14, 1940, 4.
59. "Reconstrucción en la casa del señor Desentis," *Excélsior*, January 16, 1940, 1.
60. "Era un perfecto pájaro de cuenta," *El Universal Gráfico*, January 13, 1940, 3.
61. "Era un asaltante de peligro el que mató el abogado Desentis," *Excélsior*, January 14, 1940, SS, 1, 7.
62. "Reconstrucción en la casa del señor Desentis."
63. Desentis case record, FTSJ.
64. *El Universal Gráfico*, January 16, 1940, 3.
65. Desentis case record, FTSJ.
66. Desentis case record, FTSJ; *Anales de Jurisprudencia*, 1941, tomo XXXII, 78–89.
67. *Anales de Jurisprudencia*, 1949, tomo LXIII, 117–64.
68. July 12, 1956, AP 2115/56, SJF, Quinta época, tomo CXXIX, 105.
69. Santillán Esqueda, *Delincuencia femenina*, 238–45.
70. For a similar case, that of Vita Sierra Villanueva, see Speckman Guerra, *En tela de juicio*, 339–44.
71. Sánchez Schultz case record, AGN, Galería 6, FTSJ, año 1944, caja 852, exp. 10392; "El asesinato del Capitán Sánchez ha sido venganza de politicastros," *Excélsior*, December 19, 1944, SS, 8; "Un capitán del ejército fue asesinado a mansalva," *La Prensa*, December 19, 1944, 2, 7.
72. Sánchez Schultz case record, FTSJ.
73. "El asesinato del Capitán Sánchez"; "Sangrienta tragedia en la casa del capitán Roberto Sánchez," *Excélsior*, December 19, 1944, tercera sección (hereafter TS), 9; "Un capitán del ejército"; "Un crimen de carácter político se registró anoche en Tacuba," *El Universal Gráfico*, December 20, 1944, 3.
74. "El asesinato del capitán Sánchez."
75. "El asesinato del Capitán Sánchez"; "Sangrienta tragedia"; "Un capitán del ejército."
76. "Hay dos pistas en el asesinato del capitán Sánchez Siordia," *La Prensa*, December 21, 1944, 12, 14.

77. "Está aclarado el asesinato del capitán R. Sánchez Siordia," *La Prensa*, December 22, 1944, 12.
78. Sánchez Schultz case record, FTS.
79. "La hija del Capitán Sánchez Siordia confiesa ser la autora del crimen," *La Prensa*, December 25, 1944, 13.
80. "Ana Irma Sánchez Schultz es la matadora del Capitán," *Excélsior*, December 25, 1944, TS, 1, 6; "La hija del Capitán Sánchez Siordia"; "Dice que mató en defensa de su madre," *El Universal*, December 25, 1944, 16.
81. Sánchez Schultz case record, FTSJ; "Ana Irma Sánchez Schultz es la matadora del Capitán," *Excélsior*, December 25, 1944, TS, 1, 6; "La hija del Capitán Sánchez Siordia"; "Dice que mató en defensa de su madre," *El Universal*, December 25, 1944, 16.
82. Sánchez Schultz case record, FTSJ.
83. "Dice que mató en defensa de su madre."
84. "La hija del Capitán Sánchez Siordia."
85. "La hija del Capitán Sánchez Siordia"; "El capitán R. Sánchez Siordia fue el que provocó el crimen," *La Prensa*, December 27, 1944, 15.
86. "Ana Irma Sánchez Schultz es la matadora del Capitán."
87. "Dice que mató en defensa de su madre."
88. Sánchez Schultz case record, FTSJ; "Formal prisión de Irma Sánchez," *La Prensa*, December 28, 1944, 12.
89. Sánchez Schultz case record, FTSJ; "Sangrienta tragedia en la casa del capitán Roberto Sánchez."
90. Sánchez Schultz case record, FTSJ.
91. Sánchez Schultz case record, FTSJ.
92. "Emma Perches llora, pero sin arrepentimiento," *El Universal Gráfico*, June 15, 1933, 3.
93. For the earliest news on the crime, see "Una tremenda tragedia conyugal," *La Prensa*, June 9, 1933, 2; "Drama de hogar," *El Universal*, June 9, 1933, 1; "Tuve miedo y maté," *El Universal Gráfico*, June 9, 1933, 3.
94. "Tuve miedo y maté"; "La matadora del motociclista Hernández en la penitenciaría," *La Prensa*, June 10, 1933, 2, 11; "La señora Perches de Hernández mató por temor," *La Prensa*, June 11, 1933, 1.
95. From the account of the first-instance trial in *Anales de Jurisprudencia*, tomo VII, 1934, 555–62.
96. "Emma Perches llora, pero sin arrepentimiento."
97. "El motociclista muerto por la señora Perches la engañaba," *La Prensa*, June 18, 1933, 2; "Es patético el caso de la señora Perches y de sus pequeños," *El Universal Gráfico*, June 15, 1933, 3.
98. "Quiere matarse la actora del drama de doctor Erazo," *La Prensa*, June 11, 1933, 2.
99. "Habla la mujer que mató," *El Universal*, June 10, 1933, SS, 1.

100. "¿Emma Perches que mató a su marido obró por miedo?," *La Prensa*, June 13, 1933, 11.
101. "Los balistas en el proceso de Emma Perches," *La Prensa*, June 25, 1933, 19.
102. "Emma Perches está indignada con los motociclistas," *La Prensa*, June 17, 1933, 1.
103. *Anales de Jurisprudencia*, tomo VII, 1934, 555–62.
104. The ruling in the Perches *amparo* file, SCJAC, AP, año 1935, expediente 1192/35.
105. *Legítima defensa, exculpante de*, October 9, 1936, AP 1192/35, filed by Emma Perches Frank widow of Hernández and ruled unanimously by four votes, SJF, Quinta época, tomo L, 233.
106. Perches *amparo* file, SCJAC.
107. *Amparo en revisión* file, SCJAC, año 1945, Expediente 1970/45.
108. "Una tigresa da muerte a un periodista en céntrico hotel," *La Prensa*, May 4, 1934, 1, 3, 8. For details of the case, see Luna, *La nota roja 1930*, 65–74.
109. "No soy criminal; soy una mártir," pt. 1, *La Prensa*, May 9, 1934, 1, 3, 21.
110. "No soy criminal; soy una mártir," pt. 1, 21.
111. "No soy criminal; soy una mártir," pt. 2, *La Prensa*, May 10, 1934, 1, 3, 21, 23–24.
112. "No soy criminal; soy una mártir," pt. 3, *La Prensa*, May 11, 1934, 3, 13.
113. "No soy criminal; soy una mártir," pt. 4, *La Prensa*, May 12, 1934, 3, 22.
114. Inquiry into María Soledad Rodríguez Prado, AHDF, Fondo Cárceles, Penitenciaría, Expedientes de reos 1920–49, Caja 194, Partida 3014, Expediente J/335/3014.
115. "Una tigresa da muerte a un periodista." *La Prensa*, May 4, 1934, p. 1.
116. *El Universal Gráfico*, May 4, 1934.
117. "Una tigresa da muerte a un periodista," 1, 8.
118. "Una tigresa da muerte a un periodista," 8.
119. "No soy criminal; soy una mártir," pt. 1, 3.
120. "Estaba planeado el asesinato de Quiroz Ramírez," *La Prensa*, May 5, 1934, 1, 3, 27.
121. "D. Ignacio Quiroz sabía que lo iban a matar," *El Universal Gráfico*, May 4, 1934, 3.
122. "¿La ranchera Soledad mató a su amante estando dormido?," *La Prensa*, May 6, 1934, 3, 15.
123. "Una tigresa da muerte a un periodista," 1, 8.
124. Inquiry into Rodríguez Prado, AHDF; "Chole Rodríguez formalmente presa," *La Prensa*, May 7, 1934, 2.
125. "Juro por las cenizas de mi padre que digo la verdad," *La Prensa*, May 9, 1934, 3; "Parece que Chole fue la única que disparó," *La Prensa*, May 10, 1934, 1, 3.
126. Inquiry into Rodríguez Prado, AHDF.

127. Inquiry into Rodríguez Prado, AHDF.
128. Soledad Rodríguez Prado case record of the second-instance trial, AGN, Galería 6, FTSJ, Sexta Sala, año 1935, Caja 2856, Expediente 464996.
129. La Prensa, September 25, 1935.
130. Rodríguez Prado case record, FTSJ.
131. Rodríguez Prado case record, FTSJ; "Se confirmó la pena a Chole La Ranchera," La Prensa, January 26, 1936, 9.
132. SCJAC, AP, año 1936, Expediente 1163.
133. Inquiry into Rodríguez Prado, AHDF.
134. "Otra 'cuerda' con delincuentes de ambos sexos salió rumbo a las fatídicas Islas Marías," La Prensa, April 21, 1940, 22, 24.
135. "Salió para las Islas Marías una cuerda," Excélsior, April 21, 1940, SS, 1, 6.
136. Inquiry into Rodríguez Prado, AHDF.
137. Luna, La nota roja 1930, 43–46; Gonzaga y Armendáriz, "Balazos después," 67–69; Rojas Sosa, "La ciudad," 337–38.
138. "¡Nadie mató a Guty!," La Prensa, April 7, 1932, 2, 18.
139. Ángel Peláez Villa case record of the second-instance trial, SCJAC, AP, año 1933, Expediente 5003; Efemerre, "La muerte de Guty Cárdenas," Magazine de Policía, September 1, 1952, año 11, no. 713.
140. "Guty Cárdenas muerto en una tragedia de cantina," La Prensa, April 6, 1932, 1, 3; "Hay innegable empeño en hacer un enredo alrededor de la tragedia en que pereció anoche Guty Cárdenas," El Universal Gráfico, April 6, 1932, 3; "La tragedia ocurrió a medianoche en la cantina salón Bach," Excélsior, April 6, 1932, SS, 6.
141. Ángel Peláez Villa police file, AHDF, Fondo DDF Jefatura de Policía, Investigación y seguridad pública, Servicio Secreto, "Guty Cárdenas o Augusto Cárdenas Pinelo, quien fue asesinado en la cantina Salón Bach, ubicado en la av. Madero 32 por Ángel Peláez Villa," caja 2, exp. 10, Legajo 1, 1930–32.
142. Peláez Villa police file, AHDF.
143. Peláez Villa case record, SCJAC.
144. "La tragedia ocurrió a medianoche."
145. "¡Nadie mató a Guty!"
146. "Ángel Peláez Villa confesó ya haber matado a Guty Cárdenas," La Prensa, April 8, 1932, 7.
147. Efemerre, "La muerte de Guty Cárdenas."
148. "El más alto homenaje póstumo al malogrado trovador yucateco," El Universal Gráfico, April 7, 1932, 3; "Nota de emocionante dolor fueron los funerales del artista," La Prensa, April 8, 1932, 1; "Se cantó "Rayito de Sol" que terminó en prolongado coro de sollozos," Excélsior, April 8, 1932, SS, 1, 6.
149. "Ángel Peláez Villa confesó"; "Confesó Ángel Peláez que disparó contra Guty," Excélsior, April 8, 1932, SS, 1, 6.

150. Peláez Villa case record, SCJAC. The statement was reproduced in "Ya no hay misterio," *El Universal Gráfico*, April 7, 1932, 3; "Confesó su culpa el asesino de Guty," *La Prensa*, April 8, 1932, 1, 2, 7.

151. "Ángel Peláez Villa confesó."

152. "El responsable de la muerte de Guty Cárdenas quedó formalmente preso," *El Universal Gráfico*, April 9, 1932, 3.

153. Peláez Villa case record, SCJAC.

154. "Importante careo en el proceso por la muerte de Guty," *La Prensa*, April 15, 1932, 2.

155. Peláez Villa case record, SCJAC.

156. Peláez Villa case record, SCJAC.

157. Rojas Sosa, "La ciudad"; Rojas Sosa, "El bajo mundo"; Rojas Sosa, "'Una amenaza"; Pulido Llano, *El mapa rojo*.

158. Peláez Villa case record, SCJAC.

159. *Legítima defensa*, August 12, 1931, AP 2060/30, Quinta época, tomo XXXII, 1871.

160. "Fue absuelto el matador del artista Guty Cárdenas," *La Prensa*, September 20, 1932, 2; "El matador de Guty Cárdenas fue absuelto," September 20, 1932, *Excélsior*, ss.

161. Peláez Villa case record, SCJAC.

162. Peláez Villa case record, SCJAC.

163. Peláez Villa case record, SCJAC; "La Suprema Corte dice."

164. Notes on the proof in the legal dossier Fondo Alfonso Quiroz Cuarón. For testimonies and accounts of the crime, see these 1964 articles in *Excélsior*, sección A: "Mariles sigue prófugo, su víctima agoniza," August 16, 25; "Mariles agredió a Velázquez sin mediar palabras," August 18, 43; "Mariles se presentará hoy en la Procuraduría," August 19, 37, 45. See also these 1964 *La Prensa* articles: "Humberto Mariles, émulo de Higinio Sobera de la Flor," August 15, 21, 36; "Mariles sigue prófugo," August 16, 26; "Ni con el amparo se presentó Mariles," August 18, 18, 20; "El general Mariles disparó a mansalva," August 19, 51. Additional sources are "Temen que quede impune el crimen de H. Mariles," *El Universal Gráfico*, August 21, 1964, 16; "Humberto Mariles," *Mañana*, September 5, 1964, 17. For a synthesis of the case, see Brocca, *La nota roja*, 115–23.

165. "Humberto Mariles, émulo de Higinio Sobera de la Flor," August 15 , 1964, 21.

166. "Mariles sigue prófugo" (*La Prensa*). See also "Mariles sigue prófugo, su víctima agoniza."

167. "Mariles solicitó el amparo," *Excélsior*, August 17, 1964, A38; "Mariles se presenta hoy," *La Prensa*, August 17, 1964, 27, 29; "Mariles se hace cargo de su víctima," *El Universal Gráfico*, August 17, 1964, 20.

168. "El general Mariles disparó a mansalva"; "Mariles se presentará hoy en la Procuraduría."
169. "Temen que quede impune el crimen de H. Mariles."
170. "Mariles debe ser juzgado como cualquier delincuente," *La Prensa*, August 21, 1964, 31.
171. "Mariles ya no es militar y debe tratársele como delincuente," *Excélsior*, August 21, 1964, A35; "Mariles debe ser juzgado."
172. "Ni con el amparo se presentó Mariles," *La Prensa*, August 18, 1964, 20; "Será aprehendido Mariles si no se presenta hoy ante el juez," *El Universal Gráfico*, August 18, 1964, 16; "Mariles se presentará hoy en la Procuraduría," *Excélsior*, August 19, 1964; "Mariles cree que lo salvarán sus influencias," *El Universal Gráfico*, August 19, 1964, 16; "Vence hoy el amparo del Gral. Mariles," *Excélsior*, August 20, 1964, A37; "Hoy se dictará orden de detención contra Mariles," *El Universal Gráfico*, August 20, 1964, 16; "Aflora el otro yo del general Humberto Mariles," August 20, 1964, *La Prensa*, 39; "Mariles ya no es militar."
173. "Orden de aprehensión contra Mariles Cortés," *La Prensa*, August 22, 1964, 27; "Ya buscan los agentes de policía al caballista Humberto Mariles," *El Universal Gráfico*, August 22, 1964, 16; "Mariles, prófugo de la justicia," *La Prensa*, August 23, 1964, 22.
174. "Murió el maestro albañil tiroteado por Mariles," *Excélsior*, August 24, 1964, 33; "Mariles, homicida," *La Prensa*, August 24, 1964, 38; "9 huérfanos acusan a Mariles," *El Universal Gráfico*, August 24, 1964, 20.
175. "Mariles, reo de homicidio," *Excélsior*, August 25, 1964, A40.
176. "Óbolos para los 8 huerfanitos," *Excélsior*, August 26, 1964, A1, A10; "Donativos a la familia de las víctimas de Mariles," *Excélsior*, August 27, 1964, A37; "Más donativos a la viuda de Mariles," *Excélsior*, August 29, 1964, A4; "Uruchurtu ayuda a la viuda del albañil," *Excélsior*, August 28, 1964, A5.
177. "Antecedentes anexados al expediente," *La Prensa*, June 17, 1965, 16; "Dictarán formal prisión a Mariles," *Excélsior*, June 18, 1965, A51.
178. "Mariles sigue prófugo, su víctima agoniza."
179. "Dictarán formal prisión a Mariles."
180. "Mariles," *La Prensa*, November 15, 1966, 20.
181. "Mariles, amo de la velocidad," *La Prensa*, September 12, 1964, 23, 24.
182. "Piden otra medalla de oro para Mariles," *El Universal Gráfico*, August 27, 1964, 15.
183. "Mariles sigue prófugo, su víctima agoniza."
184. "La defensa y la policía judicial dan a conocer el historial de Humberto Mariles," *Excélsior*, September 1, 1964, A31; "Vida y milagros de Humberto Mariles," *La Prensa*, September 1, 1964, 17, 22.
185. "Mariles cree que lo salvarán sus influencias"; "9 huérfanos acusan a Mariles"; "Piden otra medalla de oro para Mariles."

186. "Mariles, homicida," *La Prensa*, August 24, 1964, 38.

187. "Mariles ríe a carcajadas," *La Prensa*, August 24, 1964, 9.

188. "Acumulan pruebas para el proceso de Mariles," *El Universal Gráfico*, August 29, 15. The 1964 image of the poster appeared in various media, such as *Mañana* (September 5, 17) and *Sucesos para todos* (September 25, 25).

189. On the search, see the following 1964 articles: *Excélsior* ("Dicen que es cuestión de horas la captura de Mariles," August 26, A33; "Infructuosos cateos en busca de Mariles," September 6, D2; "Catean cinco residencias en busca de Humberto Mariles," September 10, A37; "Catean la casa de Ahumada en busca de Mariles," September 19, A42); *La Prensa* ("Catearon la residencia de Humberto Mariles," August 25, 10; "Que Mariles seguirá aún oculto," September 9, 20; "Continúa la búsqueda de Humberto Mariles," September 10, 20, 30; "Mariles continúa burlando a la justicia," September 11, 23; "Que Humberto Mariles se esconde en el Norte," September 24, 18); *El Universal Gráfico* ("La autopsia," August 25, 16, 22; "Sólo rumores sobre el paradero de Mariles," August 26, 19; "Versiones a más y mejor," September 23, 2).

190. "Que Humberto Mariles se esconde en el Norte"; "Versiones a más y mejor."

191. "Mariles cree que lo salvarán sus influencias." For the same opinion, see also "Mariles se presenta hoy."

192. "Mariles ya se bajó del caballo," *Excélsior*, August 29, 1964.

193. "Calaveras 1964 del Vatenauta," *Sucesos para Todos*, November 27, 1964, 69.

194. "Mariles, reo de homicidio."

195. "Mariles, amo de la velocidad."

196. "Humberto Mariles: De héroe a homicida," *Mañana*, September 5, 1964, 12.

197. "Mariles homicida," *Excélsior*, August 25, 1964, A6.

198. "9 huérfanos acusan a Mariles."

199. "De política," *Mañana*, April 17, 1965.

200. "¡Mariles, a la Olimpiada!," June 12, 1965, 3, 12; *La Prensa*, "Volvió Humberto Mariles," June 13, 1965, 2, 14.

201. "Mariles ya está en manos de la policía," *Excélsior*, June 14, 1965, A1, A12, A15; "Mariles se entregó," *La Prensa*, June 14, 1965, 18.

202. "Busca Mariles una sentencia benigna," Marco Aurelio Reyes, *El Universal Gráfico*, June 14, 1965, 1.

203. "Mariles será acusado de homicidio calificado," June 16, 1965, *Excélsior*, A37; "No valdrán trofeos," June 16, 1965, *La Prensa*, 2, 27.

204. "Mariles ya está en manos de la policía."

205. "Mariles se entregó."

206. *Jueves de Excélsior*, June 17, 1965, 6.

207. "Ingresó en la Cárcel Preventiva el caballista Humberto Mariles," *Excélsior*, June 15, 1965, A30; "Pretenden alegar legítima defensa," *La Prensa*, June 15, 1965, 26.

208. "Ingresó en la Cárcel Preventiva el caballista."
209. "Pretenden alegar legítima defensa."
210. "Ingresó en la Cárcel Preventiva el caballista."
211. "Prometió ayudar a los deudos de la víctima," *Excélsior*, June 16, 1965, A37; "Ayer insistió en que se defendió" and "Historia de equitación," *La Prensa*, June 16, 1965, 2, 26, 37; "Provocó su víctima a Humberto Mariles," *El Universal Gráfico*, June 16, 1965, 19.
212. "Seis militares comunicaron a Mariles que iría a una prisión militar," *Excélsior*, June 17, 1965, 24; "La SDN no aboga por Mariles," *Excélsior*, June 17, 1965, 2, 30.
213. "Más visitas y aclaración de los seis divisionarios," *La Prensa*, June 18, 1965, 47.
214. "Una viuda y ocho hijos no han olvidado," *Excélsior*, June 15, 1965, A30, A31; "Los hijos del hoy occiso recibieron $700 de 'ayuda,'" *La Prensa*, June 15, 1965, 3.
215. "Decretaron la formal prisión ayer al caballista Humberto Mariles," *Excélsior*, June 19, 1965, A22; "Los defensores, conformes salvo en algunos aspectos," *La Prensa*, June 19, 1965, 10; "Omisiones que lo beneficiarán," *El Universal Gráfico*, June 19, 1965, 20.
216. "Prospera la maniobra de Mariles," *El Universal Gráfico*, June 20, 1965, 23; "Más visitas y aclaración de los seis divisionarios"; "Se enfermó Mariles," *La Prensa*, June 21, 1965, 2, 16; "De la enfermería pasó Mariles a la Crujía I," *La Prensa*, June 22, 1965, 2, 10.
217. "Comentan la "debilidad" del juez 9°," *La Prensa*, June 19, 1965, 2, 14; "En seis meses saldrá Mariles," *El Universal Gráfico*, June 19, 1965, 20.
218. "Mariles será acusado de homicidio calificado," *Excélsior*, June 16, 1965; "No valdrán trofeos," *La Prensa*, June 16, 1965. See also "Ni un testimonio de la acusación se desvanece"; "Dictarán formal prisión a Mariles."
219. Information on the first-instance trial was taken from the second-instance trial (*Anales de Jurisprudencia*, tomo CXXIX, 1967, 141–259), *amparo* trial (SCJAC, Primera Sala, AD, año 1967, Expediente 10125), causes of violation given by the defense (*El caso del general Humberto Mariles Cortés*), expert accounts presented by both parties (Fondo Alfonso Quiroz Cuarón) and the press ("Discrepancia de los médicos," *La Prensa*, October 26, 1965, 27; "Tratan de salvar a Mariles por su glorioso pasado," *La Prensa*, November 17, 1965, 29; "Que Mariles disparó contra Velázquez al ser agredido por éste," *Excélsior*, November 25, 1965, A27).
220. "Tratan de salvar a Mariles por su glorioso pasado."
221. "Desde una celda sin lujos Mariles espera la justicia," *La Prensa*, August 14, 1965, 2, 10.
222. "Dicen que Mariles ocupará un puesto en el Comité Olímpico," *El Universal Gráfico*, October 14, 1965, 20; "Mariles es una blanca paloma," *El Universal Gráfico*, October 30, 1965, 20.

223. They based their request on Criminal Code Article 303 (which established that a wound could be considered mortal only when death was the immediate consequence, the result of alterations caused by the wound in the organ[s] or from a complication from the wound if it was incurable or if it could not be combated) and Article 305 (which indicated that a wound could not be considered mortal if it had worsened from later causes or unfortunate surgical operations).

224. "Sentencian a diez años al general Humberto Mariles," *Excélsior*, November 11, 1965, A24; "Controversia judicial provocó la sentencia del general Mariles," *El Universal Gráfico*, November 11, 1965, 16; "Mariles fue sentenciado," *La Prensa*, November 11, 1965, 1, 2, 15, 16, 28, 43.

225. Information on the first-instance trial was taken from the second-instance trial (*Anales de Jurisprudencia*, tomo CXXIX, 1967, 141–259), and *amparo* trial (SCJAC, Primera Sala, AD, año 1967, Expediente 10125).

226. Two of them were issued in 1954, fifth period of SJF: April 7, AD 1078/53, tomo CXX, 142; December 10, AD 3103/54, tomo CXXII, 1803.

227. Final judgment, May 10, 1939, AD 9003/38, SJF, Quinta época, tomo LX, 1277.

228. For the *tesis*, see Speckman Guerra, *En tela de juicio*, 413–14.

229. Information on the first-instance trial was taken from the second-instance trial (*Anales de Jurisprudencia*, tomo CXXIX, 1967, 141–259), and *amparo* trial (SCJAC, Primera Sala, AD, año 1967, Expediente 10125).

230. "Sentencian a diez años al general Humberto Mariles"; "Sentencian a Mariles," *La Prensa*, November 11, 1966, 15; "Controversia judicial provoca la sentencia del general Mariles"; "Apelarán ambas partes por la condena contra Mariles," *La Prensa*, November 14, 1966, 14, 16; "Atienden la apelación de Mariles," *La Prensa*, November 17, 1966, 19, 20.

231. "Sentencian a Mariles"; Carlos Catalán Fuentes, "Mariles: indignado," *La Prensa*, November 15, 1966, 23.

232. "Controversia judicial provoca la sentencia del general Mariles."

233. *La Prensa*, November 12, 1966, 20.

234. "Los siete días," *Impacto*, November 23, 1966, no. 873, 59.

235. "Mariles y la justicia," *La Prensa*, November 16, 1966, 9, 24.

236. *Anales de Jurisprudencia*, tomo CXXIX, 1967, 141–259.

237. "Aumentaron a veinte años la pena al general Mariles," *Excélsior*, August 16, 1967, A22; "Mariles fue notificado de su nueva condena," *La Prensa*, August 16, 1967, 2, 44, 48; "Indignado H. Mariles truena contra el Tribunal Superior," *El Universal Gráfico*, August 16, 1967, 11.

238. Roberto Blanco Moheno, "La pena a Mariles es un delito," *Impacto*, November 22, 1967, no. 925, 12, 13.

239. Columba Domínguez, "Una historia de la vida diaria y un veredicto exageradamente injusto," *Impacto*, September 24, 1967, no. 917, 21, 65.

240. *Jueves de Excélsior*, August 15, 1968, 45; *Impacto*, August 15, 1968, no. 939, 47.
241. *El caso del general*, VII–X.
242. SCJAC, Primera Sala, AP, año 1967, Expediente 10125.
243. The news was published in "El caballista está preso por homicidio," *Excélsior*, March 15, 1969, A28; "Mariles fue amparado," *La Prensa*, March 15, 1969, 2, 40.
244. "Ya amparado por la Corte," *Excélsior*, March 17, 1969, A22; "Mariles acató con resignación," *La Prensa*, March 19, 1969, 24.
245. "Trasladaron a Mariles a Sta. Marta Acatitla," *Avance*, May 7, 1969, vol. III, año III, no. 643, 1.
246. "Mariles en libertad," *El Universal Gráfico*, June 15, 1971, 2; "Entre sus familiares y amigos Mariles retornó a la equitación," *El Universal Gráfico*, June 16, 1971, 2, 9; "Mariles sería útil al equipo ecuestre," *El Universal Gráfico*, June 17, 1971, 2; "Mariles libre," *Impacto*, June 23, 1971.
247. "El desfile será un mensaje para la juventud y una sorpresa positiva," *El Universal Gráfico*, November 13, 1972, 7, 15; "Los medallistas olímpicos en el desfile del día 20," *Avance*, November 17, 1972, 3; "Mariles y Capilla en el desfile del día 20," *Avance*, November 18, 1972, 3.
248. "Mariles se dice inocente," *Avance*, año VI, no. 1926, November 28, 1972, 1, 7; "Mariles se declara inocente," *Excélsior*, November 29, 1972, 1, 10.
249. "Cateos en las casas del general y Max Rivera," *Excélsior*, November 29, 1972, 2, 10; "Mariles ante su juez," *La Prensa*, November 30, 1972, 25.
250. "Al salir de la penitenciaría de Santa Marta quedó bien vigilado," *La Prensa*, December 1, 1972; "París considera por lo menos misteriosa la muerte de Mariles," *El Universal Gráfico*, December 7, 1972, 3.
251. For follow-up on this incident, see Speckman Guerra, "Dos obstáculos."
252. This was established by the SCJ, such as in SJF, fifth period, judgments from February 25, 1955, AD 2024/54, tomo CXXIII, 1136; November 17, 1939, AD 6700/38, tomo LXII, 2504. On the concept, see Franco Guzmán, "El concurso de personas."
253. Piccato, *History of Infamy*, 131–36; Luna, *La nota roja 1930*, 21–42; de Mauleón, *El tiempo repentino*, 65–74; "El crimen de Gallegos," *Magazine de Policía*, 1939, año 1, no. 37, 11. On the photos, see Monroy Nasr, "En la escena."
254. Espejel Álvarez, "El crimen," 69–70.
255. "La señorita Jacinta Aznar asesinada misteriosamente en su hogar," *El Universal Gráfico*, February 23, 1932, 3; "Al margen del crimen" and "A macanazos fue asesinada la señorita Jacinta Aznar," *El Universal Gráfico*, February 24, 1932, 3, 14; "Unamuno amenazado," *Excélsior*, March 2, 1932, 5.
256. Espejel Álvarez, "El tinglado," 1–2.
257. Xavier Sorondo, "Unos por más y otros por menos," *Excélsior*, February 26, 1932, 5.

258. Usigli, *Ensayo de un crimen*, 26, 32, 35.

259. "A tubazos fue muerta la señorita Aznar," *La Prensa*, February 25, 1932, 2.

260. "Fue capturado el asesino de la señorita Aznar," *Excélsior*, February 27, 1932, ss, 5.

261. "El presunto asesino de la señorita Aznar detenido," *La Prensa*, February 26, 1932, 3; "Fue capturado el asesino de la señorita Aznar."

262. "Quién es el asesino de la señorita Aznar," *La Prensa*, February 27, 1932, 3, 4, 23; "Fue capturado el asesino de la señorita Aznar"; "Es falso que haya dado agua a Chinta" and "Dictamen médico," *El Universal Gráfico*, March 9, 1932, 9, 15; "Sigue el interés por la enigmática llave de la señorita Aznar," *Excélsior*, March 2, 1932, ss, 1.

263. Espejel Álvarez, "El crimen," 79.

264. "Alberto Gallegos le dijo a un amigo, en cierta ocasión, que le había puesto cerco a una 'vieja rica,'" *La Prensa*, March 1, 1932, 3, 18; "Gallegos habló a un amigo de una 'vieja rica,'" *Excélsior*, March 1, 1932, 1, 5; "En la casa de Urbina se planeó el crimen," *El Universal Gráfico*, March 2, 1932, 10, 14.

265. "Gallegos se enreda en sus declaraciones," *La Prensa*, March 4, 1932, 3, 8, 14, 15.

266. "Gallegos está ya en Belén," *El Universal Gráfico*, March 4, 1932, 9; "Gallegos se enreda en sus declaraciones"; "Gallegos formalmente preso por el homicidio de Jacinta Aznar," *La Prensa*, March 6, 1932, 1, 3.

267. For more information on Gallegos, see Gallegos prison file, AHDF, Fondo Cárceles, Penitenciaría, Expedientes de reos 1920–49, Caja 134, Partida 168bis; Gallegos Sánchez, *Mi crimen*, 6–35, his memoirs, signed by their author in the Federal District Penitentiary on April 15, 1932. Two *La Prensa* collaborators, writer Manuel Espejel Álvarez and illustrator Guillermo Nieto Hernández, oversaw the publication. See also "Fue capturado el asesino de la señorita Aznar" and "Se capturó al asesino de la señorita Aznar," *Excélsior*, February 27, 1932, ss, 5, 6; "Quién es el asesino de la señorita Aznar"; "La funesta escuela de Romero Carrasco," *El Universal Gráfico*, February 27, 1932, 1, 3, 19.

268. "Gallegos parece ya dispuesto a confesar," *El Universal Gráfico*, February 29, 1932, 3; "Quién es el asesino de la señorita Aznar"; "Alberto Gallegos le dijo a un amigo."

269. "La funesta escuela de Romero Carrasco."

270. "Un criminal mórbido," *Excélsior*, February 29, 1932, 5.

271. "Hoy puede decirse que Gallegos mató," *Excélsior*, March 11, 1932, ss, 1.

272. "Se desdice en historietas y se enreda más," *Excélsior*, March 18, 1932, ss, 1; "Digo yo como mujer," *Excélsior*, April 8, 1932, ss, 1.

273. Espejel Álvarez, "El crimen," 115–16; "Es interesante el examen psicofisiológico de Gallegos," *El Universal Gráfico*, April 9, 1932, 3.

274. Usigli, *Ensayo de un crimen*, 62.

275. Júbilo, Acotaciones del Momento, El Universal Gráfico, March 1, 1932, 6.

276. "El interés despertado por el crimen de Insurgentes," Excélsior, March 15, 1932, 6.

277. "La explotación del crimen" in Comentarios Rápidos, El Universal Grafico, March 17, 1932, 9.

278. "La criminalidad en auge," Excélsior, February 26, 1932, SS, 5; "El Señor Procurador y el aumento de la criminalidad," Excélsior, March 6, 1932, 10.

279. As Everard Meade notes, the campaign was fed with crimes that triggered indignation and was accompanied by legislative initiatives. "From Sex Strangler," 352–68.

280. In 1932 this included jurists like Telesforo Ocampo ("La benignidad de las leyes ha hecho que la criminalidad aumente," Excélsior, March 2, 1, 3; "Opiniones de dos penalistas," March 4, 5) and Manuel González Ramírez ("La pena de muerte," El Universal Gráfico, April 1, 6); journalists ("La criminalidad en auge," Excélsior, February 26, SS, 5; "La cómplice tolerancia," Excélsior, March 3, 9; "Página editorial," Excélsior, March 5, 5; "Ergatulismo," La Prensa, March 17, 1; "Los pobrecitos enfermos y la sociedad," La Prensa, March 19, 1); José Miguel Sarmiento ("La pena de muerte," La Prensa, March 24, 8; "La intimidación por medio de los castigos," La Prensa, March 28, 5); Rafael Sánchez Escobar ("Mas respeto a la justicia y menos consideración a los criminales," Excélsior, March 29, 6); Arturo Manzanos ("La pena de muerte y la reclusión," La Prensa, April 8, 8, 11); J. Gómez Portugal ("Sobre la pena de muerte" El Universal Gráfico, December 19, 9); and citizens ("La réplica de un lector," Excélsior, March 29, 5; "Una opinión femenina en pro de la pena de muerte," Excélsior, March 26, 8, 11; "Voces del público," El Universal Gráfico, December 19, 9).

281. "¿Debe restablecerse la pena de muerte?," Excélsior, March 16, 1932, 5, 6.

282. "La pena capital tiene partidarios entre los miembros del congreso," Excélsior, March 25, 1932, 1, 7. As seen in Excélsior in 1932, among the detractors were the attorney general ("El Señor Procurador y el aumento de la criminalidad," March 6, 1, 10); and attorneys José María Lozano ("Opiniones de dos penalistas"), Víctor Velázquez ("Una cuestión palpitante," March 22, 5), Federico Cervantes ("La ola del crimen y la pena de muerte," March 11, 8), and A. Núñez Alonso ("La pena de muerte," March 23, 6).

283. "¿Debe subsistir en México la pena de muerte?," El Universal Gráfico, April 2, 1932, 8.

284. "Un criminal mórbido."

285. "Una consecuencia natural," La Prensa, March 19, 1932, 9.

286. "La pena de muerte," El Universal Gráfico, April 1, 1932, 6.

287. "La ley fuga no escarmienta," Excélsior, April 1, 1932.

288. "De la pistola al tubo," El Universal Gráfico, April 6, 1932, 6.

289. Espejel Álvarez, "El crimen," 70–71.

290. "Gallegos no fue el único asesino," *La Prensa*, March 2, 1932, 14.

291. "Gallegos hoy en Insurgentes 17," *La Prensa*, March 10, 1932, 1, 3; "Gallegos ensayó la reconstrucción," *El Universal Gráfico*, March 11, 8, 15.

292. "Un testigo del salvaje criminal lo ha relatado," *Excélsior*, March 16, 1932, ss, 1, 6; "Una carta de recomendación fue la base que sirvió a la Policía Judicial para esclarecer completamente el espeluznante homicidio," *El Universal Gráfico*, March 16, 1932, 15.

293. "Un testigo del salvaje criminal lo ha relatado" and "Gallegos fue el asesino," *Excélsior*, March 16, 1932, ss, 1, 6.

294. "Sí asesinó Gallegos," *La Prensa*, March 16, 1932, 3; "Pedro Alberto Gallegos," *El Universal Gráfico*, March 16, 1932, 15.

295. "Sorpresas de rufianes," *Excélsior*, March 7, 1932, 5.

296. "Gallegos fue el asesino."

297. "Careo entre Sánchez y Gallegos," *El Universal Gráfico*, March 17, 1932.

298. "Sánchez llorando confesó todo," *La Prensa*, March 17, 1932, 18.

299. "Confesión tácita de Gallegos," *El Universal Gráfico*, March 17, 1932, cover; "Gallegos sonríe y calla," *La Prensa*, March 18, 1932, 3.

300. "Gallegos ha confesado," *La Prensa*, March 19, 1932, 2, 8; "Gallegos está escribiendo su larga confesión," *La Prensa*, March 20, 1932, 3; "Gallegos ha confesado," *Excélsior*, March 20, 1932, ss, 1.

301. "Se desdice en historietas y se enreda más," *Excélsior*, March 20, 1932, ss, 1.

302. "Gallegos sostiene ahora su inocencia absoluta," *Excélsior*, March 22, 1932, ss, 1.

303. "Gallegos es un cínico," *La Prensa*, March 22, 1932, 1, 3.

304. "Alberto Gallegos se retracta," *El Universal Gráfico*, March 22, 1932, 8, 15.

305. "Alberto Gallegos se retracta"; "La comedia ha terminado," *Excélsior*, March 23, 1932, ss, 6.

306. "Diligencias en el proceso de los embusteros," *Excélsior*, March 30, 1932, ss, 1.

307. "Eugenio Montiel sostiene que no vio matar a la señorita Aznar," *La Prensa*, May 13, 1932, 2.

308. "Ahora afirma Montiel que no conoció a Gallegos," *Excélsior*, April 24, 1932, ss, 1.

309. "Un estudio sobre Pedro A. Gallegos," *El Universal Gráfico*, April 10, 1932, 9.

310. See, for instance, the works by physicians Máximo Silva (*Higiene popular*) and Antonio Martínez Baca (*Estudios*).

311. "Otra intolerable burla de Gallegos," *El Universal Gráfico*, April 24, 1932, 8; "Otro golpe de audacia de Gallegos," *El Universal Gráfico*, May 14, 1932, 3.

312. "Denuncia de la Sra. María E. vda. de Almagro Smith contra Gallegos como presunto responsable de la muerte de su esposo," *El Universal Gráfico*, April 29, 1932, 8; "Gallegos autor de otro crimen en Córdoba," *Excélsior*, May 24, 1932, ss, 1.

313. "Las diligencias en el proceso se terminaron," *Excélsior*, June 14, 1932, SS, 1.

314. Gallegos Sánchez, *Mi crimen*.

315. "Alberto Gallegos se ha quedado sin defensores," *Excélsior*, July 2, 1932, SS, 1.

316. "Defensor de Gallegos," *La Prensa*, July 10, 1932, 1.

317. "Alberto Gallegos y socios," *La Prensa*, October 14, 1932, 2.

318. "Gallegos exhibido al desnudo," *Excélsior*, December 15, 1932, SS, 6.

319. "Gallegos exhibido al desnudo."

320. "Gallegos exhibido al desnudo."

321. "Juró que es inocente y no mató," *Excélsior*, December 16, 1932, SS, 1.

322. Cartoon by García Cabral, "La voz de la sangre," *Excélsior*, December 17, 1932, 5.

323. "Condena en su contra por veintidós años," *Excélsior*, January 13, 1933, 1; "Se dio la sentencia de Gallegos," *Excélsior*, January 13, 1933, 6.

324. "Causo indignación la pena contra Gallegos," *Excélsior*, January 15, 1933, SS, 8.

325. Gallegos *amparo* file, SCJAC, Amparo Directo, año 1933, Expediente 4648.

326. Luna, *La nota roja 1930*, 39.

327. Gallegos *amparo* file, SCJAC.

328. "Debe o no ser restaurada la pena de muerte," *El Universal Gráfico*, August 18, 1933, 6.

329. "La pena de muerte o la ley del Talión," *La Prensa*, August 24, 1933, 1.

330. See "Hoy se inaugura un interesante ciclo de conferencias," *La Prensa*, August 22, 1933, 18; "Interesantes conferencias sobre si debe o no reimplantarse la pena capital en la República," *La Prensa*, August 25, 1933, 7; "Continuaron ayer las conferencias sobre el tema de la pena de muerte," *La Prensa*, August 26, 1933, 18; "Conferencia acerca de la pena de muerte," *El Universal Gráfico*, August 22, 1933, 6; Federico Cervantes, "La verdadera justicia," *El Universal Gráfico*, August 24, 1933, 6.

331. "¡No matarás!" *El Universal Gráfico*, August 25, 1933, 6; Meade, "From Sex Strangler," 359–67.

332. "Pedro Alberto Gallegos y Raffles a las Islas Marías," *La Prensa*, August 23, 1933, 2; "Gallegos y el Raffles mexicano saldrán para el penal del pacífico," *El Universal Gráfico*, August 23, 1933, 3; "Gallegos aterrorizado," *El Universal Gráfico*, August 23, 1933, 1, 3.

333. "Gallegos fue muerto hoy," *El Universal Gráfico*, August 25, 1933, 1; "Cómo fue la muerte de Gallegos?," *El Universal Gráfico*, August 25, 1933, 2, 15; "Pedro o Alberto Gallegos muerto en la estación de Teoloyucan," *La Prensa*, August 26, 1933, 1, 12.

334. Usigli, *Ensayo de un crimen*, 212.

335. *La Prensa*, "Pedro o Alberto Gallegos muerto en la estación de Teoloyucan," August 26, 1933, 1, 12; "Gallegos fue sepultado en Cuautitlán," August 27, 1933, 1.

336. "Gallegos fue muerto hoy."

337. "Una consecuencia natural."

338. "Protestan por la muerte de Gallegos," *La Prensa*, August 28, 1933, 3, 7.

339. "La pena de muerte dentro de la ley," *La Prensa*, August 26, 1933, 1.

340. Carrancá y Trujillo, "Gallegos."

341. Usigli, *Ensayo de un crimen*, 214.

342. "Juró que es inocente y no mató," *Excélsior*, December 16, 1932, SS, 1; "Incontables personas piden un enérgico castigo para Gallegos," *El Universal Gráfico*, March 28, 1933, 3.

343. Usigli, *Ensayo de un crimen*, 124–25.

344. "Gallegos representó otra farsa," *Excélsior*, December 16, 1933, SS, 6.

345. Gallegos *amparo* file, SCJAC.

346. "Va a terminar hoy el periodo de las pruebas," *Excélsior*, July 12, 1932, SS, 1.

347. "Digo yo como mujer," *Excélsior*, SS, April 8, 1932, 1.

348. "Gallegos partidario de la pena de muerte pero no ejecutada en él mismo," *La Prensa*, March 20, 1932, 8.

349. Garmabella, *¡Reportero de policía!*, 49–56; Luna, *La nota roja, 1930*, 125–45.

350. "Horrible y cobarde asesinato" and "Don Francisco Silva es secuestrado y muerto," *Excélsior*, May 22, 1936, SS, 1, 6.

351. "Don Francisco Silva es secuestrado y muerto"; "Aparece complicada una mujer en la muerte del señor D. Francisco Silva," *Excélsior*, May 23, 1936, SS, 1, 6.

352. "Prisión de los asesinos de Silva," *Excélsior*, June 11, 1936, SS, 6.

353. "Los asesinos del señor F. J. Silva capturados," *El Universal*, June 19, 1936, 8.

354. "Esperanza García cuenta su agotada vida," *Excélsior*, June 13, 1936, SS, 6.

355. "Pavoroso relato de la muerte de Silva," *Excélsior*, June 16, 1936, SS, 1–6.

356. "Pavoroso relato de la muerte de Silva"; "G. Ortiz Ordaz incurre en muchas contradicciones," *Excélsior*, June 17, 1936, SS, 5.

357. "G. Ortiz Ordaz incurre en muchas contradicciones."

358. "Pavoroso relato de la muerte de Silva."

359. "Pídese amparo por Ortiz Ordaz y su amante María Elena Blanco," *Excélsior*, June 17, 1936, SS, 1–5.

360. "G. Ortiz Ordaz incurre en muchas contradicciones."

361. "Por fin confesó la mujer" and "También María Elena contempló el asesinato," *Excélsior*, June 19, 1936, SS, 1, 8.

362. Blanco prison file, AHDF, Fondo Cárceles, Penitenciaría, Expedientes de reos 1920–49, Caja 312, Partida 3322.

363. "Gonzalo Ortiz ha ratificado todo lo que declaró sobre el crimen," *Excélsior*, June 19, 1936, 1, 6.

364. "Se ha negado a ratificar todo lo que declaró" and "María Elena Blanco tiene ahora carácter de actriz," *Excélsior*, June 23, 1936, 1, 6.

365. Blanco prison file, AHDF.

366. "Una repugnante escena de histerismo de la vampiresa cómplice de Gonzalo Ordaz," *Excélsior*, June 24, 1936, SS, 1.

367. "Bazet desmiente a María Elena," *Excélsior*, June 28, 1936, SS, 1.

368. "Prisión de los asesinos de Silva."

369. Emilio Carrera, "María Elena implora un poco de amor," *Magazine de Policía*, September 18, 1939, 5–6.

370. "María Elena Blanco acusada de adulterio," *La Prensa*, November 1, 1937, 2.

371. "Fueron capturados los asesinos de Silva," *El Universal Gráfico*, June 1, 1936, 1, 3, 8.

372. "Esperanza García cuenta su agotada vida."

373. "Su tendencia es la de salvar a María Elena Blanco," *Excélsior*, June 17, 1936, 1.

374. "Los asesinos del señor F. J. Silva capturados"; "María Elena ingresó al escuadrón de la muerte en la Penitenciaría," *Excélsior*, June 20, 1936, SS, 1, 8.

375. "María Elena Blanco y sus colegas, blancas palomas," *Excélsior*, November 14, 1937, 1, 9.

376. "Careo entre Ordaz y María Elena," *Excélsior*, June 25, 1936, SS, 1–6.

377. "Las patrañas de María Elena las desmiente Bazet," *Excélsior*, June 27, 1936, 1, 8; "Oscar Bazet desmentirá a María Elena," *Excélsior*, June 28, 1936, 6.

378. "Oscar Bazet desmentirá a María Elena"; "Hoy será el careo Bazet-María Elena," *Excélsior*, June 30, 1936, SS, 1.

379. "Decretóse ayer la formal prisión de Bazet," *Excélsior*, July 3, 1936, SS, 1.

380. "No fue careada la siniestra María Elena," *Excélsior*, July 1, 1936, SS, 8.

381. "Ayer fueron careados María Elena, Oscar Bazet y Ordaz," *Excélsior*, July 2, 1936, 6.

382. "Decretóse ayer la formal prisión de Bazet."

383. "María Elena, gancho para asesinar al joyero," *La Prensa*, September 3, 1936, 12.

384. "María Elena Blanco acusa a Ordaz," *La Prensa*, September 4, 1936, 10.

385. Blanco, *amparo* file, SCJAC, Sentencias, Legajo 8, Expediente 505516, Amparo 307/1937.

386. "María Elena Blanco se retracta," *La Prensa*, August 17, 1937, 2.

387. "María Elena y Ordaz se siguen amando y viendo dentro de la casa negra de Lecumberri," *La Prensa*, February 2, 1937, 12.

388. "Gonzalo Ortiz Ordaz perdió su última esperanza," *La Prensa*, March 17, 1937, 12.

389. Blanco, *amparo* file, SCJAC.

390. "Concetta y María Elena Blanco serán sentenciadas a larga prisión por sus dos crímenes," *La Prensa*, May 18, 1937, 12.

391. "María Elena, gancho para asesinar al joyero."

392. "Fue revivida la tragedia en que murió el Sr. Silva" and "Los reos fueron llevados ayer a la calle Margil," *Excélsior*, November 18, 1936, SS, 1, 8.

393. "El proceso de María Elena y socios a punto de ir a Toluca," *La Prensa*, August 13, 1937, 14.
394. "Blancas palomas los que mataron al señor Silva."
395. "Pide clemencia a los jueces el defensor de Bazet," *La Prensa*, September 18, 1937, 8.
396. "María Elena Blanco y sus colegas, blancas palomas."
397. "No hay una sola prueba legal," *La Prensa*, November 13, 1937, 17.
398. "Los periodistas hicieron culpable a María Elena Blanco," *La Prensa*, November 14, 1937, 2, 15.
399. "Treinta años para María Elena Blanco," *Excélsior*, January 16, 1938, ss, 1.
400. Blanco prison file, AHDF.
401. "María Elena sonríe para no sollozar," *Excélsior*, February 1, 1938, 1.
402. Garmabella, *¡Reportero de policía!*, 55.
403. "Ortiz Ordaz muerto a puñaladas," *Excélsior*, September 3, 1938, ss, 1, 5; "Nadie vio ni escuchó nada," *Excélsior*, September 4, 1938, ss, 1; "Silencio del hampa en el crimen de Ortiz Ordaz," *Excélsior*, September 4, 1938, ss, 8; "Relata Andrés el Carpintero la tragedia penitenciara en la que pereció Ortiz Ordaz," *Excélsior*, September 6, 1938, 1, 2; "¡Quien a hierro mata a hierro muere!," *La Prensa*, September 3, 1938, 1, 2, 19.
404. "Matrimonio de María Elena," *Excélsior*, December 3, 1938, ss, 1, 4.
405. "María Elena Blanco es una histérica pasional," *La Prensa*, December 4, 1938, 2.
406. "La vampiresa no se casará," *La Prensa*, December 9, 1938, 12.
407. "María Elena es ya incapaz de llegar a la regeneración," *La Prensa*, August 6, 1936, 14.
408. "María Elena implora un poco de amor."
409. Blanco prison file, AHDF.
410. Blanco prison file, AHDF.
411. "María Elena Blanco desamparada por la Corte," *La Prensa*, April 2, 1940, 2.
412. "Salió para las Islas Marías una cuerda," *Excélsior*, April 21, 1940, ss, 1, 8. Bazet went in the same vessel.
413. "María Elena Blanco," *La Prensa*, August 12, 1940, 4.
414. "Cosas raras en el penal del Pacífico," *Excélsior*, November 9, 1942.

6. THE SUPPRESSION OF CRIMINAL COURTS

1. In García Ramírez, *La reforma*, 187–91.
2. Loaeza, "Gustavo Díaz Ordaz"; Loaeza, "Modernización"; Loaeza, "México 1968"; Rodríguez Kuri, "El presidencialismo"; Rodríguez Kuri and González Mello, "El fracaso."
3. Maza Pesqueira and Santillán Esqueda, "Movilización," 214–18, 228–32.
4. Rodríguez Kuri, "Población y sociedad," 196–97.
5. Zolov, *Refried Elvis*.

6. The boroughs were Gustavo A. Madero, Azcapotzalco, Ixtacalco, Coyoacán, Álvaro Obregón, Magdalena Contreras, Cuajimalpa, Tlalpan, Ixtapalapa, Xochimilco, Milpa Alta, Tláhuac, Miguel Hidalgo, Benito Juárez, Cuauhtémoc, and Venustiano Carranza.

7. Rodríguez Kuri, "Ciudad oficial," 422–24.

8. Loaeza, "México 1968"; Loaeza, "La política," 559–70.

9. The initiative's backers were Enrique Olivares Santana, Gilberto Suárez Torres, Vicente Juárez Carro, Guillermo Fonseca Álvarez, Víctor Manzanilla Schaffer, Enrique González Pedrero, Salvador Jiménez del Prado, Pascual Bellizia Castañeda, Ignacio Maciel Salcedo, and Norberto Mora Plancarte.

10. They also proposed dividing the Federal District into four judicial districts, expanding the power of tribunals in charge of minor crimes to lighten the caseload of other courts, contemplating consequences if the MP agent did not submit timely petitions to prevent backlogs, requiring the attendance of defense attorneys at hearings to ensure defendants' guarantees and reinforce the accusatory tone of the process, and holding summary proceedings in current cases. *Diario de Debates de la Cámara de Senadores* (hereafter *Diario de Debates Senadores*) año I, Periodo Extraordinario, Legislatura XLVIII, tomo I (9), February 9, 1971, session, 10; García Ramírez, *La reforma*, 187–91.

11. Committee members were José Rivera Pérez Campos, Luis M. Farías Martínez, Salvador Jiménez del Prado, Alejandro Carrillo Marcor, Celestino Pérez Pérez, Roberto Pizano Saucedo, and Nicanor Serrano del Castillo.

12. "Restructuración de la administración de justicia después de consultar al pueblo," El *Universal*, December 30, 1970, PS, 1, 7, 14.

13. "Opinarán sobre las reformas a los códigos el Tribunal Superior y la Suprema Corte," *Excélsior*, January 21, 1971, PS, 4A.

14. On the opinions, García Ramírez, *La reforma*, 231–49. See also 1971 articles in *Excélsior*, PS ("Quiroz Cuarón y Malo Camacho por juicios sumarios," January 13, 12A, 26A; "Una justicia retardada es una justicia denegada," January 14, 1A, 10A, "En la audiencia del Senado," January 19, 10A, 12A); *La Prensa* ("Audiencias en el senado por las reformas penales," January 9, 3, 33; Félix Fuentes Medina, "Rechazo en el Senado a los juicios sumarios," January 13, 3, 41; "Clamor contra la injusticia," January 14, 2, 45, "Inútil cambiar leyes si no hay jueces rectos," January 15, 2, 41; "Claman por el fin de juzgados mixtos," January 15, 3, 51; "Hacia mejores sistemas penales," February 10, 14, 32; "Aprobó ayer el Senado reformas al Código Penal," February 11, 3, 37; "Habrá justicia más ágil," February 11, 2, 39); El *Universal*, PS ("La justicia y el Senado," January 13, 1, 11, and January 14, 1, 6; "Cambios radicales a las iniciativas de reformas a los códigos civil y penal," February 10, 13; "Aprobó el Senado las Reformas Penales," February 11, 1, 7; "Las reformas al Código Penal fueron aprobadas," February 13, 8, 9).

15. January 12, 1971, hearing.

16. January 18, 1971, hearing.

17. January 18, 1971, hearing.

18. "Suma y resta," *Excélsior*, February 10, 1971, PS, 7A; "La justicia penal," *El Universal*, February 1, 1971, PS, 3; "Inútil cambiar leyes"; "El viejo tema de la justicia," *El Universal*, January 13, 1971, PS, 3.

19. "La autonomía presupuestal del Poder Judicial es indispensable," *El Universal*, June 21, 1971, PS, 18.

20. "El saneamiento de la justicia," *El Universal*, January 18, 1971, PS, 3; "Inútil cambiar leyes."

21. January 18, 1971, hearing.

22. January 15, 1971, hearing.

23. "Total revisión del aparato judicial," *Excélsior*, January 16, 1971, PS, 1A, 12A, 20A.

24. "Legalidad," *Excélsior*, January 20, 1971, PS, 7A.

25. January 13, 1971, hearing.

26. "Total revisión del aparato judicial."

27. "Entorpecen la justicia los salarios raquíticos," *La Prensa*, February 1, 1971, 2, 33.

28. "Nueva política," *El Nacional*, January 20, 1971, PS, 5.

29. January 13, 1971, hearing.

30. January 13, 1971, hearing.

31. "El saneamiento de la justicia."

32. "Quiroz Cuarón y Malo Camacho."

33. "Sobre el jurado popular," *El Universal*, April 28, 1965, PS, 2 and SS, B29.

34. "Descrédito total del jurado popular," *El Universal*, May 4, 1965, PS, 1, 19.

35. "Propicia el delito," *El Universal*, April 23, 1965, PS, 1, 6.

36. "Emotividad del jurado popular," *El Universal*, PS, May 3, 1965, 1, 6.

37. "México, problemas de un gran país," *Novedades*, October 31, 1970, PS, 4.

38. García Ramírez, *La reforma*, 35.

39. "La justicia penal," *El Universal*, February 1, 1971, PS, 3.

40. Rivera Vázquez, "El arbitrio."

41. García Ramírez, *La reforma*, 36.

42. January 12, 1971, hearing.

43. January 12, 1971, hearing.

44. García Ramírez, *La reforma*, 36; "Desaparecen las Cortes Penales," *El Nacional*, June 16, 1971, PS, 8.

45. "Cambios judiciales positivos," *Novedades*, June 18, 1971, 4.

46. January 12, 13, and 18, 1971, hearings.

47. "Desaparecen las Cortes Penales."

48. García Ramírez, *La reforma*, 35.

49. García Ramírez, *La reforma*, 36, 42.

50. "Cambios judiciales positivos."

51. First report of the Senate Committees on the initiative to reform the Criminal Court Code. García Ramírez, *La reforma*, 192–210. See also *Diario de Debates Senadores*, año I, Periodo Extraordinario, Legislatura XLVIII, February 9, 1971, session, tomo I, no. 9, 9–22.

52. *Diario de Senadores*, año I, Periodo Extraordinario, Legislatura XLVIII, February 10, 1971, session, tomo I (10), 18–21. Also in 1971: *Excélsior* ("Modifican los senadores hasta los vocablos en el Código Penal," February 10, PS, 1A, 10A, 11A; "Afinación de la justicia," February 12, PS, 6A); *El Universal* ("Cambios radicales a las iniciativas de reformas a los códigos civil y penal," February 10, PS, 13; "Aprobó el Senado las Reformas Penales," February 11, PS, 1, 7; "Las reformas al Código Penal fueron aprobadas," February 13, PS, 8, 9); *La Prensa* ("Hacia mejores sistemas penales," February 10, 14, 32).

53. *Diario de Senadores*, año I, Periodo Extraordinario, Legislatura XLVIII, tomo I (10 and 12), February 10 and 16, 1971, sessions, 2–10, 2–5, respectively.

54. *Diario de Debates*, año I, Período Extraordinario, Legislatura XLVIII, diario 19, February 17, 1971, session; "Aprueban los diputados el proyecto de decreto que reforma el Código Penal," *El Nacional*, February 13, 1971, PS, 7.

55. *Diario de Debates*, año I, Período Extraordinario, Legislatura XLVIII, diarios 20 and 22, February 18 and 23, 1971, sessions.

56. Decreto que Reforma Diversos Artículos del Código de Procedimientos Penales para el Distrito y Territorios Federales, *Diario Oficial*, March 19, 1971.

57. "Desaparecen las Cortes Penales."

58. "Más humana impartición de Justicia," *El Universal*, May 21, 1971, PS, 5.

59. "Legalidad."

60. January 13, 1971, session.

61. García Ramírez, *La reforma*, 6, 7.

7. CONCLUSION

1. Produced in 1946 and directed by Roberto Gavaldón, the film was inspired by a Rian James story, adapted by Gavaldón and José Revueltas.

BIBLIOGRAPHY

ARCHIVES

AGN: Archivo General de la Nación (mainly Fondo Tribunal Superior de Justicia [FTSJ]).

AHDF: Archivo Histórico del Distrito Federal (Fondo Cárceles, Fondo Departamento de Policía, and Fondo Departamento de Investigaciones de la Procuraduría General de Justicia del Distrito Federal).

AHTSJDF: Archivo Histórico del Tribunal Superior de Justicia del Distrito Federal.

FAQC: Fondo Alfonso Quiroz Cuarón in the Biblioteca Isidro Fabela.

IISUE: Instituto de Investigaciones sobre la Universidad y la Educación (Expedientes de estudiantes y de profesores).

SCJAC: Archivo Central de la Suprema Corte de Justicia de la Nación.

LEGISLATION

Constitutions

    Constitución Política de la República Mexicana, February 5, 1857.

    Constitución Política de los Estados Unidos Mexicanos, February 5, 1917.

Federal District Criminal Codes

    Código Penal para el Distrito Federal y Territorio de la Baja California sobre Delitos del Fuero Común y para toda la República sobre Delitos contra la Federación, December 7, 1871.

    Código Penal para el Distrito y Territorios Federales, September 2, 1929.

    Código Penal para el Distrito Federal en Materia de Fuero Común y para toda la República en Materia de Fuero Federal, August 13, 1931.

Federal District Criminal Procedure Codes

    Código de Procedimientos Penales para el Distrito y Territorios Federales, July 6, 1894.

    Código de Organización, de Competencia y de Procedimientos en Materia Penal para el Distrito Federal y Territorios, October 4, 1929.

    Código de Procedimientos Penales para el Distrito y Territorios Federales, August 26, 1931.

Court Organization Laws and Federal District Jury Trial Laws

Ley de Jurados en Materia Criminal para el Distrito Federal, June 15, 1869, and June 24, 1891.

Ley que Reforma la de Organización Judicial, December 28, 1907.

Ley Orgánica de los Tribunales del Fuero Común, September 9, 1919; December 29, 1922; December 31, 1928; December 30, 1932; and December 24, 1968.

PUBLISHED WORKS

Abarca, Ricardo. *El derecho penal en México*. Mexico City: Jus, 1941.

Agüero, Alejandro. "Las categorías básicas de la cultura jurisdiccional." In *De justicia de jueces a justicia de leyes: Hacia la España de 1870*, edited by Marta Lorente, 19–58. Madrid: Consejo General del Poder Judicial—Escuela Judicial, 2007.

Aguilar, Leopoldo. "La justicia del orden común en el Distrito Federal." *El Foro*, nos. 24–25 época 4 (January–June 1959): 10–15.

Aguirre, Eugenio. *El abogánster*. Mexico City: Editorial Planeta, 2014.

Alcalá-Zamora y Castillo, Niceto. "Algunas observaciones al proyecto de código procesal penal para el Distrito Federal." *Boletín del Instituto Mexicano de Derecho Comparado* 10 (January–April 1951): 9–30.

———. *Síntesis del Derecho Procesal*. Mexico City: Universidad Nacional Autónoma de México, 1966.

"Algunas opiniones sobre el nuevo Código Penal por varios autores." *Revista Mexicana de Derecho Penal* 1, no. 1, año 1 (July 1930): 122–27.

Almaraz, José. *Algunos errores y absurdos de la legislación penal de 1931*. Mexico City, 1941.

———. *Exposición de motivos del Código Penal promulgado en diciembre de 1929*. Mexico City, 1931.

———. "La especialización en lo penal." *Criminalia* 6, año 1 (February 1934): 41–43.

———. "New Mexican Penal Principles: As Revealed in the New Legislation." *Pacific Affairs* 3, no. 6 (June 1930): 531–40.

"Anteproyecto de Código Penal." *Revista de Ciencias Sociales* 1, no. 3, época 2 (1930): 123–49.

Arévalo Macías, Armando. "Más que una revisión de la ley penal, una reforma a la política de la delincuencia. Habla el doctor José Ángel Ceniceros en la encuesta abierta por 'Novedades'." *Criminalia* 11, año 20 (November 1954): 582–84.

Argüelles, Francisco. "Las modificaciones a la legislación penal de 1931." *Criminalia*, no. 9, año 22 (September 1956): 629–36.

———. "Las reformas al Código Penal vigente." *Criminalia*, no. 2, año 17 (February 1951): 75–82.

Arilla Bas, Fernando. "Breve ensayo crítico sobre el anteproyecto de reformas al Código Penal." *Criminalia*, no. 10, año 15 (October 1950): 394–401.

———. "Necesidad del procedimiento oral en materia penal." *Revista de la Escuela Libre de Derecho*, no. 2, año 1 (November 1962): 50–52.

Ávila Camacho, Manuel. *Igualdad democrática de los pueblos (México ante el conflicto mundial)*. Mexico City: Secretaría de Gobernación, 1941.

Baker, Ricard D. *Judicial Review in Mexico: A Study of the Amparo Suit.* Austin: University of Texas Press, 1971.

Barra Mexicana Colegio de Abogados (BMA). *El problema de la administración de justicia.* Mexico City: Jus, 1940.

———. *Por una Secretaría de Justicia.* Mexico City: BMA, 1961.

Ben David, Lior. "Remaking Indians, Remaking Citizens: Peruvian and Mexican Perspectives on Criminal Law and National Integration." PhD diss., Tel Aviv University.

Bobbio, Norberto. *El futuro de la democracia.* Mexico City: FCE, 1996.

Bravo Lira, Bernardino. "Arbitrio judicial y legalismo." *Revista de Historia del Derecho Ricardo Levenne,* no. 28 (1991): 7–22.

Bremauntz, Alberto. *Por una justicia al servicio del pueblo.* Mexico City: Casa de Michoacán, 1955.

Brocca, Victoria. *La nota roja, 1960–1969.* Mexico City: Diana, 1996.

Buffington, Robert. *Criminales y ciudadanos en el México Moderno.* Mexico City: Siglo Veintiuno, 2001.

Buffington, Robert, and Pablo Piccato. Introduction to *True Stories of Crime in Modern Mexico,* edited by Robert Buffington and Pablo Piccato, 1–24. Albuquerque: University of New Mexico Press, 2009.

Buffington, Robert, and Pablo Piccato. "Tales of Two Women: The Narrative Construction of Porfirian Reality." In *True Stories of Crime in Modern Mexico,* edited by Robert Buffington and Pablo Piccato, 25–56. Albuquerque: University of New Mexico Press, 2009.

Burkholder, Arno. "Construyendo una nueva relación con el Estado: El crecimiento y consolidación del diario *Excélsior* (1932–1968)." *Secuencia* (January–April 1979): 35–104.

———. "El periódico que llegó a la vida nacional. Los primeros años del diario *Excélsior* (1916–1932)." *Historia mexicana* 58, no. 4 (April–June 2009): 1369–418.

Caballero, José Antonio. "Derecho romano y codificación. Las sentencias de los jueces menores en una época de transición, 1868–1872." In *Historia del Derecho. Memoria del Congreso Internacional de Culturas y Sistemas Jurídicos Comparados,* edited by José Antonio Caballero and Oscar Cruz Barney, 269–302. Mexico City: IIJ UNAM, 2005.

Calamandrei, Piero. *Proceso y democracia. Conferencias pronunciadas en la Facultad de Derecho de la Universidad Nacional Autónoma de México.* Breviarios de derecho 33. Buenos Aires: Ediciones Jurídicas Europa-América, 1960.

Caporal Pérez, Verónica, Fabiola Bailón Vásquez, and Oscar Montiel Torres. *Diagnóstico del ciclo vital de las mujeres en situación de prostitución y su relación con el proxenetismo.* Mexico City: Oak Foundation–Centro de Estudios Sociales y Culturales Antonio de Montesinos, 2013.

Cárdenas, Raúl. "El Ministerio Público." *El Foro,* nos. 24–25, época 4 (January–June 1959): 7–10.

Cardozo, Benjamin Nathan. *La función judicial*. 1921. Reprint, Mexico City, Oxford University Press, 2000.

Carnevale, Emmanuele. "Una tercera escuela de derecho penal en Italia." *El Derecho* 3, nos. 25 and 31, época 3 (1892): 385–89, 487–90.

Carrancá y Trujillo, Raúl. "Allá van leyes." *Criminalia*, no. 1, año 2 (September 1934): 27–28.

———. *Derecho penal mexicano*. Mexico City: Limón, 1937.

———. "Gallegos." *Criminalia*, nos. 1–12, año 1 (1933–34): 12.

———. "Historia del derecho penal en México." *Criminalia*, no. 7, año 3 (March 1937): 218–23.

———. "La injusta igualdad." *Criminalia*, no. 7, año 2 (March 1935): 92.

———. "La legislación penal mexicana." In *Homenaje a Eugenio Florián*, 283–329. Mexico City, 1940.

———. "La legislación penal vigente en la República Mexicana." *Revista de la Escuela Nacional de Jurisprudencia* 2, no. 5 (January–March 1940): 39–53.

———. *Métodos y procedimientos técnicos empleados en la elaboración de la sentencia penal*. Mexico City: Botas, 1961.

———. "Sobre el valor de la prueba penal y la función de la policía judicial científica." *Criminalia*, no. 8, año 9 (April 1943): 461–64.

———. "Sobre las presunciones de legítima defensa en el código de 1931." *Criminalia*, año 6 (1939): 410–12.

———. *Teoría del juez penal mexicano*. Mexico City: Departamento del D.F., 1944.

———. *Un año de labores. Informe que en su calidad de presidente del Tribunal Superior de Justicia del Distrito Federal rindió al Tribunal Pleno*, Mexico City: TSJDF, 1945.

Ceniceros, José Ángel. "Corruptores y sobornados." *Criminalia*, no. 2, año 10 (October 1943): 71–76.

———. "De la prensa diaria: El problema de la administración de justicia." *Criminalia*, no. 6, año 9 (February 1943): 374–77.

———. *El Código Penal de 1929 y datos preliminares del nuevo Código Penal de 1931*. Mexico City: Botas, 1931.

———. "El Código Penal mexicano." In *Homenaje a Eugenio Florián*, 253–79. Mexico City, 1940.

———. "El Congreso de Palermo y la especialización judicial." *Criminalia*, no. 6, año 1 (February 1934): 43–44.

———. "El nuevo Código Penal." *El Foro* 10, no. 4 (October–December 1929): 12–15.

———. *El nuevo Código Penal de 13 de agosto de 1931 en relación con los de 7 de diciembre de 1871 y 15 de diciembre de 1929*. Mexico City: Talleres Gráficos de la Nación, 1931.

———. "La escuela positiva y su influencia en la legislación penal mexicana." *Criminalia*, no. 4, año 7 (December 1940): 200–213.

———. "La revisión de las leyes penales mexicanas." *Criminalia*, no. 8, año 16 (August 1950): 310–13.

———. "Policía de olfato y policía técnica." *Criminalia*, no. 6, año 10 (February 1944): 329–33.

———. "Realidades policiacas." *Criminalia*, no. 7, año 10 (March 1944): 396–98.

———. *Un discurso sobre el Código Penal de 1931*. Serie de Estudios Jurídicos. Mexico City: La Justicia, 1977.

Ceniceros, José Ángel, Raúl Carrancá y Trujillo, Carlos Franco Sodi, and Javier Piña y Palacios. "Las razas indígenas y la defensa social." *Criminalia*, no. 10, año 6 (1940): 517–21.

Ceniceros, José Ángel, and Luis Garrido. *La ley penal mexicana*. Mexico City: Botas, 1926.

Colín Sánchez, Guillermo. *Función social del Ministerio Público en México*. Mexico City: Jus, 1952.

Concha, Hugo. "Hacia una justicia democrática." *Reforma Judicial. Revista Mexicana de Justicia*, no. 8 (July–December 2006): 3–11.

Corona Azanza, Rocío. "'He dominado la pasión que me hizo delinquir.' Mujeres criminales en las peticiones de indulto (Guanajuato, 1920–1930)." In *Vicio, prostitución y delito. Mujeres transgresoras en los siglos XIX y XX*, edited by Elisa Speckman Guerra and Fabiola Bailón Vázquez, 309–44. Mexico City: IIH UNAM, 2016.

Cossío Díaz, José Ramón. "El juicio de amparo en el Porfiriato." In *Porfirio Díaz y el derecho. Balance crítico*, edited by Raúl Ávila Ortiz, 335–61. Mexico City: Cámara de Diputados–IIJ UNAM, 2015.

Couto, Ricardo. "Sobre la imperiosa necesidad de restaurar la Secretaría de Justicia." *El Foro*, no. 42, época 4 (July–September 1963): 19–24.

Cuellar Vázquez, Angélica. "Los jueces y el mundo de la vida." *Reforma Judicial. Revista Mexicana de Justicia*, no. 13 (January–June 2009): 25–37.

Davis, Diane. *El Leviatán urbano. La ciudad de México en el siglo XX*. Mexico City: FCE, 1999.

de la Cueva, Mario. "Razón e historia en la elaboración del derecho." *Revista de Ciencias Sociales* 1, no. 2 (1930): 37–51.

del Arenal, Jaime. *El Derecho en Occidente*. Historias Mínimas collection. Mexico City: El Colegio de México, 2016.

del Castillo, Alberto. "El surgimiento de la prensa moderna en México." In *La República de las Letras*. Vol. 2, *Publicaciones periódicas y otros impresos*, edited by Belem Clark de Lara and Elisa Speckman Guerra, 105–18. Mexico City: UNAM, 2005.

———. "El surgimiento del reportaje policiaco en México. Los inicios de un nuevo lenguaje gráfico (1888–1910)." *Cuicuilco* 5, no. 13 (May–August 1998): 163–94.

de los Reyes, Aurelio. *Sucedió en Jalisco o los cristeros.* Vol. 3, *Cine y sociedad en México.* Mexico City: IIE UNAM–INAH, 2013.

de Mauleón, Héctor. *El tiempo repentino. Crónicas de la Ciudad de México en el siglo XX.* Mexico City: Cal y Arena / Random House Mondadori, 2008.

de Pina, Rafael. *Código de Procedimientos Penales para el Distrito y Territorios Federales.* Mexico City: Ediciones Cicerón, 1952.

———. "El jurado popular." *Anales de Jurisprudencia,* 59 (1948): 441–85.

Diamond, Larry. Introduction to *Consolidating the Third Wave Democracies, Themes and Perspectives,* edited by Larry Diamond, Marc F. Plattner, Yun-han Chu, and Hung-Mao Tien, xiii–xlvii. Baltimore: Johns Hopkins University Press, 1997.

———. *The Spirit of Democracy.* New York: Henry Holt, 2008.

"Documentos para la historia del Poder Judicial de México." *La Justicia,* 13, no. 197 (January 1944): 6568.

Domínguez Carrascosa, Luis. "Reestructuración del Poder Judicial." *La Justicia* 22, no. 382 (February 1962): 7–13.

Domínguez del Río, Alfredo. *La administración de justicia en México, 1962–1972.* Mexico City: Impulso Procesal, 1973.

El caso del general Humberto Mariles Cortés. Su amparo ante la Suprema Corte de Justicia de la Nación. Mexico City, 1968.

"El jurado popular." *Criminalia,* año 8 (April 1939): 449.

"El nuevo Código de Procedimientos Penales." *La Justicia* 19, no. 260 (April 1949): 10173.

Elorduy, Edmundo. "Los delitos y las faltas de los funcionarios y empleados judiciales." *Anales de Jurisprudencia* 78 (1953): 73–92.

"El Presidente de la República desea que sea una realidad la independencia del Poder Judicial." *Criminalia,* no. 11, año 7 (July 1941): 642–44.

"El rezago judicial." *La Justicia* 9, no. 268 (December 1949): 10445.

Ernst, Carlos. "Independencia judicial y democracia." In *La función judicial. Ética y democracia,* compiled by Jorge Malem, Jesús Orozco, and Rodolfo Vázquez Barcelona, 235–44. Barcelona: Editorial Gedisa / Tribunal Electoral del Poder Judicial de la Federación / ITAM, 2003.

Espejel Álvarez, Manuel. "El crimen de la avenida Insurgentes." In *Mi crimen. Relato que del crimen de la calle de Insurgentes hace Alberto Gallegos,* edited by Manuel Espejel Álvarez and Guillermo Nieto Hernández, 59–120. Mexico City, 1932.

———. "El tinglado de la farsa." In *Mi crimen. Relato que del crimen de la calle de Insurgentes hace Alberto Gallegos,* edited by Manuel Espejel Álvarez and Guillermo Nieto Hernández, 1–4. Mexico City, 1932.

Esquivel Medina, Humberto. "El polvo de una gacetilla." *Criminalia,* no. 6, año 1 (February 1934): 47–48.

Ezquiaga Ganuzas, Francisco Javier. "Función legislativa y función judicial: La sujeción del juez a la ley." In *La función judicial. Ética y democracia,* compiled by

Jorge Malem, Jesús Orozco, and Rodolfo Vázquez, 39–56. Barcelona: Editorial Gedisa / Tribunal Electoral del Poder Judicial de la Federación / ITAM, 2003.

"Felicitan a Gustavo Díaz Ordaz por la nueva Ley Orgánica del Poder Judicial." La Justicia 29, no. 464 (February 1969): 61.

Fernández del Castillo, Germán. "El proyecto de Ley Orgánica de los Tribunales de Justicia del Fuero Común del Distrito y Territorios Federales e Islas Marías." La Justicia 18, no. 245 (January 1948): 9509–12.

———. "Nuestra realidad jurídica." Jus 3, no. 13 (August 1939): 129–35.

Fernández Reyes, Álvaro A. Crimen y suspenso en el cine mexicano, 1946–1955. Zamora: El Colegio de Michoacán, 2007.

Ferrajoli, Luigi. Democracia y garantismo. Madrid: Trotta, 2008.

Fioravanti, Maurizio. "Estado y constitución." In El Estado moderno en Europa, 13–44. Madrid: Trotta, 2004.

Fix-Zamudio, Héctor. "La administración de justicia." In Temas y problemas de la administración de justicia en México, 143–77. Mexico City: Miguel Ángel Porrúa, 1985.

Fix-Zamudio, Héctor, and José Ramón Cossío Díaz. El poder judicial en el ordenamiento mexicano. Mexico City: FCE, 1996.

Flores Flores, Graciela. "Orden judicial y justicia criminal (Ciudad de México 1824–1871)." PhD diss., UNAM, 2013.

Flores García, Fernando. "Algunos problemas de la administración de justicia." El Foro, no. 33, época 4 (April–June 1961): 10–15.

———. "Crónica del Primer Congreso Mexicano de Derecho Procesal y de las Segundas Jornadas Latinoamericanas de Derecho Procesal." Revista de la Facultad de Derecho de México 10, nos. 37–40 (January–December 1960): 15–25.

Franco Guzmán, Ricardo. "El concurso de personas en el delito." Revista de la Facultad de Derecho de México 12, no. 47 (July–September 1962): 401–16.

Franco Sodi, Carlos. "El anteproyecto del Código de Procedimientos Penales." Criminalia, no. 6, año 15 (June 1949): 222–39.

———. "Escepticismo frente a la ley y frente a los encargados de aplicarla." Criminalia, no. 1, año 17 (January 1951): 2–4.

Francoz R., Antonio. "El antiguo y el nuevo juez penal." Criminalia, no. 10, año 2 (June 1935): 134–37.

Gallegos Sánchez, Alberto. Mi crimen. Relato que del crimen de la calle de Insurgentes hace Alberto Gallegos, edited by Manuel Espejel Álvarez and Guillermo Nieto Hernández. Mexico City, 1932.

García, Trinidad. "Los abogados y la administración de justicia." In Barra Mexicana de Abogados. Conmemoración del XXV aniversario de su fundación, 77–97. Mexico City: Barra Mexicana Colegio de Abogados, 1948.

García Cordero, Fernando. La administración de justicia penal. De la Revolución Mexicana a la reforma jurídica de 1983–1984. Mexico City: Procuraduría General de la República, 1985.

García Ramírez, Sergio. "Comentario a las resoluciones de materia penal adoptadas por el Segundo Congreso Mexicano de Derecho Procesal." *Criminalia*, no. 3, año 33 (January 1967): 137–48.

———. *El sistema penal mexicano*. Mexico City: FCE, 1993.

———. *Justicia Penal*. Mexico City: Porrúa, 1982.

———. "La Academia Mexicana de Ciencias Penales y Criminalia. Medio siglo en el desarrollo del derecho penal mexicano (Una aproximación)." In *Los abogados y la formación del Estado en México*, edited by Oscar Cruz Barney, Héctor Fix Fierro, and Elisa Speckman Guerra, 759–802. Mexico City: IIJ UNAM / IIH UNAM / Ilustre y Nacional Colegio de Abogados, 2013.

———. "La división en fases del procedimiento penal mexicano." *Revista de la Escuela Nacional de Jurisprudencia* 20, nos. 79–80 (July–December 1970): 1211–36.

———. "La reforma jurídica y la administración de justicia." In *Discursos de política y justicia*. Mexico City: Instituto Mexicano de Cultura, 1988.

———. *La reforma penal de 1971*. Mexico City: Botas, 1971.

———. *Los derechos humanos y el Derecho Pena*. Sep/Setentas 254. Mexico City: SEP, 1976.

———. *Los reformadores. Beccaria, Howard y el Derecho Penal Ilustrado*. Mexico City: INACIPE / Tirant lo Blanch / IIJ UNAM, 2014.

———. "Los sistemas de enjuiciamiento penal y sus órganos de acusación." In *XII Congreso Mundial de Derecho Procesal*. Vol. 4, *Los sistemas de enjuiciamiento penal y sus órganos de acusación*, edited by Marcel Storme and Cipriano Gómez Lara, 1–182. Mexico City: IIJ UNAM, 2005.

———. *Panorama del proceso penal*. Mexico City: Porrúa, 2004.

———. "Quehacer y sentido de la Procuraduría del Distrito Federal." In *Temas jurídicos*, 21–31. Mexico City: Porrúa, 1976.

García Robles, Jorge. *La bala perdida. William S. Burroughs en México*. Mexico City: Milenio, 1995.

Garmabella, José Ramón. *¡Reportero de policía! El Güero Téllez*. Mexico City: De Bolsillo, 1982.

Garrido, Luis. "A propósito de un aniversario." *Criminalia*, no. 10, año 22 (October 1956): 710–12.

———. "El nuevo juez penal." *Criminalia*, no. 6, año 1 (February 1934): 43.

———. *Ensayos penales*. Mexico City: Botas, 1952.

———. "La doctrina mexicana de nuestro derecho penal." *Criminalia*, no. 4, año 7 (December 1940): 240–47.

———. "La justicia desvalida." *Criminalia*, no. 1, año 23 (January 1957): 61–63.

Garriga, Carlos. "Justicia animada: Dispositivos de la justicia en la monarquía católica." In *De justicia de jueces a justicia de leyes: Hacia la España de 1870*, edited by Marta Lorente, 59–106. Madrid: Consejo General del Poder Judicial / Escuela Judicial, 2007.

———. "Orden jurídico y poder político en el Antiguo Régimen." *Istor*, no. 16, año 4 (2004): 13–44.

Gaxiola, Francisco Xavier. "Sobre la creación de una Secretaría de Justicia." *El Foro*, no. 32, época 4 (January–March 1961): 19–22.

"Gestión de la Barra Mexicana sobre la nota roja (carta dirigida a las publicaciones periódicas)." *El Foro*, no. 32, época 4 (January–March 1961): 4–5.

Gómez Estrada, José Alfredo. "Elite de Estado y prácticas políticas. Una aproximación al estudio de la corrupción en México, 1920–1934." Estudios de Historia Moderna y Contemporánea de México, no. 52 (2016): 52–68.

Gonzaga y Armendáriz, Luis. "Balazos después de muchas copas. Cómo fue el asesinato de Guty Cárdenas, un ídolo." *Revista de la Universidad Autónoma de Yucatán*, nos. 239–40 (Fourth Quarter 2006–First Quarter 2007): 62–69.

González, María del Refugio, and Teresa Lozano. "La administración de justicia." In *El gobierno provincial en la Nueva España*, edited by Woodrow Borah, 75–106. Mexico City: UNAM, 1985.

González Bustamante, Juan José. "Función investigadora del Ministerio Público." *Revista de la Escuela Libre de Derecho*, no. 5, año 2 (1963): 38–45.

———. *Principios de derecho procesal penal mexicano*. Mexico City: Jus, 1941.

González de la Vega, Francisco. *Derecho penal mexicano*. Mexico City: Tipografía Previsión, 1935–37.

———. "Fue necesario derogar la legislación penal de 1929." *Criminalia*, no. 12, año 1 (August 1934): 92.

———. "J. M. Ortiz Tirado." *Criminalia*, no. 6, año 1 (February 1934): 41.

———. "La especialización en México." *Criminalia*, no. 6, año 1 (February 1934): 44–45.

———. "La evolución del derecho penal en México." *La Justicia* 9, año 9 (May 1949): 10222–29.

———. *La reforma de las leyes penales en México*. Mexico City: Relaciones Exteriores, 1935.

———. "Las Cortes Penales." *Anales de Jurisprudencia*, 12, año 6 (1936): 849–55.

González Franco, Gabriel. "El Procurador de Justicia y la recristianización." *La Justicia* 21, no. 285 (May 1951): 11067–68.

González Rodríguez, Sergio. "La avenida y el pasaje en la Ciudad de México en los años cuarenta." In *Miradas recurrentes, la ciudad de México en los siglos XIX y XX*, edited by María del Carmen Collado, 2:166–86. Mexico City: Instituto Mora / UAM, 2004.

Grossi, Paolo. *Mitología jurídica de la modernidad*. Madrid: Trotta, 2003.

Guastini, Ricardo. *Estudios sobre la interpretación jurídica*. Mexico City: Porrúa / IIJ UNAM, 2004.

Gudiño Pelayo, José de Jesús. "El papel de los jueces en la construcción de la democracia." *Reforma Judicial. Revista Mexicana de Justicia*, no. 9 (January–June 2007): 79–91.

Hart, Herbert. *Post scríptum al concepto de derecho*. Mexico City: IIJ UNAM, 2000.

Helú, Antonio. *La obligación de asesinar*. 1946. Reprint, Lecturas Mexicanas, Tercera Serie, 38. Mexico City: CONACULTA, 1991.

Hernández Islas, Josafat. "Necesidad de que los delincuentes indígenas sean juzgados por un tribunal especial." *Criminalia*, no. 12, año 5 (August 1939): 746–48.

Infante Vargas, Lucrecia. "Por nuestro género hablará el espíritu: Las mujeres en la UNAM." In *Mujeres mexicanas del siglo XX*, edited by Francisco Blanco Figueroa, 3:77–96. Mexico City: Edicol / UAM / IPN / UNAM / UAEM / UANL / UACM, 2001.

"Iniciativa del barrista Eugenio Ramos Bilderbeck, delegado ejecutivo del consejo en materia de justicia. De la innegable necesidad de la existencia de una Secretaría de Justicia." *El Foro*, no. 32, época 4 (January–March 1961): 6–8.

Jiménez, Armando. *Sitios de rompe y rasga en la Ciudad de México*. Mexico City: Océano, 1998.

Jones, Lancaster. *Estudio sobre el artículo 14 de la Constitución Federal*. Mexico City: Imprenta de José Vicente Villada, 1878.

José Agustín. *Tragicomedia mexicana*. Vol. 1, *La vida en México de 1940 a 1970*. Mexico City: Planeta, 1991.

Kalifa, Dominique. *Crimen y cultura de masas en Francia, siglos XIX–XX*. Mexico City: Instituto Mora, 2008.

Kandell, Jonathan. "Mexico's Megalopolis." In *I Saw a City Invincible: Urban Portraits of Latin America*, edited by Gilbert Joseph and Mark Szuchman, 181–201. Wilmington DE: Scholarly Resources, 1996.

"La administración de justicia. Encuesta de la Barra Mexicana de Abogados." *Jus* 5, no. 21 (April 1940): 313–27.

La administración de justicia. Opiniones de los señores Antonio Pérez Verdía, Manuel Escobedo, Gustavo R. Velasco . . . Supplement, *El Foro*. Mexico City: Barra Mexicana de Abogados, 1957.

"La administración de justicia en México." *La Justicia* 17, no. 242 (October 1947): 9300.

"La carrera judicial." *La Justicia* 19, no. 265 (September 1949): 10349.

"La función judicial." *La Justicia* 19, no. 263 (July 1949): 10285.

"La inamovilidad en el Poder Judicial." *La Justicia* 12, no. 180 (August 1942): 5752–53.

"La inamovilidad judicial." *La Justicia* 12, no. 182 (October 1942): 5835–37, and no. 254 (October 1948): 9981.

"Las reformas judiciales." *La Justicia* 21, no. 282 (February 1951): 10897.

"La Suprema Corte dice." *Criminalia*, no. 8 (April 1938): 461–66.

Leyes penales mexicanas. 3 vols. Mexico City: INACIPE, 1979.

Loaeza, Soledad. "Gustavo Díaz Ordaz. Las insuficiencias de la presidencia autoritaria." In *Presidentes Mexicanos*. Vol. 2, 1911–2000, edited by Will Fowler, 285–346. Mexico City: INHERM, 2004.

———. "La política del rumor: México, noviembre–diciembre de 1976." *Foro Internacional* 17, no. 4 (April–June 1977): 557–86.

———. "México 1968: Los orígenes de la transición." *Foro Internacional* 30, no. 1 (September 1989): 66–92.

———. "Modernización autoritaria a la sombra de la superpotencia, 1944–1968." In *Nueva Historia General de México*, 653–98. Mexico City: El Colegio de México, 2010.

Lombardo, Irma. *De la opinión a la noticia. El surgimiento de los géneros informativos en México*. Mexico City: Kiosco, 1992.

Lorente, Marta, ed. *De justicia de jueces a justicia de leyes: Hacia la España de 1870*. Madrid: Consejo General del Poder Judicial / Escuela Judicial, 2007.

Lugo, Román. "Estudio sobre la justicia penal." *Criminalia*, no. 1, año 11 (January 1945): 12–26.

Luna, Ana Luisa. *La nota roja, 1930–1939*. Mexico City: Diana, 1996.

Macedo, Miguel. "Algunas ideas sobre la reforma de los códigos." *El Foro* 7, no. 71 (May 1926): 1–2.

———. "El Código Penal mexicano." *El Foro* 4, no. 66 (December 1925): 1–7.

Machorro Narváez, Paulino. *El anteproyecto de Código Penal para el Distrito y territorios federales y para materia federal*. Mexico City: Academia Mexicana de Jurisprudencia y Legislación, 1950.

Martínez, Emilio A. "El jurado en materia criminal es una forma de procedimiento inconveniente en el país." *El Foro* 48, nos. 32–35, año 17 (February 21–25, 1897): 2, 1–2, 1–2, and 1–2.

Martínez Baca, Francisco, and Manuel Vergara. *Estudios de antropología criminal*. Puebla: Imprenta Litográfica y Encuadernación de Benjamín Lara, 1892.

Martínez Báez, Antonio. "Estudio histórico y comparativo acerca de la creación de una Secretaría de Justicia." *El Foro*, no. 32, época 4 (January–March 1961): 15–19.

Marván Laborde, Ignacio, ed. *Nueva edición del Diario de los Debates del Congreso Constituyente de 1916–1917*. Mexico City: SCJ, 2006.

Matos Escobedo, Rafael. "Control constitucional de legalidad del ejercicio de la acción penal." *La Justicia* 15, nos. 223–26 (March–June 1946): 8060–66, 8159–62, 8206–10, 8284–91.

"Mayor rigor con pandilleros, pistoleros y traficantes de drogas en una iniciativa." *La Justicia* 27, no. 451 (December 1967): 61–62.

Maza Pesqueira, Adriana, and Martha Santillán Esqueda. "Movilización y ciudadanía. Las mujeres en la escena política y social (1953–1974)." In *De liberales a liberadas. Pensamiento y movilización de las mujeres en la historia de México (1753–1975)*, edited by Adriana Maza, 198–244. Mexico City: Nueva Alianza, 2014.

Meade, Everard. "From Sex Strangler to Model Citizen: Mexico's Most Famous Murderer and the Defeat of the Death Penalty." *Mexican Studies / Estudios Mexicanos* 26, no. 2 (Summer 2010): 323–77.

Medina Caracheo, Carlos, and Carlos David Vargas Ocaña. "La vida nocturna en la ciudad de México: Centros nocturnos, cabarets y burdeles 1935–1945." Licentiate thesis, UNAM, 1996.

Medina Osalde, Claudio. "Ponencia presentada en la Primera Convención de Procuradores de Justicia del Fuero Común." *Criminalia*, no. 12, año 5 (August 1939): 741–46.

Mellado, Guillermo. *Belem por dentro y por fuera*. Criminalia Cuaderno 21. Mexico City: Criminalia, 1959.

"Memorando que se presenta al Presidente de la República acerca de la administración de la justicia local, por La Barra Mexicana, el Ilustre y Nacional Colegio de Abogados de México, la Academia de Legislación y Jurisprudencia, la Facultad de Derecho de la Universidad Autónoma y la Escuela Libre de Derecho." *El Foro*, nos. 15–17, época 4 (January–June 1957): 25–26.

Mendieta y Núñez, Lucio. *La administración pública en México*. Mexico City: Imprenta Universitaria, 1943.

Mendoza, Salvador. "El nuevo Código Penal de México." *Hispanic American Historical Review* 10, no. 3 (August 1930): 299–310.

Menéndez, José. *Memorias de "El Corbatón."* Mexico City: Ediciones Rex, 1945.

Miranda Pacheco, Sergio. *La creación del Departamento del Distrito Federal. Urbanización, política y cambio institucional*. Mexico City: IIH, 2008.

Monroy Nasr, Rebeca. "En la escena del crimen: El registro fotográfico." *Alquimia*, no. 61, año 21 (September–December 2017): 38–54.

———. *Historias para ver. Enrique Díaz, fotorreportero*. Mexico City: IIE–INAH, 2003.

Monsiváis, Carlos. "Círculos de perdición y salvación, pulquerías, cantinas, cabaret." *Diario de Campo*, 4–12. Mexico City: INAH, 2006.

———. *Los mil y un velorios. Crónica de la nota roja en México*. Mexico City: Debate, 2010.

———. "Prólogo." In *Género, poder y política en el México posrevolucionario*, compiled by Gabriela Cano, Mary Kay Vaughan, and Jocelyn Olcott, 11–37. Mexico City: FCE, 2010.

———. "Señor Presidente, ¿a usted no le da vergüenza su grandeza?" In *Tiempo de saber*, by Julio Scherer García and Carlos Monsiváis, 99–399. Mexico City: Aguilar, 2003.

Moreno Tagle, Ignacio. *Román Lugo: El fracaso de un político en la Procuraduría de Justicia*. Mexico City, 1961.

Nieto, Alejandro. *El arbitrio judicial*. Barcelona: Editorial Ariel, 2000.

Núñez Cetina, Saydi. "El homicidio en el Distrito Federal. Un estudio sobre la violencia y la justicia durante la posrevolución (1920–1940)." PhD diss., CIESAS, 2012.

———. "Reforma social, honor y justicia: Infanticidio y aborto en la ciudad de México, 1920–1940." *Signos Históricos*, no. 28 (July–December 2012): 68–113.

———. "Reforma y justicia tras la Revolución: El homicidio en la ciudad de México en los años treinta." *Legajos*, no. 3 (January–March 2010): 99–118.

Olea y Leyva, Teófilo. "Proyecto de Código Penal para los Estados Unidos Mexicanos. Memorando de observaciones formado, en su vista, por la comisión de reformas legislativas de La Barra Mexicana." *El Foro* 10, no. 3 (July–September 1929): 7–15.

Olivé, Isaac. "La nueva ley orgánica y de procedimientos penales." *Los Tribunales* 7, no. 1 (November 1929): 36–42.

Ostos, Armando Z. *Breves comentarios sobre el nuevo Código de Procedimientos Penales para el Distrito y territorios federales*. Mexico City, 1931.

Ovalle Favela, José. *Temas y problemas de la administración de justicia en México*. 2nd ed. Mexico City: Miguel Ángel Porrúa, 1985.

———. *Teoría general del proceso*. 6th ed. Mexico City, Oxford, 2005.

Padilla, Tanalís. *Después de Zapata. El movimiento jaramillista y los orígenes de la guerilla en México (1940–1962)*. Mexico City: Ediciones Akal, 2015.

Pallares, Eduardo. "El jurado popular." *La Justicia* 2, no. 23, año 2 (May 1932): 4–5.

Pardo, Ramón. "El criterio médico en derecho penal (Discurso de ingreso a la Academia de Medicina)." *Gaceta Médica de México* 63, no. 1 (1932): 5–23.

Pardo Aspe, Emilio. "Mariachis y juzgadores." *Criminalia*, no. 8, año 5 (April 1939): 453–59.

Pérez Montfort, Ricardo. "La cultura." In *México, 1930–1960. Mirando hacia adentro*. Vol. 4 of the *Historia Contemporánea de México* collection, edited by Alicia Hernández Chávez, 271–346. Madrid: Fundación Mapfre / Santillana, 2012.

Pérez Moreno, José. "Creación de escuelas científicas de policía en los estados. Ponencia presentada en el Primer Congreso de Procuradores de la República Mexicana." *Criminalia*, no. 11, año 5 (July 1939): 739–40.

Piccato, Pablo. "Altibajos de la esfera pública en México, de la dictadura republicana a la democracia corporativa. La era de la prensa." In *Independencia y Revolución: Pasado, presente y futuro*, edited by Gustavo Leyva, Brian Connaughton, Rodrigo Díaz, Nestor García Canclini, and Carlos Illades, 240–91. Mexico City: FCE / UAM, 2010.

———. "El significado político del homicidio en México en el siglo XX." *Cuicuilco* 15, no. 43 (May–August 2008): 57–80.

———. *A History of Infamy: Crime, Truth, and Justice in Mexico*. Oakland: University of California Press, 2017.

———. "Homicide as Politics in Modern Mexico." *Bulletin of Latin American Research* 32 (March 2013): 104–25.

———. "Murders of Nota Roja: Truth and Justice in Mexican Crime News." *Past and Present*, no. 223 (May 2014): 195–231.

———. "Todo homicidio es político. El asesinato en la esfera pública en el México del siglo XX." In *Formas de gobierno en México. Poder político y actores*

sociales a través del tiempo. Vol. 2, Poder político en el México moderno y contemporá-
neo, edited by Víctor Gayol, 627–54. Zamora: El Colegio de Michoacán, 2012.
———. "Una perspectiva histórica de la delincuencia en la ciudad de México en
el siglo XX." In La reforma de la justicia en México, edited by Arturo Alvarado,
615–68. Mexico City: El Colegio de México, 2008.
Piña y Palacios, Javier. "Ponencia presentada en el III Congreso Interamericano
del Ministerio Público." Revista de la Escuela Libre de Derecho, no. 5, año 2 (September 1963): 31–37.
Ponce Hernández, Alejandro. "La gestión de un nuevo orden. Reforma, profe-
sionalización y problemáticas de la policía de la Ciudad de México. 1923–
1928." Licentiate thesis, UNAM, 2018.
Porte Petit, Celestino. "Anteproyecto de Código Penal." Criminalia, no. 8, año 16
(August 1950): 317–31.
———. "El Código Penal mexicano del porvenir." Criminalia, no. 3, año 10
(November 1943): 136–70.
———. Evolución legislativa penal en México. Mexico City: Editorial Jurídica Mexi-
cana, 1965.
———. Exposición doctrinal del anteproyecto de Código Penal. Mexico City: Cultura,
1950.
Porter, Susie S. "Espacios burocráticos, normas de feminidad e identidad de la
clase media en México durante la década de 1930." In Orden social e identidad
de género. México, siglos XIX y XX, edited by María Teresa Fernández Aceves,
Carmen Ramos Escandón, and Susie Porter, 189–214. Mexico City: CIESAS/
Universidad de Guadalajara, 2007.
Portes Gil, Emilio. Autobiografía de la Revolución Mexicana. Mexico City: Instituto
Mexicano de Cultura, 1964.
Prieto Sanchís, Luis. Ideología e interpretación jurídica. Madrid: Tecnos, 1987.
"Primera Convención de Procuradores de Justicia del Fuero Común (publicación
íntegra de los trabajos)." Criminalia, no. 11, año 5 (July 1939): 642–763.
"Problemas de la justicia." La Justicia 19, no. 261 (May 1949): 10221.
Puig, Fernando. El ideal de justicia y la realidad mexicana. Mexico City, 1950.
Pulido Esteva, Diego. "El caso Quintana: Policías, periodistas y hampones en la
capital mexicana de los años veinte." In Delincuentes, policías y justicias. América
Latina, siglos XIX y XX, edited by Daniel Palma Alvarado, 312–29. Santiago de
Chile: Universidad Alberto Hurtado, 2015.
———. "Los negocios de la policía en la Ciudad de México durante la posrevolu-
ción." Trashumante, no. 6 (2015): 8–31.
Pulido Llano, Gabriela. El mapa rojo del pecado. Miedo y vida nocturna en la ciudad de
México 1940–1950. Mexico City: INAH, 2016.
"¿Qué opina usted sobre la reimplantación del jurado popular?" Criminalia, no. 1,
año 8 (September 1941): 19–20.

Quiroz Cuarón, Alfonso. "Crisis de la administración de justicia penal." *Revista de la Facultad de Derecho de México*, nos. 41–42 (January–June 1961): 319–48.

———. "La criminalidad en la República Mexicana y el costo social del homicidio." *Criminalia*, no. 3, año 36 (March 1970): 137–46.

———. "La criminalidad evoluciona." *Criminalia*, no. 3, año 9 (November 1942): 152–53.

———. "La justicia sin técnica es ineficaz." *Criminalia*, no. 11, año 33 (November 1967): 545–48.

Quiroz Cuarón, Alfonso, José Gómez Robleda, and Benjamín Argüelles Medina. *Tendencia y ritmo de la criminalidad en México*. Mexico City: Instituto de Investigaciones Estadísticas, 1939.

Quiroz Cuarón, Alfonso, and Alfredo Savido. "El juez penal clásico y el juez penal del porvenir." *Criminalia*, no. 7, año 2 (March 1935): 88–92.

Rabasa, Emilio. *El artículo 14 y el juicio constitucional*. 7th ed. Mexico City: Porrúa, 2000.

Ramírez, Alfonso Francisco. "El restablecimiento del jurado popular." *La Justicia* 2. no. 23, año 2 (May 1932): 15–16.

Ramos Bilderbeck, Eugenio. "Por una secretaría de justicia." *El Foro*, no. 32, época 4 (January–March 1961): 9–14.

Ríos Molina, Andrés. *Memorias de un loco anormal. El caso de Goyo Cárdenas*. Mexico City: Debate, 2010.

Rivera Reynaldos, Lisette Griselda. "Crímenes pasionales y relaciones de género en México, 1880–1910." *Nuevo Mundo/Mundos Nuevos*, no. 6. http://nuevomundo.revues.org/document2835.html.

———. "Criminales, criminalizadas y delatoras. Mujeres involucradas en homicidios pasionales en Michoacán, 1900–1920." In *Vicio, prostitución y delito. Mujeres transgresoras en los siglos XIX y XX*, edited by Elisa Speckman Guerra and Fabiola Bailón Vázquez, 345–70. Mexico City: IIH UNAM, 2016.

Rivera Silva, Manuel. "El positivismo y el código de 1929." *Criminalia*, no. 9, año 4 (May 1938): 567–69.

———. *El procedimiento penal*. Mexico City: Editorial Porrúa, 1944.

Rivera Vázquez, Manuel. "El arbitrio judicial en nuestras Cortes Penales." *Criminalia*, no. 1, año 8 (September 1942): 4–5.

Rodríguez Kuri, Ariel. "Ciudad oficial, 1930–1970." In *Historia política de la Ciudad de México (Desde su fundación hasta el año 2000)*, edited by Ariel Rodríguez Kuri, 417–82. Mexico City: El Colegio de México, 2012.

———. "El presidencialismo en México." *Historia y Política*, no. 11 (2004): 131–52.

———. "Población y sociedad." In *México, 1960–2000. La búsqueda de la democracia*. Vol. 5 of the *Historia Contemporánea de México* collection, edited by Marcello Carmagnani, 191–226. Madrid: Fundación Mapfre / Santillana, 2012.

Rodríguez Kuri, Ariel, and Renato González Mello. "El fracaso del éxito, 1970–1985." In *Nueva Historia General de México*, 699–746. Mexico City: El Colegio de México, 2010.

Rojas Sosa, Odette. "'El bajo mundo del pecado.' Vicio, crimen y bajos fondos en la ciudad de México, 1929–1944." In *Vicio, prostitución y delito. Mujeres transgresoras en los siglos XIX y XX*, edited by Elisa Speckman Guerra and Fabiola Bailón Vázquez, 49–84. Mexico City: IIH UNAM, 2016.

———. "La ciudad y sus peligros: Alcohol, crimen y bajos fondos. Visiones, discursos y práctica judicial, 1929–1946." PhD diss., UNAM, 2016.

———. "'Una amenaza siempre viva': Alcohólicos y toxicómanos ante la justicia. Ciudad de México, 1929–1931." In *Horrorosísimos crímenes y ejemplares castigos. Una historia sociocultural del crimen, la justicia y el castigo (México, siglos XIX y XX)*, edited by Elisa Speckman Guerra. San Luis Potosí: El Colegio de San Luis / Universidad de Aguascalientes, 2018.

Rubenstein, Anne. "La guerra contra 'las pelonas.' Las mujeres modernas y sus enemigos, Ciudad de México, 1924." In *Género, poder y política en el México posrevolucionario*, compiled by Gabriela Cano, Mary Kay Vaughan, and Jocelyn Olcott, 91–126. Mexico City: FCE, 2010.

Ruiz-Funes, Mariano. "La justicia penal y la técnica." *Criminalia*, no. 11, año 7 (July 1941): 657–61.

Ruiz Harrell, Hugo. *Código penal histórico*. Mexico City: INACIPE, 2002.

Salazar Hurtado, Daniel. "La inamovilidad judicial como factor de justicia independiente." *Criminalia*, no. 3, año 9 (November 1942): 129.

Salvatore, Ricardo. *Subalternos, derechos y justicia penal: Ensayos de historia social y cultural argentina 1829–1940*. Barcelona: Gedisa, 2010.

Sánchez-Mejorada Fernández, María Cristina. "Los elementos jurídicos y políticos en la institucionalización del gobierno del Distrito Federal a la mitad del siglo XX." In *Miradas recurrentes, la ciudad de México en los siglos XIX y XX*, edited by María del Carmen Collado, 248–68. Mexico City: Instituto Mora / UAM, 2004.

———. *Rezagos de la Modernidad: Memorias de una ciudad presente*. Mexico City: UAM, 2005.

Sánchez Ruiz, Gerardo. *La Ciudad de México en el periodo de las regencias, 1929–1997*. Mexico City: UAM–Gobierno del Distrito Federal, 1999.

Santillán Esqueda, Martha. *Delincuencia femenina. Ciudad de México 1940–1954*. Mexico City: Instituto Mora / INACIPE, 2017.

———. "Discursos de redomesticación femenina durante los procesos modernizadores en México, 1946–1958." *Historia y Grafía*, no. 31 (December 2008): 103–32.

———. "El discurso tradicionalista sobre la maternidad: *Excélsior* y las madres prolíficas durante el avilacamachismo." *Secuencia*, no. 77 (May–August 2010): 90–110.

———. "Infanticidas en la ciudad de México (1940–1950), representación y realidad." In *Presencia y realidades: Investigaciones sobre mujeres y perspectiva de género*, edited by Emilia Recéndez Guerrero, Norma Gutiérrez Hernández, and Diana Arauz Mercado, 182–90. Zacatecas: Taberna Librería / UAZ / Instituto para las Mujeres Zacatecanas / UANL / UJED / UG, 2011.

———. "'La descuartizadora de la Roma': Aborto y maternidad. Ciudad de México, década de los cuarenta." In *Crimen y justicia en la historia de México. Nuevas miradas*, edited by Salvador Cárdenas and Elisa Speckman Guerra, 355–86. Mexico City: SCJ, 2011.

———. "Mujeres delincuentes e imaginarios. Criminología, cine y nota roja en México, 1940–1950." *Varia Historia* 33, no. 62 (May–August 2017): 398–418.

———. "Mujeres *non sanctas*. Prostitución y delitos sexuales: Prácticas criminales en la Ciudad de México, 1940–1950." *Historia Social*, no. 76 (June 2013): 67–85.

———. "Mujeres y leyes posrevolucionarias. Un análisis de género en el Código Penal de 1931." *Iter Criminis*, no. 13 (April–June 2016): 125–72.

———. "Narrativas del proceso judicial: Castigo y negociación femenina en la ciudad de México, década de los cuarenta." *Historia Moderna y Contemporánea de México*, no. 48 (July–December 2014): 157–89.

———. "Posrevolución y participación política. Un ambiente conservador (1924–1953)." In *De liberales a liberadas. Pensamiento y movilización de las mujeres en la historia de México (1753–1975)*, edited by Adriana Maza, 152–97. Mexico City: Nueva Alianza, 2014.

Serna de la Garza, José María. "The Concept of Jurisprudencia in Mexican Law." *Mexican Law Review* 1, no. 2 (2009): 131–45.

Serralde, Francisco. *La organización judicial*. Mexico City: O. R. Spíndola, 1889.

Silva, Máximo. *Higiene popular: Colección de conocimientos y de consejos indispensables para evitar las enfermedades y prolongar la vida, arreglado para el uso de las familias*. Mexico City: Talleres Gráficos de la Nación, 1917.

"Sobre la justicia del fuero común." *La Justicia* 25, no. 198 (February 1955): 11673.

Sodi, Demetrio. *El jurado en México*. 1909. Reprint, Mexico City: Botas, n.d.

Speckman Guerra, Elisa. *Crimen y castigo. Legislación penal, interpretaciones de la criminalidad y administración de justicia (Ciudad de México, 1872–1910)*. Mexico City: IIH UNAM / El Colegio de México, 2007.

———. "Crónica de una muerte anunciada. La supresión del juicio por jurado en el Distrito Federal." In *El Mundo del Derecho 2. Instituciones, justicia y cultura jurídica*, edited by Andrés Lira and Elisa Speckman Guerra, 396–420. Mexico City: IIJ UNAM / eld, 2017.

———. *Del Tigre de Santa Julia, la princesa italiana y otras historias. Sistema judicial, criminalidad y justicia en la Ciudad de México (siglos XIX y XX)*. Mexico City: INACIPE / IIH UNAM, 2014.

———. "Digna flor del vicio. El caso de María Elena Blanco." In *Vicio, prostitución y delito. Mujeres transgresoras en los siglos XIX y XX*, edited by Elisa Speckman Guerra and Fabiola Bailón Vásquez, 371–408. Mexico City: IIH UNAM, 2016.

———. "Dos obstáculos en la carrera de un jinete: Incidentes delictivos de Humberto Mariles (Ciudad de México, 1964–1972)." *Mexican Studies/Estudios Mexicanos* 36, no. 3 (Autumn 2020): 356–92.

———. "El jurado popular para delitos comunes: Leyes, ideas y prácticas (Distrito Federal, 1869–1929)." In *Historia de la justicia en México. Siglos XIX y XX*, 743–88. Mexico City: SCJ, 2005.

———. *En tela de juicio. Justicia penal, homicidios célebres y opinión pública (México, siglo XX)*. Mexico City: Tirant lo Blanch / IIH UNAM, 2020.

———. "Las flores del mal: Mujeres criminales en el porfiriato." *Historia Mexicana* 47, no. 1 (July–September 1997): 183–229.

Suarez-Potts, William. *The Making of Law: The Supreme Court and Labor Legislation in Mexico, 1875–1931*. Stanford CA: Stanford University Press, 2012.

Tarello, Giovanni. *Cultura jurídica y política del derecho*. Mexico City: FCE, 1995.

Teja Zabre, Alfonso. "Doctrina de la legislación penal mexicana." In *Homenaje a Eugenio Florián*, 333–71. Mexico City, 1940.

———. "Exposición de motivos del Código Penal de 1931." In *Código Penal para el Distrito Federal en Materia de Fuero Común y para toda la República en Materia de Fuero Federal*, 7–48. Mexico City: Botas, 1936.

———. *Hacia una criminología social*. Cuadernos Criminalia. Mexico City: Criminalia, 1941.

———. "Las nuevas orientaciones del derecho penal." *Revista de Ciencias Sociales* 1, no. 3 (1930): 50–55.

Trueba, Alfonso. "Defensa de los jueces." *La Justicia* 20, no. 367 (December 1960): 36–41.

———. *Justicia Mexicana*. Puebla: José M. Cajica, 1969.

Tuñón Pablos, Julia. "Cine y cultura. La modernidad al servicio de la tradición en la trilogía de Ismael Rodríguez." In *De la mofa a la educación sentimental. Caricatura, fotografía y cine*, edited by Alejandro de la Torre Hernández, Rebeca Monroy Nasr, and Julia Tuñón Pablos, 93–126. Mexico City: INAH, 2010.

Unikel, Luis. *El desarrollo urbano de México*. Mexico City: El Colegio de México, 1976.

Urías Horcasitas, Beatriz. *Indígena y criminal. Interpretaciones del derecho y la antropología en México 1871–1921*. Mexico City: UIA, 2000.

Urueta, Jesús. "Delito y delincuentes." *Revista de Legislación y Jurisprudencia* 15, época 2 (July–December 1898): 271–74.

Usigli, Rodolfo. *Ensayo de un crimen*. Mexico City: Ediciones Cal y Arena, 2008.

Vallarta, Ignacio Luis. "Inteligencia del artículo 14 de la Constitución Federal." In *Ignacio Luis Vallarta, Archivo Inédito*, compiled by Manuel González Oropeza. Mexico City: Suprema Corte de Justicia de la Nación, 1993.

Vaughan, Mary Kay. "Introducción." In *Género, poder y política en el México posrevolucionario*, compiled by Gabriela Cano, Mary Kay Vaughan, and Jocelyn Olcott, 39–57. Mexico City: FCE, 2010.

Vela, Alberto. "Carrera judicial y jubilaciones." *Criminalia*, no. 6, año 20 (June 1954): 328–39.

———. "Funcionarios de carrera." *Criminalia*, no. 6, año 1 (February 1934): 42–43.

———. "Institución de carrera judicial y jubilaciones." *Anales de Jurisprudencia* 78 (1953): 60–69.

———. "Perdón judicial." *Criminalia*, no. 2, año 8 (October 1941): 117–20.

Vernengo, Roberto. "Interpretación del derecho." In *El derecho y la justicia*, edited by Ernesto Garzón Valdés and Francisco Laporta, 239–65. Madrid: Trotta, 1996.

Vidales Quintero, Mayra Lizzete. *Legalidad, género y violencia contra las mujeres en Sinaloa durante el Porfiriato*. Mexico City: Plaza y Valdés / UAS / Instituto Sinaloense de las Mujeres, 2009.

Whitehead, Laurence. *Democratization: Theory and Experience*. Oxford: Oxford University Press, 2002.

Zapata, Francisco. "Población y sociedad." In *México, 1930–1960. Mirando hacia adentro*. Vol. 4 of the *Historia Contemporánea de México* collection, edited by Alicia Hernández Chávez, 235–70. Madrid: Fundación Mapfre / Santillana, 2012.

Zavala, Adriana. "De *Santa* a india bonita. Género, raza y modernidad en la ciudad de México, 1921." In *Orden social e identidad de género. México, siglos XIX y XX*, edited by María Teresa Fernández Aceves, Carmen Ramos Escandón, and Susie Porter, 149–88. Mexico City: CIESAS / Universidad de Guadalajara, 2007.

Zavala, Silvio. "Nuestros legisladores y nuestras leyes." *Revista de la Facultad de Derecho y Ciencias Sociales* 1, no. 3 (October 1930): 113–19.

Zayas Lezama, Carlos Hugo, Ramón Cañedo, and Venancio González Ramiro. "Necesidad de una legislación basada en las características de las razas indígenas de nuestro país." *Criminalia*, no. 13, año 5 (August 1939): 732.

Zolov, Eric. *Refried Elvis: The Rise of the Mexican Counterculture*. Berkeley: University of California Press, 1999.

INDEX

Cárdenas, Lázaro, 57, 109, 111, 113, 169, 217

Cárdenas, Raúl, 69, 70, 73, 74, 81

Carrancá y Trujillo, Raúl, 36, 37, 47, 49, 70, 75, 104, 105, 206, 252; as president of the TSJ, 86, 113; as attorney general, 58, 82; as judge, 111, 146, 246, 247, 252

Carranza, Venustiano, 25, 26

cassation, 35

Ceniceros, José Ángel, 38, 41, 42, 44, 49, 64, 80, 89, 96, 103; as member of the code drafting committee, 39

classical school, 27, 37, 40

codification, 3, 16

collegial courts, 1, 30, 38, 54, 107, 231, 236, 237, 238

collegial system, 2, 43, 54, 61, 233, 235

confrontation, 18, 54, 62; hearing, 142, 181, 196, 198, 220, 221

correctional courts, 38, 111

corruption, 66, 76, 84, 86, 94, 95, 96, 97, 101, 102, 105, 106, 107, 181, 188, 226, 227; practices, 60, 64, 72, 81, 82, 100, 235, 236, 239, 240

criminal anthropology school, 24, 40

criminal complaints (*querellas o denuncias*), 32

criminal liability, 30, 50, 74, 127, 136, 162, 164, 240; exception of, 127, 128, 129, 130, 131, 132, 133, 137, 156, 157

cronyism, 29, 41, 87, 93, 106, 107, 112, 116, 117, 239

danger, 28, 29, 40, 49, 51, 54, 60, 137, 184, 210; concept of, 28, 30; precrime and postcrime danger, 50

death penalty, 195, 204, 205, 206, 210

De Villarreal, Concha, 63, 67, 69, 71, 74, 83, 88, 93, 97, 103

democratic state, 12, 13, 14, 46, 62, 67, 107, 117, 236, 238; system, 51, 97, 108

determinism, 30, 40

Díaz, Porfirio, 7, 20, 22, 27, 83, 94, 105, 111, 115, 210

Díaz Ordaz, Gustavo, 9, 67, 115, 230

"difficult or controversial" cases, 17, 126, 188, 209, 227, 240

drafting committee of the 1931 criminal code, 40, 47, 49, 60, 61, 127, 128, 238

"easy or clear" cases, 17, 126, 137, 144, 149, 157, 225, 227, 240

Echeverría, Luis, 187, 229, 230

eclectic school, 60

Elías Calles, Plutarco, 2, 3, 28, 31, 109, 208

equality, 10, 22, 23, 46, 48, 53, 98, 105, 107, 155, 238; mandate of, 107; principle of, 45, 238

equity, 156

Escuela Libre de Derecho (ELD), 20, 63, 86, 93, 102

European Convention, 45

Franco Sodi, Carlos, 54, 58, 66, 72, 91, 93, 100, 102, 104, 105; as judge, 55; as prosecutor, 201

García Ramírez, Sergio, 9, 13, 14, 16, 18, 97, 233, 234, 235, 237; as attorney general, 80

Garrido, Luis, 38, 45, 60, 67, 88, 89, 90, 97, 104, 233; as member of the 1931 criminal code drafting committee, 39, 40, 44; as judge, 146

gender, 11, 18, 115, 125, 132, 139, 188, 191, 228

González de la Vega, Francisco, 37, 44, 54, 67, 82,

To order or obtain more
information on these or other
University of Nebraska Press titles,
visit nebraskapress.unl.edu.